Appreciating the Chinese Difference

SUNY series in Chinese Philosophy and Culture
—————
Roger T. Ames, editor

Appreciating the Chinese Difference

Engaging Roger T. Ames
on Methods, Issues, and Roles

Edited by
Jim Behuniak

Cover art: iStock by Getty Images. Photo of Roger Ames courtesy of the University of Hawaii.

Published by State University of New York Press, Albany

© 2018 State University of New York

All rights reserved

No part of this book may be used or reproduced in any manner whatsoever without written permission. No part of this book may be stored in a retrieval system or transmitted in any form or by any means including electronic, electrostatic, magnetic tape, mechanical, photocopying, recording, or otherwise without the prior permission in writing of the publisher.

For information, contact State University of New York Press, Albany, NY
www.sunypress.edu

Library of Congress Cataloging-in-Publication Data

Names: Behuniak, James, editor.
Title: Appreciating the Chinese difference : engaging Roger T. Ames on methods, issues, and roles / edited by Jim Behuniak.
Description: Albany, NY : State University of New York, 2018. | Series: SUNY series in Chinese philosophy and culture | Includes bibliographical references and index.
Identifiers: LCCN 2017047336 | ISBN 9781438470993 (hardcover : alk. paper) | ISBN 9781438471006 (pbk. : alk. paper) | ISBN 9781438471013 (ebook)
Subjects: LCSH: Philosophy, Chinese. | Philosophy, Confucian. | Ames, Roger T., 1947–
Classification: LCC B5202 .A67 2018 | DDC 181/.11—dc23
LC record available at https://lccn.loc.gov/2017047336

10 9 8 7 6 5 4 3 2 1

Contents

Introduction   1
    Jim Behuniak

Part I: Methods

1. Roger T. Ames and the Meaning of Confucianism   13
    Thomas P. Kasulis

2. On Comparative and Post-Comparative Philosophy   31
    Hans-Georg Moeller

3. On the Importance of the Ames-Hall Collaboration   47
    Robert Cummings Neville

Part II: Issues

4. The Art of Rulership in the Context of Heaven and Earth   65
    Graham Parkes

5. Sex and Somaesthetics: Appreciating the Chinese Difference   91
    Richard Shusterman

6. Vast Continuity versus the One: Thoughts on *Daodejing 42*, *Taiyishengshui*, and the Legacy of Roger T. Ames   111
    Brook Ziporyn

7. Supplementing Ames on Creativity: A Heideggerian Interpretation of *Cheng*   133
    Chenyang Li

Part III: Roles

8. Building Bridges to Distant Shores: Pragmatic Problems with Confucian Role Ethics 159
    Stephen C. Angle

9. Does Confucianism Need a Metaphysical Theory of Human Nature? Reflections on Ames-Rosemont Role Ethics 183
    Peimin Ni

10. Roles, Community, and Morality: Comment on *Confucian Role Ethics* 203
    Daniel A. Bell

11. Performance in Confucian Role Ethics 213
    Kathleen M. Higgins

12. Role Ethics: Problems and Promise 229
    Henry Rosemont Jr.

Part IV: Replies

Roger T. Ames Responds 249
    Roger T. Ames

Contributors 295

Index 301

Introduction

Jim Behuniak

Over the last four decades, no scholar of Chinese philosophy in the English-speaking world has had a greater impact than Roger T. Ames. In fact, one needs to step back considerably to appreciate the scale of Ames's impact on the field—far enough to consider it alongside the monumental achievements made in the late nineteenth century, when the Scottish missionary and sinologist James Legge (1815–1897) defined his own epoch by first translating the Chinese classics into English.

Earnest in his desire to convey the good news of Jesus Christ to the Chinese, Legge left Aberdeen in 1839 for the Orient. During the nearly three decades that he spent in China, Legge came to appreciate the depth and density of Chinese culture. He soon realized that, in order to deliver China to the true faith, one needed to approach this ancient civilization on its own terms. "The rest of the world should really know this great empire," Legge explained, and such is now required so that "our missionary labors among the people should be conducted with sufficient intelligence and so as to secure permanent results."[1] Thus began a most remarkable career, one of transmitting China's ancient classics to the Western world. Legge's prodigious achievements include his initial 8-volume edition of the *The Chinese Classics*, and a subsequent 6-volume edition of the *Sacred Books* of Confucianism and Daoism as part of Max Müller's celebrated series, *Sacred Books of the East*. Legge's pioneering work would establish the foundation upon which twentieth-century Sinology was built.

In an interview with *Confucius Institute Magazine* in 2015, Roger Ames was asked why he found it necessary to change the English translations of so many key terms in Chinese philosophy. Specifically, he was asked why he elected to re-translate "the generally accepted 'benevolence' for *ren* 仁." Ames answered:

> The word "benevolence" is a relatively narrow, psychological disposition which bears little resemblance to the broad meaning contained in *ren* that references an entire person—the cultivated moral, aesthetic, religious, intellectual, and even physical habits that are expressed in one's relations with others.[2]

Ames returns a wholly sufficient answer. There is, however, an altogether different question that might have been asked—namely, how exactly did the word "benevolence" become the "generally accepted" translation of *ren* 仁 in the first place?

The genealogy of this particular word, in fact, has nothing to do with Chinese thought. Theologically, Legge aligned himself with the Presbyterian bishop, Joseph Butler (1692–1752). Butler devoted his philosophical talents to blunting Deism and to refuting the Egoism of the firebrand Thomas Hobbes, who in his *Leviathan* (1651) argued that human nature was essentially self-interested. In sermons such as "Upon the Love of Our Neighbor," Butler argued that "benevolence"—the desire to promote the general happiness of humankind—was an innate virtue of human nature as created by God. "Human nature is so constituted," proclaimed Butler, "that every good affection implies love of itself . . . Thus, to be righteous implies in it the love of righteousness; to be benevolent, the love of benevolence."[3] Legge saw the teachings of Bishop Butler prefigured in Confucians like Mencius, for whom "Heaven is served by obeying our Nature." Legge admitted that he could "get no other meaning" from the text. He even considered his translation of the term "Heaven" (*tian* 天) to be a compromise of sorts. As he writes, "it is much to be wished that instead of the term Heaven, vague and indefinite, Mencius had simply said 'God.' "[4]

The ideas of Bishop Butler would be inscribed directly into Legge's translations of the Chinese classics. Mencius's attitude toward self-doubting rulers, for instance, is pure Butler: "Let the prince be benevolent (*ren* 仁) and all his acts will be benevolent, let the prince be righteous (*yi* 義), and all his acts will be righteous."[5] Mencius's doctrine of human nature was, according to Legge, "as nearly as possible, identical with that of Bishop Butler," and since Butler maintained that "there is a natural principle of benevolence in man," Legge translated *ren* 仁 as "benevolence."[6] By historical accident, this peculiar translation stuck, and along with other Victorian-era coinage such as "nature" (*xing* 性), "fate" (*ming* 命), "righteousness" (*yi* 義), and "Heaven" (*tian* 天) it would persist for over a century as the standard English translation. As the *Confucius Institute Magazine* interviewer implies, such translations have become "generally accepted." Why change them now? Again, Ames's response is substantive—wholly sufficient. It does not begin, however, to answer the larger question. The *actual* reason that Ames first, and now others in the English-speaking world reconsider their translations philosophically is that the Leggian epoch has come to a close and another has begun.

Roger Ames made his first trip to Asia in 1966, a "curious 18-year-old," enrolled for one year at the Chinese University of Hong Kong. Born in Toronto and raised in England and Vancouver, Ames was instantly charmed by the new and unfamiliar ways of life that he encountered in the Chinese world. He would return to the University of British Columbia to complete his Bachelor's degree in Philosophy and Chinese before beginning graduate work with two years of coursework at National Taiwan University between 1970 and 1972. In Taiwan, he would read the classics with the inimitable Yang Youwei 楊有維, whose simultaneously exacting and antinomian style initiated Ames into the vast, interminable vocation of reading and thinking through ancient Chinese texts. After finishing his MA coursework in British Columbia, Ames studied for two additional years in Japan before pursuing his PhD at the School of Oriental and African Studies (SOAS) at the University of London between 1975 and 1978. In London, he would study under the eminent sinologist D. C. Lau (Liu Dianjue 劉殿爵). Lau had established SOAS as a center for Chinese philosophy, with a department that included A. C. Graham, Sarah Allan, and Paul Thompson. Ames benefitted from all of them, and most importantly from Graham and Lau. As teacher, mentor, collaborator, and friend, Lau especially would impart to Ames more than just a deep understanding of the Chinese classics; he would provide Ames with a model for becoming a genuine scholar in the Chinese tradition. In 1978, Ames joined the Philosophy department at the University of Hawai`i at Mānoa, where he would remain until his retirement in 2016.

Ames's earliest work, *The Art of Rulership*, focused on the political philosophy of the *Huainanzi* 淮南子. In the book's Introduction, one sees already the guiding principle behind Ames's work: the idea that no text or thinker in classical China can be adequately understood without first becoming aware of the general philosophical assumptions that shaped early Chinese discourse. In the Preface, Ames would thank his friend, David L. Hall, for having read the entire manuscript and for being "generous with important and positive criticisms." Hall, a spirited Yale-trained philosopher of culture in the pragmatic and process traditions, had recently released a pair of remarkable books, *The Uncertain Phoenix: Adventures Toward a Post-Cultural Sensibility* (1982) and *Eros and Irony: A Prelude to Philosophical Anarchism* (also 1982). The former, an essay in cross-cultural philosophy, explored the limits of Western metaphysical and technological thinking in light of alternatives suggested in the

Daoist tradition; the latter, a careful study of Greek thinking, reevaluated the cultural role of philosophy in an age that called into question its traditional epistemological purposes. In the latter's Acknowledgments, Hall thanked Ames for his "assurance that my understanding of philosophic Taoism is not altogether beside the mark." Hall and Ames each admired in the other some wanting expertise, and before long they pooled their resources to embark on a body of work that neither scholar could have produced alone.

The publication of their *Thinking Through Confucius* in 1987 would be a watershed moment in modern Chinese philosophy. In English-language scholarship, there had never been a book quite like this one in ambition and scope. Of course, it was not conceived in a vacuum. Hall and Ames drew upon the work of a number of scholars in formulating their arguments—the contributions of Peter Boodberg, Herbert Fingarette, Chad Hansen, D. C. Lau, Henry Rosemont Jr., and others were carefully considered in formulating their own positions. In his Forward to the book, Robert Cummings Neville announced without hesitation its epoch-making status: the work was "both the consummation of a century-old scholarly effort [referring to "the great projects, begun in the nineteenth century"] and the beginning of a new stage of philosophic understanding among Chinese and Western thinkers." Three decades later, Neville's estimation is confirmed—*Thinking Through Confucius* marks the beginning of the present epoch in English-language Chinese philosophy.

Neville also observed that, by calling into question "common assumptions about Chinese and Western cultures," the book "will be controversial."[7] This has also proven true. Immediately from the quarters of those producing scholarly papers on "Heaven" and "benevolence" in Chinese moral thought, *Thinking Through Confucius* was treated as a bombastic impertinence. Hall and Ames, however, were answering to what they understood to be a "real dissatisfaction" with such Victorian-era treatments voiced by scholars such as Wing-Tsit Chan, D.C. Lau, and Wm. Theodore de Bary. Such scholars "have moved, through lengthy introductions, specific papers, and commentary, to correct this situation." Something more than piecemeal redress, however, would be necessary to move the field beyond its nineteenth-century inheritance—indeed, beyond a prevailing philosophical idiom that traced back directly to eighteenth-century debates in Christian Europe. The entire classical tradition needed to be conceptually reconsidered, and in order to do this the "uncommon assumptions" that we as Western readers were bringing to our interpretations of Chinese philosophy needed to be intelligently reconstructed. The task was too ambitious for Ames or Hall to take on individually, but as collaborators they marshaled the intellectual resources and the raw nerve to make the attempt.

The significance of their ensuing trilogy of interpretative studies, *Thinking Through Confucius* (1987), *Anticipating China: Thinking Through the Narra-*

tive of Chinese and Western Culture (1995), and *Thinking from the Han: Self, Truth, and Transcendence in Chinese and Western Culture* (1998), is difficult to overstate. These works completely changed the conversation in Chinese and comparative philosophy. Since Hall and Ames were doing something not previously done—i.e., attempting to *justify* their particular readings and translations historically and philosophically—these works were difficult to ignore. Motivated by agreement, by disagreement, or by some qualification of either reaction, these works impacted nearly every research trajectory in the field.

Now that the dust has settled, it is clear that the Hall and Ames collaboration succeeded in alerting comparative philosophers to their own assumptions as historically situated inquirers, and that it helped to foreground the variability of cultural contexts in which philosophies operate—outcomes to which their postulation of "uncommon assumptions" was pursuant. Indeed, it is difficult to imagine Chinese-Western comparative philosophy ever going back to a *pre*-Hall and Ames mindset. Even those who reserve criticisms of their work display a methodological conscientiousness practically unheard of prior to the Hall and Ames collaboration. In terms of their broader argument—that classical American and Process-oriented traditions offer the most promising resources for approaching early Chinese philosophies—Hall and Ames have largely succeeded in changing attitudes in the field. Today, Brook Ziporyn represents the majority in holding that, "[the notion] that process orientations are closer to what Chinese thinkers tend to have in mind than substance ontologies and vocabularies . . . [is] by now rather uncontroversial."[8]

By the time of David Hall's death in 2001, Hall and Ames had branched out from collaborating on scholarly monographs to producing "philosophical translations" of the Chinese classics. The results, *Focusing the Familiar: A Translation and Philosophical Interpretation of the* Zhongyong (2001) and *A Philosophical Translation of* Daodejing: *"Making this Life Significant"* (2003), realized in another form the breakthroughs made in *Thinking Through Confucius*. Through substantive introductions and detailed glossaries, Hall and Ames sought to lay bare their own assumptions and to argue for their translation choices based on broader sets of patterns operative in Chinese thinking. Each text, then, was treated as a focal instance around which the entire field of early Chinese thinking could be, and needed to be, understood. Ames had, in fact, already been producing such translations with other collaborators. He worked alongside his teacher and mentor, D. C. Lau, in producing translations of *Sun Pin: The Art of Warfare* (1996) and the *Huainanzi* chapter, "Tracing Dao to its Source" (1998). Also, together with Henry Rosemont Jr., Ames completed perhaps his signature work, *The Confucian Analects: A Philosophical Translation* (1998), the most exquisite English translation of Confucius ever produced. Being so fruitful, the Ames-Rosemont collaboration would continue, resulting in another philosophical translation, *The Classic of Family Reverence: A Philosophical Translation of the* Xiaojing (2009), thus initiating another phase of Ames's collaborative career.

In addition to producing scholarship, Ames remained tremendously active in his service to his institution and to the broader field of Chinese and comparative philosophy while in Hawai'i. When Ames first arrived in 1978, the University of Hawai'i was already the uncontested center of the growing but still marginalized fields of non-Western and comparative philosophy. Under the leadership of Eliot Deutsch, its Philosophy program sustained a rich history that traced back to the first East-West Philosophers' Conferences in 1939 and 1949. As a result of the latter meeting, Charles A. Moore established the journal *Philosophy East and West*, passing editorial responsibilities on to Deutsch in 1967. Deutsch appointed Ames to be assistant editor upon his arrival in 1978, and over the next decade Ames assisted with the enormous growth that *Philosophy East and West* enjoyed under Deutsch's leadership. Deutsch passed all editorial responsibilities on to Ames in 1987, and the journal's readership continued to grow. Stronger than ever, Ames brought *Philosophy East and West* into the digital age in 2001, and in the twenty-first century it remains the flagship journal in non-Western and comparative philosophy. The conferences with which the journal is associated also flourished under Ames's tenure as director or co-director, with meetings of the East-West Philosophers' Conferences held in 1995, 2000, 2005, 2011, and 2016—each one making history in the growing field of comparative philosophy.

Ames's contributions extend well beyond such high-profile activities, creating a legacy of service seemingly impossible but for its achievement. He served as Editor for *China Review International* from 1992 to 2016, and for nearly a decade as the Director of the Center for Chinese Studies at the University of Hawai'i. He served as Co-Director and Senior Advisor for the Asian Studies Development Program (ASDP) from 1990 to 2012, during which time he worked alongside Betty Buck and Peter Hershock at the East-West Center in promoting the inclusion of Asian-related content into undergraduate curriculums. Through the ASDP, Ames was principal in securing multiple grants from the National Endowment of the Humanities, Fulbright-Hayes, Freeman, Luce, and other foundations to support this initiative. Also, with the publication of *Thinking Through Confucius*, Hall and Ames inaugurated the "Chinese Philosophy and Culture" series with SUNY Press, under which Ames served as the editor or co-editor of over 160 academic titles in Chinese philosophy—galvanizing the field with an abundance of original research while boosting the careers of dozens of upcoming scholars. Also included in this series are a number of edited volumes that Ames initiated in collaboration with scholars such as Thomas P. Kasulis, Wimal Dissanayake, J. Baird Callicott,

Joel Marks, Peter Hershock, Tsao Hsingyuan, and Carine Defoort. In addition to his long-standing collaboration with SUNY Press, Ames also served as the editor or co-editor of several volumes of papers with the University of Hawai`i Press. At the time of writing, Ames still has three co-edited volumes in Chinese philosophy forthcoming.

On a less quantifiable level, Ames's advocacy of Chinese philosophy has been carried on with door-to-door persistence for decades. He has travelled the four seas delivering talks, lectures, and workshops, encouraging and inspiring institutions to create lines for non-Western philosophers in their programs. Committed to "job creation" in Asian philosophy, Ames consistently leveraged whatever respect he earned to create opportunities for the next generation. Indeed, such generosity has been at the very heart of Ames's career and it will remain his enduring hallmark—a generosity that every student and every colleague knows as incomparable. Not surprisingly, Ames attracted PhD students from all over the world, sustaining in his era the most active doctoral program in Chinese philosophy in the United States by far. Having supervised over forty dissertations at the University of Hawai`i and serving on the committees of several dozen others, his teaching now leaves an indelible mark on the field. Also, having been a Visiting Professor at National University of Singapore and Chinese University of Hong Kong, as well as a Fulbright Professor at Wuhan University and Peking University, his influence extends well into the Chinese world. Currently residing in the Department of Philosophy at Peking University as Humanities Chair Professor, Ames's body of students continues to grow, expanding the numbers of those who already enjoy fruitful careers in Asia, Europe, and the United States.

Given such a prolific career as teacher, editor, director, chair, co-author, and advisor—not to mention colleague, mentor, friend, father, and husband—it is perhaps not surprising that Ames's later-period writings center on the importance of "roles" in achieving a meaningful human life. Following their 2009 translation of *The Chinese Classic of Family Reverence*, Ames and Rosemont each trained their energies on the development of what they labeled a "role ethics," a novel stance inspired by the Confucian tradition that regards family relations as the entry point for the cultivation of moral competence, an approach that differs markedly from both principle- and virtue-based ethical theories in the west. Its philosophical roots are foreshadowed in Ames's collaboration with Hall, with whom the publication of *The Democracy of the Dead: Dewey, Confucius, and the Hope for Democracy in China* (1999) marked a distinct shift into the fields of social and political philosophy. That particular work, which focused on the status of rights-based liberalism and democratic theory in the Chinese and Western traditions, required a more complete treatment of the status of the "individual" in these traditions. Hall and Ames would establish in greater detail the difference between the bare, autonomous "individual" residing in Western ethical and political theories and the fuller, more relational "person" described in early Confucian writings.

Ames and Rosemont had also developed this theme in their Introduction to *The Confucian Analects*, i.e., that "we express our unique personhood—*not* individualism—by the creative ways we interact with others, as children, parents, lovers, friends, and so forth, within the constraints denoted by what is meant by 'parent,' 'lover,' 'friend,' and 'neighbor.' "[9] Ten years later, *The Chinese Classic of Family Reverence* would provide a focal text around which these larger assumptions were arrayed—assumptions about what it means to be a "person" in the Confucian world. The Ames-Rosemont collaboration, while less voluminous than the Hall-Ames collaboration, has been equally impactful given the sharpness of its focus. Confucian role ethics is a compelling and provocative new entry in contemporary social and political discourse. As evinced in the present volume, scholars are currently engaged in thinking through its contemporary implications. The several papers that Ames and Rosemont have produced on role ethics have recently been collected in their *Confucian Role Ethics: A Moral Vision for the 21st Century?* (2016). Moreover, each has written his own substantive monograph on the topic: Ames, *Confucian Role Ethics: A Vocabulary* (2011) and Rosemont, *Against Individualism: A Confucian Rethinking of the Foundations of Morality, Politics, Family and Religion* (2015). As exchanges in the present volume indicate, Ames remains committed to building upon the project that he initiated together with his friend and collaborator, Henry Rosemont.

The career of Roger Ames has been such that honors, naturally, have been forthcoming. He received the Regent's Medal for Excellence in Research from the University of Hawai`i in 2012. In 2013, he was given the Confucius Culture Award by the Chinese Ministry of Culture and the Shandong 山東 government. In 2016, he received the Huilin Culture Award (*huilinwenhuajiang* 会林文化奖) from Beijing Normal University. During that same year, he was designated a "Confucian Exemplar" (*ruxuedajia* 儒学大家) by the Shandong Provincial Government. The current volume, likewise, is presented in honor of Ames's career achievements and in appreciation of his colossal service to Chinese philosophy. Brought together here are peers and colleagues with whom Roger has shared his path—not an exhaustive group, because no volume can contain such a crowd. Plus, there are no students featured in the present volume. Given the quantity and quality of those numbers, the decision was made to initiate a separate volume, *One Corner of the Square: Essays by the Students of Roger T. Ames*, which is currently in preparation. Essays in the present collection touch on several aspects of Ames's career, with the latter contributions focusing primarily on Ames's current work in Confucian role ethics. Ames's replies to these essays are forward-looking and substantive, reminding us that we pause to celebrate a career that remains very much on the active track—continuing to explore and to articulate the distinguishing features of the Chinese tradition.

History makes strange bedfellows, and Ames, ironically, sides with the most conservative Victorian-era missionaries—those who believed that Rev. Legge was being presumptuous, even heretical, in identifying parallels between Christianity and Chinese thought. For Legge had the audacity to suggest that, "Confucius—not to specify others—was raised up by God for the instruction of the Chinese people." Legge's assumption was that Confucian teachings had prepared the way for the reception of the New Testament gospels, and to his critics this was to "pull down the Old Testament to the level of Confucianism."[10] Legge had falsely regarded Confucianism as China's divinely guided prelude to its culminating encounter with Christianity, which would be its *defining moment*. In his defense of role ethics, Ames calls out the same tendency among his contemporaries. It is more than anachronistic to regard our gods as those before which the Chinese have been preparing themselves to kneel—it is completely presumptuous to read the tradition this way. Legge's conservative critics did not see in Mencius any Bishop-Butler-in-waiting; and likewise, Ames does not see in Confucius a Virtue-ethics-in-waiting, or in Mozi a Propositional-logic-in-waiting, or in Zhuangzi a Sextus-Empiricus-in-waiting. The Chinese tradition waits not for its own deliverance—not to the Christian God, and not to the gods of Occidental philosophy. We should rather hope to deliver ourselves from whatever parochial horizons prevent us from appreciating ways of thinking and living that differ from our own. Securing such deliverance is Roger Ames's mission. Professional stature and silver hair aside, that youthful glint in his eye is a curious 18-year-old beholding China for the first time and still appreciating the difference.

Notes

1. James Legge, *The Chinese Classics* (Taipei: SMC Publishing Inc., 1998), vol. 1, pg. 1.

2. *Confucius Institute Magazine* 39.4 July, 2015, pg. 6/10.

3. *The Whole Works of Joseph Butler* (London: Willian Tegg and Co., 1850), pg. 145.

4. James Legge, *The Chinese Classics* (Taipei: SMC Publishing Inc., 1998), vol. 2, pg. 448, note 1.

5. Ibid., pp. 310–311.

6. James Legge, *The Works of Mencius* (New York: Dover Publications, 1970), pg. 64, 60; see also: 56–57.

7. Roger T. Ames and David L. Hall, *Thinking Through Confucius* (Albany: State University of New York Press, 1987), pg. xiii.

8. Brook Ziporyn, *Ironies of Oneness and Difference* (Albany: State University of New York Press, 2012), pg. 21–22.

9. Roger T. Ames and Henry Rosemont Jr., tr. *The Analects of Confucius: A Philosophical Translation* (New York: Ballantine Books, 1998), pg. 27.

10. Quoted from: Norman J. Girardot, *The Victorian Translation of China: James Legge's Oriental Pilgrimage* (Berkeley: University of California Press, 2002), pp. 225, 231.

Part I

METHODS

1

Roger T. Ames and the Meaning of Confucianism

Thomas P. Kasulis

My friendship with Roger Ames dates back more than four decades to when our philosophy department at the University of Hawai'i hired him. We worked across the hall from each other and early on we established a tradition of having coffee in his office in the late afternoons after the day's work was done and before we left for home. From the very beginning Roger and I realized we were simpatico in many respects, but we also were drawn to each other out of need. My training had been primarily in Western philosophy and I had not even begun studying Japanese until I had finished my generals for the doctoral degree. Roger, on the other hand, had impressive training as a sinologist and scholar of Chinese thought, but by comparison was a relative newcomer to the systematic study of Western philosophy. So, in our regular meetings over coffee, Roger would answer my many questions about sinographs: the root meanings of key Sino-Japanese terms and their place in East Asian traditional thought. In the other direction, I would try to answer any questions Roger might have about the history of Western philosophy. An avid reader of philosophical texts, Roger was already knowledgeable about a wide range of Western philosophical ideas, but sometimes appreciated a discussion of how those ideas fit into the larger context of the development of the Western tradition.

Those afternoon conversations benefitted us both; for me at least, it was formative in how I learned to read Japanese philosophical texts both linguistically and in terms of their broader East Asian context. On Roger's part I think our interactions were a good foundation for his later comparative work and his collaborations with other colleagues more formally trained in Western philosophy, most obviously David Hall and Henry Rosemont. The real fun began, however, as we both got to understand each other and, having filled in some obvious holes in our respective training, were able to engage in boisterous but friendly argument, a pattern of interaction that I am happy to say continues today.

One incident sticks in my mind. At some academic conference we attended together, Roger Ames, the late David Hall, and I went out to dinner. As was our custom, the discussion ran long past the meal's end. We found ourselves among the last patrons in the restaurant as we were trying to settle once and for all some points about the nature of language, being, and emptiness. In the Confucian-Buddhist ratio of participants I was outnumbered two to one, but given the issue and the long tradition of Buddhist philosophy addressing it, I had ample textual and commentarial resources to manage to hold up my end of the argument. At one point toward the end of the evening, as the discussion was homing in on fundamental principles, I needed a concrete example to anchor a point about emptiness, a point that I wanted to affirm forcefully. I pointed to a water glass on the table and said (perhaps a bit more emphatically and loudly than was needed to be heard by my fellow discussants in the now quite quiet restaurant): "This glass is empty!" A young waiter scurried over with a water pitcher and apologized as he filled the glass. In my decades of philosophical and personal conversations with Roger Ames, the rich analysis and criticism of the discussions always seemed to somehow fill any void, whether concrete or abstract.

In commenting on the corpus of Roger Ames's prodigious publications and contributions to the fields of Chinese and comparative philosophy, I will focus on the way he has reinterpreted for us the meaning of the Confucian tradition, both its historical roots and its potential for addressing pressing philosophical questions of our own time. I will frame my discussion by the issue of meaning and its relevance to Ames's career as a scholar and teacher engaging the Confucian tradition.

The Meaning of Meaning

In considering how Ames has unearthed and presented to us the *meaning* of Confucianism, I suggest we keep in mind that we can talk of meaning in at least three different respects, each having its own German word. The first two were explained clearly in the nineteenth century by Gottlob Frege: *reference* or *denotation* (*Bedeutung*) and *sense* or *connotation* (*Sinn*). Thinking of meaning in terms of reference arises from the idea that words or terms point or refer to extra linguistic realities. Thus, Frege explained that when the names "the morning star" and the "evening star" both refer to the same object (the planet Venus), the two terms—as *Bedeutung*—can be said to have the same meaning. I will call that *meaning as reference*.

Of course, if we think of the larger context of the words or names, "the morning star" and "the evening star" are clearly distinguishable. One abides in that pre-dawn moment as a brilliant point of light, the last star remaining after the others have been obliterated by the oncoming illumination of a new day. The other signals the first starlight of the nightly sky awaiting its celestial companions to appear as the sun sinks behind the horizon, disappearing into dusk. That is, although "the morning star" and "evening star" may refer to the same physical object, they connect with other words and ideas (and even feelings) differently. We could say they occupy different places in the web of concepts and language or even within the stream of our experience. For Frege that indicates "the morning star" and "the evening star" are not necessarily identical in meaning—they differ as to their *Sinn*. I will call that *meaning as sense*.

To Frege's pair, I suggest adding a third kind of meaning, one that plays a key role in some philosophical fields like phenomenology and speech-act theory. It is usually expressed in German as *Meinung* or *Meinen*. Those German words are used much like the English "meaning" when we say, "I hear what you're saying, but I don't know what you *mean*;" or "What do you *mean* by that?" In making such utterances, we are usually not focusing on what the speaker is referring to or even how the speaker's statement meshes with other statements. Instead, we are trying to "get the point," or to determine what the speaker is driving at. I will call that *meaning as intention*.

To be sensitive to reference, sense, and intention as three different *dimensions* of meaning brings us to the heart of the challenge of being a scholar of comparative philosophy. That is especially true for a comparativist like Roger Ames, who both translates and interprets a non-Western tradition—indeed recognizes those two tasks to be essentially inseparable. Although to my knowledge he never explicitly makes the tripartite distinction, I would argue that much of Ames's mastery, his virtuosity, as a comparative philosopher derives from his appreciation of all three dimensions of meaning: reference, sense, and intention. From the earliest stages of his career, Ames realized that in approaching any Chinese text (indeed any text—Western as well as Asian), we must think about three sets of questions.

Meaning as Reference

What is this text referring to? What historical, social, and political context is it either directly or indirectly addressing? How can we understand the text as a philosophical response to a particular set of circumstances? In the course of developing his own philosophical outlook, Ames has become increasingly appreciative of pragmatism (in both its classical form by John Dewey and its postmodern reincarnation in Richard Rorty). In truth, however, Ames has always been pragmatic. For him, philosophy cannot be detached, or certainly *should not* be detached from its engagement with the affairs of the thinker's time and place. He *locates* the text for us so we can appreciate the intellectual climate that gave it birth.

Therefore, in approaching a Chinese text, Ames first brings his finely honed and truly impressive skills in Chinese philology and history. That has not always been the standard practice among scholars of Chinese philosophy. Many comparative philosophers from an earlier generation who specialized in the Chinese tradition either assumed their Western readers already knew that larger context or believed that philosophical ideas could transcend that context enough that it need be addressed in only a most cursory way. Of course, both that assumption and that belief were misguided. Once one reads a good sampling of Ames's works, one cannot help but appreciate how he locates the classic Chinese texts in their specific circumstances of origin. Yet, Ames's philological discussions are not simply philological in the manner of many other sinologists, nor his historical contextualizations merely historical in the manner of many area specialists in the field. As I will explain, the reason for that lies in his dual commitment to both sinology and philosophy. He negotiates the two fields in a distinctive, provocative, and creative way. To explain, I will comment on why sinologists and philosophers often find it so difficult to play nicely with each other. (The rationale for my alluding to *play* will become clearer as I proceed.)

Sinologists (like probably most other area specialists) routinely attend to the original context of words and ideas. For their analytic method, anachronism and the inaccurate understanding of the cultural-historical frame are major bugaboos. The area specialist is, therefore, suspect of any philosopher's proclivity to discuss Asian ideas without properly paying attention to how, where, and when those ideas arose. As for comparative philosophy, area specialists may even be flabbergasted by the very existence of what they consider a pseudo-discipline. To their way of thinking, comparative philosophy, by its very definition, affirms that ideas, values, and texts can, at least sometimes, be fruitfully taken beyond their geographical, historical, or cultural "area" as defined in their own specialty.

From the opposite direction, comparative philosophers may be suspicious of area specialists when they treat their research as if it were arcane and unintelligible to any but a highly restricted cabal of fellow specialists. "If you want to *really* understand this term or concept, you need to study classical Chinese and its texts for at least a decade or two (preferably under the guidance of either myself or of a colleague from an exclusive list of like-minded scholars). Otherwise, just take my word for it as an authority in the field that I know what I am talking about." In other words, an invitation to read the research is extended to the nonspecialist, but with the assumption that such readers lack the capacity to engage or further that research in any significant respect.

Roger Ames has time and again exposed such exclusivist sinologists as being blind to the fact that in their Western-language translation and discussion of a key classical Chinese term or text, their "word for it" is actually imbued with connotations from an entirely different (which is to say Western or Abrahamic) cultural and intellectual context. For example, if we use the English word "heaven" to translated "*tian*," or "righteousness" to translate "*yi*," are we not inherently making a cross-cultural comparison of a term from one geographical-cultural area with that from another? In their English interpretations and translations, the sinologists may be unknowingly engaging in comparative philosophy themselves. Whatever the inherent problems and risks involved in comparative philosophy, they must surely be exacerbated when such comparative points are offered unwittingly rather than with all the wits one can command.

The problem is compounded when Western philosophers who wish to liberate their discipline from its parochialism draw on those misleading sinological translations and explanations for their cross-cultural discussions. From the information made available to them, those Westerner thinkers have assumed that classical Chinese thinkers debated philosophical theories about righteousness, heaven, principle, moral codes, and so forth. Thus, it was perfectly reasonable from that standpoint to compare the specifics of, say, Chinese ethics, politics, or metaphysics with their western counterparts. Yet, as Ames has taught us, we should not refer to specific Chinese ethical ideas without first understanding how those "ethical" concepts function within their wider cultural, social, and historical backgrounds. That is, we must begin with questioning how moral behavior and ethical reflection operate in the Chinese setting, leaving open the possibility that in China morality might be linked to, say, the virtuosity of creative expression in a way that would seem to many Westerners to be more analogous to aesthetics than ethics. In the final analysis, therefore, we cannot unproblematically divvy up a non-Western intellectual tradition into philosophical subfields drawn from the western heritage.

I came to appreciate the significance of that last point more fully when, as a Japanese philosophy specialist, I collaborated with Roger on the *Routledge Encyclopedia of Philosophy*. As the area editor for East Asian philosophy, Roger assembled a small number of colleagues to discuss which entries to include and how to organize them. In our initial discussion, Roger raised an objection he had to the earlier encyclopedias, including what was then the standard in the field, *The Encyclopedia of Philosophy* published in 1967 by Macmillan under the general editorship of Paul Edwards. Specifically, Roger challenged the hegemony given to Western philosophical categories in the work's organization, claiming they skewed the ensuing analysis. For example, he proposed that instead of having an entry "Law, Chinese," we should have an entry on *fa* and cross-reference it after the main article on "Law" as "see also *fa*." Then, if someone wanted to learn about the classical idea of Chinese "law," that English reader would only be able to do so by first grappling with a Chinese term that has no single Western equivalent, learning how it was nuanced in different ways within the classical Confucian, Daoist, and Buddhist traditions.

As I recall, it took our little group only about fifteen minutes of discussion to conclude that Roger's suggestion was *exactly* the way we should proceed. The gist of our reasoning was that "Law, Chinese" seemed to *refer* to a Chinese object or field that was purported somehow essentially akin to "Law" as a general Western category. It was as if the English "law" and Chinese "*fa*" shared a common essence, analogous to how "morning star" and "evening star" could both denote the same thing: Venus. Our proposed approach, by contrast, would introduce our readers to the core ideas behind the Chinese concept of law by catapulting them into a constellation of traditional Chinese ideas and ways of thinking. That is, to grasp the meaning of Chinese philosophical terms, our assumption was that we needed to account for their sense as well as their reference. This brings us to the second dimension of meaning and its cluster of questions.

Meaning as Sense

When a classical Chinese philosophical writer used a particular term, what other terms or ideas did it conjure in the mind of the ancient Chinese reader? How does that conjuring bring nuance or connotation to its meaning? How is that term used in other texts from the time (poetic, historical, and exhortatory writings as well as philosophical treatises)? How does the etymology of the word or the sinograph itself reveal implicit or explicit clues to its distinctive sense?

From the standpoint of reference, words are like individual mirrors, each reflecting some unitary bit of reality. In their referential function, individual words represent or picture independent realities, preferably in a one-to-one correspondence. Richard Rorty characterized that dominant paradigm of modern Western thought in his highly influential *Philosophy and the Mirror of Nature*. It captures rather well the function of meaning as reference. For meaning as sense, however, we need to view the matter differently.

Rather than thinking of words and concepts as little mirrors reflecting bits of reality, if we are interested in their sense rather than reference dimension, it might be more fruitful to think of them as pieces in a jigsaw puzzle. Each term, like each piece of a puzzle, not only exists alone, but, in fulfilling its meaning, its very form either opens up to or penetrates into its adjoining pieces. If there is any representation involved, it only comes forth when all the pieces fit together to form a complete picture.

It is tempting to think of reference as the primary dimension of meaning and sense as an add-on. Perhaps that view derives from the naïve idea that words are learned first as ostensive gestures, as pointers to specific objects or entities. This process traces back to, for example, a baby's first word *mama* as denoting the baby's mother. Then, the theory goes, other nuances about the mother-baby relation gradually accrue to that nuclear reference and the sense of the word gradually expands its meaning into a halo of nuance and connotation. Yet, that is a rather impoverished way to construe the basic function of language. I would argue that right from the start, the word *mama* resonates with connotations of warmth, nourishment, cuddling, and singing. In saying "mama" the baby is not simply referring to an external being but is as equally and primordially evoking a rich array of connotative links. From this perspective, the meaning of the word *mama* is hugs, kisses, lullabies, smiling eyes, and a tender touch as much as it is "the woman over there who gave me birth and stays nearby." That is: the full meaning originates as much from the sense as the reference.

Meaning as sense plays two central roles in Ames's scholarship and philosophizing. First, he seems to assume that if we are going to understand Chinese thinking and expression, we need to focus at least as much, and probably more, on the dimension of sense rather than reference. For Ames, meaning is more a semantic field than an ostensive vector. Second, he maintains that if we can grasp the sense of a rather small cluster of intimately interrelated central Chinese concepts, we will obtain a key to unlocking the general thrust of Chinese philosophy in any specific context. As I will now explain, those two roles are intimately interwoven.

I begin with meaning as semantic field. Most of us at some early point in our grade school education learned that the primary and most authoritative way of determining the meaning of a particular word is to refer to a dictionary. Those of us with a philosopher's gene in our make-up likely reflected on this activity at some point, arriving at the startling and profoundly disorientating realization that the words in an unabridged dictionary define each word in terms of other words from that same dictionary. One did not have to be a logician like Gödel to surmise that language might be construed as a self-enclosed system of definitions with no semantic anchor outside itself.

Welcome to the semantic field of meaning as sense. This is the field on which Ludwig Wittgenstein saw us playing out our language games. He argued that meaning is not limited, as he once thought, to words being little pictures of states of affairs. He had in his student days assumed that what language cannot be said to picture was beyond language and had to be, as he wrote as the last sentence of *Tractatus Logico-Philosophicus*, left to silence. After distancing himself from Cambridge and engaging for some time in other activities including the teaching of primary school students, Wittgenstein came to the very different conclusion that meaning lay not in the power of words to reflect or picture an external reality but rather lay in their being moves within a prescribed language game. As he put it, "Meaning is the use." Those language games, of course, are not mere amusements but the very stuff of the *Lebensformen*, the patterns of life as we live it.

When viewed in this light, the issue then becomes that if we are to understand the meaning of Chinese philosophical terms, we must enter the classical Chinese world as it had been lived. This is the inspiration behind the pioneering and transformative early work Ames did in collaboration with David L. Hall. As they insightfully suggested in the title of their 1987 book, they did not invite us to think *about* Confucius but to think *through* Confucius, to be fellow participants in his world as a lived form of experience. Thus, when Ames and his collaborators introduce us to Confucian terms, we are not given simple dictionary definitions that pretend we can understand any key term without other key terms. Rather, as he does in collaboration with Hall in *Thinking through Confucius* and more thoroughly in 1999 with Henry Rosemont Jr., in their "philosophical translation" of the *Analects*, he introduces us to Confucius by catapulting us across the walls separating our philosophical world from that of ancient China. As a result we find ourselves in an engagement with a group of intimately interrelated terms that define the field and rules for the Chinese game of philosophy as it is played. In short: instead of explaining the terms, we are shown how to use them like a Confucian.

This tactic does present us with new concerns, however. Ultimately, if we think through to its conclusion our juvenile recognition that all the words in the dictionary are defined by other words in the dictionary, only an unabridged dictionary can give us the full picture of language as it is used and lived. In that respect, it might seem that we would need to know *all* the Confucian words if we are truly to understand *any* of them. To fathom the complete sense of meaning as it is played out by the speakers of a given language game would seem to mean we need all the words just as we need all the pieces of the jigsaw puzzle to comprehend the full picture of what the puzzle portrays. If that is right, then it would seem the task of thinking through Confucius would require us to know *all* the words in *all* the Confucian texts. But such scope is in practice impossible, even to a specialist.

For the sake of Ames's enterprise, to give his readers a mastery of the entire lexicon of Confucian terms might be a theoretical ideal, but fortunately it is not necessary for getting the project underway. Ames and his colleagues realized that it should be possible to find a web of interconnected key concepts or words that would serve as the basic parameters within which all the fundamental Confucian points can be located and played out, establishing the boundaries and rules for its philosophical language game, as it were. The tactical issue, though, was which cluster of concepts could, when taken together, establish the needed parameters. Judging from the final product, I suspect the strategy was something like the following.

First, we note that a striking characteristic of Confucianism is its exegetical intertextuality. The extent of this proclivity for consciously and conscientiously writing texts to build on previous texts was brought home to me many years ago when I studied Japanese Edo-period Confucianism for a year under the tutelage of Professor Koyasu Nobukuni of Ōsaka University. For our study guide, he photocopied a Chinese-language text from that era that purported to be a study of the *Analects*. What struck me was its format. A line from Confucius was followed by whatever Mencius or Xunzi had written (most likely in a few sentences each) about the line or perhaps a key point in that line. Then came Zhuxi's commentary on what Mencius and Xunzi had said about that original line. (Now we have perhaps a page of commentary). Then came what the Japanese Confucian, Itō Jinsai, said about that whole corpus of commentary, perhaps in a couple of pages. Finally, there was Ogyū Sorai's commentary in two or three pages addressing the whole kit and caboodle.

Of course, those East Asian commentators were not necessarily agreeing with each other. In fact, they often used their commentaries to diverge from or subordinate the interpretations of others. All along the way, however, they were spinning off the original words of Confucius. That is, despite their differences, there was never disagreement over what the issue was or over which terms or concepts were pivotal. In thinking through Confucius in this way, the commentators were investigating the sense rather than reference of the original statement from the *Analects*. The referents of words are always quite fixed, but the senses are always organically growing and blossoming forth (organicism is another favorite motif in Roger Ames's gestalt of early Chinese thought). That commentarial tradition, well known to Ames and his collaborators, was likely an inspiration for trying to identify the basic cluster of words, terms, and concepts that were the seeds that grew and bore fruit as the Confucian tradition. Thus, the two points I mentioned—the focus on meaning as sense in the task of unearthing the roots of Confucianism and the construction of a cluster of key concepts to define the parameters of the tradition—merge at this point. Before Roger Ames and his co-authors, much of the Western scholarship amounted to a summary of the commentarial tradition as a path to explaining Confucianism. What was new in the Ames-led project was that it was in the end more a commentary in itself, a commentary written in English. Like all good commentaries, however, it was firmly based in the originary texts. Its operative principle was that to study Confucianism was to think through those texts rather than think about them.

Still, however carefully they might try to represent the weight of the Confucian canon in picking their terms, there was still the danger of radical misinterpretation. The Chinese say a journey of a thousand *li* starts with a single step, but we might add that the step had better be in the right direction. Choosing the appropriate and most pedagogically effective seminal concepts was not a simple matter of gathering concordances and determining which terms occurred most frequently in the ancient Chinese texts. The project was not simply to see which ideas were most discussed, but more pointedly, to determine which ones *normatively* shaped the tradition, defining what a Confucian *ought* to think about.

Notice that this observation returns us to the dimension of meaning as sense. Think back to my example of the infant's saying "mama." In discussing the sense as contrasted with the referent of that word, I introduced affective, interpersonal, and behavior factors. In Ames's most current iteration, this indicates that Confucianism makes senses as the modeling of *roles*, a function not just cognitive but also affective, not just intellectual but also somatic, not just theoretical but also practical. And most importantly of all: not just descriptive but also prescriptive. Once he took this line of analysis, Ames realized that he had found a way to avoid projecting Western categories onto Chinese categories and he shaped his idea in his 2011 book as "Confucian role ethics."

There remains, however, the question of how Ames can determine whether the decided upon cluster of seminal concepts are indeed the right ones. Can they really, if properly nurtured, lead to the human flourishing as we find it in the Confucian tradition? Being a pragmatist in spirit, Ames places the purported truth of his analysis in whether it "works." Here the proof of the pudding lies in whether that cluster of concepts can successfully explain to a neophyte the basic character of Confucian philosophy. In his interpretative scholarship, Ames has argued that we can understand Chinese Confucian philosophy only if we start by surveying and carefully marking the parameters defining its conceptual field, its arena of ideas within the boundaries of which its particular philosophical language game is played. Ames's essays and books have been working through the Confucian philosophical enterprise by taking for his point of departure the key terms and concepts that yield something like the overall Confucian/Chinese worldview.

Just as importantly, though, there is the practical test of the approach. Here we find another element of John Dewey in Roger Ames. The real test for Ames is to appraise the ideas as heuristic tools in the laboratory of education (the stress on education is also, of course, clearly Confucian in spirit as well). In following this line of thought to this point, we should note that we have already drifted into the third dimension of meaning—intention.

Meaning as Intention

In asking whether there is pedagogical value in his characterization of Confucianism, Ames believes the real test is to see whether a novice can use the core cluster of categories as an entrée to experiencing for oneself, at least imaginatively, what Confucianism is trying to achieve. From the standpoint of intention, we cannot know the meaning of Confucianism by merely understanding all the points Confucius was referencing or all the connotations that allowed him to make sense of the forms of life he advocated. To fully appreciate the meaning of Confucianism, we must also engage its intentions. What is Confucianism getting at? Where is it trying to lead us? Of what is it trying to persuade us? What are its assumptions about personal transformation? Those questions emerge from the third dimension of meaning and escort us into the domain of education.

Roger's reputation as an outstanding teacher derives in part, of course, from his personable style, his attention to the details of his pedagogical craft, and his care for students. Just as importantly, though, is the transformative function of his teaching. Using his schema of key Confucian terms and— just as crucially—embodying the role of the true Confucian teacher, Roger does not teach *about* Confucianism but teaches *through* Confucianism. This activity is not limited to the classrooms at the University of Hawai'i either. A spinoff of his teaching career has been to demonstrate convincingly the pragmatic value of studying the philosophy of an Asian culture as an initial gestalt for interpreting the culture at large. Working in collaboration with another philosopher, Peter Hershock of the East-West Center, Roger has helped create and direct a highly effective program that has proven just how powerful philosophy can be as an *entrée* to understanding different cultures. I am referring to the Asian Studies Development Program, a joint venture of the UH Department of Philosophy and the East-West Center dating from 1991 and continuing today.

The ASDP is an assemblage of programs—summer institutes, workshops, field experiences in Asia, website and curricular development, and so forth—for training college teachers who are not specialists in Asian cultures, but who want to introduce their students to more Asian materials in a variety of disciplines. Previously, most such training programs have begun with the literature, history, arts, or anthropological behaviors of the target culture. Roger and Peter have shown, however, that philosophy as well can be a most effective starting point. If done properly, it can be an effective launching point for engaging the culture, giving a map for subsequently studying the country's literature, arts, history, and so forth. This is only true, however, if the philosophical introduction is properly constructed. Roger started by using his cluster of key ideas and terms to explain China and then asked me to do something similar with Japan. ASDP's scope has subsequently expanded to cover South and Southeast Asia as well.

The stellar success of the program is attested to not only by its receiving renewed federal and private funding for well over a decade now, but also, and more importantly, by the achievements of its participants who have developed new courses and exciting curricular innovations in institutions throughout the country. This has demonstrated not only the effectiveness of starting with a cluster of philosophical ideas as an entrance into understanding foreign cultures, but also has disproven the idea that only an area specialist can teach students something valuable about Asian cultures.

Assessing the Contributions of Roger Ames and Prospects for the Future

In the spirit of a true *Festschrift*, I will conclude by briefly bringing a critical eye to Roger Ames's body of work, raising questions and issues for further reflection and possible future paths for thinking through Confucianism. In the spirit of olden days, I will pour myself another cup of coffee and initiate a critical discussion, if not an argument. When Roger and I argue, however firm our differences of philosophical conviction, it is ultimately an act of mutual support like two apes grooming each other. In our case, though, when we identify and remove bugs, it is from our wooly ideas. Or, to resort to a sports metaphor (part of a language game often engaged in my university), our arguments are more intrasquad scrimmages than games against an opponent. In both cases we play our language game as competitively and intensely as possible, but the primary purpose—unlike a game against an opponent—is to make each other better at what we do. And in doing so, to take special care not to cause personal injury.

For my summary critique, I will focus on one of Roger's most recent philosophical formulations: Confucian role ethics. For much of this essay, I have looked to the origins of Roger's thinking. So, it is fitting in my conclusion to look to where it has brought him, at least up to now. Thus, I am not looking at his role ethics as a theory in itself, but more as another trail marker in helping us to think through Roger Ames's course of work. To some of these questions, Roger has given answers in his writings, at least partial or tentative ones. For my purposes here, however, I do not want to address details, but rather to give a holistic vision of issues that Roger's work as teacher and scholar raise for me.

I have fundamentally one question: what does Ames's theory *mean*? I suggest we follow the template we have already used. To what does the theory of Confucian role ethics *refer*? How does the theory make *sense* of ethics by defining the field and rules for its language game and for engaging its forms of life? Where does the theory *intend* to lead us and of what is it trying to persuade us?

The Reference of Confucian Role Ethics

In a rather obvious way, the theory refers to the way the Chinese live their moral life, to the way they achieve virtuosity in acting appropriately to what our humanity demands of us. In short: the theory refers, at least initially, to China. But which China? Ancient China? It initially portrays ancient China, but it also suggests that at least some of its ancient worldview affects China even today (which is why it works so well in the ASDP program even for those participants who are most focused on modern China). But then, are we considering the ancient China of history or a venerable Confucian imaginary of an ancient golden age? From some postmodern standpoints, it may not make much of a difference since we are as driven by our imaginaries as we are our facts of positivistic history (which is its own imaginative reconstruction of events).

Yet, from a practical point of view, the answer does make a difference. If the theory at least partially, perhaps in an originary way, refers to ancient Chinese forms of life, we should probably test it chiefly through historical research (philological, textual, archeological, etc.). If, on the other hand, the theory is more an ideal picture of a society that for rhetorical purposes its proponents framed as an ancient truth, then its narrative is more utopian than empirical. In that case, the grounds for its assessment would require different methods, more strictly grounded in philosophical analysis in the way we evaluate other utopian visions (Augustine's *City of God* or Thomas More's *Utopia*, for instance). If Confucianism presents us with a utopian rather than historical account, for example, we might look more closely into its coherence, the possible consequences of its enactment, and its implications for inspiring further theories and practices. So, before we can assess the truth of Ames's theory, we must be clear about what counts as the criteria for evaluation. And that depends on how we judge the genre of the Confucian texts, perhaps along the methodological lines of Rudolf Bultmann's "form criticism" in biblical studies.

The mention of Bultmann (who was noted for his method of "demythologization") suggests yet another possibility. Perhaps Confucius's portrayal of the virtues and performances of the sagely kings of old more resembles a religious myth. Religious myths can be in the form of historical narratives, but whether they are factually true as historical fact is far less important than what they tell us about the religion's fundamental worldview, its philosophical anthropology, and its core values. For example, the Christian myth found in the Gospel of Luke portrays the familiar account of Jesus's being born in a manger. The birth narrative exemplifies many Christian core teachings such as the primary value of humility, the presence of the divine as completely immanent and incarnate, the universality of the Christian message (the narrative includes poor shepherds, the three magi kings, the celestial choir of angels, animals, and an astronomical event). Christians would maintain those core values in the narrative even if someone could prove the event portrayed never occurred. In a parallel way, would Confucians still uphold the truth of the *Analects* even if it turns out there were no sagely kings in ancient China upon whose virtues Confucius had focused his narrative? This question of truth relates more to sense than reference.

The Sense of Confucian Role Ethics

Given what I said earlier about Ames's philosophical orientation, the sense of Confucian role theory is probably in some ways more significant to him than its referent. Ames's work has been criticized by some sinologists who are limited to a positivistic understanding of evidence and who are apt to criticize how historically and philologically "authentic" is Ames's depiction of ancient China. Ames has addressed many of those concerns—very well in my opinion—but the nature of area studies scholarship is such that some of its advocates will never fully agree with him. That is understandable because Ames recognizes that the meaning of Confucianism, and by extension the meaning of Confucian role ethics, is constructive, holistic, and creative. (Ames considers the *poesis* in ancient Greek thought to be analogous in some ways with ancient Chinese thought.) That is, Confucian role ethics involves sense as well as reference.

This dimension of sense allows for real comparative work to occur. While comparison has its pitfalls, as I have explained with the attempt to consider individual terms like *law* and *fa* to be analogous, it is much more philosophically interesting and valuable to compare holistic gestalts or worldviews. Ames and his co-authors have excelled in nuanced juxtapositions of the ancient Chinese and ancient Greek worldviews as well as the stark contrasts between traditional Chinese thought and the thinking typical of the Western Enlightenment. Such comparative projects are still in their emergent phase but Ames's Confucian role ethics presents us with fertile ground to till even if it is only as of now a point of departure. Much more thinking, much of it foundational, has to be done by all of us engaged in comparative philosophy, regardless of Asian focus.

For example, let us return to the idea of each culture having its own philosophical language games, each with its own clearly defined playing field and rules. The approach for analyzing similarity and difference can then be seen to have various possibilities. For example, is the relation between role ethics and traditional Western ethics like the one between chess and checkers? If so, then the domain, the playing board, is the same, but the game has different moves, rules, and strategies. Or does role ethics raise the possibility that the very enterprise of comparative ethics can only function on a trivial and superficial level, like ruminating on the similarities and differences between Chinese and Western checkers? The two share neither playing field nor rules so why engage in any detailed comparison at all? Why should we even call Chinese checkers "checkers?" The nomenclature probably derives from some Westerners seeing two people move pieces on a board and being reminded of checkers because the pieces jump each other. Such a naïve comparison based in projecting one's culture onto another is akin to naively correlating *yi* with "righteousness." If that is the case, then perhaps Confucian role ethics has no place within the language game of comparative ethics as it has usually been played, but instead is a provocation to do something other than ethics in the way it has usually been conducted in the West. This brings me to the dimension of the meaning of role ethics as its intentional dimension.

The Intention of Confucian Role Ethics

Where is Roger Ames really trying to take us? As he suggests in his introduction to *Role Ethics*, it is to a better world. His project is constructive, not simply analytic; prescriptive, not simply descriptive. In addressing this enterprise, Ames is still, I believe, trying to feel his way. At times I see his intention as meta-ethical as well as ethical. That is, he seems to be trying to develop his account of Chinese role ethics into a global discussion of key ethical and social issues. The implication in so doing, however, is that role ethics would have to be excised from its Chinese milieu. For role ethics to have meta-ethical valence, Chinese thought can be no more than a particular (well-developed and provocative) instance of how it works. But to be applicable in a global philosophical discussion, role ethics would eventually have to assume a more cross-cultural characterization. Only then can role ethics maximize its critical role in the development of philosophical meta-ethical theory.

Incidentally, this raises further issues concerning the cultural embeddedness of any theory of role ethics (whether Ames's or not). Namely, someone might argue, for example, that *homo sapiens* is intrinsically social, but the manifestation of social relations is always necessarily cultural. This raises the possibility that, say, the roles of parent or child and of husband and wife might exist everywhere, but its characters might still differ in important ways across cultures. Even in China, with the changes in family size, geographical dispersion of extended families, and so forth, does the traditional performance of familiar roles have to undergo some alteration? If we go in this direction, the issues start looking more sociological than philosophical and I suspect that is not Ames's intent. But then the issue remains of how to negotiate the idea of "role" in a way that is true to the formidable insights Ames has found in the Chinese tradition yet still be open to the possibility of cultural diversity and social differentiation.

In the end, I think Ames's intention is probably more subtle than any of the options I have articulated. Here I may be projecting some of my own experience onto his, but I think the value of thinking through X (whether Confucianism, Daoism, Buddhism, Islam, Christianity, or whatever) is not to stay within X. That is, when those of us who were not born Confucians undertake the task of thinking through Confucius, we have used our intelligence, imagination, empathy, and creativity to imagine a different "way" of playing out the forms of life. This suggests that the integration of Confucian role ethics into our moral life does not necessarily mean we must become Confucians. The concept and practice of justice in the West has historically been profoundly influenced by engaging the idea of justice in the Hebrew Bible, but that does not mean the West became Jewish. The ancient Hebrew ideas so thoroughly dissolved into the Western ideal that many western people do not even recognize the contribution made by that encounter with Jewish thought.

Analogously, I can imagine a point at which some ideals within Confucian role ethics so permeate global philosophical discussions that they are no longer considered Confucian at all. Roger Ames's theory of role ethics may have, biographically speaking, been inspired by his lifelong encounter with Confucianism, but the theory itself need not be considered Confucian. The Western expressionist movement in art may have been inspired by the encounter with Japanese art, but that does not make expressionism "Japanese." And as expressionism developed further in the West, it did not have to continue to return to Japanese sources for further inspiration. In fact, as with the connection of western ideas of justice to Judaism, the link between expressionism and Japanese woodblock prints may not even be known to many people.

In the final analysis, from my standpoint, and at least to some extent Roger's too I suspect, the long-range intention of thinking through Confucius need not at all be to become a Confucian or even a better Confucian. The real benefit to thinking through Confucius is to expand philosophical horizons, to think what we had never thought of thinking, and to be enriched as philosophers, citizens, and human beings by that experience. Viewed in that light, role ethics is not only philosophically provocative; it also possesses the pragmatic potential for helping us heal some of the wounds of our world in our time. But we have to engage collectively in making the theory "work." Then it cannot be simply Confucian or merely Chinese in its relevance, but would have to become global and universal in its implications. We need not convert the world to Confucianism in order to develop our world in a way inspired by some of its ideas. In its meaning as reference and sense, Confucian role ethics has already shown itself to be a major success through the impact of Roger Ames's scholarship and teaching. The next stage has to be a more collective philosophical enterprise inspired by Confucian role ethics in a way that takes it beyond its own geographical borders and inherent limitations of being a culturally dependent language game. In that respect, the ultimate intention of Ames's role theory may be for it not to remain "Confucian" or "Chinese" but to be more universal than any one cultural tradition can ever be.

At this point I end my discussion with Roger and his work, looking forward to another cup of coffee on another day.

2

On Comparative and Post-Comparative Philosophy

Hans-Georg Moeller

Introduction: Comparative Philosophy as a Feature of Modernity

The history of comparative philosophy, as it is understood and practiced academically today, dates back to the intensification of the cultural and economic contacts between Europe and the "Orient" in early modernity. In the seventeenth century, Far Eastern and, in particular, Chinese, philosophy emerged as a subject of European intellectual curiosity with the reports on Chinese civilization and translations of Chinese canonical texts sent back from Jesuit missionaries, such as Matteo Ricci, who had immediate access to the imperial court and thus also to the intellectual elite of the Chinese empire. In this sense, comparative philosophy and modernity are historically connected. East-West comparative philosophy is a modern phenomenon: it arose in the context of the modernization of European society and of its simultaneous global expansion.

Historically, East-West philosophy thus differs from intra-European, or, for that matter, intra-Chinese comparative philosophy. Of course, philosophy had always been comparative: Aristotle had already compared himself with Plato and other Greek philosophers he knew of; medieval Christian philosophy had compared itself with the Greeks. Likewise, the book of *Zhuangzi* concludes with a whole chapter on early Chinese comparative philosophy, and the Neo-Confucians of the Song and Ming dynasties were busy comparing themselves with the Buddhists. However, in these cases, some sort of genealogical continuity between the two or more sides which were compared was assumed. The radical others, the "barbarians" or the "heathens" were not really considered worthy of a serious comparison and could, culturally speaking, remain an object of curiosity or simply be ignored. Niklas Luhmann says of the barbarians of old: "They were left with their own social order. We did not have anything to do with it." While, as Luhmann adds, one was still "free to convert them or to enslave them, or to cheat them when exchanging goods,"[1] there was no need to seriously reflect on their "meaning." Along with the transition toward modernity, however, such cognitive exclusion becomes less practicable. The space where the others can hide out of sight increasingly vanishes. Comparative philosophy thus not only fulfils the function of identity construction in the face of those who seem different, or at least not yet quite like "us"—whoever "us" and "they" are—but also, and perhaps increasingly so under the conditions of globalization, to cultivate attitudes toward and a semantics of inclusion of those who can no longer be dismissed as meaningless barbarians, since "we" now indeed *do* have something to do with "them."

In their *Communist Manifesto*, Marx and Engels characterized the situation of a globalizing economy in the nineteenth century in quite colorful language: "The need of a constantly expanding market for its products chases the bourgeoisie over the whole surface of the globe. It must nestle everywhere, settle everywhere, establish connections everywhere."[2] The academic profession of today has inherited this predicament from industrial capitalism. In the wake of globally established communicative "connections"—which are by no means confined to economic ties—even philosophy nowadays cannot but also nestle everywhere and settle everywhere. The global extension of practically all social function systems, including the academic system, is geared toward all-inclusion. Specific forms of inclusion vary, and thus it is no surprise that comparative philosophy, over the course of a few centuries, also developed a variety of ways of making sense of or *de-barbarizing the barbarians*.

Four Historical Forms of Comparative Philosophy

In the somewhat notorious beginning of his lectures on the *History of Philosophy*, Hegel provides an account—in part directly and in part indirectly—of possible attitudes in comparative philosophy.[3] In the context of his remarks on the "first" (in the sense of "primal") philosophy, namely the philosophy of the "Orient," Hegel outlines what was generally known about Chinese philosophy at his time, referring explicitly to Gottfried Wilhelm Leibniz, who was, arguably, the most relevant European East-West comparative philosopher before him.⁴ Leibniz represents a largely welcoming and actively interested approach to Chinese thought that reflects the European curiosity about this newly found foreign civilization at the other end of the world. This curiosity had led to a first wave of *Chinoiserie* that influenced the fashion trends of the European bourgeoisie in the eighteenth century, particularly with respect to gardening and porcelain.

As Hegel mentions, Confucius "made a great sensation in Leibniz's time."⁵ The Roman Catholic missionaries at the Imperial Court in China reported often favorably on the level of cultivation of the Chinese elite and admired their sense of and concern for history, along with what they perceived as a complex and effective political and social organization of the Chinese empire. They were impressed by the rich textual tradition in China and the highly developed Confucian moral semantics which thoroughly informed public life through an elaborate ritual code. Leibniz concluded from the information provided by the missionaries that Europeans could actually learn something from the Chinese. To Leibniz, Chinese moral teachings seemed to be capable of improving European manners, and he believed that they could contribute to making European society more refined and virtuous.

Leibniz had an equally welcoming opinion of Chinese logic and language. As an early Universalist, Leibniz hoped to be able to outline foundational mathematical and logical patterns, and he believed that these had been already expressed, at least in rudimentary form, in the Chinese classics—namely in the symbolic mapping of the relationships between the "principles" of Yin and Yang in the Book of Changes (*Yijing*). Leibniz also believed that the Chinese writing system was ideographic; he thought that it would thus be an excellent candidate for a future universal script and language, which would not be tied to the phonetic peculiarities of any particular language, but rather based only on ideas which, as he believed, were universally shared.

In sum, Leibniz undertook comparative philosophy as a project of *ornamentation, incorporation,* and *universalization.* Quite in accordance with the material *Chinoiserie* that was clearly visible both outside and inside the European courts to which he was attached, Leibniz hoped to adorn European moral taste and political manners through Chinese imports. The incorporation of Chinese thought, he believed, could help identify the basic patterns of reason, and the characters of the Chinese script would be an important tool for ultimately achieving the communicative unification of humankind. Simply put, Leibniz already pursued a more or less benign goal which has often been formulated by comparative philosophers: namely that both sides could profit from a dialogue with one another and thus improve not only mutual understanding, but also self-understanding and, eventually, some sort of general human hermeneutic progress.

More than one hundred years after Leibniz, when Hegel presented his lectures on the history of philosophy, the European attitude toward the Far East had undergone some severe changes. In the first half of the nineteenth century Imperialism was moving toward its pinnacle, and it also met with increasing resistance and conflict. Hegel no longer shared Leibniz's view of the "Orientals" as a quaint counterpart of European reason useable to embellish the common world that was about to be built. For Hegel, the Orientals were not some lost brothers who were found again. Instead, he employed the metaphorics of childhood and immaturity to describe them and their philosophy.

The distinction between maturity and immaturity was central to the semantics of the Enlightenment. "Enlightenment is man's emergence from his self-incurred immaturity," famously, is the very first sentence of Kant's programmatic essay "An Answer to the Question: 'What is Enlightenment?'"[6] Only the enlightened human is a mature human. Those who have not gone through the process of modernization and its philosophical enlightenment are thus by definition immature. Hegel's view of the Orientals, including the Chinese, follows this simple pattern. He begins his remarks on oriental philosophy by stating that "its position is preliminary" and he concludes his outline of Chinese philosophy by maintaining that "if Philosophy has got no further than to such expression, it still stands on its most elementary stage."[7]

Hegel could perhaps also be classified as a Universalist; but for him, more than for Leibniz, reason had a history and was continuously developing. Therefore, his technique of including non-European into the "world spirit" was different from that of Leibniz. Genealogically, the Orientals can only be included at the beginning, or, better—because the beginning may smack too much of origin—even slightly before that. Hegel thus essentially conceives of non-European thought as "primitive." Accordingly, Hegel represents what may be called a "primitivist" type of comparative philosophy. The Chinese, in particular, have remained in an infantile state of "not yet" for Hegel. In this way, unlike the barbarians, they belong to our family, but only like children do: we have to take care of them, educate them, and discipline them; but, insofar as we are enlightened, we cannot yet regard them as worthy interlocutors. In the *Lectures on the Philosophy of World History*, Hegel says:

> Among the Chinese, for example, no form of individual assent whatsoever is required; if they were taken to task for this as a deficiency in their constitution, they would consider it just as absurd as if children of all ages were asked to participate in a family council. The Chinese are not yet conscious of their own nature as free subjectivity; they do not yet realise that the essential property of ethicality and justice is contained within the latter,

which is not yet present to them and their end, their product, and their object.[8]

Hegel's "primitivism," however, also touches upon another form of comparative philosophy. When commenting on Daoist philosophy in the *History of Philosophy*, Hegel quotes chapter 14 of the *Daodejing*. This chapter refers to the *Dao* as hardly visible, audible, and touchable, and thus as "minute," "silent," and "smooth." The translation Hegel uses, however, transliterates these three words as "I," "Hi" and "Wei." When read aloud in sequence (I-Hi-Wei), they sound in German somewhat similar to the name of the Hebrew God, Jehovah, as well as of "the African kingly name of Juba and also of Jovis."[9] Hegel apparently believed that the Daoists intuitively shared some metaphysical insights with other world religions. Of course, the assumption that the three characters in question were actually pronounced in ancient Chinese akin to the ancient pronunciation of the ancient Hebrew word for Jehovah is highly problematic. Be that as it may, it is interesting to see how Hegel reads some basic Judeo-Christian contents into non-European texts and in this way universalizes and decontextualizes them.

Here, another method of comparative philosophy comes to the fore that has been practiced in various guises and that may be called a form of *interpolation*. Through (often extremely vague and/or liberal) translations into a European language, non-European texts can sound and read as if they were written in some ancient European language and operated with an essentially European vocabulary. Once one has settled on a specific translation or interpretation, this translation or interpretation often takes on its own life, so to speak, and one works with it as if it were in the original text. When Hegel quotes other passages from the *Daodejing* in the *History of Philosophy*, he uncritically accepts, for instance, the translation of the core term *dao* 道 as "reason" (*Vernunft*) or of *yin* 阴 and *yang* 阳 as "principles" (*Prinzipien*) of darkness and light.[10]

By the nineteenth and early twentieth centuries, Protestant missionaries from continental Europe and the Anglo-American world had replaced the Roman Catholic missionaries of earlier centuries as the main intellectual mediators between China and the West. They produced translations of a variety of texts, including the most famous philosophical works. These translations were much more accessible than previous ones; they were published in various local European languages rather than only in Latin or French, and they were readily available in bookstores or libraries. Among the most influential missionary translators were the Scotsman James Legge[11] and the German Richard Wilhelm.[12] Both translators infused Chinese philosophy with a Christian vocabulary and Christian semantics. On the basis of these translations it was easy to find the seeds of all sorts of European ideas in the Far East—and in particular, of course, Christian ones. In short, it seemed that God was already known to the Chinese, but had not yet fully revealed Himself to them. This was now the task to be fulfilled by the missionaries.

Given the relatively wide audience reached by the missionary translations of the late nineteenth and early twentieth centuries, it was not surprising that Chinese philosophy now began to emerge as a *spiritual* complement or even outright alternative to a waning Judeo-Christian religiosity in Europe. The Jewish religious philosopher Martin Buber, for instance, developed his thought under a significant influence from Daoism while a first wave of a "New Age" syncretism began to rise amongst a wider intellectual readership.[13] A new form of "global" religiosity, now often called "spirituality," grew in modern European society at the time when the secularized new European nation states had removed themselves to a great extent from the direct influence of the Christian churches and its clerics.

In sum, four general forms of comparative philosophy as de-barbarization developed between the seventeenth and the twentieth centuries at a time when Europe modernized and globalized itself: (1) an approach of incorporation of and improvement by Oriental philosophy *a la* Leibniz, (2) a "primitivist" inclusion of Chinese thought into the development of the "world spirit" *a la* Hegel, (3) an interpolation of European religions and philosophy into ancient Chinese texts *a la* Richard Wilhelm, and (4) a syncretic embrace of Chinese Philosophy as a major source for the foundation of post-Christian modern "spirituality."

Chinese Academic Philosophy as Comparative Philosophy

Only in recent decades has comparative philosophy been accepted into the philosophical academic curriculum of Western universities. Until the second half of the twentieth century, comparative philosophy was typically only undertaken by major philosophers with aspirations for a "world philosophy" (such as Leibniz, Hegel, or Martin Buber) or by "Orientalists" at universities or in missionary service. Unlike the academic field of Religious Studies, which largely developed as an offshoot of anthropology and related disciplines and thus affirmed a plurality of religions, academic philosophy in the West was hardly open to the notion of philosophies in the plural. Even the concept of a world philosophy still conceived of philosophy in the singular—philosophy was believed to be somehow one larger epistemic activity. Rather than acknowledging the existence or possibility of a diversity of philosophies, the Hegelian question of how to include oriental philosophy into an encompassing world philosophy dominated the field—accompanied by the question which Hegel had already asked himself, namely, whether Chinese philosophy (for instance) actually was philosophy at all and not instead religion or something different altogether, such as a form of popular "wisdom."[14]

That comparative philosophy was eventually included into global academic philosophy was not the least due to the fact that it had become a, if not *the*, major form of philosophy in non-Western regions. In China, as in many other "oriental" and other non-European countries, a radical transition toward modern Western social and political structures was initiated in the nineteenth century. While the imperial court of the Qing Dynasty was hesitant to introduce radical reforms, it still gradually adopted Western social and political institutions and tried to adopt "Western learning" not only in technology and the natural sciences, but also in the cultural sphere. When the imperial system collapsed in 1911 and a republic was established, the modernization process accelerated. Modern universities were founded or expanded, and much wider cultural changes took place. The old focus on studying the classics was largely abandoned, and along with it the classical Chinese language as the medium for official and public communication. The May 4th movement in 1919 demanded further modernization and Westernization and called for "Mr. S and Mr. D"—science and democracy—to make their way to China. This made it obvious that the new generation of intellectuals was committed to radical social change.[15]

In this period, an intense East-West exchange took place. While in Europe and America people read traditional Chinese poetry and the works attributed to Confucius and Laozi, Chinese people read contemporary Western literature and the works of, for instance, Nietzsche and Marx. Leading Western philosophers of the time went to China and spent an extended period of time there, most importantly John Dewey, Bertrand Russell, and Hans Driesch whose now largely forgotten vitalist philosophy was quite influential in both China and the West at the time.[16]

Chinese students not only listened to the lectures of these and other Western thinkers but went abroad to Japan—where modernization efforts were a step ahead—as well as to the United States and to Europe. In America, for instance, the major twentieth-century philosopher Feng Youlan studied with Dewey at Columbia University in New York, while others went to France or to Germany, where major philosophers such as Martin Heidegger were frequented by visitors and pupils from the Far East.[17] Along with the establishment of European-style Western universities, academic philosophy was established in China. The new generation of Western-trained young philosophers introduced Western methodologies and a Western metaphysical vocabulary. Hu Shi and Feng Youlan published histories of Chinese philosophy. This was an entirely new category in China. The works which were now understood as philosophical texts—following the interpretations of Hegel and others—had been referred to in the Chinese tradition as "classics" (*jing* 经) or as works of the "masters" (*zi* 子). While such texts had been transmitted over centuries and carefully annotated and edited by the literati of many generations, they had never been conceived of as constituting a specific philosophical history in the Western sense.[18]

In addition to a larger historical overview of Chinese philosophy, Feng Youlan wrote a comprehensive outline of the history of Chinese philosophy. Here he followed the Hegelian approach and looked at Chinese philosophy in terms of a genealogical unfolding of the Chinese "spirit" (*jingshen* 精神). Consequently, it was translated into English as *The Spirit of Chinese Philosophy*.[19] This work is representative of the efforts of the time to "translate" portions of the Chinese classical texts into a conceptual philosophical terminology and historical and systematic framework that was to a large extent taken from modern Western philosophy. The task that Chinese philosophers like Feng Youlan set for themselves was the reinvention of classical Chinese thinking in terms of modern Western philosophy. Based on their work, modern Chinese academic philosophy emerged during the first half of the twentieth century essentially as comparative philosophy. When Chinese philosophers were not directly engaging in comparisons with Western philosophy, they would tend to interpret their own heritage in Western terms: a Chinese metaphysics was reconstructed along with a Chinese ethics and epistemology, and several attempts were made at a general classification of the philosophies of the world and at relating Chinese philosophy to Western and Indian philosophies. An early example is Feng Youlan's Columbia University PhD thesis, which was published under the title *A Comparative Study of Life Ideals* (Shanghai: Shangwu, 1924).

Chinese philosophers, however, worked not only toward the integration of their tradition into the intellectual history of the world and, in order to facilitate this, on the reinterpretation of their ancient texts in the technical vocabulary of Western philosophy. They also worked toward establishing what German scholars have called a *Selbstbehauptungsdikurs* or "self-assertion discourse."[20] One example of this is Feng Youlan's article on "Chinese Philosophy and a Future World Philosophy," published in 1948.[21] Here, Feng argued for a new world philosophy under the guidance of traditional Chinese thought which would overcome what he perceived as a lack of spiritual cultivation in the Western tradition while enriching the Chinese tradition with the rationalism and scientific precision he believed to by representative of Western thought. Feng's article thus represented broader philosophical movements in non-Western countries, such as the Chinese New Confucian philosophy and the Neo-Buddhism of the Kyoto School in Japan, which aimed at correcting the shortcomings of Western philosophy. New Confucian thinkers wanted not only to integrate their own philosophy into global philosophy, but ultimately to "Confucianize" world philosophy. In this way, comparative philosophers in Asia could also emphasize the differences between Eastern and Western philosophies which, in their view, would necessitate a dialogue, and, eventually, a "sublation" of the differences in a higher unit. Often, as in Feng Youlan's case, they envisioned this unit to be founded on their own heritage.[22] No longer satisfied with mere *self*-de-barbarization, major Chinese philosophers such as Feng Youlan also made some attempts at de-barbarizing the West. In effect, they thereby perpetuated the de-barbarization project of comparative philosophy that they had found themselves subjected to.

Contrastive Philosophy and Its Critics

While as de-barbarization comparative philosophy is ultimately geared toward the inclusion and appropriation of the "other," it must also preserve the otherness of the other, at least to a certain extent, since there cannot be a comparison without a distinction. This is the case for comparative philosophy in both the East and the West. Comparative philosophy has its contrastive side, and some comparative philosophers leaned more heavily in this direction. Nearly twenty-five years ago, my former teacher at the Chinese Studies department of Bonn University, Rolf Trauzettel, published an essay with the programmatic and slightly provocative title "Denken die Chinese anders? Komparatistische Thesen zur chinesischen Philosophiegeschichte"—"Do the Chinese think differently? Comparative theses on the history of Chinese philosophy."[23] Trauzettel's answer to the question was an emphatic "Yes." According to him, Chinese philosophy differs significantly from Western philosophy in three major ways: (1) Unlike Western philosophy, Chinese philosophy insolubly integrates thinking and perception (as manifested in the concept of *xin* 心, or the heart-mind—as the organ of thought and perception); (2) Chinese philosophical thought is "self-less" (*ichlos*), unlike modern Western philosophy, it does not presuppose a thinking subject; and (3) Chinese Philosophy is end-oriented (*zielorientiert*), unlike Western philosophy, it therefore did not develop a general philosophical methodology that is not tied to any particular object or objective.

In a different manner, the French comparative philosopher François Jullien has outlined his own version of key differences between Chinese and Western thinking. Jullien has published numerous books on "contrastive philosophy" in recent years that have been translated into a number of languages.[24] Currently, Jullien is arguably the most successful and influential Western comparative-contrastive thinker; but in turn, as is to be expected, he is also one of the most criticized.[25] Typically, the main objections contrastive philosophers have to face are of a political nature in a wider sense: *they don't de-barbarize enough*. They are accused of "reifying" an other which can lead to (a) an Orientalist creation of an "exotic" alien; (b) the denial of universal rationality and thus rational agency to that other; and/or (c) a relativism which undermines universal norms.[26] A related accusation found repeatedly is that contrastive thinkers generalize too much and paint too homogenous a portrait of another culture, denying it internal diversity and development.[27]

The critics of the contrastive philosophers may be divided into two main groups. Some argue ethically like Heiner Roetz[28] and maintain that the assumption of different rationalities undermines universally binding norms and is thus morally unacceptable. Others, like Edward Slingerland,[29] aim at proving through case studies or by statistical means that generalizations about cultures are empirically untenable. In slightly different ways, both groups show their unwavering commitment to the project of early modernity by chastising their comparative predecessors for not having gone far enough in their efforts at de-barbarizing the barbarians.

Re-Barbarizing Ourselves: An Appreciation of Roger Ames's Post-Comparative Confucianism

After this overview of some aspects of the history and current state of comparative philosophy, I will conclude with a brief reflection on the state of comparative philosophy in contemporary contexts. I will specifically address the work of Roger Ames and his *Confucian Role Ethics*.

Modernity has been defined in numerous ways, and many believe that history has already passed the modern stage altogether and that we have now entered the postmodern era. I do not want to comment on these issues in the context of this paper. Instead, I adopt the conception of modernity of Niklas Luhmann. According to Luhmann, modern society emerged in Europe between the sixteenth and eighteenth centuries and, in the time since, constitutes global "world society."[30] The basic structural feature of modern society is "functional differentiation." In modern society, social life is divided into a number of social systems, such as the economy, law, the academic world, or the mass media, each of which has developed its own forms of communication.

All social systems are now globally in place. While regional differences remain—different currencies and different laws, for instance—common basic structures and forms of communication are nevertheless established: currencies can be exchanged, and the distinction between legality and illegality regulates what can be socially expected in most places in the world. Similarly, academic communication, including philosophy, functions worldwide along the lines of the same structures: a paper such as this one communicates in similar ways, regardless of whether it is published in Europe, North America, or East Asia.

There are two central aspects of a functionally differentiated world society. These are (1) the tendency toward all-inclusion, and (2) the coexistence of multiple systems-rationalities. First, all communication systems tend to address everyone: everyone is, politically speaking, supposed to be governed by a government; goods can be purchased by everyone who can pay for them; and the knowledge produced by science is true for all. Second, there is no foundational coherence or shared rationality that would ultimately bind all communication systems to an underlying rationality. That which is legal is not necessarily economically profitable. That which is scientifically true is not necessarily distributed as information by the mass media. Politically effective communication is not necessarily religiously uplifting, and so on.

These aspects of modern society confirm an observation made above. Along with the modern tendency toward all-inclusion or de-barbarization, comparative philosophy works toward the globalization of philosophy. Communication that, in earlier times, had not been regarded as philosophical is now included into philosophical discourse. As we have seen, efforts toward inclusion are by no means restricted to the Western world, but equally undertaken by non-Western academics. Perhaps more interestingly, however, this inclusion does not necessarily lead to "consensus," a "fusion of horizons," or a "future world philosophy." Modern society is highly complex and not integrated by one underlying rationality or common set of cognitive operations. Not only do prices not correspond to laws nor politics to scientific truth, but prices differ from one another, and academic truths—even in analytic philosophy—are rarely in agreement.

Luhmann accordingly gives up "the assumption of parallel views of a unified world."[31] Related to this assumption, he identifies a series of "epistemic blockages," or further erroneous assumptions, that a theory of modern society should leave behind. Among them is the assumption "that more communication and socially reflected communication [. . .] contribute to understanding instead of having the opposite effect."[32] This means that, paradoxically, the more we engage in comparative philosophy the less we understand one another in the sense of approaching a definite or substantial conception of either the "other" or "ourselves." In fact, we are left with an increasing number of often conflicting descriptions or "narratives." Similarly, the history of comparative philosophy did not lead to an over-all consensus, on, let us say, the "spirit of Chinese philosophy" or rational or cognitive universals, but to a variety of differing positions—some of which I discuss in this paper.

It looks as if in earlier times comparative philosophy were still largely concerned with identity formation and the attempt to incorporate that which seemed extra-rational, or at least to measure it against the rational. This lead to the idea of an inter-cultural dialogue which was hoped to bring about, if not the reunification of philosophy, then at least a deeper mutual understanding, or, in the works of Roetz and Slingerland, a complete de-barbarization through the identification of universal rational or cognitive features.

Under current academic conditions these grand projects seem to give way to less general attempts to include non-Western philosophical traditions, such as Confucianism, into various current philosophical discourses. These new discourses may be called, for lack of a better term, "post-comparative." Such attempts gradually move beyond the "de-barbarization" approach of comparative philosophy and aim more precisely at making non-Western traditions significant within current philosophical debates. They "re-barbarize," so to speak, current philosophy and challenge it internally by creating a break-away semantics derived from traditions at the fringes of mainstream discourses. A post-comparative philosophy complements a focus on de-barbarizing the other (e.g. "China" or "the East") with a focus on re-barbarizing ourselves—and "we" are no longer "Westerners," but "our" mainstream philosophical discourses wherever they may take place.

Over the past few decades, Roger Ames's work can be regarded as the most comprehensive and momentous effort to make traditional Confucian texts and their interpretations significant in current philosophical contexts. While some of his critics, such as Roetz and Slingerland, have repeatedly criticized him for not participating fully enough in the de-barbarization project of modern comparative philosophy, they have, intentionally or not, missed what I perceive to be the most decisive contribution that Ames, along with his collaborators David Hall and Henry Rosemont Jr., has made to expand the established horizon of de-barbarization. This contribution lies, in Ames's own terminology, in the formation of a philosophical *vocabulary* that does not evolve from within the currently dominating philosophical discourses but, to the contrary, substantially challenges these discourses by confronting them with an "alien" semantics.

Ames's and Rosemont's "philosophical translation" of the Confucian *Analects*,[33] with its extensive terminological reflections and glossary, already signals this focus on the establishment of an alternative vocabulary that neither imposes an existing current semantics on ancient Chinese texts nor simply inserts a few Chinese ideas or words into such a semantics. Built on efforts such as these, Ames's *Confucian Role Ethics* finally formulates a comprehensive alternative vocabulary to current mainstream ethics.[34] The decisive *philosophical* point of the hermeneutic creation of a Confucian *role ethics* is not so much to say something entirely new about traditional Chinese philosophy, but rather to quite thoroughly question contemporary individualism-centered moral philosophies. Similarly, the significance of Henry Rosemont's work on Confucian ethics lies primarily in its ability to challenge individualism-centered approaches to human rights issues. In other words, both Ames and Rosemont employ comparative philosophy in order to eventually develop a post-comparative philosophy in its own right.

The post-comparative core of Roger Ames's Confucianism connects with Richard Rorty's understanding of philosophy as an explorative engagement with language, texts, and vocabularies. As such, unlike traditional comparative philosophy, it is not geared toward the determination of any cultural or universal identities. Instead, it constructs a rather novel network of technical terms, metaphors, conceptual ideas, and normative claims from readings of ancient Confucian texts. It is not my intention here to present an analysis, summary, or critique of Ames's role ethics, but it should be clear to anyone vaguely familiar with it that its purpose is not primarily historical or philological, but philosophical. This is not to say that historically and philologically informed interpretations of ancient Chinese texts are not central to Ames's work—they are and must necessarily be. Any philosophical vocabulary has to emerge out of a context, and it can only construct meaning by reference to this context. The post-comparative dimension of *Confucian Role Ethics* is thereby firmly grounded and embedded in the comparative dimension of Ames's work. The two dimensions, the comparative and post-comparative, mutually support and influence one another. It is important to see them in conjunction in order to appreciate each of them. If, as some of Ames's critics tend to do, one reduces one to the other, a poor and one-sided picture ensues. I, for one, do not blame Roger Ames for the deficits of this picture.

Notes

1. Niklas Luhmann, "Beyond Barbarism," in *Luhmann Explained: From Souls to Systems*, Hans-Georg Moeller (Chicago: Open Court, 2006), 271.

2. Karl Marx and Friedrich Engels, *The Communist Manifesto*, trans. Samuel Moore (London: Penguin, 1967), 83.

3. On Hegel, Leibniz, and comparative philosophy see the first chapter in Roger T. Ames, *Confucian Role Ethics: A Vocabulary* (Honolulu: University of Hawai'i Press, 2011), 1–40.

4. See Gottfried Wilhelm Leibniz, *Writings on China*, trans. Daniel J. Cook and Henry Rosemont Jr. (Chicago: Open Court, 1994). See also: Franklin Perkins, *Leibniz and China: A Commerce of Light* (Cambridge: Cambridge University Press, 2007).

5. G. W. F. Hegel, *Lectures on the History of Philosophy*, trans. E. S. Haldane (New York: Humanities Press, 1963), vol. 1, 120.

6. Immanuel Kant, *Kant's Political Writings*, ed. Hans Reiss (Cambridge: Cambridge University Press, 1970), 54.

7. G. W. F. Hegel, *Lectures on the History of Philosophy*, trans. E. S. Haldane (New York: Humanities Press, 1963), vol. 1, 125.

8. G. W. F. Hegel, *Lectures on the Philosophy of World History*, trans. H. B. Nisbett (Cambridge: Cambridge University Press, 1975), 121–22.

9. G. W. F. Hegel, *Lectures on the History of Philosophy*, trans. E. S. Haldane (New York: Humanities Press, 1963), vol. 1, 125.

10. Hegel, *Lectures on the History of Philosophy*, 122.

11. On James Legge see Norman J. Girardot. *The Victorian Translation of China: James Legge's Oriental Pilgrimage* (Berkeley: University of California Press, 2002).

12. On Richard Wilhelm see Klaus Hirsch, ed., *Richard Wilhelm: Theologe, Missionar und Sinologe* (Frankfurt/M.: Verlag für Interkulturelle Kommunikation, 2006).

13. On Martin Buber and Chinese philosophy see Jonathan R. Herman, *I and Tao: Martin Buber's Encounter with Chuang Tzu* (Albany: State University of New York Press, 1996).

14. G. W. F. Hegel, *Lectures on the History of Philosophy*, trans. E. S. Haldane (New York: Humanities Press, 1963), vol. 1, 121.

15. See Peter Zarrow, ed., *China in War and Revolution: 1895–1949* (New York: Routledge, 2005).

16. See the case study by Ku-ming (Kevin) Chang, "Politics of Life and Science: The Introduction of Hans Driesch's Vitalism to Post-WWI China." Accessed March 10, 2015. http://harvard-yenching.org/sites/harvard-yenching.org/files/featurefiles/Kevin%20/Kuming_Politics%20of%20Life%20and%20Science.pdf.

17. See Graham Parkes, *Heidegger and Asian Thought* (Honolulu: University of Hawai'i Press, 1987), 1–14.

18. On the development of Chinese academic philosophy in the context of modernization and the history of the twentieth century see John Makeham, ed., *Learning to Emulate the Wise: The Genesis of Chinese Philosophy as an Academic Discipline in Twentieth-Century China* (Hong Kong: The Chinese University Press, 2012).

19. In the 1930s, Feng Youlan published a history of Chinese philosophy in two volumes entitled *Zhonguo Zhexue Shi* 中国哲学史 (Shanghai: Shangwu, 1934). It was later published, in Derk Bodde's translation as *A History of Chinese Philosophy* (Princeton, NJ: Princeton University Press: 1952–1953). A shorter and more "philosophical" history of Chinese philosophy under the title *Xin Yuandao* 新原道 was published in 1945 (Chongqing: Shangwu). It was later translated by E. R. Hughes and published under the title *The Spirit of Chinese Philosophy* (London: Kegan Paul, 1947).

20. See Iwo Amelung, Matthias Koch, Joachim Kurtz, Eun-Jeung Kee, and Sven Saaler, eds., *Selbstbehauptungsdiskurse in Asien: China-Japan-Korea* (Munich: Iudicium, 2003).

21. Feng Youlan, "Chinese Philosophy and a Future World Philosophy," *The Philosophical Review* 57 (1948): 539–49.

22. See Hans-Georg Moeller, "Daoism as Academic Philosophy: Feng Youlan's New Metaphysics (*Xin Lixue*)," in *Learning to Emulate the Wise: The Genesis of Chinese Philosophy as an Academic Discipline in Twentieth-Century China*, ed. John Makeham (Hong Kong: Chinese University Press, 2012), 217–35.

23. *Saeculum* 41 (1990): 79–99.

24. A representative book is François Jullien, *A Treatise on Efficacy: Between Western and Chinese Thinking* (Honolulu: University of Hawai'i Press, 2011).

25. See Jean François Billeter, *Contre François Jullien* (Paris: Alia, 2006).

26. For a rejection of these objections see Roger T. Ames, *Confucian Role Ethics: A Vocabulary* (Honolulu: University of Hawai'i Press, 2011), 22.

27. See Ralph Weber "What about the Billeter-Jullien Debate? And What Was It about? A Response to Thorsten Botz-Bornstein," *Philosophy East and West* 64:1 (2014): 228–37.

28. See for instance Heiner Roetz, "What It *Means* to Take Chinese Ethics Seriously," in *Taking Confucian Ethics Seriously: Contemporary Theories and Applications*, ed. Philip J. Ivanhoe, Julia Tao and Kam-Por Yu (Albany: State University of New York Press, 2010), 13–26.

29. See Edward Slingerland, "Body and Mind in Early China: An Integrated Humanities-Science Approach," *Journal of the American Academy of Religion* 81:1 (2013): 1–50.

30. See Niklas Luhmann, *Theory of Society*, trans. Rhodes Barrett (Stanford: Stanford University Press, 2012, 2013); and *Observations on Modernity*, trans. William Whobrey (Stanford, CA: Stanford University Press, 1998). See also William Rasch, *Niklas Luhmann's Modernity: The Paradoxes of Differentiation* (Stanford, CA: Stanford University Press, 2000), Hans-Georg Moeller, *The Radical Luhmann* (New York: Columbia University Press, 2011).

31. Niklas Luhmann, *Observations on Modernity* (Stanford, CA: Stanford University Press, 1998), 28.

32. Luhmann, *Observations on Modernity*, 29–30.

33. *The Analects of Confucius: A Philosophical Translation* (New York: Ballantine Books, 1998).

34. Roger T. Ames, *Confucian Role Ethics: A Vocabulary* (Honolulu: University of Hawai'i Press, 2011).

3

On the Importance of the Ames-Hall Collaboration

ROBERT CUMMINGS NEVILLE

Introduction

The collaboration between Roger Ames and David L. Hall decisively changed the course of Chinese/Western comparative philosophy and in doing so brought comparative philosophy to a vastly broader public than it had enjoyed before. The collaboration began with the preparation of their first major publication together, *Thinking Through Confucius*, in 1987 and lasted until Hall's premature death in 2001.[1] Three subsequent monographs of their collaboration appeared: *Anticipating China: Thinking through the Narratives of Chinese and Western Culture* (1995), *Thinking from the Han: Self, Truth, and Transcendence in Chinese and Western Culture* (1998), and *The Democracy of the Dead: Dewey, Confucius, and the Hope for Democracy in China* (1999).[2] They also collaborated on two major translations, one of the *Daodejing* and the other of the *Zhongyong*, each with a commentary.[3] I count about a dozen articles, book chapters, critical studies, and responses to critiques of their work that they wrote together.[4] They also went to conferences together. Although they only collaborated for fifteen years or so, the collaboration was intense and grew in its complexity. Ames had other publications not involved with Hall, and other collaborations, including important ones with Henry Rosemont. But I am going to focus here on Ames's work with Hall, dealing with institutional, intellectual, and finally personal matters.

I came to know Ames personally and intellectually through David Hall. At the 1973 meeting of the American Academy of Religion, I saw a man fondly petting Hall's just-published *The Civilization of Experience: A Whiteheadian Theory of Culture*.[5] Because I had read the manuscript for Fordham Press and recommended it highly, I told the man it was a very good book. He mopped his brow, sighed "Whew!" and said "Thank goodness it's good! I wrote it." We became fast friends from that moment. Whereas I had helped put a cover on his first book, my wife, Beth, designed the covers for his next two. He became part of our household, visiting on holidays and teaching addition and subtraction to our younger daughter. For several years, Hall, Kuang-ming Wu, and I had a traveling road show, going to colleges and conferences to talk about comparative philosophy, Chinese philosophy, and American Platonism (Jonathan Edwards, Ralph Waldo Emerson, John Dewey, etc.). We all thought so much alike, however, each with a PhD from Yale, that our brief conversations about collaborating in publications went nowhere. Then Hall met Ames and found the perfect authorial collaborator, his peer in a different field with relevant expertise who would add greatly to what Hall already knew and who would not fight him over the small stuff. That was the beginning of one of the most serious collaborations in philosophical history.

In this essay I shall discuss some of the theoretical innovations Ames and Hall made in comparative philosophy and then some of their delightfully contentious claims about China and the West. I will conclude with some observations about the role of friendship in their collaboration.

Reimagining Comparative Philosophy

One of the important motivations for Ames and Hall to undertake this comparative project, which was beyond the fields in which they had been trained, was the realization that the culture presupposed by the comparative enterprise itself, which had been going on since the great European translators of the nineteenth century, was Western culture, by and large. This constituted a deep bias because it was the Western questions and categories that guided the comparative inquiry. What would the comparative inquiry look like if it were arising out of Chinese culture? In order to address that question, it was necessary to create a philosophy of culture that could establish the independence of China's philosophical culture. Coming to appreciate the uniqueness of Chinese philosophical culture over against the West then allowed for a reappraisal of Western comparative culture itself. The need to distinguish Chinese from Western philosophical cultures at the cultural level naturally sets up a search for binary comparisons, the Chinese versus the West. This stage of oppositional thinking was necessary to establish a fair philosophical culture, China and the West together, in terms of which the uniqueness of each can be appreciated. Toward the end of this essay I quote a long passage from a recent article by Ames that lists elements in the Chinese cultural perspective that would be very difficult, though not impossible, to express in terms native to the cultures prominent in the West.

Ames's official education has been mainly as a Sinologist with a career of producing translations of Chinese texts with up-to-date historical contextualizing. Expert in the Chinese language, especially in philological matters, Ames has remained true to this "Fach" down to his amazing recent book, *Confucian Role Ethics: A Vocabulary*.[6] It is a brilliant new form of philology with chapters as essays on how to translate basic Chinese philosophical terms and moves. The "how to translate" issues are hardly about word equivalences, however; they are philosophical issues about how to present Confucian philosophy to English readers. I suspect that from the beginning Ames was a philosopher at heart, working in the disciplinary medium of Sinology.

Hall, by contrast, did not know Chinese and was trained as a Western philosopher who, on his own, took up an interest in China. Hall's motivation for the turn East was dissatisfaction with the Western philosophical traditions' attempts to put a categoreal grid down on top of more open experience—what he later would call, with Ames, "second problematic" thinking. He thought Plato and the aesthetic elements in the American tradition were exceptions, but too weak and compromised to return philosophy to the "first problematic" thinking of what Emerson would call "original experience." When he found Ames, he discovered astonishing access to Chinese philosophies that he judged to be open to "first problematic" thinking. Also, Ames *knows* something over and above what Hall considered his own "speculative" thinking.

But what is the medium in which they could work together? It could not be Sinology with a Western philosophical interpretation tacked on. Nor could it be a Western philosophical comparison with newly translated Chinese proof texts, although F. S. C. Northrop had made good comparative headway with that in his *The Meeting of East and West* (Northrop was a teacher of both Hall and me).[7] What Ames and Hall decided was that they should do "philosophy of culture." The philosophy side allowed of speculative comparisons with newly invented categories (e.g., first and second problematic thinking). The culture side gave a strong empirical bias through the Sinological apparatus.

"Philosophy of culture" was part of the subtitle of Hall's early book on Whitehead. Hall was insightful in seeing Whitehead as a philosopher of culture, even in his technical books such as *Process and Reality*. But Whitehead had no empirical side to his philosophy of culture beyond simply being a well-educated, urbane, and aesthetically sensitive philosopher. What Ames and Hall had to do was to devise a philosophical and empirically checkable (at least through texts) strategy for cultural analysis. Whereas Whitehead gave a philosophical commentary on culture and its problems, Ames and Hall had to cope with understanding what culture is, without falling into what they took to be the reductionisms of cultural anthropology. Cultural anthropologists rarely analyze *philosophical* cultures.

The precise nature of the Ames and Hall comparative cultures methodologies has been analyzed in splendid detail by Robert W. Smid in his *Methodologies of Comparative Philosophy: The Pragmatist and Process Traditions*.[8] There is no need to do that analytical work again, especially to try to squeeze it into a short essay such as this one. My purpose here is not to explain their collaborative method of philosophy of culture but to make some comments on it.

Ames and Hall collaborated by thinking through Chinese and Western philosophical culture at the level of cultural philosophical categories that they had to create, or rebaptize from earlier comparativists and Sinologists such as A. C. Graham.[9] This resulted in them realizing that the great Chinese texts need to be translated anew with an eye to their Chinese cultural embodiment, at the same time that the concepts of philosophers both East and West had to be reanalyzed as instances of cultural expressions. The result was a broad set of generalizations distinguishing the two cultures. In a strict sense, they were not comparing philosophers so much as philosophies as expressive of cultures. Although they wrote a great deal about Confucius, the individual who authored the *Analects*, their focus was on what Confucius's words meant in reflecting and shaping Chinese culture.

This was hard for many of us to understand, at least at the beginning (I speak for myself). We missed the pitch of their comparisons. Some Sinologists were nervous about the heavily interpretive phrases used to translate debatable Chinese terms. Some philosophers such as I could always think of exceptions to the generalizations. I take myself to be a contemporary philosopher, building a philosophy for a global conversation that builds heavily on Confucianism while extending it, and on Platonism while extending it too. It has been frustrating for me to think of Chinese and Western cultures as distinct rather than as containing a great many mutually divergent philosophers among whom one must walk critically. In Western thought I am a Platonist, not an Aristotelian, and in Confucianism I follow the line of Xunzi much more than that of Mencius. I favor reading the history of philosophy as figures in debate and dialogue, rather than as expressions of a more pervasive culture, because I want to appropriate some points for a new philosophy and detach my commitments from others. Though systematic philosophy has been seriously unpopular throughout most of my career, I have long argued for the legitimacy and cultural need for the development of a new and relevant philosophy. But this is a weakness on my part when it comes to understanding philosophy of culture and its particular usefulness. Therefore, what are some of the advantages of the genre of philosophy of culture?

Advantages of Philosophy of Culture

The first and most obvious advantage is that philosophy is an element of culture, if not the kind of cultural element usually studied by anthropologists. Moreover, there are lots of cultures with very complex historical, geographical, climatic, economic, and geopolitical connections among them. How philosophies vary among these different kinds of cultural conditions is important for understanding the philosophies, and for assessing them philosophically. The philosophical dialectic of understanding and weighing different philosophies does not consist only in a line of argument, as some neo-Pragmatists such as Robert Brandom might argue.[10] What counts as argument differs from one philosophy to the next and this is often as much a function of the philosophies' cultures as of their defense of their respective argumentations.

The second is that philosophies very often are in critical dialectical relation to their own cultures as they understand them. Confucius was in opposition to the savage culture of his historical period, one that he attributed to a decline in observance of proper rituals, among other things, and that he aimed to counter by improving his culture's rituals. Plato took opposition to the cultural relativism he saw in Sophism, with the assumed conclusion that might makes right and that persuasion, even with bad reasons, is the only discourse that counts politically. Like Confucius, Plato thought that education rather than military power was the way to reform his culture, although his Academy had a very non-Chinese sense of that in which education consists. Plato moreover developed his own philosophy that there are real differences in the values of things and that responsibility includes being accountable to what is really good. The point is, Confucius, Plato, and to be sure many other philosophers saw their task to be the criticism and reformation of their society's culture.

Third, the dialectical relation of philosophers to their cultures is itself part of culture in a higher sense. That is, the cultures include the critical activities of their philosophers. It is commonplace to say that philosophy arose globally with the rise of literacy and other accouterments of Axial Age developments.[11] Different cultures express this differently. Ames and Hall's philosophy of culture operates at this level of general development, where philosophers who might be critical of their cultures are themselves part of the larger cultural development.

Fourth, it is just plain helpful, in fact necessary, to understand how philosophers relate to their cultural backgrounds, what they assume unconsciously, what they defend or oppose, and how their audience would have heard and interpreted them. This is not just the issue of how philosophers fit into their historical setting, although that is crucial. It is the issue of how that setting is a cultural background for the cultural activity of philosophers.

Fifth, philosophy of culture can be a creative, brilliant, inspiring, innovative direction in philosophy and the literary arts that opens the way to important new avenues of inquiry and thought, and this is surely true of the contributions of Ames and Hall. The virtues I mentioned in the previous four points could be nicely manifest but with dull, ill-focused recycling of old ideas. Ames and Hall's philosophy of culture comparing China and the West is astonishingly exciting and electrifying. Beginning English-speaking students who had no orientation for reading Chinese philosophers suddenly had the cultural hooks to orient themselves. Suddenly they read Western philosophers in a new way. Mature scholars who knew what the Chinese philosophers said were now told what they *meant*, culturally speaking (which is where most real meaning lies, according to Ames and Hall). Some of these mature scholars just blew smoke from their ears. Others argued vociferously for alternative interpretations of the culture at hand. Some lifted up their favorite philosophers who did not fit the cultural paradigm. Yet others joined to enrich and expand the comparative discussion.[12] All the while the scholarly community was absorbing new finds of ancient texts that called for a reevaluation of the last couple of centuries of scholarly interpretation, a process to which the comparative philosophy of culture was integral. The Ames and Hall collaboration lifted East/West comparative philosophy from the province of a few super-specialists to a prominent exciting position in a large intellectual landscape of global philosophy and understanding.

Proposals about China and the West

Now I would like to comment on several of the important ideas that have been lifted up for analysis and reflection in the Ames and Hall collaboration. In order to make sure that I am dealing with the part of the collaboration with which Ames is thoroughly comfortable, I will sometimes take his solo late work, *Confucian Role Ethics*, and his very recent essay, "Reading the *Zhongyong* 'metaphysically,'" as his lenses to reflect back on certain issues in the collaboration.[13] I will discuss (1) the first and second problematics already mentioned, (2) the issues in claiming that Western philosophy is characterized by transcendence while China is not, thinking instead in terms of correlations, and (3) the treatment of individuality and metaphysics.

First and Second Problematics

The distinction between first and second problematics is used throughout the Ames-Hall collaboration and has continued into Ames's recent writings. Its most theoretical exposition probably is in *Anticipating China*, chapter 2. More a thematic distinction than a categoreal one, the distinction is an extraordinarily helpful heuristic device for throwing light on many different problems. Sometimes the distinction signifies the difference between an aesthetic approach to the world (first problematic) and a rationalistic one (second problematic). Sometimes it signifies a more metaphysical difference: the position that each individual has his or her own perspective on the world with no overarching unity (metaphysical chaos, first problematic) and the position that there is an overarching order, or several of them, within which individuals are defined (metaphysical cosmos, second problematic). Sometimes it signifies a somewhat passive reverence for things, letting them be (first problematic), versus a readiness to impose order on things, fixing them up according to some human purpose or scheme (second problematic). Ames and Hall associated first problematic thinking with Chinese culture and second problematic thinking with Western culture. They then pointed out that second problematic thinking has gotten the world into a lot of trouble and advocated the virtues of first order thinking. (They, of course, wrote with much greater sophistication and qualification than in the above, but I think this was their original point.)

The obvious difficulty with such large-scale generalizations about cultures is that they have so many exceptions. The Chinese emphasize aesthetic perception and deference, but they also have been great classifiers: who would think that all things could be understood in terms of the hexagram patterns of the *Yijing*? Western Aristotelians perfected a kind of classification in the genus-species scheme, but Platonists, including the American tradition from Edwards to Emerson to the pragmatists, have insisted that the aesthetic gets the last word, even in mathematics.

Though a difficulty, the application of the first and second problematic distinction to Chinese and Western cultures has the ironic virtue of making progress through the elaboration of the exceptions. The distinction itself is deepened as apparent exceptions are brought to light. Moreover, the inquiries into the exceptions often take the form of setting the exceptional philosopher over against an otherwise dominant cultural trait. And I confess also that after nearly three decades of worrying this bone, I have come to believe that Ames and Hall are basically right in their characterization of the cultural backgrounds within which Chinese and Western philosophers have worked since ancient times. Rationalizing philosophers are counter-cultural in China and the aesthetic Platonists are counter-cultural in the West. To the extent that each problematic draws out and provokes the other, as is apparent on even not-so-close analysis, the weight is on the aesthetic in Chinese cultures and on the rational order in Western ones, I think.

Note that the enterprise of cultural comparison is itself a second problematic endeavor. It aims to develop contrasting themes and categories by virtue of which each culture is epitomized or simplified in relation to the other. The comparisons are helpful to the extent that the contrasting themes and categories can be specified in terms of one another. Whitehead was very clear that simplification is necessary if there is to be a human reaction to something, including reactions of comprehension. He warned that one of philosophy's jobs is the policing of the simplifications, appealing aesthetically to what is left out.[14] But even the best, most self-conscious simplifications do violence to what they do not carry forward. This is the violence that pains those who object to Ames and Hall's comparative endeavor.

Transcendence and Correlative Causation

Consider one of the most notorious contrasts Ames and Hall have made between Chinese and Western philosophical cultures. They claim that Western cultures think that ultimate explanations make reference to transcendent causes, such that the cause is not modified by the effect but the effect is wholly dependent on the cause, with strict asymmetry. By contrast, Chinese cultures think of causation in terms of correlations, as in the moving correlations of *yin* and *yang*; the emphasis on correlation comes from the outstanding work of A. C. Graham. The Chinese, claim Ames and Hall, do not have the West's preoccupation with finding an ontological ground, a God, or a One from which all things flow. Rather, the Chinese preoccupation is with locating the flow of things within correlates, *yin* and *yang*, Principle and Material Force, and so forth. Sometimes the subtext here seems to be that the Chinese are ethical and not religious, whereas the West is religious but with dubious ethics dependent on the whim of an arbitrary divinity.[15] Because we secular people do not believe in a transcendent divinity, with or without whims, it is lucky we have the Chinese alternative with a correlative ultimate cosmology that orients us to the proximate issues of the moral life. Although Ames and Hall would never say anything as crude as this, it is the way many people interpret the upshot of their contrast between Chinese and Western cultures.

My own position is that philosophers *ought* to acknowledge and articulate an ultimate ontological ground of all things determinate.[16] It does not matter whether the determinate world consists in *yin-yang* vibrations, Samkhya *gunas*, Aristotelian substances, or the energies of positive and dark matters. All those different views say the world is determinately something. The analysis of determinateness itself, I claim, argues for an ontological creative act that makes determinate things be mutually relevant but still somewhat external to one another. If there is anything determinate whatsoever, under any description, its possibility and actuality are owed to an ontological creative act that is not itself determinate except as the creator of whatever is determinate. There have been very few philosophers in China or elsewhere who have analyzed determinateness itself, a topic of utmost abstraction. Most have tried to show how their particular cosmologies are possible or real. Ames and Hall are right that this kind of question in China is answered by finding correlates that make the middle movement real. In the West, most often the search for an ontological ground has limited itself to Very Big Determinate Things, such as an intentional God who is all-powerful, all-wise, and all-good, or who is the Act of To Be, or the Ontological One that contains all possible diversity. These are impossible, according to my argument, because they are all versions of something determinate and would themselves have to be related to other determinate things by an ontologically prior creative act.

The cultural upshot of my argument, supposing it to be interesting and valid, is complicated. To the extent that the West has supposed that there is an ontologically transcendent *thing*, that is, something determinate, its culture is mistaken if the point is taken literally. So the demise of such a God in secular consciousness is a good thing. That the Chinese never had such a conception of an ontological God, at least not since the pre-*Zhou* heyday of *Shangdi*, has saved a lot of effort criticizing ontological supernaturalism, which is a good thing. But suppose that both Chinese and Western cultures (and South Asian cultures in their own ways) have grappled with the conditions for a plurality of determinate things, however those things have been conceived. Because there are indeed determinate things, it would require a powerful anti-curiosity not to wonder about their conditions. So I suspect that both Western and Chinese cultures developed symbols for what I call the ontological creative act that aim to get at those conditions, even if they must be false if taken literally.

Western cultures have taken the idea of a person, a personal creative agent, as the metaphor to build up into a conception of the ontological creative ground. Part of the value in this is that we might come to know or understand something about the world by knowing the character or will of its creator, conceived as an intentional agent, a Person. This has contributed to the Western affinity for the principle that nothing can be in the effect that is not already in the cause; thus the ontological ground—God, the Act of To Be, the One—must already contain the reality of, or at least the plan for, the created world. The result has been that the West has very often been preoccupied with the ontological ground because that is supposed to explain so much that is relevant to daily life and high civilization. But the ontological ground cannot contain the reality, or explain the specific realities, of the created world if it creates everything determinate. Nothing is to be learned about the character of the created world by looking to the ontological ground; we just have to look to see what is created, and what the conditions for being determinate are. In this respect, Chinese culture is quite right not to become preoccupied with the ontological ground. It won't help much with daily life or high civilization, questions about which need to be addressed to the harmonizing of the correlative conditions, supposing this cosmology to be true. So it makes good sense to read Chinese culture as primarily ethical in the sense of being concerned about the harmonizing of correlates, and only marginally ontological in the sense of inquiring into the conditions for determinateness, for instance, the possibility of *yin-yang* movements. Yet when Chinese philosophical culture does look to the ontological ultimates, for instance, the *Dao* that cannot be named, or Wangbi's Non-being, or Zhou Dunyi's Non-being that gives rise to the Great Ultimate from which *yang* emerges and then the retreat into *yin*, it perceives exactly the point that most Western philosophical culture misses: creation produces novelty. Relative to the cause, the created effect arises spontaneously. Of course, the cause cannot be a determinate thing, and so it is slightly perverse to speak of it as a cause. There is only the ontological act of creation whose terminus is the world of determinate things, whatever that is and however it works. Non-being (*wuji*) is not a *thing* that *causes* the Great Ultimate (*taiji*). The Chinese metaphor of ultimate spontaneous emergence is a good corrective to the Western metaphor of a cause that contains the effect *in nuce*. Moreover, one would not learn much about the world that spontaneously arises by looking at the state of affairs without the spontaneous arising. Look rather at what arises, that is, at the ethical matters relative to correlations.

To be sure, predicting and justifying affairs is not the only reason Western cultures look to God as if hunting for an explanatory personal character or intention. Nor is looking for the ways to harmonize things the only reason Chinese cultures look to ultimate matters. For both there is a kind of piety or awe at the gratuitous, arbitrary, totally surprising radical contingency of determinate existence. Western culture tends to express this piety in the metaphors of worshipping a king who makes that happen on a cosmic scale.

Chinese culture tends to express this piety in the aesthetic moods of vacuity, tranquility, mystery, empty depths.

Indeed, the reason I have come to appreciate and accept Ames and Hall's claim that China has mainly first problematic thinking is that its style of ontological piety, showing up in poetry, painting, the arts of humane living, and all the preoccupations of high civilization, is this aesthetics of mysterious radical contingency. Even the person next door is a mysterious wonder. The reason Ames and Hall are mainly right about the association of second problematic thinking with the West is that its cultural style of piety imagines that the world is the expression of the mind of God, the creator on whom everything depends with radical contingency. Whitehead attributed the early modern rise of mathematizing science to the earlier medieval European faith that the rational mind of God would create a world that is deep down rational. Of course, the professional Western philosophers and theologians had sophisticated expressions of this; but at the cultural level, there was the expectation that the fundamental character of the world was based on a fundamental character in the intentionality of its creator. So the West had a pervasive interest in and preoccupation with the transcendent creator that China lacked, because spontaneous emergence has no predictive powers for what emerges.

I hope in these last several paragraphs to have illustrated something of the comparative philosophy of culture I supported at the beginning. This is distinct from history of philosophy in comparative perspective, which would trace the textual development and deviations of theories of rational order in the West and historically evolving approaches to the discernment of principles of harmonization of correlative changes in China with the concomitant evolution of the virtues of what Ames and Hall call the "exemplary person."

Individuals and Metaphysics

This brings me to one last point of comparative philosophy of culture in their work, developed in very rich detail by Ames after Hall's death, especially in *Confucian Role Ethics* and "Reading the *Zhongyong* 'metaphysically.'" The topic is the nature of human individuality. According to Ames and Hall, for instance in *Thinking from the Han*, the culturally dominant view of individuality in the West is derivative from the idea of substance. A substance is a thing that possesses its properties, or a subject to which properties can be predicated. Accordingly, a person is an individual with character traits who acts "in character" in the situations of life. People change, to be sure, and so traits of character can be acquired and lost. Where an individual does not have a character directing behavior in a situation, the individual has a will that decides. The will might or might not be "free," as debated by various philosophies, but it stems from the individual as a substance. At the current time, this substance approach to individuality finds vigorous expression in Anglo-American "virtue ethics," which is popular and takes inspiration from Alasdair MacIntyre's *After Virtue* that is explicit in its appropriation of Aristotelianism. Moreover, many contemporary comparativists find it extremely useful to liken Confucian ethics to virtue ethics. Surely the Confucian tradition has much to say about the development of virtues.

But Ames counters that Confucianism is primarily a *role* ethics, not a virtue ethics except insofar as virtues are needed to play roles well. Role ethics are essentially relational, not properties of individuals. Individuals are actors and reactors in multileveled situations, always in process relative to the processes around them. Their responses are aesthetically shaped in complex ways and articulate their environments in aesthetic focus-field delineations. In a *tour de force* of metaphysical imagination, Ames develops from the *Zhongyong* (*Focusing the Familiar*, as translated by him and Hall) a list of traits that distinguishes a Confucian metaphysics from the metaphysics of substantial individuality. The list is worth quoting here (without the Chinese characters):

1. Human "becomings": gerundive, relationally constituted notion of persons (a dynamic matrix of unique relations);

2. Doctrine of internal (vital, existential) relations;

3. The uniqueness of particulars;

4. Reflexivity, collaboration, multilateralism in relations;

5. A focus-field rather than part-whole understanding of particulars and their context;

6. An inseparability of one and many (of the continuity among and the uniqueness of things;

7. A centered and unbounded holism, an unsummed totality;

8. The interdependence of the formal and the informal, the determinate and the indeterminate;

9. Analogy and correlativity (*ars contextualis*) as the method of creative advance;

10. The centrality of moral imagination;

11. A processual and emergent cosmic order;

12. A human-centered religiousness achieved through a sense of felt worth and belonging;
13. Ongoing disclosure;
14. Plurality as diversity rather than as variety;
15. Provisional and fallibilistic order;
16. *Creatio in situ* as increased significance or meaning in relations;
17. A Whiteheadian aesthetic order;
18. First-order problematic;
19. A *shi* "causality" in which all contextualizing factors are relevant;
20. A narrative, event identity;
21. A principle of individuation that moves from contextual relations to particular focus;
22. Processive forms as the rhythm or cadence of experience;
23. Everything affects everything else;
24. Something becomes something else;
25. *Tiandi* as an unbounded "horizon" concept;
26. *Tiyong* as "trans-*form*-ing";
27. Nothing is unconditional;
28. Religiousness versus religion;
29. The appeal to the historical and empirical;
30. A confident meliorism;
31. The primacy of wisdom in *philosophia*;
32. Correlative (rather than dualistic) *yin-yang* categories.[17]

These phrases might not be immediately intelligible to people who do not know Ames and Hall's work, but they cumulatively give an indication of the philosophical culture they find in Confucianism, and I largely agree.

In *Confucian Role Ethics* Ames argues brilliantly that the "Confucian project" is to attain relational virtuosity.[18] The virtues are not possessed by individuals in a substantialist sense but by individuals functioning in their many relations. I myself would balance this expression of the Mencian form of Confucianism with one expressing Xunzi's emphasis on rituals.[19] The roles in role ethics are roles in rituals. Xunzi's insights have to do with the reality of rituals as such. Because of family rituals, we can have ongoing, growing families. Economic rituals give us dynamic economies. Political rituals give us politically ordered and changing societies. High civilization gives us the multiple-layered and diverse environments within which human life can have consummate quality. Alongside the Confucian project of attaining individual relational virtuosity, consummate individuals, I would place the Confucian project of correcting, building, and sustaining the rituals that individuals play so as to have high civilization (or, as is usually the case, to achieve high civilization, or to correct deficiencies of not-so-high civilizations). Rituals are general patterns of interaction and most of them can be played in a variety of ways. Each individual individuates his or her ways of playing the rituals, and part of becoming a consummate individual is to individuate the ways of playing the matrix of rituals that contextualizes personal life. As Confucius himself fulminated against the inadequate ritualization of his situation, so the Confucian project includes attention to the rituals themselves, not only to the attainment of virtuosity in playing them in the consummate life. I make this point about ritual not to criticize Ames's role ethics but to complement his account.

Friendship in Collaboration

I want to conclude with some comments on the personal side of collaboration, especially the roles of friendship. It was obvious to all who knew them together that Roger Ames and David Hall became close friends. Writers can collaborate in authoring books and papers without being friends, so long as they are civil and contribute complementary materials. When friendship is involved, however, the collaboration becomes a project in itself, something like the way a ritual is more than the ritual players playing. This is the way it was with David and Roger. In a great many contexts, each one of them was "Hall and Ames" (David was usually listed first because he was the older of the two). Perhaps there were moments when each one wanted to be dis-linked from the other, but by-and-large they grew into their linked collaborative identity, personally as well as professionally, individuating their roles together. When David died, Roger was in charge of his ashes, and he shared them. He sent me half with instructions to scatter them around places on the East Coast that were important to David. Then he invited me and many others to a memorial service near his home in Hawai`i, where David had spent so much time; while I read some of David's favorite Daoist texts, Roger's sons paddled a surfboard out into the sea and dumped the other half of the ashes into the waters. To me, at least, Roger's consummate act of collaboration with David was to share him with others who loved and grieved him.

Since then, through nearly fifteen years, Roger and I have developed a mutual friendship of our own, no longer mainly derivative from the friendships each of us had with David. This is another kind of collaboration too. We do not write together. But we think in collaboration as friendly correctors of the other's insights and emphases. I hope this essay has illustrated the kind of collaboration with Roger that I have come to prize so highly. The essay is not the argument of a thesis, although it contains bits of argument. Rather it is a tribute to a friend who has taught many of us to collaborate in the exploration of the philosophic cultures of China and the West. I am grateful to be admitted to this collaboration.

Notes

1. Roger T. Ames and David L. Hall, *Thinking Through Confucius* (Albany: State University of New York Press, 1987).

2. Roger T. Ames and David L. Hall, *Anticipating China: Thinking through the Narratives of Chinese and Western Culture* (Albany: State University of New York Press, 1995), *Thinking from the Han: Self, Truth, and Transcendence in Chinese and Western Culture* (Albany: State University of New York Press, 1998), and *The Democracy of the Dead: Dewey, Confucius, and the Hope for Democracy in China* (Chicago and LaSalle, IL, Open Court, 1999).

3. *Dao De Jing: Making This Life Significant: A Philosophical Translation* (New York: Ballantine, 2003). *Focusing the Familiar: A Translation and Philosophical Interpretation of the Zhongyong* (Honolulu, HI: University of Hawai`i Press, 2001).

4. See the bibliography of David Hall in *Metaphilosophy and Chinese Thought: Interpreting David Hall*, edited, with a prologue, by Ewing Chinn and Henry Rosemont Jr. (New York: Global Scholarly Publications, 2005), 201–05.

5. *The Civilization of Experience: A Whiteheadian Philosophy of Culture* (New York: Fordham University Press, 1973).

6. Roger T. Ames, *Confucian Role Ethics: A Vocabulary* (Sha Tin: Chinese University Press; Honolulu, HI: University of Hawai`i Press, 2011).

7. F. S. C. Northrop, *The Meeting of East and West: An Inquiry Concerning World Understanding* (New York: Macmillan, 1946). Northrop's subtitle is a take-off on David Hume's *An Inquiry Concerning Human Understanding*. The point is that there was and still is no global *human* understanding and that Hume's assumption that European understanding is the only game in town was remarkably ignorant.

8. See Robert W. Smid, *Methodologies of Comparative Philosophy: The Pragmatist and Process Traditions* (Albany: State University of New York Press, 2009), chapter

3. Speaking of collaborations, Smid's volume started off as a PhD dissertation under my direction at Boston University. In addition to the very long and fulsome chapter on Ames and Hall, it contains analyses of the comparative work of William Ernest Hocking, F.S. C. Northrop, and myself. It was published in Roger T. Ames's *SUNY Series in Chinese Philosophy and Culture* and is dedicated to me. I shall return in the last section to the sense in which Ames and I have a collaboration.

9. See A. C. Graham, *Disputers of the Dao: Philosophic Argument in Ancient China* (La Salle, IL; Open Court, 1989).

10. See Robert B. Brandom, *Perspectives on Pragmatism: Classical, Recent, and Contemporary* (Cambridge, MA: Harvard University Press, 2011).

11. This and many other points emerging in the Axial Age have been much discussed lately. The recent mastwork on the Axial Age is Robert N. Bellah's *Religion in Human Evolution: From the Paleolithic to the Axial Age* (Cambridge, MA: Harvard University Press, 2011).

12. See Smid's discussion of Ames and Hall and their critics in *Methodologies of Comparative Philosophy*, chapter 3.

13. Roger T. Ames, "Reading the *Zhongyong* 'metaphysically,'" in *Chinese Metaphysics and its Problems* ed. Chenyang Li and Franklin Perkins (Cambridge, UK: Cambridge University Press, 2015), chapter 5. The *Zhongyong* was one of the works Ames and Hall translated together and so the later essay is in light of that collaboration.

14. See Alfred North Whitehead's last two published essays, "Mathematics and the Good" and "Immortality," in *The Philosophy of Alfred North Whitehead, The Library of Living Philosophers*, ed. Paul Arthur Schilpp (New York: Tudor Publishing Co., 1941), pp. 666–700.

15. Ames devotes the last chapter of *Confucian Role Ethics* to Confucian religiousness that is human centered and does not much involve organized religion.

16. This is a huge claim, but I have defended it in a huge three-volume project: *Ultimates: Philosophical Theology Volume One, Existence: Philosophical Theology Volume Two*, and *Religion: Philosophical Theology Volume Three*. The first volume defends the theory of the ontological creative act sketched here, and the third volume gives an interpretation of Confucian religiosity.

17. Ames, "Reading the *Zhongyong* 'metaphysically,' " 104.

18. See especially chapter 3.

19. My case is argued in my *Ritual and Deference: Extending Chinese Philosophy in a Comparative Context* (Albany: State University of New York Press, 2008), a volume that appears in Ames's SUNY Series in Chinese Philosophy and Culture.

Part II
ISSUES

4

The Art of Rulership in the Context of Heaven and Earth

GRAHAM PARKES

A major difference between traditional political philosophy in China and the West is this: whereas classical Chinese thought always considers the establishment and maintenance of political order in the context of the natural world, this has rarely been a consideration in the Western traditions. Although correspondences between microcosm and macrocosm are central to much Neo-Platonic thought, Islamic philosophy, and Medieval and Renaissance thinking, these traditions rarely advocate modeling political order on the order of the cosmos. (One reason for this being that God takes precedence over the natural world.) The attention paid to the powers of Heaven and Earth throughout the Chinese tradition suggests that political philosophy in the West might have been missing something important. And since the current dominance of Western-style political institutions with their disregard of the natural world has brought us to the brink of environmental catastrophe, we have good reason to question their ideological bases in the light of Chinese philosophy, and ask whether this different way of thinking doesn't have some ideas worth adopting and adapting.

Environmental catastrophe wasn't looming nearly so large in the early 1980s when Roger Ames wrote his pioneering "Study in Ancient Political Chinese Thought," *The Art of Rulership*.[1] But looking at those ancient texts in political philosophy now, in the context of global warming, one is struck by how much they emphasize the importance for political rule of understanding and cultivating the ways of Heaven and Earth. The chapter that follows is both a complement and a compliment to *The Art of Rulership*, elaborating some of its themes concerning the natural world. Because of geographical proximity, I was one of the first to receive a copy of that work when it came out in 1983. I am sorry the acknowledgment is so belated.

The Mandate of Heaven

Whereas Western philosophies have tended to focus on the social and political in isolation from the natural world, ancient Chinese thought always considers "the three realms"—Heaven, Earth, humans—"as one." The notion of Heaven (*tian*) evolved over the centuries, from originally meaning a sky God who ruled the cosmos, then *fate* in the sense of an all-encompassing power beyond human control, the *sky* (as in "the heavens") and the rest of the natural world ("Heaven-and-Earth"), and eventually to an impersonal standard for human conduct. At no time did it signify a transcendent realm beyond this world, as in the dualistic metaphysics of the Platonist or Christian traditions, since the three realms were always regarded as belonging together, as one. And from the continuous interaction between Heaven and Earth come the "myriad things," including human beings.

By the time philosophy got underway in China, "Heaven" had become a relatively impersonal force of nature that reigned over the worlds of Earth and humans beneath it, ordering and regulating "All under Heaven" (*tianxia*), the whole World. Although Heaven was in some sense a higher power than Earth, the two were also complementary; and as "Heaven-and-Earth" in the sense of the natural world they were on a par with each other, like *yang* and *yin*. Insofar as human existence is always understood as unfolding from the interactions among the Heavenly and Earthly powers, good government will bring order to it by appreciating that any human society flourishes, or fails to flourish, always in this broader context of the natural world.

Patterns of order obtain across the three realms such that, just as Heaven reigns over the world beneath, so in the human realm the ruler reigns likewise—and for this reason the king, or emperor, was known as the "Son of Heaven" (*tianzi*). (Moving again from macrocosm to microcosm: the father rules the family, and the heart-mind orders the body politic that is the individual.) And just as the Heavens are open and expansive rather than closed or self-centered, and behave impartially toward all they oversee, the good human ruler practices these same virtues. He accords with the will of Heaven by correlating human activities with the patterning of natural processes. Since the Chinese understand the world as a field of relations, it's natural to think of the individual always in the context of the family, and the family in the society, and then the world of nature, and finally in the context of the whole World—"All under Heaven."

In ancient times the Son of Heaven had the unique privilege of worshipping Heaven as the supreme deity and communing with it through ritual sacrifices. Whereas in the Western world rulers were legitimated by the Divine Right of Kings, the rule of the emperors in China was justified by the Mandate of Heaven (*tianming*), whereby the ruler reigns by virtue of, and in accordance with, Heaven's will.

A prime manifestation of the order of Heaven, aside from the paths of the sun and moon, is the movements of the planets and stars. "[The] celestial sign for the 'transfer of the Mandate' and the founding of a new dynasty was a triple conjunction of Jupiter, Saturn, and Mars, sometimes briefly joined by the faster moving Venus and Mercury, which occurs approximately every 516 years."[2] And indeed, the successions to the Xia (possibly around 2092 BCE?) and the Shang (1576) and the Zhou Dynasties (1059) did take place in conjunction with the most remarkable astronomical events. To retain the Mandate of Heaven, the ruler must have advisors who understand astrology and can help him adjust his rule to the larger patterns of the heavens.

The idea of the Mandate of Heaven originated from the succession whereby the Zhou Dynasty overthrew the Shang in the eleventh century BCE. The Zhou claimed that the previous rulers had forfeited the Mandate of Heaven through their misrule, and took the success of their own rebellion as evidence that the Zhou king had received Heaven's Mandate to take over. The Duke of Zhou explained that "the Mandate was bestowed by Heaven in recognition of the potency of the founding king and withdrawn because of the diminished potency of the previous king."[3] It's all a matter of the potency of the ruler, which he "gets" (a connotation of the term *de*) from the powers of Heaven and Earth. Confucius famously says that what has "given life to and nourished excellence [potency] in him" is not he himself, but rather Heaven.[4]

In the *Analects* the Mandate of Heaven is mentioned only twice, but in significant contexts. In recounting what he was capable of at various ages, the Master says that, after "taking his place" in society by the time he was thirty, he was able twenty years later to "understand Heaven's Mandate." This suggests that it took time, years of experience and reflection, for him to see his life as a teacher, and the life of the self-cultivated ruler, in the context not just of social and historical strictures but also of what's given by the natural world and the biological body.

Confucius also cites the Mandate of Heaven as the first of three sources of awe for the cultivated gentleman (preceding "great men" and "the words of the sages"). By contrast, the petty person, narrowly focused on self-interest, is incapable of understanding these, and especially anything as broad as Heaven's Mandate and the awe-inspiring order it manifests above and below.⁵

Mozi held a view of the Son of Heaven that is similar to the Confucians'.

> The three high counselors and feudal lords devote themselves to administering the government but they do not make up their own standard. There is the Son of Heaven to govern them. The Son of Heaven does not make up his own standard. There is Heaven to govern him.

The best emperor governs as the Son of Heaven by being empty of his own ideas, and thus impartial. Letting himself be governed by Heaven he allows the empire to be ordered by the forces of Heaven and Earth working through him as human intermediary. Mozi says of the "sage-kings" of the past who "accorded with Heaven's will:"

> On high they honored Heaven, in the middle realm they served the ghosts and spirits, and below they cared for human beings. And so Heaven's will proclaimed, "These men impartially care for those I care for and impartially benefit those I benefit. Their care for the people is extensive and the benefit they bring is substantial." And so Heaven made it come to pass that they each became the Son of Heaven and were given the wealth of the whole World.⁶

The Mandate of Heaven is granted to great rulers so that they can let society accord with its natural environing conditions. If the ruler ignores the Mandate and governs for his own interests, if he fails to pay attention to the rhythms of the natural world when performing the rituals required by his position, the result will be inefficient agriculture, crop failure, starvation and misery—all signs that he has lost the Mandate and had better look for a different line of work.

When asked about a particular succession between emperors of dynasties, Mencius insisted that it is Heaven—and not a human being, even an emperor—who gives the empire to a new ruler, not directly but rather by "revealing itself through its acts and deeds."

> When the new emperor was put in charge of sacrifices, the hundred gods enjoyed them. This showed that Heaven accepted him. When he was put in charge of affairs, they were kept in order and the people were content. This showed that the people had accepted him. Hence I said, "The Emperor cannot give the Empire to another."⁷

The Mandate of Heaven can thus be discerned not only by the way the forces of Heaven and Earth respond to an emperor when he performs ritual sacrifices, but also, and more importantly, by the reaction of the people to their conditions. Mencius often emphasizes that a ruler is legitimated by the people's long-term flourishing, and that their misery is a sign that the ruler has lost Heaven's Mandate.[8]

The Historical Record

Let's consider an objection to my claim that philosophical ideas from the Chinese tradition are relevant for the current environmental crisis: namely, China's poor environmental record. If such ideas didn't protect the environment in the past, how can they be of any help now, in these changed and changing times? Well, a brief survey of the environmental history, together with what the philosophers were saying about the natural world around them, shows that the problem lies not with the ideas but with a simple failure to implement them.[9] Far more than their counterparts in the West, the Chinese thinkers warned time and again against environmental exploitation. Can't we perhaps learn from this history and avoid failing yet again?

China has always been subject to devastating floods and droughts. The heavens dealt out so much destruction that the ancients—as in many cultures—came to believe that an angry Sky God was orchestrating these extreme weather events. In times of excess rain the Yellow River would burst through the levees built to contain it, to lethal effect. A catastrophic breach in the year 1117 is said to have killed a million people. As the population density increased the fatalities did too. In 1886 two million died when the Yellow River flooded. The polar opposite, lack of rain, could be even more deadly: in 1876, after three years of drought, some thirteen million people died from lack of water or food.[10]

Under such conditions projects to conserve water for drinking and irrigation of crops are a necessity. After nine years of flooding, an old story goes, the legendary first ruler of the Central Kingdom, Yu the Great, founder of the Xia dynasty, had many dikes constructed to contain the rivers. Ever since then it has been the responsibility of China's rulers to manage the country's system of waterways, which are used for transportation as well as irrigation. No society has achieved such great feats in the realm of hydrological engineering as the Chinese, who over the millennia have constructed complex systems of seawalls, levees, irrigation channels, dikes, watermills, and canals over a vast expanse of terrain. Mark Elvin has given a comprehensive account of these achievements in his definitive environmental history of China, *The Retreat of the Elephants*.[11]

Skills in irrigation allowed agriculture to become highly developed early on, but the evidence shows that the land was often so intensively cultivated that "migratory farming," where people continually relocate in order to find better land, was a pervasive practice.[12] The spread of agriculture during the first millennium BCE required the clearing of vast tracts of land for cultivation. The early Chinese, like many other peoples, found forests unsettling and antithetical to the spread of civilization, so they cleared land for settlement as well as farming. (This resulted in the "retreat of the elephants" who used to inhabit much of the land.[13]) What distinguishes the Chinese case from others is that the mistrust of forests and exploitation of the earth and its waters went hand in hand with an extraordinary reverence for natural landscape ("mountains and waters"), as evidenced in their celebration over many centuries in the most consummate poetry and landscape painting.

The Chinese deforested the land to the point of major damage. Not only did they use wood for fuel, and for building ships, carts, bridges, and buildings, but since the custom was to bury the dead in coffins they also used a great deal of wood for funerals, in amounts proportional to a steadily growing population. Deforestation became steadily more widespread, and by the eighteenth and nineteenth centuries there was a severe shortage of timber in most parts of the country. Europe also suffered from a serious depletion of resources, reaching its most severe in the sixteenth century, but was able to resolve the problem by colonizing other countries and exploiting *their* natural resources. Lacking the military might of the European powers, and with political philosophies that didn't encourage colonial adventures, China was unable to follow their example and had to make do with less. On top of everything else, population pressure was a perennial problem.

In spite of decades of government bans on using wood for all but the most necessary purposes, China's current reserves of wood per person are only one-eighth of the world average, and it is now one of the most un-forested countries in the world.[14] We now know what most ancient cultures didn't: that deforestation leads to a variety of ecological problems. Forests prevent erosion of topsoil; through regulating snowmelt, they ensure a good supply of fresh water; and they provide habitat for birds, animals, and plants (sources of food when agriculture fails). Deforestation is thus a major factor behind the current environmental degradation in China.

China finally has a president in Xi Jinping who acknowledges the country's "ecological vulnerability" and especially its "scarcity of forest resources," and urges the people to plant trees for the "arduous mission of afforestation and ecological improvement." He is thinking in a longer time frame than his predecessors—and also longer than the average Western politician nowadays, whose thinking extends only as far as the time of the next election.[15] Thanks to the way Chinese politics are constituted, President Xi is likely, by contrast, to be in charge for quite some time.

Documents dating back to the eleventh century BCE show an awareness on the part of the authorities of the need to restrain people from over-exploitation of natural resources. The oldest of these observes that local governors were responsible "for protecting rivers, mountains, forests, birds and other animals."[16] A well-known story from the sixth century BCE tells of a high official who reproaches a Duke for fishing too early in the season, before the young fish have grown up. He cites the regulated fishing practices advocated "in ancient times" by the official known as "guardian of the waters." When the people follow such regulations, this helps "the bright *qi* energies to rise." The official "guardian of the animals" would enact corresponding regulations prohibiting the hunting or trapping of animals that are too young.

> Furthermore, in the mountains the sprouts growing from coppiced trunks were not to be chopped off. In the wetlands, it was forbidden to cut the tender sprouts. . . . It was obligatory to protect the fledglings and the eggs of birds. As for insects, the eggs and pupae of ants were to be left untouched. The teaching of ancient times is that all beings should propagate themselves in abundance.

Another document, from the time when Confucius was a young man, records a high government minister expressing concern about possible ill effects on agricultural land of deforestation and draining of marshes.[17] Such passages demonstrate an awareness stretching back three thousand years of the nature of ecological interactions and the need to restrain human interventions in them. However, as new developments in technology gradually granted people greater power over the natural world, under pressure from a growing population they continued to intensify their impact on the land.

Mark Elvin characterizes China's chronic problem with the environment as "the exploitation of the environment at a rate overstressing its natural resilience and exceeding its capacity for self-renewal within a humanly relevant time frame." It's also a very contemporary problem for the world right now. And why can't we act to slow global warming? Elvin's diagnosis of the situation throughout much of China's history still applies: "What has made the process hard to restrain by conscious action, even when there has been a fairly widespread appreciation of its damaging effects," he continues, is *"the pay-off in power."*[18] In military, economic, and political power, rather than the power of the fine example or the philosopher's ideas. These latter are integral with the powers of Heaven and Earth, and are according to the Confucian thinkers the best kind of power to use in governing.

Confucian Regulations

Exploitation of the natural world for human purposes has often elicited misgivings on the part of China's major philosophers. The first to raise doubts about deforestation was Mencius.

> There was a time when the trees were luxuriant on the Ox Mountain, but since it is on the outskirts of a great city, the trees are constantly lopped by axes. Is it any wonder that they are no longer fine? With the respite they get in the day and in the night, and the moistening by the rain and the dew, there is certainly no lack of new shoots coming out, but then the cattle and sheep come to graze upon the mountain. That is why it is as bald as it is. People, seeing only its baldness, tend to think that it never had any trees. But can this possibly be the nature of a mountain?[19]

No, it can't be: the nature of a mountain is to be covered with trees, and it's the double neglect by humans (unsustainable extraction of timber and permitting over-grazing) that's compromising that nature.

Appeals like this tended to fall on deaf ears, in Mencius's time and after. Even so, the historical record shows that at least some people appreciated the interconnections between trees and other components of ecosystems, and especially the way forests prevent erosion of topsoil. The phenomenon was often couched in the language of the Five Agents, as in this explanation by Yu Sen, a commissioner for watercourses in the late seventeenth century.

> The functioning of the Five Agents is such that failure to overcome is failure to generate. If now trees are scarce, wood will not overcome soil, and the nature of soil will be light and easily blown away, while the human character will become crude and fierce. If trees are plentiful, the soil will not fly up, and men will revert to refinement and good order.[20]

This is an excellent example of the cycles of the Five Agents in interaction, and involving humans.

Another crucial function that forests perform is the regulation of snowmelt, thereby ensuring a good supply of fresh water. And they naturally provide habitat for birds, animals, and plants—sources of food when agriculture fails. But these compelling ecological reasons for avoiding deforestation had no purchase in an era where wars demanded large quantities of timber.

Mencius goes on to draw an analogy between the Ox Mountain and the human being: just as the mountain loses its nature when deprived of its natural cover of vegetation, so if we humans "let go our true heart" we lose the natural endowment of humanity and become like animals. There's an implication that it also works the other way round: the same desires that are destroying our natural environment are also eating away at our own nature as humans. If we fail to protect the natural covering of the mountain, we end up no better than the animals that help denude it. For Mencius, it's a matter of "educating the heart" through keeping one's desires to a minimum.[21]

A crucial part of the ruler's task is then to restrain people's greed when it threatens to disrupt the natural propensities of Heaven and Earth. Being innocent of free market ideology, Mencius understands that in situations where people's short-term focus on their own gain prevents their seeing the larger picture, somebody has to intervene with regulations.

> If you do not interfere with the busy seasons in the fields [by conscripting the men for a war], there will be more grain than the people can eat; if you do not allow nets with too fine a mesh to be used in large ponds, there will be more fish and turtles than they can eat; if hatchets and axes are permitted in the forests on the hills only in the proper seasons, there will be more timber than they can use.[22]

When there's a sufficiency of foodstuffs to sustain life, and enough timber to properly house the dead, the people will be contented.

However, human nature being the way it is, people will use nets with a fine mesh if it's to their advantage and they can get away with it, and they'll hack down trees in all seasons if they can turn a profit by doing so. When resources are scarce, different groups will compete for them and before long there will be wars. And wars are notoriously devastating to the natural environment. Not only do armies fell trees and mine for material with horrific intensity, but they gain further advantage if they can destroy the enemy's resource base by burning crops, or poisoning water supplies, or flooding their terrain.

As Mark Elvin has shown, those parties or states that were the most efficient short-term exploiters of human and natural resources tended to win their wars. Those that reshaped the environment through agriculture, water-control, and extraction of fuel and minerals, without regard for the longer-term consequences for the environment, were usually the victors—who would then find themselves dominating a land that was becoming progressively poorer in resources.[23] He cites from the definitive account by Donald Hughes of the environmental devastation wreaked by ancient Greece and Rome, where one finds the same prevalence of "social-Darwinist brutality" and wars:

> The most damaging aspect of Greek and Roman social organization as it affected the environment was its direction toward war. . . . Ancient cities and empires were warrior-dominated societies, never at peace for very long. . . . Nonrenewable resources were consumed, and renewable resources exploited faster than was sustainable. As a result, the lands where Western civilization received its formative impulse were gradually drained.[24]

Elvin comments that the brutality of the Eurasian classical world went with less self-understanding on the part of the perpetrators, and that the remarkable feature of the Chinese case is that the brutality appeared to be "more aware of its own nature."

Seldom were wars more internecine than during the Warring States Period in China (475–221 BCE), which is also when philosophy first began to flourish widely and to encourage awareness of nature's vulnerability. Some of the most prominent philosophers argued for protecting the natural environment and warned of the dangers of damaging it. Unfortunately, rulers with benign attitudes toward nature are not especially apt to flourish during times of war, and even after this period the number who were in this respect enlightened remained small. Economic development then became the goal, in favor of which environmental sustainability was regularly sacrificed. In general the highest officials favored securing their own power over caring for the natural environment, even if their counterparts at the level of local government were on occasion able to enact beneficial regulations.

Confucian philosophy would in general endorse the enterprise of engaging the powers of Heaven and Earth for the benefit of human society, and could be criticized from a Daoist perspective for focusing so much on the human realm as to become blind to exploitation of the natural world. However, the Confucian emphasis on sufficiency and moderation means that use of natural resources is to be kept within limits. And since the ruler's primary responsibility is always the well-being of the people, it would be unjust for him to exploit those resources for personal gain.

In spite of this, Xunzi in particular has been characterized as an anthropocentric Confucian who advocates the exploitation of nature for the sake of humans, but this is a misrepresentation. In fact, he follows the Confucian tradition of aligning good government with the natural order, and he situates human beings—and the self-cultivated especially—firmly between the powers of nature.

> The gentleman is the triadic partner of Heaven and Earth, the summation of the myriad things, and the father and mother of the people. . . . The [five Confucian] relationships between lord and minister [etc.] . . . share with Heaven and Earth the same organizing principle.[25]

The ruler reigns in concert with the forces of nature, drawing inspiration and strength from them, on the basis of his experience of interaction within the family. And when Xunzi encourages intervention in the course of nature for the benefit of human beings, this engagement has to be timely and to respect natural limits.

> How can glorifying Heaven and contemplating it,
>   be as good as tending its creatures and regulating them?
> How can obeying Heaven and singing it hymns of praise
>   be better than regulating what Heaven has mandated and using it?
> How can anxiously watching for the season and awaiting what it brings,
>   be as good as responding with activities that are seasonal?
> How can depending on things to increase naturally
>   be better than developing their natural capacities so as to transform them?
> How can contemplating things and expecting them to serve you
>   be better than administering them according to the opportunities they present?
> How can brooding over the origins of things
>   be better than assisting what perfects them?[26]

This passage has been read as advocating the exploitation of the natural world, but Xunzi understands the relationship as an ongoing interaction, more complex and mutually responsive than exploitation. The regulating and using and administering go along with tending and responding and developing and assisting. Note that it's the *natural* capacities of things that we are to develop, rather than remaking their cores (as in nuclear fission or genetic modification) to suit human purposes. This is classic Chinese sage behavior: intervening gently so as to enhance what is already going on, by nature—though the Daoists would want to downplay the "for human benefit" aspect.

Xunzi is more concerned than Mencius about the human tendency to let desires get out of hand, and points out that unrestrained desires on the part of the few often jeopardize the use of "the commons" by the many. In discussing "The Regulations of a Sage King" he emphasizes that a primary duty of the ruler is to forestall environmental destruction by enacting seasonal regulations.

> If it is the season when the grasses and trees are in the splendor of their flowering and sprouting new leaves, axes and halberds are not permitted in the mountain forest so as not to end their lives prematurely or interrupt their maturation. If it is the season when the giant sea turtles, water lizards, fish, freshwater turtles, loach, and eels are depositing their eggs, nets and poisons are not permitted in the marshes. . . .
>
> The ponds, lakes, pools, streams, and marshes being strictly closed during the proper season is the reason that fish and turtles are in plentiful abundance and the Hundred Clans have surplus for other uses. The cutting and pruning, growing and planting, not being out of their proper season is the reason the mountain forests are not denuded and the Hundred Clans have more than enough timber.[27]

The traditional Confucian attitude toward the natural world combined a respect for the powers of Heaven and Earth with a sense that some human beings were capable of understanding natural patterns well enough to turn some propensities to human advantage. But it's also recognized that the wise among human beings would know how to restrain this utility-driven enterprise when appropriate, and that the sage-ruler will sometimes have to regulate the activities of those whose desires render them less than wise.

The Confucian thinkers realized early on the importance of integrating the political with the natural order. The *Zhongyong* emphasizes that "for the person who would be the true king over the World" the way to rule is the Middle Way: "Established between the heavens and the earth, this Way does not run contrary to their operations." The best ruler will be the sage, and Confucius is cited as exemplary.

> Only if one is able to make the most of the natural tendencies of processes and events can one assist in the transforming and nourishing activities of heaven and earth. . . .
>
> Confucius modeled himself above on the rhythm of the turning seasons, and below he was attuned to the patterns of water and earth. He is comparable to the heavens and the earth,

sheltering and supporting everything that is. He is comparable to the progress of the four seasons, and the alternating brightnesses of the sun and moon.[28]

Anyone capable of self-cultivation can eventually, by aligning one's energies with the forces of nature, come to amplify and modulate them, and thereby benefit the whole world.

Numerous passages in the Confucian classics advise the ruler how best to govern according to the seasons. The way *not* to govern—and this applies to the ruler of the individual body as well as to the ruler of the state—is by having a fixed image of goals to be pursued in disregard of environment or time of year. The earliest Chinese calendar with philosophical import is to be found in the "Almanac" chapters of the first twelve books of the *Annals of Lü Buwei*, one for each month of the year. A consideration of the first chapter of the first book, for the first month of spring, can give us a sense of the whole.

The almanacs begin with four brief sections. The first situates the month astrologically, giving the sun's location in the zodiac, and naming the constellations that dominate at dawn and dusk. The second lists the month's correlates among the Five Creatures (scaly, feathered, naked [humans], furred, shelled), the Five Notes (of the pentatonic scale), the Five Numbers, the Five Tastes (sour, bitter, sweet, acrid, salt), and the Five Viscera (spleen, lungs, heart, kidneys, liver). Then comes a short description of contemporary processes in the natural world, such as "The east wind melts the ice, dormant creatures begin to stir." The last section concerns the Emperor: which apartment of the imperial Hall of Light he resides in (he has to move every month to the appropriate one), the accouterments of his chariot, the color of his robes and kind of his ornaments, the nature of the food he eats—all of which must be in accordance with the month.[29]

Then comes the ritual that the Emperor has to conduct at each time of year, the background to which is the increase of *qi* energies during spring and summer and their diminution during autumn and winter, as well as the *yinyang* alternations throughout the seasons. In outlining the ruler's duties, the calendrical chapters of the *Annals* focus on the Five Potencies that drive the Five Agents. Angus Graham paraphrases elegantly:

> Thus at the beginning of the year . . . the Grand Historiographer reports "Such-and-such a day is the start of spring; the fullness of Potency is in Wood." The ruler, wearing blue-green, then leads out his nobles to welcome spring in the East suburb, rewards civil officials, issues orders to be merciful and bountiful to the

people, pushes the plough three times to encourage farming, and commands the superintendent of agriculture to take up residence in the East suburb.

Correspondingly, when "the chill winds come, the white dew falls and the cold cicada chirps," the Historiographer reports "Such-and-such a day is the start of autumn; the fullness of Potency is in Metal."[30]

And so forth, for each of the twelve months, always aligning the ruler's activities with the prevailing Agent and Potency.

After the Almanac sections comes a description of the measures that must be taken at the particular time of year to protect the environment. In the first month of spring, for example:

> The Son of Heaven puts in order the statutes regulating sacrifice, and commands that in making offerings to the mountains and forests, streams and marshes, no female animals be used as victims. He issues orders to prevent the felling of trees; to prohibit the overturning of nests; to forbid the killing of very young creatures . . . fledgling birds, fawns, and eggs.

The basic principles are summed up as three general prohibitions:

> Do not transgress the Dao of Heaven;
> Do not contravene the pattern of order on Earth;
> Do not disrupt the guiding principles of humans.[31]

As long as the ruler and his advisors understand the Way of Nature and how the Five Agents work, and take care to appoint the most competent officials, agriculture will thrive, the people will be happy, and the ruler will be seen to enjoy the Mandate of Heaven.

The Daoist Sage-Ruler

Not long after the time of Confucius the classical Daoist thinkers stressed even more strongly the need to integrate the orders of society and nature. Whereas Confucius developed a comprehensive humanism aimed at the good of society as a whole, the *Laozi* advocates a distinctly non-anthropocentric political philosophy for the purpose of integrating human existence with the processes of the natural world, the energies of Heaven and Earth.

In the context of the unity of Heaven, humans, and Earth, Daoists would say that Confucians are too narrowly focused on the middle realm of human society, and so lack a robust engagement with the natural world above and below. For Confucius, the Way (*dao*) is generally the way of humans (the way of the sage, the way of the ancestors, and so forth), whereas the Daoist focus is softer and wider—on the Way as the unifying pattern of all three realms.

The *Laozi*'s view of the natural world is eminently realistic: even though the powers of Heaven and Earth provide all that human beings need to survive—and thrive, as long as they manage it properly—they are not especially concerned with the human species.

> Heaven and Earth are not humane. . . .
> The space between Heaven and Earth—
> Isn't it just like a bellows?
> Even though empty it is not exhausted.
> Pump it and more and more comes out.[32]

The worldview is trans-humanist and un-anthropocentric, insofar as humans are understood as beings irrevocably subject to the powers of Heaven and Earth. And so the Daoist sage-ruler empties himself of personal likes and dislikes to become a medium for the impartiality of those greater powers, letting them inform the social realm in its continuity with the natural. Roger Ames has pointed out this theme in the *Zhuangzi* too: "because the ruler shows no partiality, the country is properly ordered."[33]

The *Laozi* at one point lists the "four greats" (meaning great things or processes) in the world: the Way, Heaven, Earth, and the King. Notice that even the greatest of humans comes last among the four. This ordering is then reversed when each great emulates, or models itself on, the next greater—or, more literally, "takes it as a law:"

> Human beings [through the King] emulate Earth,
> Earth emulates Heaven,
> Heaven emulates Way-making,
> Way-making emulates what is spontaneously so.[34]

This remarkably trans-anthropocentric approach to governing may appear paradoxical, but it actually makes sense insofar as any polity can thrive only in the context of a sustaining environment, and following the ways of nature is a good way to begin. When peoples ignore this, they risk, if their circumstances become straitened, going under.[35] As with Mencius, Daoist politics are concerned to restrain the desires of those who are incapable of self-restraint, so that human wants will not eclipse the will of Heaven (which is empty of desire). The *Laozi* thus calls for a distinctive form of representative government, in which the ruler represents in the human world the interests of Heaven and Earth and the myriad things.[36]

The text sometimes refers to the Way of Heaven and Earth as "unworked wood," signifying natural simplicity before human culture has shaped it.

> Were the nobles and kings able to respect this,
> All things would defer of their own accord.
> The heavens and the earth would come together
> To send down their sweet honey,
> And without being so ordered
> The common people would see that it is distributed equitably.

The sage-ruler, as one whose awareness of natural energies allows him to align himself with them, is thus able to say:

> We do things non-coercively
> And the people develop along their own lines;
> We cherish equilibrium
> And the common people order themselves;
> We are non-interfering in our governance
> And the common people prosper themselves;
> We are objectless in our desires
> And the common people are of themselves like unworked wood.[37]

Acknowledging the dynamic equilibrium that characterizes most natural processes, the *Laozi* observes that "the Way of Heaven is to let some go where there is excess, and to augment where there is not enough." The way of the human tends, perversely, to do the opposite: "It is to take away from those who do not have enough in order to give more to those who already have too much." (Hard not to think of current regimes in the United States and United Kingdom.) A sage ruler who by contrast follows the natural course would win the world: "Who then in having too much is able to draw on this excess to make an offering to the world? There that can take what he himself has in excess and offer this to the World? Perhaps only those who are way-making."[38]

Insofar as the *Laozi* offers a philosophy of images rather than concepts, the images are drawn mostly from the natural world. Water, and especially rivers, where the water flows continuously from a source, is the significant image in the present context.[39] There is a prime example of flowing water as an image for life, and all existence, in the *Analects*:

> The Master was standing on a riverbank, and observed, "Isn't life's passing just like this, never ceasing day or night!"

The broader point is that, as in the Buddhist view, *everything* passes away, eventually. The whole world is flow—as Heraclitus also remarked, at the beginning of the Western philosophical tradition.[40]

Xunzi writes about water in a similar vein:

> Confucius was once gazing at the water flowing eastward. Zigong questioned Confucius about it, saying: "Why is it that whenever a gentleman sees a great stream, he feels the necessity to contemplate?"
>
> Confucius replied: "Ah! Water—it bestows itself everywhere, on all living things, yet there is no assertion: in this it resembles Potency. Its direction of flow is to descend toward the low ground, and whether its course is winding or straight, it necessarily follows its natural principle: in this it resembles rightness. Things float along on its surface and its depths cannot be fathomed: in this it resembles knowledge. Its vast rushing waters are neither subdued nor exhausted: in this it resembles the Way."

As Roger Ames remarks, this fine image of the way potency emanates and the sympathetic resonance it elicits, by way of *wuwei*, is an idea common to both the Daoist and Confucian traditions.[41]

Although the *Laozi* called *dao* one of the "greats," it did so only tentatively (since to call it great would preclude its being small—which of course it also is, though without being any kind of thing). The passage goes on to say that its greatness comes from its "passing away:"

> If forced to give it a name,
> I would call it great.
> Being great it is called passing away,
> Passing, it is called distancing.
> Distancing, it is called returning.[42]

The Way is great because its passing away—the same word as Confucius used of the river—is constant and inexhaustible, like a spring that never dries up. It goes far after coming, but then turns back: think of the cycles of *yin* and *yang*, where the increase in *yin* gives way, after the maximum, to an increase in *yang*—and so on, endlessly.

Another passage in the *Laozi* explicitly associates the flow of *dao* with water.

> The highest efficacy is like water.
> It is because water benefits everything
> Yet vies to dwell in places loathed by the crowd
> That it comes nearest to proper way-making.[43]

These lines are followed by a series of attributes of the good ruler, among which is his power to create order. And just as water settles in the lowest places, which most people shun, so the ruler governs best from below.

> What enables the rivers to be king over all the valleys
> Is that they are good at staying lower than them. . . .
> This is the reason that the sage in wanting to stand above the people
> Must put themselves below them in what they have to say.[44]

The Daoist view is not only that human beings will flourish if they emulate natural processes, but also that this happens primarily because the best ruler is the most consummate emulator—of water especially.

During imperial times (beginning with the unification of China under the Qin Dynasty in 221 BCE), the Chinese greatly expanded their numerous water-control projects. As mentioned earlier, they soon encountered the core problem with large-scale systems of this kind, which is that they're inherently unstable. They are always far more expensive to maintain than to build in the first place, since the necessary structures—sea-walls, levees, and polders used to claim land for cultivation—are subject to constant wear and tear. And in the case of rivers and waterways the continuous buildup of sediment means that the dredging of channels and heightening of dykes generate a perpetual burden of human work. Mark Elvin offers a comprehensive account of how such massive projects lock people in to an unusually high-maintenance enterprise with steadily diminishing returns.[45]

The instigators and directors of these hydrological projects were apparently ignorant of the wisdom of the Daoist thinkers on the topic of water. As the *Laozi* remarks:

> Nothing in the world is as soft and weak as water,
> And yet in attacking what is hard and strong
> There is nothing that can surpass it. . . .
> There is no one in the world that does not know
> That the soft prevails over the hard,
> And the weak prevails over the strong,
> And yet none are able to act accordingly.[46]

The ancient Chinese engineers apparently never appreciated the nature of this power at the core of their hydrological projects: they were certainly never able to harness it satisfactorily.

A Daoist would doubt the wisdom of building dams—especially large examples of "the hard and strong"—in the first place. The *Laozi* also says, "Those who would grasp things lose them." Which is never more true than in the case of water, whose flowing tends to elude human control.[47] If you try to grasp water by making a fist you get only a few drops: what works is to cup your hands—a more open and far less aggressive action.

The history of China's hydrological failures seems to confirm the *Laozi*'s acknowledgment of "rivers and seas" as "kings of the hundred valleys," a high position that derives from their habit of "staying low." If humans persist in trying to lord it over the aquatic powers, they remain blind to the more general Daoist admonition "not to contend" against the powers of Heaven and Earth.

Syncretic Studies

The most comprehensive account of political rule that's grounded in the realms of Heaven and Earth comes from the *Huang-Lao Boshu* (Silk Texts), manuscripts that were discovered in 1973 in the excavation of the tombs at Mawangdui, which had been sealed in 168 BCE. The *Huang-Lao* is a syncretistic work, predominantly Daoist, but also influenced by Legalism: the "Lao" refers to Laozi, and the "Huang" to the legendary Yellow Emperor, Huangdi. The political philosophy it contains is distinguished by its having actually been put into practice in the courts of the Western Han (early second century BCE), before Confucianism became the official state philosophy.

> Again, Huang-Lao assumes the unity of the three realms, Heaven-humans-Earth.
>
> The way of one who realizes kingly rulership of the empire consists of a heavenly component, a human component, and an earthly component. When these three are employed in line with each other . . . one will possess the whole World.[48]

The political ideas are based on what Western thinkers would call a philosophical naturalism—the view that that natural world is the basis for human existence and so provides standards of some kind—and the proposed system of law derives from natural law. Insofar as Heaven and Earth are taken as exemplary, we find the natural order cited as a justification for orders of rank within human society. Just as there is high and low in the world of nature, so in the human world there is noble and base. And again the ruler is encouraged to reward and punish in keeping with the time of year: "To realize achievements during three seasons and to punish and execute during one season is the way of Heaven and Earth."[49]

Since the Way of Heaven and Earth manifests itself in complementary alternation between the forces of *yin* and *yang*, humans are enjoined to synchronize their activities with these alternations. The *Huang-Lao* also extends the operations of *yinyang* in natural phenomena (the seasons, dark-light, cold-hot, etc.) to human beings in their social activities (female-male, family relations, and so forth). Just as *yin* and *yang* alternate as active and passive forces in the natural order of things, so the ruler is advised to employ not only aggressive (masculine) initiative but also receptive (feminine) reserve. And indeed any time the ruler acts in ways contrary to the forces of *yin* and *yang*, "at worst the state will perish, and at the least the ruler will meet with disaster."[50]

The text's recommendations pertain, as one would expect, not only to the activities of the outstanding person of the ruler, but also to those of the individual.

> Only after one lines them up in accordance with the constant Way of Heaven and Earth will one determine wherein lies the cause of disaster and fortune, life and death, survival and demise, prosperity and decline. For this reason, one will not deviate from principle in one's actions but will sort out the World.[51]

Sorting out the World sounds like an eminently worthwhile enterprise, but one might well ask how humans are supposed to know "the constant Way of Heaven and Earth." "Nature" is always, as we say today in quote marks, a social construction: there's no such thing as heaven and earth in any real sense, since they are always experienced through some social and historical perspective or other. The *Huang-Lao* is aware of this issue, and proposes a straightforward solution:

> The way to apprehend and understand is simply to be empty and have nothing. . . . In his observations in the World, the one who grasps the Way is without grasping, without fixed positions, without impositional action, without personal biases.

After practicing this process of emptying, one eventually comes to experience the natural order directly, and to "understand without confusion."[52]

We find similar ideas in the *Huainanzi*, elaborated in greater detail. The "Art of Rulership" chapter begins by recommending again that the ruler's activities and techniques should follow the natural order.

> The art of rulership consists in
> managing without interfering
> and issuing wordless instructions. . . .
> The ruler's conduct is a model for the world.
> His advancing and withdrawing respond to the seasons,
> his movement and rest comply with proper patterns. . . .
> Affairs emerge from what is natural,
> so that nothing issues from the ruler himself.

Because the ruler is attuned to the powers of nature and his actions "respond to the seasons . . . with proper patterns," there is no need for him to issue explicit instructions or interfere in the affairs of the people.

The ruler gets attuned by refining the *qi* energies from Heaven and Earth that constitute his person, and can thus act as a medium for the quintessential *qi* of those greater powers. Like the legendary emperor known as the "Divine Farmer," Shen Nong, he is thereby able to transform the people by emanating his "spiritual" or "godlike power."[53] This kind of "spirit transformation" has a powerful and extensive reach: "A great shout can be heard at most only within a hundred paces, but the human will can project over a thousand *li*."

In a passage consonant with Xunzi's invoking of the vast water-like emanations of potency through *wuwei*, the *Huainanzi* echoes Huang-Lao philosophy:

> If the ruler is pure, tranquil, and non-active,
> Heaven will provide the seasons for him.
> If the ruler is modest, frugal, and keeps to moderation,
> Earth will yield its wealth for him. . . .
>
> Thus the ruler covers the world with his Potency. He does not act from his own wisdom, but follows what will bring benefit to the myriad people.

The more the ruler is able to channel the powers of Heaven and Earth to the benefit of the people, the more awesome his potency becomes in turn:

> If the ruler defends the people against what does them harm and opens a way for the people to have what brings them benefit,

then his awesomeness will spread like the bursting of a dike or the breaking of a dam.[54]

Interesting that the one who protects people from water-caused disasters should resemble such a force of nature in his power.

The *Huainanzi* often invokes "an age of Utmost Potency" in the distant past, where human activity—and especially the minimal activity of the sage—is what maintains harmony with the environment. In that era,

> The sage simply inhaled and exhaled the *qi* of *yin* and *yang*, and none of the myriad things failed to flourish as they acknowledged the sages' Potency in harmonious compliance. At this time nothing was directed or arranged: separately and autonomously things completed themselves.[55]

Those were the days, indeed. Roger Ames has remarked the strong Daoist strain in this political philosophy, whereby "when each particular is allowed to express its own natural potential without being distorted by external constraints, these elements will collectively function in a thoroughly integrated natural order."[56]

"The people of antiquity" are imagined to be able to "make their *qi* energy the same as that of Heaven and Earth," and so they were able to "wander in an era of unity." They could do this thanks to the pervasiveness of sympathetic resonance (*ganying*) throughout the field of *qi* energies. Although Ames notes the importance of the narrower Han Confucian idea of "the mutual influence of the human and nature" (*tian ren xiang ying*), he doesn't mention the discussion of sympathetic resonance in chapter 6 of the *Huainanzi*.[57] As a condition of everything in the energy field, sympathetic resonance accounts for interactions not only between human beings and natural phenomena, but also between the potency of rulers and the responses of the people.

According to the *Huainanzi*, when contemporary people come into conflict through competing to fulfill their desires, the ensuing disturbance of *qi* energy brings in its train, by sympathetic resonance, mayhem in the natural world too.

> When the hearts of high and low become estranged from each other, noxious *qi* rises like a vapor; when ruler and minister are not in harmony, the five grains do not produce a yield.[58]

This in turn ushers in an age of decline, when awareness of the Way is steadily diminished and human desires are given free rein.

Coming down to the age of decline:
People delved in mountains for precious stones.
They engraved metal and carved jade,
Pried open oysters and clams to get pearls,
Smelted bronze and iron,
And the myriad things were not nurtured.

People ripped open pregnant animals and killed young ones . . .
They overturned nests and broke eggs . . .
They bored wood to get fire,
Cut timber to build terraces,
Burned forests to make fields,
Drained marshes to catch fish,
So tortoises and dragons no longer frequented the earth. . . .

Thus yin and yang became twisted and tangled;
The four seasons lost their proper order;
Thunderclaps caused things to overturn and break.

Nature made chaotic, disasters and catastrophes, the myriad things thrown into confusion by ill-considered human intervention. There follows a series of extreme weather events, such that "the myriad things suffered premature deaths:" and on top of that "there were innumerable instances of misshapen shoots, non-blossoming flowers, and pendant fruit that died out of season."

Blissfully unaware, the rich simply strove—as they often do—to get richer, "building great mansions, houses, and palaces" and adorning them with lavish artistry. The powerful among them grew yet more self-indulgent, to the point where such sumptuous extravagance "did not suffice to fulfill the desires of the rulers of men." The result was further degradation of the natural environment and those whose livelihoods most immediately depended upon it, "the common people." The silver lining to this dark cloud is that such dismal times provide an opportunity and challenge for a ruler of a quite different kind, one empty of desires and concerned above all for the welfare of the people.[59]

Stories like this—where the human race degenerates through the arrogant exploitation of the natural world for the satisfaction of extravagant desires, and thereby provokes a destructive response—are by no means confined to ancient China. Such authors as Hesiod, Ovid, and Pliny in the Western tradition call attention to similar patterns, often through the figure of Prometheus, where the backlash often comes in the form of a flood (as in the Book of Genesis).[60] So are we really surprised now when, after throwing off the energy balance of the planet by emitting enormous quantities of greenhouse gases, we find ourselves subject to more devastating storms and flooding and other natural disasters?

We are now in an age of decline where extravagance still fails to fulfill human desires, and the backlash from the global warming we have been fueling for decades is imminent—in the form of droughts as well as floods. Governments in the West have always governed as if their states, and human societies generally, existed in a vacuum, and as if the ever-present context of the natural world were of no relevance. Nor have political philosophers in the Western traditions ever suggested that this might be shortsighted. And what you get when you ignore the natural context is the risky situation the world is now in.

The Chinese thinkers have generally paid close attention to the context of Heaven and Earth, and many of their rulers did too. Now is the time to retrieve and act on this ancient wisdom. Doing so will benefit not only the Chinese but also the rest of us.

Notes

1. Roger T. Ames, *The Art of Rulership: A Study in Ancient Chinese Political Thought* (Honolulu: University of Hawai`i Press, 1983).

2. John Knoblock, in *Xunzi: A Translation and Study of the Complete Works* (Stanford, CA: Stanford University Press, 1988), 3 vols., 2:16–17.

3. See Wing-tsit Chan, *A Source Book in Chinese Philosophy* (Princeton, NJ: Princeton University Press, 1963), 5–7.

4. Confucius, *Analects* 7.23, in Roger T. Ames and Henry Rosemont Jr. *The Analects of Confucius: A Philosophical Translation* (New York: Ballantine Books, 1999), 116.

5. Confucius, *Analects*, 2.4, 16.8.

6. Mozi, "The Will of Heaven," in *Readings in Classical Chinese Philosophy*, eds., Philip J. Ivanhoe and Bryan W. Van Norden (New York & London: Seven Bridges Press, 2001), 87–88.

7. *Mencius*, translated with an introduction and notes by D. C. Lau, revised edition (London: Penguin, 2004), 5A:5.

8. *Mencius*, 4A:9, 7B:14; 1B:6 and 1B:8.

9. See Mark Elvin, "Three Thousand Years of Unsustainable Growth: China's environment from archaic times to the present," *East-Asian History* 6 (1993): 7.

10. Mark Elvin, *The Retreat of the Elephants: An Environmental History of China* (New Haven, CT, and London: Yale University Press, 2004), 26; Elizabeth C. Economy, *The River Runs Black: The Environmental Challenge to China's Future* (Ithaca, NY: Cornell University Press, 2004), 41.

11. Elvin, *Retreat*, chapter 7, "Water and the Costs of System Sustainability."
12. Duan Chang-qun et al., "Relocation of Ancient Civilization Centers in Ancient China," *Ambio* 27, No. 7 (Nov., 1998): 572–75. Cited in Economy, *The River*, 37.
13. Elvin, *Retreat*, 9.
14. Elvin, *Retreat*, 85, 20.
15. Xi Jinping, *The Governance of China* (Beijing: Foreign Languages Press, 2014), 229–30.
16. Concerning the "Rite of Zhou: Regional Officer," cited in Economy, *The River*, 29.
17. Guoyu, "Tales from the Various States," cited in Elvin, "Three Thousand Years," 16–17.
18. Mark Elvin, "The Environmental Legacy of Imperial China," *China Quarterly*, 156 (1998): 742–43 (emphasis added).
19. *Mencius*, 6A:8.
20. Sen Yu, "On the Growing of Trees," cited in Helen Dunstan, "Official Thinking on Environmental Issues and the State's Environmental Roles in Eighteenth-Century China," in Mark Elvin and Ts'ui-jung Liu, eds., *Sediments of Time: Environment and Society in Chinese History* (Cambridge: Cambridge University Press, 1998), 602.
21. *Mencius*, 7B:35.
22. *Mencius*, 1A:3.
23. See Elvin, chapter 5, "War and the Logic of Short-term Advantage," *Retreat*.
24. Donald Hughes, *Pan's Travail: Environmental Problems of the Ancient Greeks and Romans* (Baltimore, MD: Johns Hopkins University Press, 1994), 198–99.
25. *Xunzi*, 9.15, 2:103.
26. *Xunzi*, 17.10, 3:20–21.
27. *Xunzi*, 9.16b, 2:105. See also *Huainanzi*, 9.28, 331.
28. Roger T. Ames and David L. Hall, *Focusing the Familiar: A Translation and Philosophical Interpretation of the* Zhongyong (Honolulu: University of Hawai'i Press, 2001), 110–11, 105.
29. John Knoblock and Jeffrey Riegel, *The Annals of Lü Buwei* (Stanford, CA: Stanford University Press, 2000), 1/1.1, 60–61.
30. *The Annals*, paraphrased by A. C. Graham, *Disputers of the Dao: Philosophical Argument in Ancient China* (La Salle, IL: Open Court, 1989), 351.
31. *The Annals*, 1/1.5, 63. For the third month of spring the proscription reads:

> Allow out of the Nine Gates of the city no one with barbs and hand nets for hunting, or rabbit snares and nets, or gauze netting for birds, or poisoned food to feed to animals. . . . In this month, the Son of Heaven orders that foresters not allow the mulberry and silkworm oak to be felled. 3/1.4–1.5, 97.

32. Roger T. Ames and David L. Hall, *Daodejing: "Making This Life Significant"* (New York: Ballantine Books, 2003), chapter 5 (translation modified).
33. *Zhuangzi*, 25, cited in Ames, *Art*, 46.

34. *Daodejing*, 25 (translation modified).

35. See, for example, the stories in Jared Diamond, *Collapse: How Societies Choose to Fail or Succeed* (New York: Penguin, 2005).

36. See the insightful treatment of this idea by Hans-Georg Moeller in "Paradox Politics," chapter 4 of *The Philosophy of the Daodejing* (New York: Columbia University Press, 2006).

37. *Daodejing*, 32, also 37; *Daodejing* 57.

38. *Daodejing*, 77.

39. An excellent source on this topic is Sarah Allan, *The Way of Water and Sprouts of Virtue* (Albany: State University of New York Press, 1997).

40. Confucius, *Analects*, 9.17; Mencius discusses Confucius on the topic of flowing water in *Mencius*, 4B:18. Charles Kahn, *The Art and Thought of Heraclitus* (Cambridge: Cambridge University Press, 1979), fragments L and LI (pp. 166–69), Diels 12, 91.

41. Xunzi, 28.5, 3:248. Cited in Ames, *Art*, 31–32.

42. *Daodejing*, 25 (translation modified).

43. *Daodejing*, 8.

44. *Daodejing*, 66.

45. Elvin, *Retreat*, 116–18; 113; 26.

46. *Daodejing*, 78.

47. *Daodejing*, 64.

48. Cited in Randall Peerenboom, *Law and Morality in Ancient China: The Silk Manuscripts of Huang-Lao* (Albany: State University of New York Press, 1993), 28. This excellent study and its translations are the basis for much of the rest of this section.

49. Peerenboom, *Law and Morality*, 29; *Huang-Lao Boshu*, 57:65b, cited and translated by Peerenboom, p. 44.

50. *Huang-Lao Boshu*, 83:164b, 51:40b (Peerenboom, 45, 46).

51. *Huang-Lao Boshu*, 57:69a (Peerenboom, 47).

52. *Huang-Lao Boshu*, 43:3a, 53:52a (Peerenboom, 71).

53. *Huainanzi*, 9.1, 295–96; 9.2, 296; 9.3, 297; 9.4, 299. For discussions of this "godlike transformation," see the index entries for *shenhua* in Ames, *Art*.

54. *Huainanzi*, 9.14, 307–08; 9.26, 327–28.

55. Liu An, *The Huainanzi: A guide to the theory and practice of government in early Han China*, trans. John S. Major et al. (New York: Columbia University Press, 2010), 2.10, pp. 98–99.

56. Ames, *Art*, 148.

57. Ames, *Art*, 58, 134–35.

58. *Huainanzi*, 8.3, 271; 8.2, 270.

59. *Huainanzi*, 8.1, 268–70; 8.6, 275–77.

60. See Hesiod, *Works and Days*, lines 109–201; Ovid, *Metamorphoses*, Book I, 6–8; Pliny, *Natural History*, Book xxxiii, chapter 1; *Genesis* 6.

5

Sex and Somaesthetics

Appreciating the Chinese Difference

RICHARD SHUSTERMAN

Introduction: Somaesthetics and Chinese Philosophy

When I first presented the project of somaesthetics in the late 1990s at a large international conference in Ottawa, Canada, the public's response was extremely positive. Enthusiasm, however, focused on two topics neither of which I discussed in my paper: food and sex. The reaction did not entirely surprise me because my pragmatist aesthetics was already well known for celebrating pleasure and full-bodied experience, while the pleasures of food and sex are not only the most familiar of our somatic pleasures but moreover eminently pragmatic for personal and species survival. I immediately understood that my initial somaesthetic inquiries should not pursue these topics which, though central to life, are provocatively unconventional and marginal for academic philosophy. Having already experienced enough notoriety for my sympathetic study of rap music in *Pragmatist Aesthetics*,[1] I decided that my somaesthetic focus should be on more meditative, spiritual somatic practices, which Asian philosophical traditions had embraced and articulated far more fully than Western philosophy had done.

Early in the new millennium, I was fortunate to be invited as a special Research Professor at Hiroshima University to develop my work in somaesthetics. I was equally lucky that a young philosopher from Peking University, Peng Feng, decided to translate two of my books that dealt with that topic and with pragmatism more generally. These happy events, however, exposed a problem. I always write prefaces for translations of my books to contexualize them within the new culture, as I regard books not as objects to be fetishized but as tools which should be adapted to the circumstances of use in their new cultural context. Moreover, to have a fruitful dialogue with my Japanese hosts, I should also know something of the philosophical traditions that inform their culture, and I realized that Chinese philosophy was central to it. But I did not know how I should begin to learn East Asian philosophy, having never studied it in my student days in Jerusalem and Oxford, nor in my subsequent professional career in philosophy.

My third stroke of luck in this affair was finding Roger Ames to instruct me. I never took a course with Ames, nor even sat in on one. But he has been for almost fifteen years, my teacher of Chinese philosophy. I had met him only briefly and rather superficially when his department tried, unsuccessfully, to recruit me (in the winter of 1987–1988) as a Full Professor, and therefore flew me out to tempt me with the charms of Honolulu. Having no interest then in Asian culture, I preferred to remain at Philadelphia's Temple University with its strong program in analytic aesthetics. But more than ten years later, when I was already in Hiroshima and suddenly eager to explore East Asian thought, I still remembered Ames's intellectual energy and reputation as a scholar of sinology, so I decided to send him an email asking for some bibliographical pointers regarding basic texts and essential secondary literature in Chinese philosophy that might help nourish my research in somaesthetics.

Wondering whether he would even bother to answer, I was delighted that he responded not only with a lengthy list of texts and instructions on how best to approach them, but also a series of attached files of articles (published and unpublished) that he thought would be helpful. Ames went still further by sending me a half-dozen books (not only his own translations and monographs but also those of some authors he admired). He sustained and reinforced such gestures of generosity by responding to the many questions I had in reading Chinese philosophical materials and by reviewing my initial efforts to invoke Chinese sources in my writing. He was always encouraging even when critical of my early misreadings. When I was anxious about teaching a doctoral seminar in East Asian aesthetics when I returned to Temple, Ames reassuringly offered to help me, which he did. Whenever the students posed questions I could not answer, I told them "Just wait till I ask Professor Ames," and he always responded immediately and in rich detail, as he still does today whenever I ask him a question about Chinese philosophy. The intellectual nourishment and consequently strong reception that somaesthetics has received in China are deeply indebted to the instruction he gave me.[2]

From Roger Ames I learned more than factual information. I learned to appreciate the precious difference of what a teacher means in Chinese culture; it is not simply a job but a calling that involves deep moral commitment and devotion to one's study and to caring for one's students. It is teaching not by mere words but by actions and attitudes. If I grew increasingly appreciative of Confucianism, it was largely because of the compelling way that Ames exemplified its doctrines, attitudes, and ideals. If studying Confucian thought produced a teacher like Roger Ames, then that body of thought (I reckoned) must truly be worth studying. I had already been interested in the idea of philosophy as a way of life or art of living, and I had studied some of its past Western masters, but Ames showed me how such a life can be nobly pursued today when one takes one's teaching more seriously, broadly, and generously than most of even our best university teachers do. I remember how he affectionately gave me his tie, so that I would be more elegantly dressed at a conference we attended in Singapore, instructing me with generous understatement that my designer suit would not be sufficient to show my respect for the Chinese hosts who had invited me there for the first time.

In other words, Ames taught not merely ancient philosophical doctrine but also practical cultural knowledge for best pursuing a philosophical life today. As somaesthetics became increasingly popular in China and I began to research its erotic dimensions, Ames joined my most trusted Chinese friends in advising me to wait prudently a bit longer before publishing such work there. Respecting their superior knowledge of the Chinese difference, I have complied. Because this book will be essentially an American product read in primarily Western philosophical contexts, I feel more comfortable in taking up the topic of eroticism here, also because it is a topic that Ames has not really treated in his amazingly wide-ranging work on Chinese thought. This topic moreover is useful in showing the dangers of exaggerating the Chinese difference by erecting it as the exotic other to serve our philosophical fantasies or desires. Properly appreciating difference means justly estimating it rather than blindly positing it as a radical other. Justly estimating it means recognizing underlying commonalities despite the differences, in the same way that the complementary logic of meaning recognizes that the very notions of difference and sameness reciprocally imply and rely on each other.

Foucault and Chinese Sexology

China, the world's longest continuous civilization, can also boast of the oldest surviving studies of lovemaking. Sexual theorizing reaches back to the founding texts of Chinese thought and permeates its multiple fields of inquiry: from the divinatory cosmology and metaphysics of the *Yijing* or *Book of Changes* (the oldest of classical Chinese texts) to the medical theories of *The Yellow Emperor's Classic of Internal Medicine*, and further into the ethics of

Confucius and the ascetic Daoist doctrines of Laozi and Zhuangzi. Because sex pervades so many aspects of life, it finds expression in many fields of thought. Much classical Chinese sexual theory has therefore been formulated in works primarily focused on other, broader topics. However, there does exist a distinct genre of texts in Chinese erotic theory, variously known as the "sex handbooks" or "manuals of the art of the bedchamber."[3]

Apart from students of sinology, most contemporary intellectuals have learned about the rich tradition of Chinese sexology through the influential writings of Michel Foucault. Unfortunately, despite his enthusiastic interest in this field, Foucault has gravely misunderstood it. This essay thus begins by revising Foucault's misinterpretations, while explaining the aesthetic motivation of his misreading. The celebrated author of the *History of Sexuality* (only half of whose six projected volumes was completed when he died in 1984), Foucault was motivated by his research of the past by a passionate interest in the integration of erotic artistry into today's aesthetic stylization of life. His focus of advocatory theorizing concerned gay lovemaking, and more particularly consensual homosexual S/M, which Foucault celebrates as "a whole new art of sexual practice which tries to explore all the internal possibilities of sexual conduct" and to establish an "aesthetic appreciation of the sexual act as such." This art, a "mixture of rules and openness," combines consensual codes (that significantly script sexual behavior) with experiments "to innovate and create variations that will enhance the pleasure of the act" by introducing novelty, variety, and uncertainty that otherwise would be lacking in the sexual act.[4] Moreover, despite its use of scripting and special fictional frames of performance (e.g., the sexual dungeon), this sexual activity is not portrayed by Foucault as isolated from the rest of one's life and subjectivity. Instead, one's formation as a sexual subject forms an important part of creatively shaping one's self in terms of one's "aesthetics of existence."[5]

Foucault's sexual theorizing was not principally inspired by the Asian erotic arts but rather by his study of ancient Greek and Roman erotic theory and by his own erotic experience. But he crucially enlists what he calls the Asian "*ars erotica*" as suggesting a valuable alternative to our modern Western "*scientia sexualis*."[6] In contrast to our sexual science whose discourse of truth combines the ancient tool of confession with the modern "imperative of medicalization" (HS 68) of sexual behavior and function, the Asian erotic arts draw their truth "from pleasure itself, understood as a practice and accumulated as experience" (HS 57). In these arts, sexual pleasure "is not considered in relation to an absolute law of the permitted and the forbidden, nor by reference to a criterion of utility, but first and foremost in relation to itself; it is experienced as pleasure, evaluated in terms of its intensity, its specific quality, its duration, its reverberations in the body and the soul."

Moreover, the experienced pleasure and knowledge from *ars erotica* "must be deflected back into the sexual practice itself in order to shape it as though from within and amplify its effects. In this way, there is formed a knowledge that must remain secret, not because of an element of infamy that might attach to its object, but because of the need to hold it in the greatest reserve, since, according to tradition, it would lose its effectiveness and its virtue by being divulged. Consequently, the relationship to the master who holds the secrets is of paramount importance; only he, working alone, can transmit this art in an esoteric manner and as the culmination of an initiation in which he guides the disciple's progress with unfailing skill and severity." The results of "this masterful art," Foucault concludes, "are said to transfigure the one fortunate enough to receive its privileges: an absolute mastery of the body, singular bliss, obliviousness to time and limits, the elixir of life, the exile of death and its threats" (HS 57).

Refining, in a later interview, his views on *ars erotica* and summarizing the differences between Greek, Christian, and Chinese cultural attitudes to sexual practice in terms of the three factors of "act, pleasure, and desire," Foucault claims that, in contrast to the Greeks who focused on the act and its control as "the important element" by defining the quantity, rhythm, occasion, and circumstances of its performance, but also in contrast to the Christians who focused on desire in terms of how to fight it and extirpate its slightest roots while limiting or even avoiding pleasure when performing the act, the Chinese elevated pleasure as the highest, most valuable factor in sex. "In Chinese erotics, if one believes Van Gulik, the important element was pleasure, which it was necessary to increase, intensify, and prolong as much as possible in delaying the act itself, and to the limit of abstaining from it."[7] As this interview indicates, Foucault's understanding of Asian *ars erotica* rests largely on the Chinese sources compiled, translated, and analyzed by Robert van Gulik's groundbreaking classic *Sexual Life in Ancient China*. Foucault, however, misreads not only the cited texts, but also van Gulik's explicit commentary in the following important ways.[8]

First, it is wrong to characterize the classical Chinese texts of *ars erotica* in sharp contrast to sexual science and the medical approach to sex. These writings were instead very much concerned and largely motivated by health issues; so much so that when they are listed in the bibliographical sections of the ancient written histories of the various dynasties, they often appear under the heading of medical books or, when listed separately, after the medical books (SL 71, 121, 193). Though these sexual handbooks are described by Van Gulik as treating "the Art of the Bedchamber," the actual Chinese terms used do not refer to "art" in a distinctive aesthetic sense but rather denotes the very general sense of "technique" or "skill" acquired by learning. Van Gulik repeatedly affirms that the "handbooks of sex . . . constituted a special branch of medical literature" because their two primary goals of sexual intercourse were focused on promoting health—that of the husband, his wife, and the child to be conceived (SL 72).[9] "Primarily," he argues, "the sexual act was to achieve the woman's conceiving" (preferably a male child) so as to perpetuate the family. "Secondly, the sexual act was to strengthen the man's vitality by making him absorb the woman's *yin* essence [held to be an invigorating power], while at the same time the woman would derive physical benefit from the stirring of her latent *yin* nature" (SL 46).

Together these dual aims result in a dialectical sexual economy. Since "a man's semen [where his *yang* force is concentrated] is his most precious possession, the source not only of his health but of his very life[,] every emission of semen will diminish this vital force, unless compensated by the acquiring of an equivalent amount of *yin* essence from the woman" (SL 47). Therefore, a man's sexual activity should seek to ensure that his female partners be given full satisfaction so that he can absorb the *yin* essence that will flow from their multiple orgasms, "but he should allow himself to reach orgasm only on certain specified occasions," notably those most suitable for conceiving a child with his wife. "If a man continually changes the woman with whom he copulates the benefit will be great. If in one night one can copulate with more than ten women it is best. If one always copulates with one and the same woman her vital essence will gradually grow weaker and in the end she will be in no fit condition to give the man benefit. Moreover, the woman herself will become emaciated" (SL 138). A plurality of wives and concubines is thus recommended to provide this abundance of *yin*, since relying on a single woman for multiple orgasms would eventually drain her of the *yin* essence needed both to maintain her own health (and consequent power to conceive) and to increase the health of her male partner. By copulating with many women each night without reaching orgasm while saving his semen only for occasional ejaculations, a man not only increases his vitality and *yang* (i.e., male) essence, but in doing so raises his chances of conceiving a male child to perpetuate the patriarchal family.

These principles of sexual logic, explains Van Gulik, "implied that the man had to learn to prolong the coitus as much as possible without reaching orgasm; for the longer the member stays inside, the more *yin* essence the man will absorb, thereby augmenting and strengthening his vital force" (SL 46). The sex handbooks therefore provide men with special techniques to "prevent ejaculation either by mental discipline or by such physical means as compressing the seminal duct with his fingers. Then his *yang*-essence, intensified by its contact with the woman's *yin* will flow upwards along the spinal column and fortify his brain and his entire system. If therefore the man limits his emissions to the days when the woman is liable to conceive, his loss of *yang* essence on those occasions will be compensated by the obtaining of children perfect in body and mind"[10] (SL 47). A man who thus preserves his semen through such *coitus reservatus* while absorbing the *yin* of many women that he brings to orgasm will not only sustain his health but also become more youthful and age-resistant, even (according to some of the more radical Daoist texts) to the point of achieving immortality.[11] To quote one of the Tang Dynasty texts that Van Gulik supplies, "If one can copulate with twelve women without once emitting semen, one will remain young and handsome forever. If a man can copulate with 93 women and still control himself, he will attain immortality" (SL 194). Though most potent in the woman's genitalia, the invigorating flows of *yin* could also be drawn from the secretions of her mouth and breast, both in erotic foreplay and in the act of coitus itself. These secretions were often referred to as the "Medicine of the Three Peaks" (SL 96, 283).

Coitus reservatus served another health-related function—the emotional stability and peace of mind that depends on a harmoniously managed and satisfied household of women. Already in the ancient Confucian *Book of Rites* (*Liji*), a man's sexual duty to both his wives and concubines was firmly asserted and even inscribed in strict protocols of order and frequency of intercourse, whose violation was "a grave offense." As the *Liji* states: "Even if a concubine is growing older, as long as she has not yet reached the age of fifty, the husband shall copulate with her once every five days. She on her part shall, when she is led to his couch, be cleanly washed, neatly attired, have her hair combed and properly done up, and wear a long robe and properly fastened house shoes" (SL 60). These duties (apart from brief respites in periods of mourning) only ceased when the husband "reached the age of seventy" (SL60). Without saving his *yang* through *coitus reservatus*, and without the erotic ability to consistently give his wives and concubines real sexual (and emotional) gratification, a husband with a large household of women could easily exhaust himself without satisfying his females, thus creating a disgruntled, disorderly home whose ill-repute as mismanaged "could ruin a man's reputation and break his career" (SL109).

It should already be clear from this brief account (and there is an overwhelming wealth of further evidence in Van Gulik) that, *pace* Foucault, Chinese *ars erotica* was very deeply motivated by health issues and crucially concerned with medical matters and sexual science (albeit not in the dominant forms of modern Western medical science). Foucault surely errs in claiming that Chinese erotic theory regards sexual pleasure as more important than the sexual act because the highest goal is pleasure which it aims "to increase, intensify, prolong as much as possible in delaying the act itself, and to the limit of abstaining from it." Instead, the act itself is what the Chinese male seeks to prolong so as to magnify his *yin* and *yang* powers along with the salutary benefits they bring. Foucault apparently confuses the sexual act with the act of orgasm rather than the act of coitus or the broader act of lovemaking whose complete erotic performance would include foreplay, coitus (which could issue in orgasm), and also post-coital acts. Pleasure is indeed significant for Chinese erotic theory but it is integrally tied to the sexual act and cannot be increased by being separated from it.

Though sexual union is sometimes celebrated as "the supreme joy of man" and the "climax of human emotions," sexual pleasure cannot be the highest goal in lovemaking, since health interests clearly trump it (SL 70, 203). Indeed, Chinese *ars erotica* often warns against an overriding focus on pleasure as dangerously unhealthy. After explaining that that "the essence of the Art of the Bedchamber" is "to copulate on one night with ten different women without emitting semen even a single time," one treatise clearly warns: "A man must not engage in sexual intercourse merely to satisfy his lust. He must strive to control his sexual desire so as to be able to nurture his vital essence. He must not force his body to sexual extravagance in order to enjoy carnal pleasure, giving free rein to his passion. On the contrary, a man must think of how the act will benefit his health and thus keep himself free from disease. This is the subtle secret of the Art of the Bedchamber."[12] Another text warns that, "Intercourse between man and woman should not be for the purpose of lustful pleasure. People today do not understand the meaning of self-cultivation. They force themselves to perform the act and therefore most often harm their *jing* and damage their *qi*" (W 128–29).

In short, pleasure is certainly valued, but its importance in classical Chinese sexual theory was embedded into broader goals of health and proper management of self and household. The prevailing view was that sexual pleasure should be used to regulate and refine one's body, mind, and character through the ritual shaping of lovemaking's rules or techniques. As one Former Han Dynasty document puts it: " 'The ancients created sexual pleasure thereby to regulate all human affairs.' If one regulates his sexual pleasure he will feel at peace and attain a high age. If, on the other hand, one abandons himself to its pleasure disregarding the rules set forth in the abovementioned treatises [i.e., the sex handbooks] one will fall ill and harm one's very life" (SL70–71).

Why does Foucault so gravely misconstrue the Chinese *ars erotica* as primarily concerned with maximizing pleasure? Looking for a contrasting culture to challenge the dour sexual science of the West and highlight erotic artistry as a key element in his project of a self-styling "aesthetics of existence" grounded in pleasures, Foucault projects this theoretical desire onto Chinese sexual theory by exoticizing it as that radical other, erecting it as a pleasure-seeking, aesthetic *ars erotica* in order to provide a contrast to *scientia sexualis*. Fixated on sexual pleasure, he failed to see that Chinese erotic arts were primarily designed for health, procreation, and the harmonious management of a polygamous household. This blindness was surely intensified by Foucault's inattention to the philosophical, social, and cultural background in which Chinese erotic theory was embedded and functioned, an inattention apparently due to ignorance of Chinese thought.

Aesthetics and Ethics

Of course, the fact that Chinese *ars erotica* had these practical aims does not mean that they cannot have a significant aesthetic character and related pleasures. Such a misguided inference rests on the common error of assuming (because of the dogma of aesthetic disinterestedness) that functionality and aesthetic quality are incompatible. Religious paintings and sculptures have spiritual functions while protest songs have political goals; but this does not preclude their having aesthetic value and being appreciated for their aesthetic qualities even while we appreciate their other functions. Such appreciation of function can even feed back into our aesthetic appreciation by adding dimensions of meaning to the aesthetic experience of these works. Intrinsic value is not inconsistent with instrumental value. We can appreciate the intrinsic taste of a meal we are eating even if we know that the meal is also nourishing us. Likewise our intrinsic enjoyment of good sex is no less intrinsic in knowing that it is also good for us.

One can indeed make a case for the presence of aesthetic dimensions in the classic Chinese erotic arts, as these are described in the texts presented by Van Gulik. These aesthetic elements can be discerned in certain remarks relating to the cosmic meanings of the sexual relations between man and woman, to issues of harmonizing the couple's energies through foreplay, to the aesthetic arrangement of "the bedstead" as the stage of the erotic encounter, and to the harmonized blending of different erotic movements and pleasures, including the orchestration of different styles, depths, speed, and rhythms of the penetrating strokes of the penis. Moreover, if we take a broader view of the role that sex plays in a person's life and character, we will see that *ars erotica* is not only crucial to the central Chinese quest for health or "nurturing life" (*yang sheng*) but also forms part of the ethical project of aesthetic self-cultivation. This is because sex, if properly managed, gives beauty, invigorating pleasure, and harmony to one's character and intimate relationships; but if mismanaged, it easily engenders disturbing disorder, painful exhaustion, and destructive discord.

In classical Chinese culture, just as there was a profound blending of ethics and aesthetics, so there was also a significant overlap between virtue and erotic attraction. Rulers, lords, and generals were considered objects of passionate desire not simply because of social supremacy or brute dominance but because they were seen as endowed with a special excellence, virtue, or qualitative power (*de* 德) that made them aesthetically attractive even if they were not physically beautiful in external appearance. The intimate association of virtue with attractiveness in ancient Chinese culture is exemplified by another term for virtue, *meide* 美德, in which *de* is prefaced by the character for beauty (*mei* 美).[13] People of humbler social status might also be blessed with extraordinary *de* that made them irresistibly attractive. We find a striking example in the *Zhuangzi* chapter, "The Sign of Virtue Complete": "In Wei there was an ugly man named Ai Taito. But when men were around him, they thought only of him and couldn't break away, and when women saw him, they ran begging to their fathers and mothers, saying, 'I'd rather be this gentleman's concubine than another man's wife!'—there were more than ten such cases and it hasn't stopped yet." This is because, despite physical ugliness, he radiated with perfect harmony the inner power or virtue that animates the body, which is what people really love and desire when they are attracted to another human's body.[14]

Such radiating harmony was a highly prized goal in the pursuit of virtuous excellence through self-cultivation that is essential to classical Chinese culture. The aesthetic dimension of virtue explains the centrality of art and ritual in Confucian ethics. For art is not only a source of personal pleasure; it also gives grace and beauty to the social functions of everyday life. Art and ritual further provide a crucial means of ethical education that refines both individual and society by cultivating a sense of good order and propriety while instilling an enjoyably shared experience of harmony and meaning. As Confucius stressed, "In referring time and again to observing ritual propriety (*li*), how could I just be talking about gifts of jade and silk? And in referring time and again to making music (*yue*), how could I just be talking about bells and drums?"[15] He thus urged his disciples, "My young friends, why don't you study the *Songs*? Reciting the *Songs* can arouse your sensibilities, strengthen your powers of observation, enhance your ability to get on with others, and sharpen your critical skills. Close at hand it enables you to serve your father, and away at court it enables you to serve your lord" (A17.9). Likewise, without ritual one would not know "where to stand" or how to behave, and the broader goal of "achieving harmony" in both self and society "is the most valuable function of observing ritual" (A16.13, A1.12).

This aesthetic model of good government through refining character and harmony has an erotic dimension because it works by exemplary attraction, desire, and emulation rather than by commandments, threats, and punishments. "The exemplary person attracts friends through refinement (*wen*), and thereby promotes virtuous conduct (*ren*)." Attracted to such people, we want "to stand shoulder to shoulder with them" by emulating their virtue (A12.24, 4.1, 4.17). So "if people are proper in personal conduct, others will follow suit without need of command. But if they are not proper, even when they command, others will not obey" (A13.6). Good conduct is also understood aesthetically; it is not a mere matter of mechanical or grudging compliance with ethical rules but also requires maintaining the proper appearances that express the proper feelings. Hence the Confucian emphasis on "the proper countenance," "demeanor," and "expression" that virtuous excellence displays and that contribute, through aesthetic appeal, to social harmony and good government (A8.4). Given this intimate connection between aesthetics, ethics, and politics, a ruler's large number of wives and concubines did not simply indicate his political power but symbolized also his presumably strong aesthetic attraction through excellence that his governing eminence implied and that was reinforced through a variety of impressive aesthetic means (exquisite wardrobes, jewels, accessories, carriages, court poets and artists, and special musical and dance performances that only he was permitted to stage).

The essential blending of aesthetic and erotic skills and pleasures is personified in the mythical figure of Su Nu, who before gaining fame as the legendary instructress of *ars erotica* (including such eponymous works as the *Classic of Su Nu*, *Prescriptions of Su Nu*, and the *Wondrous Discourse of Su Nu*) was known as a goddess so "skilled in music" (and such "an excellent singer") that when "the Yellow Emperor heard her play a zither with fifty strings, he became so moved that he decided that this instrument was too dangerous for man, and had it split into two smaller zithers, of 25 strings each" (SL 74). The erotic-aesthetic blending symbolized by Su Nu finds further expression in her linkage to the fertility cults (of rivers and lakes and of the god of grain) and to the beauty of shells whose shape she could assume, a shape that aesthetically evoked female erotic power by its accepted "resemblance to the vulva" (SL 74). The mingling of musical and sexual mastery that Su Nu embodies is echoed in the prevalent musical metaphors of Chinese erotic theory, which frequently refers to female genitalia as zither and to the male organ as flute, both requiring consummate playing skills to produce the richest harmonies and the greatest pleasures.

Beyond such mythical figures and metaphors, the Chinese tradition of mixing aesthetics and erotics finds expression in the pervasive role of professional women entertainers who combined the fine arts with *ars erotica*. Van Gulik insists that until the nineteenth century, "brothels where educated men went for sexual intercourse only were rare," because erotic desire and gratification included an essential aesthetic, artistic dimension (SL 65–66).

Harmonies of Lovemaking

Pervasively shaping the formative background of Chinese aesthetics, the arts of music and cuisine highlight the beauties of harmony and variety through mixing and blending. Aesthetic pleasure is heightened by combining different notes and different ingredients in a unifying way so that they complement or enhance rather than detract from each other, resulting in a satisfying richness of non-coercive unity in variety. Such delightful aesthetic harmony provides a paradigm that extends beyond the fine arts to the realm of social relations, politics, and the ethical art of living. Not surprisingly, the principle of harmony likewise permeates Chinese sexology, constituting both a crucial means and central aim for successful lovemaking. Its formative role finds expression in multiple, overlapping forms of erotic harmony: not only between the sexual partners but also harmonies within the lovers themselves and also beyond them with their environing conditions of time and place. A person's "*qi* is weak and out of harmony," Su Nu explains, because of a failure to harmonize *yin* and *yang* through harmonious sexual relations, but those who know the *dao* of *ars erotica* "will be happy in their hearts and the power of their *qi* will be strong," making them vigorous and "free of illness." "All debility in man," she continues, "is due to violation of the *dao* of intercourse between *yin* and *yang*. Women are superior to men in the same way that water is superior to fire. This knowledge is like the ability to blend the 'five flavors' in a pot to make delicious soup. Those who know the *dao* of *yin* and *yang* can fully realize the 'five pleasures'; those who do not will die before their time without ever knowing this joy" (W 85). This *dao* "consists in settling the *qi*, calming the mind, and harmonizing the emotions" (W 85–86).

Harmony is the crucial key to knowing this *dao*, as confirmed by the *Essentials of the Jade Chamber*. "There is no mystery to the *Dao* of intercourse. It is simply to be free and unhurried and to value harmony above all" (W 100). Chinese action theory more generally argues that it is dangerous to act on what is outside the self until one's inner self is in harmonious order.[16] The purpose of unpressured, unhurried lovemaking is to maximize harmonies (of movement, feeling, etc.) because relaxed slowness allows greater control in managing one's own bodily feelings, movements, secretions, and energies, and consequently also those of one's lover. In recommending "harmonizing the saliva" as one of "eight benefits" of good sex, the *Discourse on the Highest Dao* clearly connects harmony and leisurely slowness: "Engage in the act without haste or rapidity, moving in and out harmoniously. This is called harmonizing the saliva." (W 81) But even before the coital act, calm slowness is crucial for allowing the man to properly harmonize his own *qi*[17] while engaging in foreplay to arouse his partner's passion, which in turn contributes to and must be harmonized with his own before engaging in the coital act. "The *dao* of mounting women is first to engage in slow foreplay so as to harmonize your spirits and arouse her desire, and only after a long time to unite" (W 101). Otherwise, if lovers "perform the act before *yin* and *yang* have been properly harmonized," they will likely suffer from the "ill . . . called 'overflow of *jing*,'" a form of premature ejaculation where "the *jing* overflows in mid-course (W 90).

The reciprocal erotic harmony that ensures the most rewarding arousal is not merely a matter of fleshly sensation but of heartfelt emotion. "*Yin* and *yang* respond to each other's influence," so if either one of the partners is not emotionally "desirous," then "their hearts are not in harmony and their *jing qi* is not aroused" (W 86). Conversely, an initially unaroused lover of meager penis size and firmness can gain both genital size and strength through the flow of *qi* awakened by loving harmony: "When two hearts are in harmony and the *qi* flows freely throughout the body, then the short and small becomes longer and larger, the soft and the weak naturally firm and hard" (W 130). The harmonious circulation of *qi* throughout the body is not only an enabling condition for good lovemaking but also one of its cherished aims because it produces good health and good offspring.

Erotic harmony must take account of the environmental factors of time and place. There were strict constraints on proper location. Foreplay and intercourse (indeed, for Confucians, any touching at all between the married couple) should be confined to the bedroom so as to ensure a relaxed, unhurried, and aesthetic atmosphere. Indeed, some texts literally limit contact to the bedstead alone, which (as Van Gulik describes it) was "really a small room in itself" within the bedroom (SL 59 107). Other constraints of location (more geographical in nature) were sometimes stipulated: "The environs of mountains and rivers, altars to the gods of heaven and earth, wells, and stoves are . . . taboos" (W 122). There are likewise "taboos for the time of intercourse," based on times when one's body-mind or soma is not in harmony or when the heavens are unharmonious or inauspicious: "when one is hungry, full, and drunk; mentally exhausted and physically fatigued; distressed and anxiety ridden; recently recovered from an illness; in mourning, or during the woman's menses" or "when one has just washed the hair, is fatigued from travel, or when feeling great joy or anger." Likewise, "one should not have intercourse when heaven and earth are dark and trembling, when there is swift lightning, violent winds, and heavy rain, nor . . . bitter cold and intense heat," and other "inauspicious days of the almanac," including "solar and lunar eclipses" (W 122, 137). Some texts moreover advise certain hours of the day as erotically more auspicious in terms of having greater *yang* energy (generally between midnight and dawn) (W 121).

Like the arts of music and cuisine to which it has been compared, lovemaking is a temporal art of performance. It takes time to perform, but also time to enjoy or savor. Proper timing, moreover, is crucial to aesthetic success and is more than a matter of choosing the proper season, day, or hour. Good timing is essential to harmony which requires coordinating arousal tempos so that "partners come together at the proper time" when the "two hearts are in harmony and the *qi* flows freely throughout the body" (W 130). It further involves an appropriate temporal structure, requiring the right sequencing, rhythms, and intervals of actions. Many texts establish an essential "sequence" of lovemaking movements, proposing a ritual order rich in symbolic meaning. As man is identified with the *yang* of heaven, while woman with the *yin* of earth, and as "Heaven revolves to the left and earth rotates to the right," so "the man must rotate to the left, and the woman must revolve to the right. Man thrusts downward from above, and woman receives him from below. To come together in this way is called 'heavenly peace and earthly fulfillment' "[18] (W 108). By linking the movements of lovemaking to planetary motions, Chinese eroticism magnifies its meaning and aesthetic power by enriching its harmonies with those of celestial bodies. "To have intercourse in harmony with the stars, even if wealthy and honored offspring are not produced, is still beneficial to oneself," both aesthetically and healthwise, since harmony is essential to both kinds of value. Moreover, such ritualized order, replete with reflective pause, also serves to prevent sexual passion from overrunning its options of aesthetic shaping that can bring heightened benefits of pleasure and health.

We find this idea of ritual order already in China's earliest erotic texts, such as *Uniting Yin and Yang*. In formulating "the method for uniting *yin* and *yang*," it instructs the lover to "carry out the *dao* of dalliance step by step" and slowly. "Although full of passion do not act" until the time is right to move to the next step. "First, when her *qi* rises and her face becomes flushed, slowly exhale. Second, when her nipples become hard and her nose perspires, slowly embrace her. Third, when her tongue spreads and becomes lubricious, slowly press her. Fourth, when secretions appear below and her thighs are damp, slowly take hold of her. Fifth, when her throat is dry and she swallows saliva, slowly agitate her." The text goes on to specify the various modes and movements of "stabbing, penetration, and thrusting" in terms of "ten movements" and "ten refinements," along with the woman's "five signs of desire" and "eight movements" indicative of her state of arousal (W 78–79).

Ritualizing, however, should never be a matter of rigid, mechanical uniformity; it rather seeks to enrich its aesthetic power by creatively adjusting to particular contexts and offering some pleasing variety to establish more satisfying harmonies. In the words of the same *Dong Xuanzi* that recommends the cosmically inspired ritual order of movements, "The principles of deep and shallow, slow and fast, thrusting and twisting, and east and west do not follow a single path, but have 10,000 strands. For example, there is slow thrusting like a gold carp toying with the hook, or the tense urgency of a flock of birds facing a stiff wind." Every action, every pause should be chosen to harmonize with the woman's condition and "adapt to her pace." Thus "pulling in and drawing out, up and down, following and receiving, left and right, going forth and returning, withdrawing and entering, separation and closeness, all need to be orchestrated and properly adjusted. One must not forever sing the same old tune in every circumstance" (W 108).

Aesthetic values of variety and harmony find further expression in Chinese views of erotic pleasure. The varied sensual delights from the diverse senses should be harmoniously blended with pleasures of affective concord with one's partner and environment. Pleasurable feelings of health and energy combine with cognitive pleasures of form and meaning—including the knowledge that one is working on the ethical duties of sustaining health or creating new life, and that one is following hallowed ritual tradition in performing the act of love in the appropriate way. There are also the pleasures of empowerment in demonstrating one's erotic mastery, which includes also the enjoyment of self-mastery through restraint. Finally, the intense delights of ardent passion are balanced and blended with the pleasures of masterful calm and reflective composure.

Reflection, Passion, and Self-Mastery

What is the aesthetic and ethical importance of calm and reflection that are repeatedly emphasized in Chinese *ars erotica*? First, the pleasure of aesthetic experience is intensified by reflective awareness of that enjoyment and explicit attention to what one is enjoying. Savoring extends and deepens one's pleasure; and since savoring takes time and tranquil reflection, we find another reason for thoughtful leisured slowness in lovemaking. Second, calm reflection is needed for mastery of technique. To perform the proper movements in the appropriate places and at the right times, one must be clearly aware of what one is doing with one's own body and one's lover's. Not only your own state of arousal and performed actions but also those of your lover must be carefully monitored so that they can be properly orchestrated to achieve the right rhythm and harmony.

Because it requires calm composure and critical reflection, technical mastery in Chinese *ars erotica* demands superior *self-mastery* in order to control one's passion. The lover needs to mindfully regulate his level of arousal even at the height of passion so that this passion does not exceed his control and prematurely explode into ejaculation; and, in order for this vigilant control to be effective, slowness is once again advised. While "inserting soft and withdrawing hard," instructs a Tang text *Health Benefits of the Bedchamber*, "the pace of advancing and retreating should be very slow and, when passions are aroused, rest. Do not throw yourself into it with abandon," but instead use a pause to calm the mind and settle one's energy: "Slow the breath, close the eyes, lie on your back and guide the *qi* internally" (W 116).

Another text elaborates, "As your passion mounts, do not allow yourself to become overly excited or reach the point of intense ecstasy, and then it will be easy to control yourself in intercourse. One must perform the act slowly, entering soft and withdrawing hard. Execute three shallow and one deep thrusts eighty-one times as one round. If the *jing* becomes slightly aroused, immediately stop and retreat . . . When resting, allow an inch or so to remain inside, and after the heart's fire has calmed, continue the procedure as earlier. Now execute the five shallow and one deep method, and finally nine shallow and one deep." Through such reflective monitoring and critical control (that also involves "the locking technique" to prevent ejaculation) one can "capture the spoils" of the woman's orgasmic energy (W 139–40).

Tranquility and critical reflection are further necessary for the meditative discipline of directing the absorbed and enhanced *qi* to the proper energy centers so that its benefits of health, beauty, and pleasure can then be circulated throughout the body. If mastery of one's breathing serves to calm the lover's mind, then such calm reciprocally enables him better mastery of the extraordinary breathing techniques for absorbing and circulating the *qi* acquired from his lovemaking. The crucial role of breathing in settling the mind for erotic success must have been obvious in the original Chinese context, where mind and heart are identified and denoted by the very same word or character (*xin* 心). The ancients knew what current science confirms: breathing strongly affects heart rate and feelings of calm.

Finally, serene composure in experiencing intense passion is aesthetically appealing in itself—an ideal of harmony, of masterfully controlled but still vibrant life-energy sustained at its optimum beyond which it will explode or dissipate. "Only one who understands the *dao* is able to suppress emotion in the presence of the [erotic] object and be dispassionate in the midst of passion" (W 141). To achieve this level of mastery, Chinese erotic texts recommend various methods: critical reflection, slowness of movement, pausing, withdrawing, slowing the breath, closing the eyes (both for inner concentration and to avoid overstimulation in seeing one's partner's passionate beauty). Some texts even offer training advice to develop this erotic calm composure (W 139–40).

Spontaneity and Reflection

Besides its intrinsic importance for Chinese *ars erotica*, the advocacy of reflection in lovemaking raises a much larger issue in both Western and Chinese theory of action. William James, Maurice Merleau-Ponty, and a great many other Western thinkers have argued that skilled action is more effective when it is spontaneous and that reflecting on the action (such as monitoring one's movements and consciously controlling them) will destroy the smooth flow of spontaneity and gravely detract from one's performance. In Daoist philosophy, with its central concepts of *ziran* and *wuwei* (often translated in terms of spontaneous, natural action), we see a similar insistence on spontaneity and an apparent rejection of reflective, calculating consciousness in action. The key attitude seems to be "just do it," but do not think about how you are doing it. In the *Zhuangzi* "Artisan Zhui could draw as true as a compass or a T square because his fingers changed along with things and he didn't let his mind get in the way" (Z 206). The *Liezi* expresses the same idea of unreflective, spontaneous action, not only arguing that a drunken man, by being largely unconscious, is likely to be less injured in falling from a cart than a conscious man who stiffens and tries to brace his fall, but also that the good swimmer says, "I do it without knowing how I do it."[19] The book's distinguished translator, A. C. Graham, formulates this attitude as "thinking does [one] harm instead of good" and that "it is especially dangerous to be conscious of oneself" (L 32).

But alongside this unreflective spontaneity, these texts also contain passages affirming thoughtful attention to oneself. "When I speak of good hearing, I do not mean listening to others. I mean simply listening to your self. When I speak of good eyesight, I do not mean looking at others; I mean simply looking at yourself. He who does not look at himself but looks at others, who does not get hold of himself but gets hold of others, is getting what other men have got and failing to get what he himself has got. He finds joy in what brings joy to other men, but finds no joy in what would bring joy to himself" (Z 102–03). "So I examine what is within me and I am never blocked off from the Way" (Z 319). At one point, even bodily action or movement is said to be improved by looking inward to establish a stable sense of self from which action can more effectively emerge. "If you do not perceive the sincerity within yourself and yet try to move forth, each movement will miss the mark" (Z 245).

The *Liezi* likewise affirms self-examination: "You busy yourself with outward travel and do not know how to busy yourself with inward contemplation . . . [through which] we find sufficiency in ourselves" (L 82). And with respect to skilled action, the *Liezi* similarly suggests that underlying masterful performance is a mastery of self, achieved through attention to oneself, because underlying the self is the unfathomable, empowering Way that guides us best. Thus, the musician insists on first finding the harmony in himself before venturing to play: "What I have in mind is not in the strings, what I am aiming at is not in the notes. Unless I grasp it inwardly in my heart, it will not answer from the instrument outside me" (L 107).

How does one reconcile this apparent conflict between attending to self and unreflective self-forgetting spontaneity as being the key to effective performance? One strategy I outline in previous texts involves interchanging phases or stages.[20] Although spontaneous unreflective action may be most effective for skilled performers, in the earlier stages of learning any sensorimotor skill (like riding a bicycle or playing an instrument) we must direct careful, critical attention to the body parts, postures, and movements engaged in that action. Moreover, even if we are highly skilled, when environmental circumstances or bodily conditions change as they often do (whether through injury, illness, travel, fatigue, diet, etc.), we may need to relearn or adapt the skills through critical reflection.

Chinese *ars erotica* suggests a more radical thesis: that in the midst of what might seem to be the most natural and ardent of acts, when we are carried forward spontaneously by the natural *qi* of desire, we nonetheless should engage in deliberately critical reflection to perform at our best, carefully noting the number and style of strokes while carefully monitoring our breathing and level of passion, as well as thoughtfully discriminating all the different movements and signs of arousal of one's female partner. In the act of love, where the cosmic dualisms of *yin* and *yang*, heaven and earth, man and woman are joined together in harmonious union, can it be that the Daoist sex masters are also proposing a union of the apparent duality of spontaneity and reflection? There may be, ultimately, no absolute contradiction between them. Perhaps one can be reflectively spontaneous or spontaneously reflective. Perhaps such thoughtful spontaneity means being fully present in one's soma by being attentively and critically present in thought and action to all the diverse dimensions of the erotic situation that impact one's soma and that include one's partner's movements and energies, as well as one's own and those of the entire environmental force field that one's lovemaking both inhabits and helps create. If this seems beyond the normal powers of human attention, we might still suggest (adapting a strategy of Mencius) that while these capacities may in principle be possible as an endowment of nature, it requires a sage to achieve them—and also perhaps a lifetime of practice.[21]

Notes

1. Richard Shusterman, *Pragmatist Aesthetics: Living Beauty, Rethinking Art* (Oxford: Blackwell, 1992).

2. One recent example is the symposium on "Richard Shusterman's Somaesthetics" in *Frontiers of Philosophy in China*, 10:2 (2015), 163–211, to which Roger Ames contributed an essay on "Bodyheartminding (*Xin* 心)."

3. The Chinese terms are *fang shu* or *fang zhong shu* meaning literally "bedroom technique" or "inside the bedroom technique." These texts, though sharing many themes, do not present one monolithic theory, instead displaying variations in different historical periods and according to the different philosophical ideologies and aims that inspired their authors. For more detailed information on this genre of Chinese sexology, see especially R. H. van Gulik, *Sexual Life in Ancient China: A Preliminary Survey of Chinese Sex and Society from ca. 1500 B.C. till 1644 A.D.* (Leiden: Brill, 2003), hereafter cited as SL, and Douglas Wile, *Art of the Bedchamber The Chinese Sexual Yoga Classics Including Women's Solo Meditation Texts* (Albany: State University of New York Press, 1992), hereafter cited as W.

4. Michel Foucault, "Sexual Choice, Sexual Act" in *Essential Works of Michel Foucault*, vol. 1 (New York: New Press, 1997), 151–52. For a detailed critical analysis of Foucault's somaesthetics of sex as part of his idea of philosophy as an art of living, see Richard Shusterman *Body Consciousness: A Philosophy of Mindfulness and Somaesthetics* (Cambridge: Cambridge University Press, 2008), ch. 1.

5. Michel Foucault, *History of Sexuality*, vol. 2 (New York: Pantheon, 1986), 12, 89–93; hereafter cited as HS2.

6. Michel Foucault, *History of Sexuality*, vol. 1 (New York: Pantheon, 1980), 57–71; hereafter cited as HS.

7. An English version of this interview "On the Genealogy of Ethics: An Overview of Work in Progress" is published in Herbert Dreyfus and Paul Rabinow (eds.), *Michel Foucault: Beyond Structuralism and Hermeneutics* (Chicago: University of Chicago Press, 1983), but I cite the more complete French version revised by Foucault and published in his *Dits et Ecrits, vol. 2: 1976-1988* (Paris: Gallimard, 2001), 1428–1450; quotations, 1441. In this interview, Foucault claims the ancient Greeks and Romans lacked an elaborate *ars erotica* comparable to that of the Chinese (see 1434).

8. R. H. van Gulik, *Sexual Life in Ancient China: A Preliminary Survey of Chinese Sex and Society from ca. 1500 B.C. till 1644 A.D.* (Leiden: Brill, 2003), hereafter cited as SL.

9. Foucault's emphasis on the essential esoteric nature of these arts is also misleading. For many periods of China's long history the handbooks of sex, which were frequently illustrated, "circulated widely" and "were well known and the methods given by them widely practiced" not only by esoteric specialists but "by the people in general." The handbooks' circulation began to decline in the Sung period, and still more in the Ming period with its greater Confucian prudishness, but the handbooks' practices and "principles still pervaded sexual life" (SL 79, 94, 121, 192, 228, 268).

10. It followed from this logic that male masturbation was "forbidden (except for extreme occasions) and nocturnal emissions were viewed with concern." As long as it did not involve ejaculation, homosexuality was not condemned in classical Chinese culture but nor did it form part of the ancient sexual handbooks (SL 48).

11. In one document from the Later Han Period, we read of a Taoist master who "lived to the age of over 150 years by practicing the art of having sexual intercourse with women," and that by such art "one's grey hair will turn black again and new teeth will replace those that have fallen out" (SL 71).

12. This text also discusses the method for controlling ejaculation and making its energy "ascend and benefit the brain" (SL 193–94). Other passages repeatedly emphasize that the multiplicity of partners has health not pleasure as its dominant aim.

13. The term is found in Xunzi, Bk. 32:3, where Knoblock renders it as "inner power" in *Xunzi*, trans. John Knoblock (Stanford, CA: Stanford University Press, 1988), vol. 3, 266.

14. *Chuang-Tzu*, trans. Burton Watson (New York: Columbia University Press, 1968), 72; hereafter cited as Z.

15. *The Analects of Confucius: A Philosophical Translation*, trans. Roger T. Ames and Henry Rosemont (New York: Ballantine, 1998), 17.11, 206; hereafter cited as A.

16. For elaboration of this idea see "Body Consciousness and Performance: Somaesthetics East and West," in Richard Shusterman, *Thinking through the Body* (Cambridge: Cambridge University Press, 2012).

17. Only "when the three harmonious *qi* are aroused" will the penis be "sturdy and strong" and ready for intercourse (W 80).

18. Nonetheless, in later specifying thirty different "postures of intercourse," this same text describes some positions where the woman places herself above the man (W 109).

19. A. C. Graham (trans.), *The Book of Lieh-tzu* (New York: Columbia University Press, 1990), 44; hereafter cited as L.

20. See *Body Consciousness* and *Thinking through the Body*.

21. Cf: "Though the body's functions are the endowment of nature (*tian*), it is only the Sage who can properly manipulate them." *Mencius: A New Translation*, trans. W. A. C. H. Dobson (Toronto: Toronto University Press, 1969), 144 (7A.38).

6

Vast Continuity versus the One

Thoughts on *Daodejing 42*, *Taiyishengshui*, and the Legacy of Roger T. Ames

Brook Ziporyn

The character *yi* (一) occurs fifteen times in the received eighty-one chapter (Wang Bi) version of the *Daodejing*. Of these, eleven, or possibly twelve instances (chapter 12 is an ambiguous case) seem to require translation as nouns. Twice (in chapters 10 and 22) the character is the object of the transitive verb *bao* (抱), "to embrace." Seven times (all in chapter 39) it is the object of the transitive verb *de* (得), "to attain." Once, in chapter 42, it is the object of the transitive verb *sheng* (生), "to give rise to"—and immediately thereafter, is made the *subject* of the same transitive verb. This clear nominalization has led most translators to translate with rather august, often capitalized words like "Oneness," "Unity," or even "The One." The discovery of the bamboo slips of a text that has come to be known as "The Great One Gives Rise To Water" *Taiyishengshui* (太一生水) belonging to the *Laozi C* bundle at Guodian, has strengthened the impression, for some, that this *yi* in the *Daodejing* refers to some specific particular entity, and one which plays a key role in a cosmogony, thereby further encouraging translations such as "The One," with its vaguely Neo-Platonic echoes. This linkage of the *Daodejing*'s *yi* with an entity called *Taiyi* has further suggested what might be called a metaphysical or even religious significance for this specific entity with the key role in a cosmogony, due to the growing awareness of the existence of a Warring States period cult in the state of Chu devoted to a deity of this name.[1]

Now this kind of hasty inference is precisely the kind of thing the formidable oeuvre of Roger Ames has been battling for many decades: the equation of superficially similar-sounding tropes in early Chinese philosophical works with familiar Western categories. The issue raised by this kind of interpretive problem lands us in the very heart of the legacy of Ames, illustrating both the brilliance of his approach, its implications, and the aspects that arouse objections from its nay-sayers. *The suspension of knee-jerk associations*, both grammatical and philosophical, has allowed Ames to give us fresh eyes with which to see many thorny problems in Chinese thought.

This is nowhere more impressively in evidence than in the brilliant translation offered by Ames, along with his collaborator David Hall,[2] of *Daodejing* 42, one of the chapters in which the supposed linkage to cosmogony, and thus the role of a specific entity involved in that process, is most pronounced, especially in that, like *Taiyishengshui*, it directly links *yi* to *sheng*.

The Chinese runs as follows:

道生一, 一生二, 二生三, 三生萬物。萬物負陰而抱陽, 沖氣以為和。

Reading *yi* as an uninflected dictionary-reflex word like "One," the reader is confronted with what looks like a sort of cosmic number mysticism, perhaps along the lines of the numerical derivations found in some later *Zhouyi* commentary, extrapolating from the calculations related to hexagram construction and yarrow-stalk sorting in the divination process. Here one begins thinking Pythagoras or Plotinus, or else just plugs in the words one unreflectingly "sees" in the Chinese text: "Dao produces the One, the One produces the Two, the Two produces the Three. . . ." Dao is supposed to mean something like "The Way." Why would it produce anything? What is there about a "way" that produces? And why would it produce "The One"? What could that be? Perhaps something beyond perception and thought, as we find in Plotinus—even more non-empirical than a first principle—since all of this sounds very non-empirical; after all, where is "The" Dao? Where is "The One"? What we experience is manifestly multiple, changing, multidirectional; so this One must be an invisible reality beyond our perceptual reach—accessible only to some special faculty like speculative reason, dialectic, or, alternately, mystical intuition or religious experience—or something that happened back at the beginning of time, when everything was being "produced." It sounds immediately as if all this is something that happened or happens behind the curtain, the deep intelligible structure of the world, the source or underlying principle that directs, controls, or commands the empirical world. Read in this way, we have here only a very slight variation on familiar Western metaphysical themes, and a nice comfirmation of a universal "perennial philosophy" blossoming in slightly different forms wherever there are human beings of deep insight and good will: it is not all that different from the oneness insisted upon by the Hebrew prophets, or Plotinus, or the Upanishadic rishis. All humanity more or less agrees on the main things.

The Amesian method simultaneously suspends the grammatical and the theoretical assumptions informing this kind of reading, which go hand in hand. Grammatically, we notice first that a definite article has been supplied in the knee-jerk translation. Sitting out there all alone, this *yi* seems to be a noun, and a noun that starkly asks for the definite article. But of course, in classical Chinese there are no articles, definite or indefinite; nor is there a morphological distinction between gerunds, nouns, and verbs, all of which can be depicted with the same graph. Could it be "Dao produces one, one produces two, two produces three . . ."? Meaning what? Dao produces *some* one . . . ? What would that mean? One of what? "Dao produces a one, a one produces a two. . . ." Just remembering to leave out the knee-jerk aspects of our usual translation starts to open new possibilities. But it is the global suspension of our usual assumptions that really opens a way forward, and this is what we find in the Ames translation of the passage. In the Hall and Ames translation of *Daodejing*, published after David Hall's untimely demise, we find the following translation of the passage in question:

> Way-making gives rise to continuity.
> Continuity gives rise to difference,
> Difference gives rise to plurality,
> And plurality gives rise to the manifold of everything that is happening.
>
> Everything carries *yin* on its shoulders and *yang* in its arms
> And blends these vital energies (*qi*) to make them harmonious. . . .[3]

Immediately a complete thought emerges: "Dao" has been de-reified, construed as a verb, to honor the "process" orientation the authors argue should be prioritized in interpretations of early Chinese thought, as rehearsed in their Introduction; confronted with an ambiguity, as we always are in reading early Chinese texts, we must have recourse to a hermeneutic circle that works within the horizon of an evolving global interpretative orientation. Instead of "The Way" we have "way-making," in the sense of clearing or producing a way by one's own motion, "making one's way" in the world and in so doing leaving behind one a clearing, a way to be followed. And to create a path in this way obviously does give rise to, at whatever level however local or global, *continuity*—that is precisely what "way-making" is. It is the creation of continuity. The making of a way is a connecting of various points in space. It is the clearing of a path that facilitates the unhindered communication and motion between two places that were previously disconnected or obstructed. To move from one place to another is to create a habitual connection, to begin to carve a groove in the world through which things can flow. To move is to facilitate that flow, to show a new way of moving or reinforce an existing way to a new degree. Simply to be is to move, the authors argue, and to move is to make a way. To make a way is to make continuity. We already begin to see an *intrinsic* logic to this previously enigmatic passage.

The translation of *yi* as "continuity" is a stroke of genius, of a kind that requires the practiced application of one's "childlike mind" to familiar passages; one thinks here, somewhat whimsically but not completely recklessly, of the significance attached in Chinese spiritual traditions to tropes, like the "infant's mind" *chizi zhi xin* 赤子之心 of Mencius or the "beginner's mind" (*chuxin* 初心) in some strains of Chan Buddhism. Ames is, among all working sinologists, the person who has best preserved his childlike mind: the mind that sees things afresh, the mind of wonder and unrestricted free-association all non-native readers probably bring to their first encounters with the marvels of the Chinese written language and the tradition in which it is embedded. The shock of difference, the popcorn of new possibilities, the sudden melting away of old habits and assumptions, the millionfold expansion of possibilities for thought—what learner of classical Chinese has not tasted that sensation when the peculiarities of this linguistic system were first dawning on him or her? No tense, no singular and plural, no punctuation, no noun/verb morphological difference, no noun/verb agreement, no conjugations, no declensions, no frustrating exceptionless grammar! Grammar as a probability function rather than rules that can be applied with authority to determine their instantiations! Must we not rethink what "making sense" even means in such a system?

What happens to most learners of this language and culture after the first few weeks or months of such excitement and shock, however, is that they are convinced to calm down, to start to gradually integrate this initially strange system into accepted habits, linguistic forms, cultural theories; the vivid liberation of those first few months or years of study is ground down into just more knowledge about the world, *within* the systems of handling knowledge that existed prior to the encounter: the frameworks of knowledge are allowed to control the data, so the overexcited young learner is chastened and taught to rein in his exuberance: no, no, there's only one kind of sense to make, once you come to inhabit the language you will see it follows the general rules linguists have found for all languages, all that *universal human kind* of sense-making and valuing; this culture follows the general laws that all cultures *must* follow—as delineated over long periods of time by political scientists, economists, linguists, sociologists *working entirely within the non-Chinese model*, for both their theoretical constructs and their data. The uniqueness of the case is dismissed; all things human must follow the same laws. (Never mind that the question about what "laws" and "following" are is exactly one of the questions raised by the Chinese case.) This childlike exuberance of the initial encounter is then systematically made into an object of opprobrium: it is taken as a sign of not yet getting it. Rare is the student who persists in the original dream, follows through on it. Ames is one who has done so all the way to the end.

Ames is, strictly speaking, a genuinely *sui generis* figure—though I once had a dream in which he was conflated with former U.S. President Bill Clinton, another unique figure in his own chosen field, and one whose exceptional positivity, warmth, and fluency, as well as general personal vibe, somewhat resemble those of Professor Ames, *mutatis mutandis*. But if actually forced to compare him to someone in a completely unrelated field, I might venture to call Professor Ames the George Lucas of contemporary Sinology. Besides another instance of that same warm and unflappable personal vibe, Ames and Lucas are both self-standing institutions, single-minded presiders over their own discursive empires, who seem to have created *ex nihilo* a complete systematic universe of contemplation, following through to riff on the details of every corner and side of it. And the vision he has made fully real is a uniquely important one because of its relation to the childlike dream, the boyhood fantasy: he alone has stayed true to his childlike mind.

The tone of printed statements is easily misconstrued, so I want to make it clear that I do not *at all* mean this sarcastically; I don't mean to imply, winkingly or slyly, that Ames is therefore a "fantasist," that his vision is as unrelated to reality as Lucas's vision of the universe. No. Ames has made his case through the superior sensitivity to the Chinese texts that his openness has allowed him. He has a case to make based on irrefutable linguistic subtleties agreed upon by all competent readers. A very interesting and exemplary case is chapter 25 of the same *Daodejing* translation. This is another place where we would expect Ames to have to eat his words and abandon his overreaching claim that there is no transcendence and no independent agent of creation in the "Chinese worldview": it is probably the most oft-cited instance of a knock-down example of a transcendental status for the Dao in the *Daodejing*, as Something that is independent and prior to the empirical universe. Hell, it even *says* there is something *duli*, which is the modern Chinese word for "independent"—the actual *source* of the phrase used to translate the English word "independent." Here is the Chinese of the passage:

有物混成，先天地生。寂兮寥兮，獨立不改，周行而不殆，可以為天下母。

Glaringly, "something" (*wu*) is already complete (*cheng*) "prior to" (*xian*) the arising of heaven and earth, and this something is "unchanging" (*bugai*) and "stands alone" (*duli*). The first reaction is to take this as knock-down evidence that refutes any claim that nothing in this world-view can be complete in-itself independently of the rest of the world, that there is nothing unchanging, that there is no equivalent to the transcendent first principles and creator gods of the Western tradition. The knee-jerk reading is thus something like this: "There is something, fully completed before the arising of heaven and earth, silent and empty, independent and unchanging, acting everywhere without being endangered by anything." Sounds very transcendent indeed. But here is the Hall and Ames translation:

> There was some process that formed spontaneously
> Emerging before the heavens and the earth.
> Silent and empty,
> Standing alone as all that is, it does not suffer alteration.
> [All pervading, it does not pause.][4]

A skeptic will raise eyebrows at what might seem to be sneaky substitutions: "process" for *wu*, usually translated as the more static and concrete "thing," "as all that is" added after that suspicious *duli*, eliminating the implication of transcendence at a stroke, seemingly importing immanence by translator's fiat. These choices are justified purely by the reference to the global interpretation of the tradition, the prior assumption of process-orientation and non-transcendence. Outside of that context they cannot be justified (although it might be pointed out that the English word "thing" is just as laden with alien interpretative assumptions as the English word "process"), but if that context is accepted, so that the author's assumptions would have to fit within it, they are reasonable and artful choices. The question for a translator in a passage like this is whether there is anything *in the passage itself* which signals the appropriateness of this context.[5] And here is where Ames's sinological sensitivity makes the case plausible. For the other two instances of seeming special-pleading—the explaining-away of "prior" and of "unchanging"—really do rest on solid sinological observations. The first can be found in the footnote to the second line quoted here: "All of the terms for 'world,' such as *tiandi* 天地 and *qiankun* 乾坤, are bipolar and correlative, entailing 'copulation' in the sense of joining together. Even *yuzhou* 宇宙 as the rounded eaves and the phallic ridgepole is a sexual image. The emergence of *dao* is prior to these familiar images of conception and birthing."[6] What is noticed by the Amesian "childlike mind" here is the undeniable fact that the very term for "world" carries a particular structure encoded explicitly in the passage: it is not a neutral ontological marker, but a specifically structured two-termed contrastive phrase, delineating two extremes of a larger continuity. To say that "way-making" is prior to the two ends of any particular way is very different from claiming that, say, the One or God or the intelligible realm precedes the material world. It may just mean that the two endpoints of any process are joined by that very process, and that in that sense the process is prior to the two end-points as explicitly connected, as explicitly "endpoints of this process." This then fits snugly with the process and non-transcendent assumptions claimed for the larger tradition, simply another instance of illustrating that the process always precedes whatever relatively static byproducts are later abstracted from it. The point is thus not imported into the text arbitrarily, but attaches to something that is grounded in an agreed-upon aspect of the language.

Even more impressive is the following footnote, which explains the translation of the offending *bugai* not as "unchanging" but as "does not suffer alteration."[7] The point here rests entirely on an observation about the different possible words for "change" in the tradition, making a point that any competent reader of the language will have to accept. *Gai* 改 is not *bian* 變 or *hua* 化 or *qian* 遷. Why *gai* in this passage? The note points out that *gai*, alone among these words often translated as "change," is used to mean "to be corrected," unlike all the other terms, which are never used in this way.[8] In fact, this moral-normative sense is perhaps the dominant use of the term *gai* in pre-*Daodejing* Confucian and Mohist texts, which *never* use it to mean natural or value-neutral change. The relevance of this point to the passage in question has not been pointed out before, to my knowledge. This means that this term is *transitive* in a much more emphatic way than any of the other terms for "change," but also that it carries a strong normative implication that none of the other terms carry. Hence the translation "suffer alteration": to be altered *by something else*. What changes spontaneously is not changed by something else. The passage now fits snugly into the claim of non-transcendence. Indeed, the direction of this transitive verb is indeterminate; riffing on the implications, we might now ponder the possibility of "it stands alone but never corrects anyone or anything; it goes everywhere but never endangers anyone or anything," a meaning that fits nicely not just within the larger assumed cultural context of nontranscendence but very specifically within the local context of the *Daodejing*, for example the assertion in chapter 34 that *dao*, although it some special central status in relation to things in that they all (spontaneously) "return" to it, nevertheless "does not act as their master" (*wanwuguiyan erbuweizhu* 萬物歸焉, 而不為主). This now reads almost as a gloss on *duli er bugai*: unique but not because it controls anyone—in fact, it is precisely because it does not control them that they make themselves uniquely dependent upon it, such that it "stands alone." Because it does not correct them, they all make themselves subordinate to it spontaneously (in Amesian language, they show "deference" to it), and because they all thus come to "belong to it," they are in that sense parts of it, there is indeed nothing outside it—it "stands alone." We might go a step further and carry the indeterminacy of the direction of the transitive verbs here all the way into the translation: "Stands alone yet without correcting or being corrected by anything; goes everywhere yet without endangering or being endangered by anything." This too would not be out of place in the *Daodejing* considered as a whole. But the point here is that, whether or not we want to go this far or just stick with the relatively conservative tweak provided in the Hall and Ames translation, this is not arbitrarily added by translator's fiat, nor indeed merely limply assumed on the basis of the prior commitment to the global hermeneutic of the tradition (which might be justifiable but is not necessarily convincing). Rather, it is based on a *new observation*, facilitated by the preservation of the fresh eyes of the childlike mind, by suspending the knee-jerk assumption about the undeniable philological characteristics of the passage in question. Indeed, it then connects fruitfully to larger points drawn from the global hermeneutic.[9] This is of course not a knockdown argument for this interpretation of the passage, but it does make it at least as plausible as its competitors, on objective grounds.

This brings us back to the passage in chapter 42. For, freed of the associations with Pythagorean-Platonic hypostatization of number as model of all apodictic knowledge—prized for its objectivity, its freedom from ambiguity, its enabling of perfect separation of concepts into abstractly distinct and unmixed forms, its priority to its instantiations—and of any requirement to distinguish between noun, verb, gerund, definite and indefinite article, what is *yi*? Oneness, one-itude, unity, unification. Indeed, given the emphasis on process and verbal forms, we might think "unification" would be the preferred choice here, rather than the more static-sounding "continuity." But the word "unification" can imply an achieved and finalized totality, which the authors have already argued is precisely what is not assumed in a cosmos devoid of precisely those Pythagorean-Platonic (and further Aristotelian, Christian, etc.) assumptions. This is due not only to the emphasis on "process," implied by the non-separation of nouns and verbs, but is precisely what is implied in

Tang Junyi's oft-invoked "non-separation of one-and-many" (*yiduobufenguan* 一多不分觀) claimed here to be endemic to Chinese thought: for a *one* that is not separated from the *many*, that is not to be even conceptually separated from multiplicity, is precisely a repudiation of the Pythagorean-Platonic notion of number as the realm where these separations are, at last, uniquely possible, thus opening a way to real knowledge. A one that is not separated from many, even conceptually, is not a "one." It is something else entirely. I've called it "coherence"—a notion meant to include from the beginning a built-in ineradicable equiprimordiality of unity and multiplicity. And that is just what the translation here finds: the word "continuity." For continuity is manifestly both one and many: it is the connectedness of a manifold, requiring even-handedly both the connection and the manifold, prioritizing neither.

The riches of the approach continue to present themselves in the following line: "continuity gives rise to difference." The commentary on the text, however, does not exploit the possibilities here, and arguably strays from the text more than is easily justified. "In this chapter, *dao* is said to engender both 'one' and 'many,' both 'continuity' and 'difference.' "[10] But this attributes both continuity and difference equally to *dao*, without providing an explanation for the sequence unambiguously present in the text, the difference in levels of mediation. The text does not say, 道生一, 生二, 生三," (which would be a transformation like that found in the Guodian variant of a similar passage in the difficult chapter 40); rather, it says: 道生一, 一生二, 二生三。 Hall and Ames do not help their case by sliding over important distinctions like this in their commentary. Why the distinction of levels, why the definite sequence? This is something that has to be addressed. Indeed, the commentary to this chapter exemplifies not only here but much more grievously on the following page the sort of bulldozing overreach that raises the hackles of the anti-Ames party, and weakens the Amesian case, which is, as I've already indicated, sufficiently strong to stand without exaggerating its claims to less defensible territory. On the next page we find the assertion: "If we chose to view this process of proliferation and differentiation from the perspective of the particular in its production of continuity, we could as legitimately claim that:

> The myriad things engender three,
> Three two,
> Two one,
> And one, dao."[11]

Indeed, *we* could legitimately claim this *if we* chose to view things that way—but does the *Daodejing* do so? Certainly not explicitly, and certainly not in this chapter, where the opposite is asserted, without emendation. The comment here does not literally say that the *Daodejing* does or should be read as holding that position, but surely a casual reader would assume that this is the implication. And indeed, it is quite defensible to argue that this reversibility is indeed found *elsewhere* in the tradition, very plausibly as a further development of the kinds of ideas Hall and Ames are pointing out in the text of the *Daodejing*: in parts of the *Zhuangzi*, in the *Zhouyi* commentarial tradition, in the "Zhongyong," in Guo Xiang, in Chinese Buddhism of various stripes, possibly in the thought of Wang Yangming and certain of his followers. That the implicit reversibility is something that was indeed picked up and developed to great effect is indeed supremely important and interesting; but one feels a disservice is done not only to the text and to the process of development of further complexities in the later tradition through conflict and inventive resolution of conflict, but to the evenhandedness of the commentary when it is introduced as part of the commentary to this chapter. This occurs without noting that the *Daodejing* never makes any move like this, but maintains throughout the perspective that puts *dao* in a special, nonreversible position, rather than speaking of it as somehow reciprocally generated by things—however defensible this proposition may be on the premises of the text itself or further ponderings found (perhaps only!) in the Chinese tradition.

That said, let us try to pursue the line of thought suggested by the Amesian intervention, but maintaining the sequence and levels of mediation stipulated in the text itself. For here the idea follows the contours developed in the interpretation of *tiandi* in the difficult passage in chapter 25, discussed above. The specific contrast of heaven and earth is formed by bringing them into relation to each other; they are constituted as a pair with a specific determining difference only by this contrast, by this connection. It seems at least plausible to assert that continuity does indeed give rise to difference; no thing in isolation has the property of being "different from" something else. To attribute "difference" to something is already to relate it to something else, to be viewing it in continuity with something. Difference presupposes continuity. It is true that continuity also presupposes difference, but any given *specific* difference, this particular determinate difference, membership in a pair, such as is indicated by the term *er* when construed in this way, importantly presupposes the prior way-making in a way that the way-making does not necessarily presuppose the specificity of that difference. Pair-making requires way-making. Things are not just paired; what we call heaven or what we call earth are only so determined when a linkage is being made between them. In other made ways, other types of continuity, the very thing we are pointing to and calling earth can have different lines of contrast drawn around it, boundaried with a different extent of reference, and thus called something else: "mountain" as opposed to "lake," for example, if paired according to one of the dyadic trigram schemas. The point is that we distinguish between the locally contained "mountain" and the larger category "earth" not by attending to a unique cutting-at-the-joints of nature, but as a function of a particular making of a way, of a continuity. The distinction between "mountain" and "earth" is constituted only by what we are contrasting to what we are pointing to or holding in mind when we refer to it. What makes that thing up there specifically "heaven" is its pairing with earth, which is to say, the continuity engendered by the making of a way with these two specific endpoints.

It is worth pausing to consider the richness of the chosen words, "continuity," "difference," "plurality." As we have said, "continuity" is importantly different from "One," "The One," "Oneness," "Unity," and even "Unification." We might wish to extend this further, and ensure that even the nouns we end up with are not taken as strictly singular, as indeed they cannot be in the Chinese. Pluralizing them all would give us, "Way-makings give rise to continuities, continuities give rise to differences, differences give rise to pluralities. . . ." Not one plurality, but a plurality of pluralities! Any particular way-making gives rise to its own set of continuities, which give rise to its own system of differences, and thence its own unique system of pluralities, which do not necessitate the exclusion of other systems of plurality. This would be in keeping with another of the global cultural interpretations urged by Hall and Ames: the rejection of any single-ordered cosmos. Daos give rise not to order, but to *orders*! Indeed, is this not precisely the import of the focus-field model at the center of the Amesian interepration? Each being is an "insistent particular" that not only is subsumed but subsumes all other particulars in its own unique act of world-making. I would not argue that the *Daodejing* already enunciates this vision of the world, which is made most explicit in what I have elsewhere called the "intersubsumptive" view of some Chinese Buddhist schools. But already we have an important hint of it precisely in the last line of the sequence here, in the Amesian interpretation of "three" as "diversity." The "thirdness" thrown at us here, once released from its interpretation as an ordinal number, ties not just into the next line, where we have a sense of mediation between two extremes, but associatively to the common alternate graph for "three," 參, often used as a verb in pre-Han texts, not least in the famous phrase from the *Xunzi* and the *Liji*, "to form a triad with heaven and earth." The same term has the implication of "participation" more generally, a linking not as the prior and presupposed continuity underlying the setting up of any extremes, but an accomplished specific continuity established by human presence as mediation between two already defined and opposed extremes. But another sinological association suddenly comes before us once we have accustomed ourselves to the Amesian reading of this passage: the binome *cenci* 參差, meaning disarray or unevenness, lurks in the background of this usage perhaps. This would surely bring us even closer to the meaning of "diversity" in the sense outlined above: not of individual items in a single-ordered cosmos, but of infinitely diverse alternate "orders" forming the fields around the varying foci of each mediating particular. Again, I do not think anything like this view is actually established in the *Daodejing*. But the fact that the text moves with a halo of implications that leave this open, albeit peripherally, is surely a significant result of the Amesian childlike mind and its method.[12]

The handling of the transcendence versus reciprocity issue—unilateral causal priority as opposed to cooperative intercausality or "co-creativity"—is of course the heart of the question in all these cases. We see a further wrinkle in how the problem is approached in the Hall and Ames translation of the *Taiyishengshui* itself, which is appended to the *Daodejing* translation. For as noted, and as forcefully presented in the very title of the text, this excavated work has been taken as knock-down evidence for the existence of a true first-cause cosmogony in the era of the *Daodejing*'s composition, since this text is "quite simply the earliest record of Chinese cosmogony that we have."[13] Unsurprisingly, Hall and Ames find this conclusion over-hasty: "The Great One is identified as the first among the defining terms in the Daoist cosmology," and yet, "all of these correlated elements constituting the cosmos collaborate to produce each other and the totality. Said another way, the Great One is not a transcendent, ordering principle—a single source—that stands independent of the world it produces. Rather, it is coterminous with this world, hidden within it, and circulating everywhere."[14] The commentary here is of course grappling with the same issue we have just confronted in the commentary to chapter 42: is this a one-way causal sequence metaphysics with a transcendent first cause, or a reversible reciprocal cocreative immanent process philosophy? Its answer here seems to be, somehow, *both*. "Produce each other" seems to want to claim that the Great One too is produced by the other elements that it produces. The reason given to offset the objection that this is being just bluntly asserted, flying in the face of the plain sense of the text, merely the fiat of the global context hermeneutic circle, is suggested by the next sentence in the commentary: "While the Great One gives birth to the waters, it also lies hidden in them, and these same waters collaterally assist it in giving birth to the heavens and the earth."[15] This tells us that the seemingly brazen "both-and" explanation given here—yes, the Great One is first, but at the same time, everything collaborates to reciprocally create everything else, including the Great One—rests on two particular facets which are in fact found in the local text, and which do require explanation: the theme of "reversion" (*fan*) and the theme of "hiddenness" (*cang*). For the text starts like this: 太一生水, 水反輔

太一, 是以成天。天反輔太一, 是以成地, and so on. This does seem to suggest some degree of priority for the Great One along with some degree of cooperation: the Great One gives birth to the waters, and the waters "turn back" and assist the Great One to produce Heaven. Then Heaven somehow collaborates with the Great One to produce Earth. The equation seems still to be neatly and unproblematically sequential: Great One produces water unassisted, but then Great One plus Water = Heaven, Great One plus Heaven = Earth, and so on. This temporal sequence and priority is deliberately muted in the Hall and Ames translation: "In the Great One giving birth to the waters, the waters collaterally assist the Great One, thereby producing the heavens. . . ." and so on.[16] The processes are here depicted as simultaneous and inseparable: "*In its giving birth* . . . ," suggesting that just while the Great One is giving birth to the waters, the waters are at that moment already assisting the Great One and producing the heavens thereby. Here again, we must pause to consider questions of method and the assumptions behind them. At first this seems outrageous: almost any reader of the original text will automatically take it as a clear temporal sequence: first this happens, then that happens, then with the elements generated when that happened, a third thing is able to happen, and so on. But again we look with the childlike mind, and see, as in all Chinese writing, there is really no explicit tense in the grammar. The language *can* be read, when the automatic demands of tense are suspended, as functioning in a kind of eternal present unless otherwise stated. We really can go back and reread the text in this way, as all gerunds: "the Great One is giving birth to water and water reverting to assisting the Great One, producing the heavens, which are mixing back in with the Great One to produce the earth, which. . . ." With new eyes a new possibility opens up—not by hermeneutic fiat, but rooted in a renewed sensitivity to a sinological subtlety in the text itself, facilitated by the suspension of Indo-European grammatical and metaphysical assumptions.

But here too there seems to be obvious overreach. None of this remotely suggests that the Great One itself is also produced by these elements it produces. A neutral observer would have to grant that the priority of the Great One wins in the end, at least in this text; such reciprocity that we see here—in the "reverting" of things to assist the Great One in creation and the "immanence" (= hiddenness, *cang* 藏) of the Great One in its products is clearly part of a one-way sequence and one-way schema of prioritization, which the text never reverses. We see this in the use of the key term *fu* 輔, "to assist," which generally suggests not mere "cooperation" but a clear relationship of one-way subordination, though it is importantly true that in the succeeding lines we find the term used for nonhierarchical cooperation and mutual assistance, in repeated use of the phrase *xiangfu* 相輔. But it is not clear whether this should be back-read into initial stages of the process; in the absence of overt usage some kind of priority does seem to be emphasized for the Great One in the initial use of *fu* without *xiang* (after all, if the nonhierarchical sense were intended for the first steps, it seems like it would have been just as easy and elegant to write, say, *taiyi yu shui xiangfu, shiyichengtian* 太一與水相輔, 是以成天, etc. And even that would not retract the single-agent birthing of the text's first line: *Taiyi* alone seems to be what gives rise to water).

A bit later in the text we have the assertion of immanence: "是故太一藏於水, 行於時," which Hall and Ames render, "Thus it is that the Great One is hidden away in the waters, and travels with the seasons."[17] If the Great One is a cause, it is at least what Spinoza called an "immanent cause," rather than a "transitive cause"; it never becomes separated from its effects. This certainly establishes a strong sense of immanence, but this in itself does not eliminate the possibility of unchanged priority: the one-way dependence of things on the Great One is not necessarily compromised by its constant co-presence in them. Temporal priority is not the only kind of priority that can foreclose full existential interdependence. Nevertheless, what we learn from the Amesian method of fresh eyes, even when it overreaches and asserts full reversibility where there is rather only a hint and a nimbus of reversibility-structure awaiting further development, is that "it is the Great One that gives birth to the heavens and the earth" does *not* mean the Great One is a sole first cause that produces *all things* by fiat, or unassistedly. It is in this sense, indeed very far from the basic premise of divine omnipotence of a Creator God, which severely constrains the extent to which created beings can contribute to the creation, maintenance, improvement, completion of anything, that being the prerogative of God. Here the Great One is assisted in creation not only by humans (at most, in some versions of monotheism, human beings "husband" or "steward" or somehow "help perfect" the world, e.g., the Jewish notion of *tikkun olam*; but animals, not to mention material things such as *water*, certainly are not involved in doing any of the cosmic creative work) but by whatever it produces; by itself it produces only water, but from then on all creativity is collaborative, albeit in a highly prioritized and one-way hierarchical manner, which does not quite manage to bounce back and assert that the Great One itself is generated by this process.

But this pushes the question upon us: what exactly *is* this Great One? This is where we get further unexpected benefits from applying the Amesian eyes, well worth the small price of occasional interpretive overreach. What do we suddenly see when we look at the phrase *taiyi*, if we revert to the translation insights already applied to *Daodejing* 42? Not "the" Great One. Not "A" Great One. Not a Great "One." Rather, perhaps, something like: "Vast Continuity." How different would our thinking process be if we read: "Vast continuity produces water, which then interacts with the vast continuity to help produce the heavens. The heavens relate back to the vast continuity to help produce the earth. . . ."[18] "Vast continuity is hidden in the waters, moves along with the seasons. . . ." Suddenly we have a very different picture. The word "continuity" frontloads the co-presence of multiplicity, and thereby of immanence; unlike "The" Great "One," it does not make us assume that the "producing" here is producing something *outside itself*, or even *additional to itself*, which then presents all the quandaries of what degree of interaction and cooperation and precedence exist between these separate entities. Instead, we see the arising of water *within the expanse of a vast continuity*, like a wrinkle in a blanket, or a pimple on skin: it is a modification of a pre-existing continuity, which however remains part of that continuity. Vast continuity now reads like a way of describing space itself, the physical extended universe, *in which* and *from which* various physical objects come to exist, but without thereby ceasing to be part of the spatial system, or leaving the fabric of continuity which is space. Yet space arguably remains the prior condition even when it is co-present and co-extensive with any particular spatial item. The water may arise and perish, but the space, seemingly, cannot. Hence, even if they are both there for as long as we know, it makes some sense for the space, the continuity, to be said to be "prior." Whatever creative process the water is involved in, we can then sensibly speak of it as "the water, in collaboration with the space," doing the creating. The water remains the subordinate partner, because the next thing to be created will also be part of space, part of the vast continuity, but not necessarily part of the water; but also because whatever water does is *ipso facto* also being done by the continuity that is co-present with the water, and co-present in it as always having priority. Suddenly the rest of the passage makes some degree of sense, and we see in what respect we can speak of both a priority relation, with a one-way prior term which is everywhere pervading its subordinate products, and the full reciprocal cooperation of creative work. Again we must remember to take into account the question that arose in the comments made on *Daodejing* 25, i.e., whether what is caused here is "the universe as such" or rather "heaven and earth as a matched pair in particular," a consideration encouraged by the ruminations on the *naming* of heaven and earth that come later in the *Taiyishengshui* text. What is produced in a vast continuity is its divisions into provisionally separate entities that presuppose it, divisions within that prior vast continuity itself. Vast continuity does not produce all Being as such, since it is itself priorly there, is itself already being. But it is in fact the prior condition for any specific, nameable (i.e., provisionally separate) entity, the ground of comparison and contrast necessary for a distinction to be made. Water is only watery against the continuity of space surrounding it. But water is itself just more continuity: indeed, it is perhaps singled out as the first product in the sequence precisely because it illustrates "continuity" more directly than any other element in the empirical world. If divided, it immediately rejoins, always "flowing together," resilient to division precisely because it is supremely soft and yielding, persisting due to its very noncontending softness—precisely the virtues of water singled out in the *Daodejing*, and also valorized in the *Taiyishengshui*.[19] Water is the closest approximation to pure continuity, "close to *Dao*," as *Daodejing* 8 says, the least complex derivative of continuity *per se*, the most basic element in continuity. Water presupposes prior continuity, contrasts to surrounding continuity, but also exemplifies and extends continuity, and then modifies and contributes to the activity of this continuity.

All of this becomes immediately coherent to the mind's eye simply by suspending Indo-European grammatical assumptions that have slipped into our mind while translating—by experimenting instead with the no-article, deconcretized, tenseless, numberless version of the same ideas, and seeing what happens. When textual issues are thereby clarified, as here, we have warrant to adopt that translation and that interpretation as an advance in understanding.

But turning back to the comparative issues, there are still further boons to be gleaned from this approach. We now can perhaps come closer to understanding the seemingly paradoxical idea of simultaneous priority and single first cause combined with some cooperative cosmic creation. All we had to do was take the immanence really seriously, and to do this all we had to do was to suspend the mistaken linguistic assumption that giving birth necessarily implied that the produced was outside or definitively ontologically "other than" the producer rather than a part of it, or just a division within it; this was easily accomplished just by substituting the indefinite "vast continuity" for proper noun "The Great One." We noted above that this structure of priority with immanence and subsequent collaboration is far from monotheism. But is it so far from the Plotinian One? In Plotinus too we see the One emanating a first hypostasis, which then comes to play a role in the emanation of all further existences, step by step, in each case also with the cooperation of the always immanently present original One. And yet the Plotinian One, unlike the continuities stipulated in the Chinese texts, does end up being compatible with a certain form of exclusion and ontological otherness, in spite of its exceptionless immanence. Plotinus insists that the One is not any specific entity, and yet it has the power to exclude some existents, just as it would if it were a proper noun, naming a particular entity—for "to exclude other entities" is precisely what it means to "be" a specific entity. For Plotinus's One is said to be *less* present progressively in all its emanations, and when it gets to the last emanation, *matter*, it is almost completely undetectable. In matter Plotinus sees not extended substance, a continuum with wrinkles and bumps in it that we loosely call "things," but genuinely distinct substances, really separate from one another, something like the (by now commonsensical) finite substances of Aristotle: each a crappy, partial, and inadequate instantiation of the "Oneness" which all things need to exist at all, but already dominated almost to the point of non-existence by the opposite principle: dissolution, separation, division, non-Oneness. This is the essence of Plotinus's "theodicy," and accounts for his ability to devalue matter, a move that has huge ethical and metaphysical consequences. This would not be the case for strict immanence, which would not allow "the" One to be anything ontologically other to, or insufficiently present in *any* instantiation of being, however meager. The oneness of any finite one would really be the unbroken same-and-different continuity that was discoverable everywhere; not even a genuinely distinct "part" of this continuity, but just further continuity—continuity with every other aspect of continuity.

Now our comparative considerations allow us to entertain a hugely consequential question: could it be that the peculiarities of Indo-European language, including the Greek language Plotinus was writing in, with its requirement for morphological distinctions and articles, tweaked Plotinus's thought into a direction that allowed this weird idea—an all-inclusive immanent One crucial to all ontological reality that was nevertheless exclusive of some entities—to seem natural to him and his readers? That "the" One became the name of an entity, and sounded *and felt* like a numerical one—unity *as opposed to* multiplicity—rather than "continuity," which is immediately always both unity and difference, and does not name a particular entity? The idea, carefully considered, makes no sense; why has it seemed so intuitive and convincing for so many centuries? The puzzling weirdness now seems to be not in the Chinese case, but in the European case.

If we follow this line of thought, we are enabled to see a question that is rarely raised, as well as a possible solution to this question. For this weirdness allows us to see another weirdness that has been quite central to Occidental thinking for over two millennia: monotheism. Monotheism means precisely the assertion of a Oneness *instead of* a multiplicity: *one God, as opposed to* many gods. A oneness whose very essence is a virulent exclusivism, a mocking polemic against idolatry, rather than the one god as *including* all other gods, or appearing as all other gods, which is what a neutral observer might expect. One way to think about the dominant European form of monotheism, Christianity, is to trace an encounter between Hebrew monotheistic mythology and Plato's introduction of a nameless singular divinity, "the deity" (*ho theos*), likely motivated by something like Socrates's enthusiastic welcome, reported in the *Phaedo*, of Anaxagoras's idea of *nous* as *arche*: mind as the true source of the world. This is crucially the idea of a *single, controlling mind* as the final and sole reason for why things are as they are: the special characteristic of minds, as opposed to any other candidate for *arche*, is that, as here conceived, minds are always striving to do what they consider "best" in any situation, what is good to them and for them. It is crucial that there be *one* mind at the source of all things for the problem of contending conceptions of good to be solved. From this we get the speculations about the creative demiurge of the *Timeaus*. Why are things as they are? Because the mind of the demiurge built them that way. Why are things this way rather than that way? Because that is what that mind thought would be best—which is to say, therefore, that is what *is* best. Plotinus goes beyond the demiurge, who is demoted to the status of emanated hypostasis but remains the final account of why things are as they are, and still with reference to its conception of what is good. The role of the good and the One are now conflated more explicitly in The One beyond *nous* to which *nous* nonetheless looks and which it tries to approximate in conceiving the Good. Oneness as *an* entity, and as linked to a noetic conception of goodness, i.e., of *choice*, introduces for us the hopefully by-now strange-sounding idea of a Oneness that is nonetheless exclusive. For choice is, by definition, exclusive. Plotinus's non-mind One, which is necessary to all ontic reality, has nonetheless been made compatible with a choice-making, exclusive, good-mongering, specifically named entity, mind as opposed to non-mind, Oneness as opposed to an impossible but nonetheless ontologically obstructive non-Oneness. Suddenly this does not sound so different from the jealous God of the Old Testament. They meet, they fall in love. *Voila*, Christianity is born—and is able to make abundant use of Neo-Platonic motifs in the construction of its theology.

That theology, however, was a Trojan horse. My account above of how we might think of a truly *non-exclusive One*, oneness not as the name of a specific entity opposed to diversity, but as true immanence and continuity, somewhat in the manner of space *in which* things arise, and which remains exhaustively co-present with whatever arises. The notion that "Oneness" which is always necessarily and simultaneously diversity does not name any specific entity, which is not in fact *any one*, owes much to the thought of Spinoza.[20] I would like to cast Spinoza here as perhaps the first thinker in the European tradition who, for various accidental reasons, found himself in a position where he could again observe monotheism without prejudice, from outside, taking traditional monotheistic theology more literally at its word, more literally than the theologians who propounded it, perceiving that its real implication undermined the tenets of the exoteric monotheistic doctrine. This is true of his deployment of the Ontological Proof, and of his deployment of the Privation Theory of evil. In both cases, he uses these hoary old monotheistic tropes to disprove the conclusions of monotheism. But it is also true of his deployment of the very idea of the *Oneness of God*. Spinoza sees quite clearly that the Oneness of God *does not mean that there is One God*! The Oneness of God means instead that there is no particular entity named God—and this matters because it finally erases the implication that the One God could somehow exclude some "other" things. In his early *Metaphysical Thoughts*, appended to his *Principles of Cartesian Philosophy*, Spinoza writes:

> They say that this term [the One] signifies something real outside the intellect. But they cannot explain what this adds to being, and this is a clear indication that they are confusing beings of reason with real being and are thereby rendering confused that which they clearly understand. But we on our part say that unity is in no way distinct from the thing itself or additional to being and is merely a mode of thinking whereby we separate a thing from other things that are similar to it or agree with it in some respect.
>
> The opposite of unity is plurality, which likewise obviously adds nothing to things, nor is it anything but a mode of thinking, just as we clearly and distinctly understand. Nor do I see what more remains to be said regarding a thing so clear, except that here it should be noted that, insofar as we separate God from other beings, he can be said to be one; but insofar as we conceive that there cannot be more than one of the same nature, he is called unique. In truth, if we wished to look into the matter more rigourously, we might perhaps show that God is only improperly called one and unique.[21]

Spinoza was careful not to push his luck by saying this too loudly or emphatically, since he had a lot riding on making the case that his own doctrine was simply reasserting, more rigorously, what all monotheists already accepted: that God was One. But he continued to mention this insight—that God is not really "One"—explicitly and indeed forthrightly in private letters. Explaining the above passage to Jarig Jellis, in Letter L, written in 1674 (three years before his death), Spinoza says, ". . . a thing can only be said to be one or single in respect of its existence and not of its essence: for we do not conceive things under numbers until they have been subsumed under a common class. . . . Hence it seems clear that nothing can be called one or single unless some other thing has first been conceived which (as has been said) agrees with it. But since the existence of God is His essence itself, and since we can form no general idea of His essence, it is certain that he who calls God one or single has no true idea of God, or is speaking of Him inappropriately."[22]

Spinoza is using monotheistic theological concepts against monotheism itself. This is the process later described by Feuerbach: "*Pantheism is* the *necessary consequence* of theology (or of theism). It is *consistent* theology. *Atheism* is the *necessary consequence* of pantheism. It is *consistent* pantheism."[23] Spinoza is *thinking through* the idea of Oneness: he has perceived that it cannot be not the name of existing entity as opposed to other entities, but must rather be the name for existence itself. Spinoza (writing in Latin, *without* definite or indefinite articles!), has seen that it is not "the" "One," but in fact *continuity*: in his terms, "indivisibility," which pertains to the nature of Substance as such (as do necessary existence and necessary infinity expressed in infinite ways, which are of course not necessarily part of the question set or the answer set in the *Daodejing* or *Taiyishengshui*). The ontologically significant One now can no longer be a choice-making, purposeful mind, as in the *Timeaus* and orthodox monotheism, nor can it be a particular entity that in some manner excludes or has reduced instantiation in some real things, as in Plotinus. It is not "the" One any longer: it is continuity, coterminous with multiplicity and diversity. This puts us in the position to suggest that perhaps we stumble over the character *yi* in the *Daodejing* because our notion of oneness has long been filtered through the very strange, Indo-European-grammar-dependent synthesis of the all-inclusive "oceanic" oneness of extended substance with the vociferously exclusive, purposeful, choice-making deity of the *Pheado* and the *Timeaus* and the Old and New Testaments, or "the" dwindingly emanating impersonal One of Plotinus, or some confused hybrid of the two. This is immediately obvious to us if we suspend our knee-jerk grammatical and metaphysical assumptions when thinking about oneness, when *looking* at our Chinese texts with fresh eyes. We latter-day students of these texts owe a profound debt to Roger Ames for making his way through them first, and thereby providing us with an exemplar of how it is done, so that we can in turn make our way.

Notes

1. Li Ling 李零, "An Archeological Study of Taiyi (Grand One) Worship," translated by Donald Harper. *Early Medieval China* 2 (1995–1996).

2. Since the translation was published many years after Hall's untimely death, it seems fair to consider the final edit, and especially the word-choice in the translation, mainly the work of Ames, always the sinological authority in this team throughout their many collaborations.

3. Roger T. Ames and David L. Hall, *Dao De Jing: Making This Life Significant, A Philosophical Translation, Featuring the Recently Discovered Bamboo Texts* (New York: Ballantine Books, 2003), 142–43.

4. Ames and Hall, *op. cit.*, 115.

5. Even without the considerations to follow, there are some good reasons drawn not only from the shakier global cultural context but also from the more concrete textual local context to argue for something like this interpretation, in particular in the line parallel to the "unchanging" line in the WB edition. I myself have argued that these two lines together form two poles of a single paradoxical statement, and thus that the "independent and not-changing" is meant as only half the story, not to be taken literally or definitely. (See *Ironies of Oneness and Difference*, pp. 276–77, n. 20). Hall and Ames make a similar point, *DDJ*, 210, n. 67.

6. Hall and Ames, *DDJ*, 210.

7. Ibid.

8. Though *hua* can sometimes have a transitive normative sense, it never appears in the *Analects* or the earliest parts of the *Mozi*; even when it does take on the normative sense of "to civilize, convert, transform," the sense remains strongly tilted toward spontaneity, implying being moved or inspired by something or someone that brings about an unintentional but positive change, in sharp contrast to the deliberate, hands-on, agent-heavy corrective operation implied by *gai*.

9. In this case, this point now comes into contact with a question I have pondered and argued in the case of the "Neo-Daoist" writer Guo Xiang. I have argued that when Guo Xiang states that "the nature" (*xing*), which is "self-so" (*ziran*), is "unchanging" (*bugai*), he means precisely that it "can change but cannot *be* changed." (See *The Penumbra Unbound*, pp. 143–46). There too Guo speaks fulsomely of its "transformation" (*bian, hua*). The highlighting of the normative and transitive senses of the term *gai* adds a very helpful dimension to this point. I wish I had noticed it myself at the time I was writing that!

10. Ames and Hall, *op. cit.*, 143.

11. Ibid., 144.

12. We could indeed experiment further with this method by keeping to gerunds all the way through, thereby avoiding either limiting the meaning to either the singular or the plural, thereby arguably hewing even closer to the original text. Then we might expect a translation of the beginning of chapter 42 that looked something like this: "Way-making unifies; Unifying contrasts; Contrasting diversifies; Diversifying ramifies into everything."

13. Ames and Hall, *op. cit.*, 226.

14. Ibid., 227.

15. Ibid.

16. Ibid., 229.

17. Ibid.

18. If we choose to accept the global interpretative context urged by Hall and Ames and accordingly dampen the one-way agency, we would have something like, "Water arises from and within a prior vast continuity, which then interacts with that vast continuity to produce the heavens, which then interact with that vast continuity to produce the earth. . . ."

19. Note that even Spinoza uses precisely water when he needs a concrete illustration of the indivisibility of substance. See EIp15s.

20. And I note with some pleasure the coincidental fact that Tang Junyi, a man very sensitive to the nuances of thought and of words, and a close student of the intellectual continuities in both Western and Chinese philosophical traditions, translates Spinoza's "substance" precisely as *taiyi*. See *Xinwu yu rensheng* (Taipei: Xuesheng shuju, 1989), 237–44. In this imaginary dialogue, Spinoza is speaking in verse, in the first person.

21. Spinoza, *Principles of Cartesian Philosophy*, translated by Stanley Shirley (Indianapolis, IN: Hackett Publishing Company, 1998), 106.

22. *Correspondence of Spinoza*, translated by A. Wolf (New York: Lincoln MacVeagh, The Dial Press, 1928), 269–270.

23. Ludwig Feuerbach, "Preliminary Theses on the Reform of Philosophy," in Ludwig Feuerbach, translated by Zawar Hunfi, *The Fiery Brook: Selected Writings* (New York and London: Verso, 2013), 153.

7

Supplementing Ames on Creativity
A Heideggerian Interpretation of *Cheng*

CHENYANG LI

Of all concepts of classic Chinese philosophy, *cheng* 誠 is one of the most difficult to decipher. The matter is not only of translating the term into English or another language. Even in Chinese, its meaning is so indefinite and elusive that the prominent Chinese philosopher Zhang Dainian has called it "the most unintelligible concept in Chinese philosophy."[1] Yet, *cheng* is undoubtedly an important concept; no serious student of Chinese philosophy can avoid encountering it.[2] In this chapter, I examine various efforts that have been made to interpret *cheng* and show how these interpretations have shed light on different dimensions of the concept. I also show that, although Roger Ames has made important contributions in this regard, his interpretation is nevertheless lacking in an important way, and that a crucial aspect of *cheng* has yet to be elucidated. This lack can be filled by a Heideggerian reading.[3] In such an interpretation, *cheng* is a mode of being human in the most fundamental sense. As an essential characteristic of humanity, *cheng* signifies authentic human existence. Through *cheng*, humanity, heaven, and the world become, and maintain, what they are and what they ought to be. *Cheng* reflects truth, creativity, and reality, the three key dimensions of the Confucian human ontology. To offer such a reading is not to suggest that ancient Chinese thinkers philosophized as Heidegger. It indicates, however, that different philosophical traditions can share important insights even though they may possess varied ways of thinking and justification. My focus here is on pre-Qin Confucian thought, primarily on *cheng* in the *Great Learning*, the *Zhongyong*, and the *Mencius*, the three classic texts in which *cheng* plays a substantial role.

Interpretation of *Cheng* in English Scholarship

One of the earliest Western scholars who attempted to interpret *cheng* was James Legge. He interpreted *cheng* as "sincerity," making it primarily an ethico-psychological concept. According to *The Oxford English Dictionary*, "sincere," the adjective form of "sincerity," is derivative of the Latin word "*sincerus*," meaning "clean, pure, sound." In another interpretation, "sincerity" comes from the Latin word "*sine*," i.e., "without," and "*cera*," i.e., "wax." The word originally meant that good sculpture artists do not use wax to hide defects in their productions. In either reading, "sincerity" can mean the original state without artificial disguise. Legge used the word mainly as a psychological concept. One of the reasons he stuck to "sincerity" in interpreting *cheng* may be due to his taking on the *Great Learning* before tackling the *Zhongyong* in following the sequence of Zhu Xi's *Four Books*. In the *Great Learning*, "*cheng*" is used in close connection to *yi* 意, "intention" or "determination." It is evidently psychological in connotation. To make one's *yi* "*cheng*" (誠其意) means to set a sincere heart onto something. Legge also extended this translation to the *Zhongyong*. He wrote,

> The second clause of par. 5-誠之不可揜如此, appears altogether synonymous with the 誠於中必形於外, in the 大學傳 [*Great Learning*], chap. vi.a, to which chapter we have seen that the whole of chap. i, pars. 2, 3, has a remarkable similarity.[4]

Interpreting *cheng* as sincerity seems straightforward and unproblematic in the *Great Learning*. It is in the *Zhongyong*, however, that Legge encountered difficulties. Section 20 of the *Zhongyong* states:

> 誠者, 天之道也。誠之者, 人之道也。誠者, 不勉而中。不思而得, 從容中道, 聖人也。誠之者, 擇善而固執之者也。

Legge translated it as follows:

> Sincerity is the way of Heaven. The attainment of sincerity is the way of men. He who possesses sincerity is he who, without an effort, hits what is right, and apprehends, without the exercise of

thought; he is the sage who naturally and easily embodies the right way. He who attains to sincerity is he who chooses what is good, and firmly holds it fast.[5]

"The way of Heaven," however, is obviously not confined to the human person. Using "sincerity" as a psychological state to describe Heaven hardly makes sense. Recognizing the difficulty, Legge wrote,

> However, we may be driven to find a recondite, mystical, meaning for 誠, in the 4th part of this work.[6]

Commenting on Section 21, at the beginning of the 4th part of the *Zhongyong*, Legge wrote,

> The ideal of humanity—the perfect character belonging to the sage, which ranks him on a level with Heaven—is indicated by 誠, and we have no single term in English, which can be considered as the complete equivalent of that character.[7]

And he added quickly,

> The Chinese themselves had great difficulty in arriving at that definition of it which is now generally acquiesced in.[8]

Legge's case shows that, while his interpretation of *cheng* may work in the *Great Learning*, it is far from being appropriate when it comes to the *Zhongyong*.

Wing-tsit Chan's work on interpreting *cheng* seems to have been influenced by Legge. For instance, Chan translated Section 20 of the *Zhongyong* in close resemblance to Legge, as follows:

> Sincerity is the Way of Heaven. To think how to be sincere is the way of man. He who is sincere is one who hits upon what is right without effort and apprehends without thinking. He is naturally and easily in harmony with the Way. Such a man is a sage. He who tries to be sincere is one who chooses the good and holds fast to it.[9]

Attributing sincerity to Heaven, Chan encounters the same problem as Legge. Following Legge, Chan translated "*cheng zhe, wu zhi zhongshi* (誠者, 物之終始)" as "sincerity is the beginning and end of things."[10] However, if sincerity is a psychological state, how can it be the beginning and the end of things in the world? In an attempt to resolve this difficulty, Chan broadened his renditions of *cheng* and wrote,

> The quality that brings man and Nature together is *cheng*, sincerity, truth or reality. The extensive discussion of this idea in the Classic makes it at once psychological, metaphysical, and religious. Sincerity is not just a state of mind, but an active force that is always transforming things and completing things, and drawing man and Heaven (*Tien*, Nature) together in the same current.[11]

Chan's account points out a key meaning of *cheng*, namely, it is an active force that transforms things and completes things, and brings humanity and Heaven into unity. However, saying that this force is "sincerity" is clearly forced; the English word simply does not have such a connotation. Chan's treatment seems to display Legge's influence. Linking *cheng* to truth and reality brings it closer to the meanings of the word in the *Zhongyong*. Unfortunately, Chan did not elaborate on these linkages in explicating *cheng*. Commenting on *cheng* as a creative force, Chan wrote, "In so far as it is mystical, it tends to be transcendental."[12] Chan did not explain what he meant by "transcendental." If it means "beyond the human realm," justifying such a reading is difficult, because in Confucianism the human realm is not separate from Heaven or earth.

Recognizing the difficulties associated with translating *cheng* as sincerity, both Donald Munro and A. C. Graham avoided psychologizing *cheng* and opted for "integrity." Munro wrote,

> My translation of *cheng* as "integrity" rather than "sincerity" comes from the term's sense as a completeness that contains all natural attributes, none of which is fraudulent or missing.[13]

This rendering allows Munro to translate "*cheng zhe, zi cheng ye* 誠者, 自成也" in the *Zhongyong* as "integrity is that whereby things complete themselves."[14] In cases like this, "integrity" clearly has an advantage over "sincerity."

Graham expanded this rendering to the *Great Learning*, where "sincerity" seems to have stronger grounding than "integrity." He translated "*cheng yi* 誠意" as "integrating the intention." He wrote,

> *Cheng* "integrity" derives from *cheng* 成 "becoming whole," used (in contrast with *sheng* 生 "be born") of the maturation of a specific

thing . . . we use "integrity, integral, and integrate" to combine the two senses, wholeness and sincerity.[15]

Using "integrity" for *cheng*, Graham translated Section 20 of the *Zhongyong* as follows:

> Integrity is the Way of Heaven, integrating is the Way of man. The man who is integral is on centre without endeavour, succeeds without thinking, is effortless on the Way; he is the sage. The man who integrates is one who chooses the good and holds on to it firmly.[16]

Graham's rendering seems to have been motivated by his effort to offer a consistent interpretation of *cheng* in both the *Great Learning* and the *Zhongyong*. His translation of "*cheng yi*" as "integrating the intention" suggests that he read the meaning of *cheng* in the *Zhongyong* back into the *Great Learning*, or it would be difficult to comprehend how he came to the idea of "integrating the intention" from "*cheng yi*."

Munro apparently approached the matter in the opposite direction from Graham. For Munro, the proper meaning of *cheng* is "sincerity," which "referred to the unwavering attempt to realize the specific social virtues." Such an attempt is undoubtedly a human effort. On the basis of this, Munro asserted, "*cheng* was then read into nature."[17] Such a reading-back into nature can be found in the *Mencius* as well as in the *Zhongyong*, both of which belong to the Si-Meng School of Confucianism. Munro's reading could be supported in two scenarios. First, the word "*cheng*" originally described a psychological state. Given the etymological connection of *cheng* 誠 with its homophone 成 (to complete),[18] however, such a conjecture is difficult to sustain. Second, the *Great Learning*, in which *cheng* carries a close psychological connotation, was written before the *Zhongyong* and the *Mencius*, in which *cheng* appears with broader meanings. However, Munro provided neither as evidence. Therefore, he has not convincingly established that *cheng* as a personal (psychological) state was read back into nature to acquire broader meanings such as integrity, truth, and reality.

In his *Centrality and Commonality*, Tu Weiming followed Wing-tsit Chan's interpretation of *cheng*, but emphasized its senses of "truth" and "reality." Tu wrote,

> *Cheng* as the Way of Heaven is certainly different from "sincerity" as a personal quality. To say that Heaven is *sincere* seems to

translate the idea of an honest person into a general description of the Way of Heaven.[19]

For Tu, however, such a reading of *cheng* back into the world is a misinterpretation. Unlike Munro, Tu maintained that, when the *Zhongyong* describes the way of Heaven as *cheng*, it does not say that Heaven is like a person. On the contrary, it means that *cheng* is unmistakably a quality of Heaven, and that humans should follow this heavenly quality to be *cheng*. Thus, Tu placed "sincerity" in quotation marks and considered *cheng* as "a primary concept in the construction of a moral metaphysics."[20] Toward that end, Tu quoted Lau's translation of *cheng* in the *Mencius* for support. Lau interpreted *cheng* as "true." For instance, the *Mencius* states:

反身不誠, 不悅於親矣. 誠身有道. 不明乎善, 不誠其身矣. 是故誠者, 天之道也. 思誠者, 人之道也. 至誠而不動者, 未之有也. 不誠未有能動者也. (4A12)

Lau translated the passage as follows:

If upon looking within he finds that he has not been true to himself, he will not please his parents. There is a way for him to become true to himself. If he does not understand goodness he cannot be true to himself. Hence being true is the Way of Heaven; to reflect upon this is the Way of man. There has never been a man totally true to himself who fails to move others. On the other hand, one who is not true to himself can never hope to move others.[21]

"Being true" is key to Lau's understanding of *cheng*. As Zhang Dainian maintained, there is a close affinity between the concept of *cheng* in Confucianism and the concept of "*zhen* 真" (true, truth) in Daoism: "what Daoists calls *zhen*, Confucians call *cheng*."[22] In this connection, it makes good sense to interpret *cheng* in terms of "truth," as Lau did. Being true is a way of being for the person. It is not merely psychological, but also ethical and ontological. In this sense, Lau translated "*bu ming hu shan, bu cheng qi shen yi* 不明乎善, 不誠其身矣" as, "if he does not understand goodness he cannot be true to himself." This rendering is much better than either Legge's ("if a man does not understand what is good, he will not attain sincerity in himself"[23]) or Chan's translation ("If one does not understand what is good, he will not be sincere with oneself"[24]). Legge's and Chan's translations imply that understanding the good is a precondition of being sincere, and hence one could understand what is good without being sincere. This implication is problematic because in Confucianism one has to learn to understand the good (or to become enlightened with the good), and dedication, including being sincere, is required in learning about the good.

Aided by Lau's interpretation, Tu went further to link *cheng* directly to the Confucian ideal of the unity of Heaven and humanity. Tu wrote,

> *Cheng*, so conceived, is a human reality, or a principle of subjectivity, by which a person becomes "true" or "sincere" to himself; in so doing, he can also form a unity with Heaven.[25]

Thus, in Tu, *cheng* is first of all a metaphysical concept. It refers to the human reality and the ultimate human existence in unity with Heaven. He maintains that such human existence is the unfolding, and hence the realization of the goodness in human nature (*xing* 性).[26] From this perspective, *cheng* is not only existence but also activity, not only one of self-realization but also of helping to realize others in the world. In this sense, *cheng* is "creativity."

Drawing on Tu Weiming's understanding of *cheng* in terms of creativity, Roger Ames and David Hall translated *cheng* as "creativity." Ames and Hall wrote,

> Construed by appeal to a world of process, both "sincerity," as the absence of duplicity, and "integrity," the state of being sound or whole, must involve the *process* of "becoming one" or "becoming whole." The dynamic of becoming whole, construed aesthetically, is precisely what is meant by a creative process. It is thus that *cheng* is to be understood as *creativity*.[27]

Reading "*wu* 物" in the *Zhongyong* as "process" or "event," Ames and Hall thus interpreted "*bu cheng ze wu wu* 不誠則無物" as "without this creativity, there are no events."[28] Whereas Tu Weiming emphasized the religio-ontological sense of *cheng* and closely associated it with the unity of Heaven and humanity (*tian ren he yi* 天人合一), Ames and Hall focused on its sociopolitical meaning. On Ames and Hall's "focus-field" ontology, human existence is to emerge in a social "field." They wrote,

> We might appeal to the relationship between personal realization and the flourishing community to make this description of creativity more concrete. The basis of community is not a ready made individual, but rather a "functional" or "instrumental" inchoate heart-mind (*xin* 心) emergent from productive relations. It is

through communication that the knowledge, beliefs, and aspirations of the individual are formed. Human realization is achieved not by whole-hearted participation in communal life forms, but by life in community that forms one whole-heartedly. We do not speak because we have minds, but become like-minded by speaking to one another in a communicating community.[29]

It should be noted that Ames and Hall did not deny that *cheng* has a psychological dimension. Even in that regard, however, they saw that "it describes a commitment to one's creative purposes, a solemn affirmation of one's process of self-actualization."[30] Nor did they rule out the sense of integrity from *cheng*. Integrity, to them, meant living in "trustworthy and true" relationships with fellow human beings. They said,

> *Cheng* translated as "creativity" underscores the integrative process itself, while its translation as "integrity" denotes the culmination of any such integrating process. *Cheng* as "sincerity" underscores the emotional tone—the subjective form of feeling—that makes this creative process uniquely perspectival. As we have suggested, the cluster of translations is present as a seamless range of meaning in each occurrence of the term *cheng*.[31]

Like Tu Weiming, Ames and Hall also regarded humanity as a "co-creating" force. While Tu called humanity the "co-creator" with Heaven, Ames and Hall maintained that humans are "co-creative beings that have a central role in realizing both individual selves and the eventful worlds around them."[32] Understanding *cheng* in terms of creativity has enabled Ames and Hall to produce a powerful and apt translation of the important Section 23 of the *Zhongyong*:

誠則形, 形則著, 著則明, 明則動, 動則變, 變則化, 唯天下至誠為能化.

> When there is creativity there is something determinate; when there is something determinate, it is manifest; when it is manifest, there is understanding; when there is understanding, others are affected; when others are affected, they change; when they change, they are transformed. And only those of utmost creativity (*zhicheng* 至誠) in the world are able to effect transformation.[33]

In his more recent work of *Role Ethics*, Ames interprets *cheng* in *Mencius* 7A4 in terms of both "integrative and creative." He writes,

The character *cheng* in this passage is conventionally translated as "sincerity" or "integrity." In most occurrences in the classical corpus it does carry this meaning, and this *Mencius* passage is no exception. But in a processive and transactional world, sincerity is the bond that unites one in one's relations with others, and that makes the process of personal co-creativity possible. Under such circumstances, "integrity" is not simply retaining what you "have" or being who you "are": It is what you "do" and "become" in *integrating* effectively with family and community. *Cheng* is thus the ground of an *integrative and creative process* of becoming consummately human.[34]

In doing so, Ames connects the dots between "sincerity," "integrity," and "creativity." His interpretation culminates in creativity, with both ontological and ethical significance. As a creative process, *cheng* is in close connection with the notion of "*shengsheng* 生生" (creative creativity) in the *Yijing*.

However, there are two weak links in Ames's conceptualization of the various meaning of *cheng*. First, while taking "creativity" as its core meaning, Ames nevertheless has accepted "sincerity" as one unquestionable interpretation and has moved too quickly in embracing it into his understanding of *cheng*. Ames takes *cheng* in the sense of sincerity to be "an essential affective ground for deepening one's relations with others, and in so doing, for achieving real personal growth."[35] He writes, "sincerity is the bond that unites one in one's relations with others, and that makes the process of personal co-creativity possible."[36] In his view, being sincere to others enables one to strengthen human relationships and to be better prepared in joining the co-creative process in the world. In this understanding, *cheng* as sincerity pretty much stays within the psychological and social dimensions. It is not framed explicitly as a special mode of being true in the ontological context of human *being*. Second, as far as Ames bases his interpretation on ontology, his ontological view is too fluid, too unstructured. The sense of "reality" that Tu Weiming has endeavored to expound is left out or simply consumed in Ames's extensive processive ontology. In his philosophical framework, Ames gives little room to "being," to the human reality; everything is in the flux of "becoming." Reality has been replaced with process. Persons have been dissolved into relations. In this respect, Ames has departed too far from the worldview as developed by the ancient Confucians.

In my view, conceptually, the dimension of sincerity in *cheng* should be grounded in the notion of human reality. The human being has its relatively steady structure; it is not always in flux. In an important sense, one can step into the same river more than once. We need to preserve what D. C. Lau and Tu Weiming have accomplished in deciphering the notion of *cheng*. In their view, the "sincerity" dimension of *cheng* is best understood as being true to oneself and to others. We should understand sincerity as a mode of being, as being true. Being true is being, or more precisely, a state of being, a way of being. Only in this understanding, only by grounding it on being true can we closely connect sincerity as a psychological concept to *cheng* as a more fundamentally ontological or metaphysical concept.

Following this line of thinking, we can say that the Confucian notion of *cheng* possesses three main dimensions.[37] First, it is trueness or truth. In this sense, to be *cheng* means being true to oneself, to other people, and to the world. Being true is a matter of truth. This meaning encompasses sincerity (i.e., being sincere) but frames it on an ontological ground. When understood as a person's internal state, sincerity is not purely a mental property; it is also a way of ones being who he is and what he is. It suggests authenticity. A sincere person is a true or truthful and an authentic person.[38] Second, *cheng* implies creativity. One important characteristic of *cheng* in the *Zhongyong* is that *cheng* has the capacity to transform the world. It can complete itself (*cheng ji* 成己) and complete things (*cheng wu* 成物). Such a process never ceases (*wu xi* 無息). Together with truth, this meaning of creativity covers the two senses that Munro uses for "integrity," namely wholeness and sincerity. Munro uses "wholeness" to express *cheng*'s role in completing oneself and others. This sense is better communicated in terms of "creativity" as Ames and Hall have admirably shown. Third, *cheng* means reality. It does not just refer to whatever there is. Reality in the sense of *cheng* signifies how the world truly exists. As Tu Weiming remarked, "*cheng* definitely points to a human reality which is not only the basis of self-knowledge but also the ground of man's identification with Heaven."[39] In Confucianism, this ground is the ultimate reality.

A Heideggerian Approach

How are truth, reality, and creativity related in *cheng*? How can we link these three dimensions of *cheng* together conceptually to better make sense of the concept? I believe that Heidegger's scheme of truth can shed important light on this question. Like Ames, Heidegger's world is far from being static, but it is not as fluid and processive as Ames's either. By situating Da-sein's world within referential contextuality, Heidegger provides a framework of being with appropriate stability. His framework enables creativity to take place with reality, enables reality to serve as a fertile ground for creativity and truth, and enables truth to become realized through creativity.

Countering the prevailing conception of truth in the West, Heidegger developed a notion of truth through an ontological twist, or a "return" to its Greek roots, as he saw it. In both *Being and Time* and *On the Essence of Truth*, Heidegger explicitly criticized the Western traditional concept of truth that reduces truth to a matter of "correctness" of the relation of the intellect to the known object. Heidegger objected to the notion that an assertion can "agree" with an object or reality, which is a non-assertion.[40] He maintained that truth cannot possibly have the structure of an agreement between knowing and the object in the sense of a likening of one entity (the subject) to another (the object). Correspondence between the statement and the thing cannot signify a thing-like approximation between dissimilar kinds of things.[41]

Then, what can truth be? Heidegger proposed:

> To say that a statement *is true* means that it discovers [uncovers] the beings in themselves. It asserts, it shows, it lets beings "be seen" (*apophansis*) in their discoveredness [uncoveredness]. The *being-true* (*truth*) of the statement must be understood as *discovering* [*uncovering*].[42]

For Heidegger, an assertion can "correspond with" or be "in agreement with" an object only in the sense that an assertion points out or reveals what has been hidden. The truth of an assertion, or more appropriately, an assertion's *being* true, lies in its "being-uncovering."

If a statement's being true lies in its "being-uncovering," and if that is the essence or underlying meaning of truth, then non-linguistic entities can also be true, namely, when they are encountered in Da-sein's world of referential functionality and get fully uncovered in the way they are what they are. For instance, a hammer is being true when the being of the hammer is unveiled in the world—when it is found in a context in which hammers exist; when a hammer functions in a typical hammering way, not as, say, a paperweight. Thus understood, the "locus" of truth is not in language *per se*, but in the entire realm of being. The ontological status of being true is no longer merely that of knowing, but also that of being. The semantic concept of truth now has turned into an ontological one with a shift in emphasis from "being *true*" to "*being* true."

Heidegger regarded truth as "true-being" or "being-true (*Wahrsein*)," and defined "being true" as "*aletheia* (ἀλήθεια)." He used three terms for truth: unveil/reveal (*enthüllen*), uncover/discover (*entdecken*), and disclose (*erschliessen*). Heidegger explained the difference between them as follows:

> We shall call the unveiling of an extant being—for example, nature in the broadest sense—*uncovering*. The unveiling of the being that we ourselves are, the Da-sein, and that has existence as its mode of being, we shall call not uncovering but *disclosure, opening up*.[43]

In uncovering and disclosing entities, Da-sein opens up its world of being and realizes truth.

Da-sein's being-true makes the truth (trueness) of entities possible. Then, in what way does Da-sein uncover entities in the world? Heidegger maintains that Da-sein cannot uncover entities unless it is itself disclosed to the world. He uses "disclose" (*erschliessen*) and "disclosedness" to mean "to lay open" and "the character of having been laid open."[44] To say that Da-sein is laid open is to say that Da-sein is being-in-the-world in which Da-sein unveils itself in a referential whole; it is within this referential totality that Da-sein makes sense of its being. Only within this holistic contexture are things what they are in the way they are, and thus have meaning. In other words, the uncoveredness of entities within-the-world is *grounded* in the world's disclosedness; and disclosedness is the basic character of Da-sein "in accordance with which it *is* its 'there [*Da*].'"[45]

In this disclosedness Da-sein obtains familiarity with its world, and upon this familiarity lies the very possibility of Da-sein's explicit ontologico-existential interpretation of relations and entities in the world.[46] The disclosedness in the form of familiarity is, in turn, constitutive of Da-sein. In this disclosedness lies the very being of Da-sein. In such a way, truth is a fundamental character or state (*existentiale*) of Da-sein; or in Heidegger's own words, disclosedness is the primordial truth and the truth of existence.[47] He stated,

> In that Da-sein essentially *is* its disclosedness, and, as disclosed, discloses and discovers [uncovers], it is essentially "true." Da-sein is "*in the truth*."[48]

Heidegger maintained that the above assertion has meaning ontologically. Instead of an "agreement" between two things, truth is that in which Da-sein uncovers entities in the world. It is a way of Da-sein's being—"a being toward discovered [uncovered] beings."[49] In truth, whereas entities are being uncovered, Da-sein is being disclosed and is uncovering. The "roots" of entities being what they are in the world can only be found in Da-sein, and the foundation of their being true is in Da-sein. Truth is a way of being of Da-sein itself, of Da-sein's existence.

In this understanding, truth in its primary sense is the disclosing of Da-sein; when Da-sein uncovers entities, truth is manifested through the being of entities. Thus, entities are true in the secondary sense, namely when they are uncovered by Da-sein.[50] Semantic truth, truth as a characteristic of a statement, comes only in the tertiary sense, only when entities are uncovered as being true through Da-sein's being in the truth. For instance, the statement that "this is a hammer" is true when it uncovers the object in question as a hammer; the hammer is what it is, i.e., acquires its true being, when it is uncovered in Da-sein's world of referential nexus, which obtains only because Da-sein discloses. Accordingly, a statement is true when it works to uncover entities in ways they are in the world. Entities obtain their being and hence their true existence when they are uncovered by Da-sein. Da-sein is not only the ultimate source of truth, but also the ultimate source of reality, in the sense that things exist as they are only within Da-sein's world of a meaningful referential framework.

Now let us see how a Heideggerian reading of the Confucian *cheng* can help us grasp the linkage of various dimensions of this notion. We begin with the meaning of truth. As indicated by Zhang Dainian, *cheng* in Confucianism is the counterpart of "truth" (*zhen* 真) in Daoism.[51] *Zhen* means being true or truthfulness, as opposed to artificiality (*wei* 偽). This sense is reflected in the notion of *cheng* in Confucianism. Zhang used as an example the statement of "*xiu ci li qi cheng* 修辭立其誠," namely, the purpose and criterion for good writing (scholarship) is truth or truthfulness.[52] In the *Mencius*, *cheng* is used in a similar sense. For instance, the text records a conversation in which Mencius's interlocutor said, "Confucius said, at that time the world was in great danger. Was what he said not true (*cheng*)?"[53] In usages like this, *cheng* has to do with beliefs and statements being true. *Cheng* also refers to a person's psychological state. In discussing the sage King Shun's attitude toward his brother, Mencius said that Shun "truly believed (*cheng xin* 誠信) him and was happy for him; where is disingenuousness?"[54] In this use, *cheng* expresses the meaning of sincerity. *Cheng* as a quality of knowing and *cheng* as a state of psychological activity are special modes of being true in the sense of truth. They are manifestations of being true to oneself and are rooted in being true to oneself. A person who is true to oneself must be sincere toward oneself and toward others, and must have a clear sense of reality without delusion. In the *Zhongyong*, being true to oneself is called *cheng shen* (誠身), or "to make oneself true." If we are to force this expression in English, we would say "to *true* oneself," with "true" used as a verb.[55] To *true* oneself is to open oneself up, to make oneself authentic. Along this line, Tu Weiming wrote:

> The person who embodies *cheng* to the utmost is also a most genuine human being. It is in this sense that he completely realizes his own nature. The person who realizes his own nature to the full becomes a paradigm of authentic humanity.[56]

For the Mencian branch of Confucianism, to which the *Zhongyong* is attributed, human nature is Heaven-endowed and hence is in accord with the Way.[57] To be authentic is to be true to one's nature.

In Heidegger, Da-sein's being true is in its disclosedness. Heidegger said in an interview that "man is only man when he stands within the disclosing of being."[58] That is, a human is human in the proper sense only when one stands in truth. When Da-sein discloses, it manifests authenticity and uncovers entities in the world. Heidegger wrote,

> Da-sein discloses itself to itself in and as its ownmost potentiality-of-being. This *authentic* disclosedness shows the phenomenon of the most primordial truth in the mode of authenticity. The most primordial and authentic disclosedness in which Da-sein can be as a potentiality-of-being is the *truth of existence*.[59]

Being-true is the authentic way of Da-sein's being. It is the ultimate realization of Da-sein's innermost potentiality-for-being. Da-sein's disclosedness and authenticity do not consist in conforming to anything; it is Da-sein's way of being-in-the-world through choosing its choice in life. Authenticity, however, does not mean that Da-sein simply chooses a way of being, not even just a unique way of being. Many people more or less choose their ways of life, yet they may not all be said to be authentic. Authenticity requires Da-sein to choose the way that it has to choose. In this sense, there is an apparent paradox: on the one hand, Da-sein is free and makes its own choice; on the other, its choice ought not to be just any choice. For Heidegger, authenticity is linked to the unique singularity of Da-sein's own death. Heidegger wrote,

> The more authentically Da-sein resolves itself, that is, understands itself unambiguously in terms of its ownmost eminent possibility in anticipating death, the more unequivocal and inevitable is the choice in finding the possibility of its existence.[60]

Da-sein as being-toward-death brings with it the finitude of existence. This finitude takes Da-sein back from its endless possibilities "nearby" and to "the simplicity of fate," namely "a possibility that it inherited and yet has chosen."[61] This statement points to a constructed common humanity shared by authentic human beings.

By Taylor Carman's account, Heidegger's authenticity consists in two components: resoluteness (*Entschlossenheit*) and forerunning (*Vorlaufen*).[62] It is a kind of hybrid of Aristotelian *phronēsis* and Kierkegaardian faith.[63] With the former, one needs to exercise practical wisdom because an authentic life is not prescribable from any rule book. On the latter, there is no absolute assurance in life; ultimately, one has to make up one's mind on how to live. In comparison, Charles Guignon's reading is more concrete and brings it much closer to the Confucian conception of *cheng*. Interpreting authenticity largely from Heidegger's negation of inauthenticity, Guignon emphasizes that, contrary to just drifting along with the latest trends, authentic Da-sein "remembers" its rootedness in the wider unfolding of its culture, and

> [i]t experiences its life as indebted to the larger drama of a shared history. As a result, authenticity involves encountering one's possibilities as drawn from the "wellsprings" of a "heritage" and living one's life as part of the "mission" or "destiny" definitive of one's historical community as a whole. (BT 435–36)[64]

This way of reading differentiates Heidegger from the radical, "naked" freedom of Sartrean existentialism. For Heidegger, authentic existence is rooted profoundly in its destiny, namely "the occurrence of the community, of a people."[65] Heidegger concluded, "the fateful destiny of Da-sein is and with its 'generation' constitutes the complete, authentic occurrence of Da-sein."[66] Being authentic is not only being true to oneself, but also to one's community, or even more broadly, to humanity.

In Heidegger, Da-sein's being true is closely connected to its world of existence. In the sense of "world" relevant to our discussion here, it denotes the human reality. He said,

> "Worldliness" is an ontological concept and designates the structure of a constitutive factor of being-in-the-world . . . "World" is ontologically not a determination of *those* beings which Da-sein is essentially is *not*, but rather a characteristic of Da-sein itself.[67]

Da-sein's world is with "a contexture of functionality."[68] Without it, entities cannot be what they are in the world. Therefore, "*There is* ["*gibt es*"] *truth only insofar as Da-sein is and as long as it is. Beings are discovered only when Da-sein is, and only as long as Da-sein is are they disclosed.*"[69] This does not necessarily mean that Heidegger was an idealist.[70] However, as far as the world in which we live is already and always a humanized world, our "worldliness" is undeniably a human creation. Moreover, Da-sein for Heidegger will be not mere presence in the sense in which the word "existence" is often used in modern philosophy. Da-sein means "to be there." It is more analogous to an act, a happening, and hence a process, than to a *status* (what stands, what remains). However, such a happening always takes place against a background of Da-sein's contextual framework that is already "there." Da-sein's being-in-the-world means participatory creation of the humanized world and participatory enrichment of the world in a fundamental way. In such an important sense, truth as Da-sein's disclosedness and uncovering in the world is creation. Heidegger did not use the term "creation," which is usually associated with God in the West. We can use the word in the sense of establishment or attainment because, in Heidegger, Da-sein's world is one that can be established and obtained only with its disclosedness and uncoveredness. Da-sein's disclosedness not only bestows on the world its "worldliness," thereby making it an undisputable reality, but also maintains it as such. The foundation of reality in Da-sein's worldliness lies in its truth.

This kind of creation or establishment is not the kind that Kant attributes to the "*Ich denke*" ("I-think"), because Heideggerian creation is achieved through Da-sein's deep involvement in the world. "To be" in the world is not merely to think; Da-sein is involved in the world by such ways as understanding (*Verstehen*), forerunning (*befindlichkeit*), and care (*Sorge*). Furthermore, Da-sein's creation should be understood as mutual-creation, in which Da-sein both shapes its world and at the same time is shaped by it. I will label this mutual transformational relationship "bi-creation." Unlike the common notion of creation by God, bi-creation is not *creatio ex nihilo* (creation out of nothing).[71] In bi-creation, Da-sein generates meaning for its world and enriches its referential framework of functionality and meaning. In the meantime, Da-sein is also inevitably shaped, or re-created anew in its world. Da-sein is "thrown" into the world that already exists in the first place. But, Da-sein is not a passive entity and is fundamentally different in that Da-sein re-acts to the world and is able to shape and re-shape its world. Da-sein finds itself in a world with forests, rivers, mountains, and wind. Through disclosedness Da-sein makes this world filled with timber, water power, and quarries of rock.[72] The world in the latter sense, with a "worldliness" in Heidegger's characterization, is an outcome of Da-sein's bi-creation. It is the reality in which Da-sein finds itself. Thus, in Da-sein's disclosedness emerges truth, creativity, and reality.

Now we return once again to the Confucian notion of *cheng*. In order to achieve trueness to oneself, a person needs to illuminate goodness (*ming shan* 明善). Goodness, as illustrated in the *Zhongyong*, is not something readily available as a given, but something to be established through the human co-creation with Heaven. The active human participation in the Heavenly way is humans "being true." This process can also be characterized as bi-creation. On the one hand, humanity is not an arbitrary creator in any sense. It is destined toward the Way of Heaven. Individual persons need to cultivate themselves in order to come into attunement with the Way. On the other hand, humanity is definitely a creative force and aims to bring out a humanized world. This is not to say that human beings create mountains and rivers on earth (though they could). But it is through human creation that this world becomes a morally significant human reality. It is in the process of humanizing the world, human beings themselves become (more fully) humanized. It is in the process of co-creating the world, humanity becomes re-created. To be *cheng* is to be true to one's Heavenly endowed nature, and to be true to one's Heavenly endowed nature is to realize it in the world. In this process there is transformational creativity. Section 26 of the *Zhongyong* states,

> *Cheng* is ceaseless. Being ceaseless, it is lasting. Being lasting, it is manifesting. Being manifesting, it is infinite. Being infinite, it is extensive and deep . . . It is because it is infinite and lasting that it can complete all things.[73]

As such, *cheng* is the force that not only enables us to complete ourselves, but also to complete all other things in the world.

Conceived as creativity, Tu Weiming wrote about *cheng* as follows,

> [*Cheng*] is that which brings about the transforming and nourishing process of heaven and earth. As creativity, *cheng* is "ceaseless" (*bu xi* 不息). Because of its ceaselessness it does not create in a single act beyond the spatiotemporal sequence. Rather, it creates in a continuous and unending process in time and space. It is therefore a "lasting" (*jiu* 久) event.

Thus,

> It is simultaneously a self-subsistent and self-fulfilling process of creation that produces life unceasingly.[74]

In Ames and Hall's description,

> Creativity (*cheng* 誠) as a transactional, processive, and cooperative endeavor, has the element of affirming things as they are and participating in the process of drawing out novel possibilities from the circumstances.[75]

The Confucian world is never a given, static world. It is co-created by humanity with Heaven and is constantly renewed. *Cheng* represents such a perpetual dynamism in such a world.

As the true human way of being, *cheng* is to be achieved and realized in the human co-creation with Heaven. It points to the ultimate yet ever changing reality, of which humans are a part. This human reality, it should be noted, is not confined to the human person; it is manifest in the entire realm of human existence. It implies that in actualizing our Heaven-endowed nature into reality, we make our world a human world. Such a world is a "furnished" one, one with all kinds of entities in relationship with humanity. In the Confucian view, without *cheng* such a reality is impossible, since humanity is not only a creative force but also a constituting party in its realization. The *Zhongyong* states, "without *cheng* there is nothing 不誠無物." In Confucianism, creativity and reality are the two sides of the same coin of *cheng*. The concept of *cheng* encompasses the idea and the ideal that, in being true, humanity co-creates the worldly reality with Heaven.

Finally, it should be noted that *cheng* in Confucianism should not be understood as a finalized state in a person. Rather, it is a process that calls for constant renewal. In Heidegger, truth does not exist apart from untruth. He wrote,

> The full existential and ontological meaning of the statement 'Da-sein is in the truth' also says equiprimordially that 'Da-sein is in untruth.'[76]

Falling is characteristic of Da-sein's being-in-the-world. Its falling into untruth is by no means accidental. For Heidegger, the world is a "with-world," always the one shared with others.[77] This characteristic determines that Da-sein is not free from everyday falling. Heidegger said,

> The self of everyday Da-sein is the *they-self* which we distinguish from the *authentic self*, the self which has explicitly grasped itself. As the they-self, Da-sein is *dispersed* in the they and must first find itself. This dispersion characterizes the "subject" of the kind of being which we know as heedful absorption in the world nearest encountered. If *Da-sein* is familiar with itself as the they-self, this also means that the they prescribes the nearest interpretations of the world and of being-in-the-world.[78]

In the dispersion of the "they," Da-sein follows the convenient and usually popular interpretations of the world. This is so because, in an everyday manner, the "they" itself articulates the referential context of significance for Da-sein. Furthermore, because Da-sein is essentially "being-with," the "they" is essentially part of Da-sein's positive constitution.[79] Paradoxically, Da-sein's authentic being is not a state detached entirely from the "they," "*but is an* existentiell *modification of the they as an essential existential.*"[80] In its *existentiell* as well as *existential* being, Da-sein is at both the ontic and ontological level. Not free from the "they" in its everydayness, Da-sein's life is at once both authentic and unauthentic. These two types of existence do not and cannot exclude one another. They both constitute Da-sein's being. Because of this co-occurrence, the very being of Da-sein is in tension, hence in a struggle, between truth and untruth. Just as there are various degrees of inauthenticity, there can be various degrees of authenticity with Da-sein. To live an authentic life is thus to be constantly on guard against falling into untruth. Thus, living an authentic life is like Sisyphus rolling the stone uphill: one may never overcome the struggle between truth and untruth, yet it is in this struggle that truth takes place.

Similarly, Confucians see self-realization through *cheng* as a constant life-long endeavor. The very notions of self-realization and self-cultivation imply that one is not yet fully *cheng*, that there are both truth and untruth. A person of full truth is one who is completely one with Heaven. Confucius is said to have achieved this stage when he was seventy years old. Confucius supposedly became a "sage." Presumably, this rarely happens among ordinary people. In effect, therefore, the Confucian belief is that one's struggling between *cheng* and *uncheng*, truth and untruth, never ends. *Cheng* is forever ceaseless.

To conclude, a Heideggerian reading sheds new light on our understanding of the Confucian notion of *cheng*. From such a perspective, we can see *cheng* as being true to oneself, as a creative force, and as a human reality. In Heidegger, Da-sein's authentic existence requires it to disclose and uncover, which can be understood as a creative process that makes beings in the world meaningful and serves as the foundation of the reality of its "worldliness." In the same vein, *cheng* is the mode of human existence in which humanity obtains its authentic being by transforming the world into a humanized world. In being true to oneself, the person of *cheng* co-creates with Heaven a human reality and achieves one's authentic existence by promoting the Way in the world. In this sense, *cheng* is trueness (truth), creativity, and reality. Perhaps the difference of fluidity of being between Heidegger and Ames is a matter of degree, since both see the human reality as a generating process. Nevertheless, by setting human creativity within an already established yet continually renewing referential framework, Heidegger's philosophy presents more stability for being than Ames provides. A Heideggerian reading of *cheng* furnishes a root metaphor that serves as a foundation for comprehending all three dimensions of *cheng*.[81]

Notes

1. Zhang Dainian 張岱年, *Zhongguo zhe xue shi fang fa lun fa fan* 中國哲學史方法論发凡 (*An Introduction to the Methodologies for Studying the History of Chinese Philosophy*) (Beijing: Zhonghua Shuju, 2005), 124.

2. For a comprehensive study of *cheng*, see Yanming An, *The Idea of Cheng (Sincerity/Reality) in the History of Chinese Philosophy* (New York: Global Scholarly Publications, 2005).

3. I first made this connection in *The Tao Encounters the West: Explorations in Comparative Philosophy* (Albany: State University of New York Press, 1999), ch. 2.

4. James Legge, *Confucius: Confucian Analects, the Great Learning, & the Doctrine of the Mean* (New York: Dover Publications, Inc., 1971), 397.

5. Legge, *Confucius: Confucian Analects, the Great Learning, & the Doctrine of the Mean*, 413.

6. Legge, *Confucius: Confucian Analects, the Great Learning, & the Doctrine of the Mean*, 397.

7. Legge, *Confucius: Confucian Analects, the Great Learning, & the Doctrine of the Mean*, 413–14.

8. Legge, *Confucius: Confucian Analects, the Great Learning, & the Doctrine of the Mean*, 414.

9. Wing-tsit Chan, *A Source Book in Chinese Philosophy* (Princeton, NJ: Princeton University Press, 1963), 107.

10. Chan, *A Source Book in Chinese Philosophy*, 108. Legge's translation is that "sincerity is the end of the beginning of things." (Legge, 418)

11. Chan, *A Source Book in Chinese Philosophy*, 96.

12. Ibid.

13. Donald Munro, *Images of Human Nature: A Sung Portrait* (Princeton, NJ: Princeton University Press, 1988), 120.

14. Munro, *Images of Human Nature: A Sung Portrait*, 119.

15. A. C. Graham, *Disputers of the Tao: Philosophical Argument in Ancient China* (La Salle, IL: Open Court, 1989), 133.

16. Graham, *Disputers of the Tao: Philosophical Argument in Ancient China*, 135.

17. Munro, *Images of Human Nature: A Sung Portrait*, 33–34.

18. Chapter 25 of the *Zhongyong* states, 誠者, 自成也, namely that *cheng* means "self-completion." (cf. Munro, 119)

19. Tu Weiming, *Centrality and Commonality: An Essay on Confucian Religiousness* (Albany: State University of New York Press, 1989), 71.

20. Tu, *Centrality and Commonality: An Essay on Confucian Religiousness*, 4.

21. D. C. Lau, *Mencius* (trans. Middlesex, England: Penguin Books, 1976), 123.

22. Zhang Dainian 張岱年, *A Concise Discussion of the Key Concepts in Ancient Chinese Philosophy* 中國古典哲學概念範疇要論 (Beijing: Zhongguo Shehui Kexue Chubanshe, 1989), 230.

23. Legge, *Confucius: Confucian Analects, the Great Learning, & the Doctrine of the Mean*, 411.

24. Chan, *A Source Book in Chinese Philosophy*, 107.
25. Tu, *Centrality and Commonality: An Essay on Confucian Religiousness*, 73.
26. Tu, *Centrality and Commonality: An Essay on Confucian Religiousness*, 77.
27. Roger T. Ames and David Hall, *Focusing the Familiar: A Translation and Philosophical Interpretation of the* Zhongyong (Honolulu: The University of Hawai`i Press, 2001), 32. Also see Roger T. Ames, *Confucian Role Ethics: A Vocabulary,* Honolulu: University of Hawai`i Press, 2011: 307n68.
28. Ames and Hall, *Focusing the Familiar: A Translation and Philosophical Interpretation of the* Zhongyong, 32.
29. Ames and Hall, *Focusing the Familiar: A Translation and Philosophical Interpretation of the* Zhongyong, 33.
30. Ibid.
31. Ames and Hall, *Focusing the Familiar: A Translation and Philosophical Interpretation of the* Zhongyong, 38.
32. Ames and Hall, *Focusing the Familiar: A Translation and Philosophical Interpretation of the* Zhongyong, 34.
33. Ames and Hall, *Focusing the Familiar: A Translation and Philosophical Interpretation of the* Zhongyong, 105.
34. Ames, *Confucian Role Ethics: A Vocabulary*, 67.
35. Ames, *Confucian Role Ethics: A Vocabulary*, 206.
36. Ames, *Confucian Role Ethics: A Vocabulary*, 67.
37. For a different reading, see An, *The Idea of Cheng (Sincerity/Reality) in the History of Chinese Philosophy*, 7, who held the two basic meanings of *cheng* to be "sincerity" and "reality."
38. For an illustration of *cheng* as a Confucian personal virtue, see Chenyang Li, *The Tao Encounters the West: Explorations in Comparative Philosophy* (Albany: State University of New York Press, 1999), chapter 2.
39. Tu, *Centrality and Commonality: An Essay on Confucian Religiousness*, 72.
40. Martin Heidegger, *Being and Time* (trans. Joan Stambaugh, Albany: State University of New York Press, 1996), 199/216.
41. Martin Heidegger, *Basic Writings* (ed. David Farrell Krell, New York: Harper Collins, 1993), 123.
42. Heidegger, *Basic Writings*, 201/218. Joan Stambaugh translated *entdecken* as "discover." "*Entdecken*" consists of "*ent*," to remove, and "*decken*," to cover. In English, "discover" can mean either coming to know something that is unknown before, or removing the cover of something to reveal it. Given this ambiguity, "discover" is less appropriate than "uncover," which is the translation of John Macquarrie and Edward Robinson (*Being and Time*, New York: SCM Press Ltd., 1962).
43. Martin. Heidegger, *The Basic Problems of Phenomenology* (trans. Albert Hofstadter, Bloomington, IN.: Indiana University Press, 1975), 215.
44. Heidegger, *Being and Time*, trans. Macquarrie and Robinson, 105/75.
45. Ibid.
46. Heidegger, *Being and Time*, trans. Stambaugh, 81/86.
47. Heidegger, *Being and Time*, 273/297.

48. Heidegger, *Being and Time*, 203/221.
49. Heidegger, *Being and Time*, 207/225.
50. Heidegger, *Being and Time*, 203/220.
51. Zhang, *Zhongguo zhe xue shi fang fa lun fa fan* 中國哲學史方法論发凡, 230.
52. Ibid.
53. *Mencius*, 5A2. Liang Tao reads this as "孔子說: '這時候, 天下真是岌岌可危!' 不知這話真是這樣嗎?" See Liang Tao 梁濤, *Interpreting the Mencius* 孟子解讀 (Beijing: Renmin University of China Press, 2010), 244.
54. *Mencius*, 5A2. Liang Tao reads this as "舜真誠地相信而感到高興, 怎麼能說是假裝的呢?" See Liang Tao, *Interpreting the Mencius* 孟子解讀, 240.
55. As a verb, "true" in English usually does not have this sense. It means to make level, balanced, or to bring to a desired state.
56. Tu, *Centrality and Commonality: An Essay on Confucian Religiousness*, 77–78.
57. *Mencius*, 7A1.
58. Interview in *Listening* 6 (1971), 35. Quoted from Barry Allen, *Truth In Philosophy*. (Cambridge, MA: Harvard University Press 1993), 82.
59. Heidegger, *Being and Time*, 204/221. Italics in the original.
60. Heidegger, *Being and Time*, 351/384.
61. Ibid.
62. Taylor Carman, "Authenticity." *A Companion to Heidegger*, ed. H. L. Dreyfus and M. Wrathall (Oxford: Blackwell, 2005), 285–96.
63. Carman, "Authenticity," 291–92.
64. Charles B. Guignon, "Authenticity, Moral Values, and Psychotherapy," in *Cambridge Companion to Heidegger*, ed. Charles B. Guignon (Cambridge: Cambridge University Press, 1993/2006), 287. "BT" pages in the quote refers to John Macquarrie and Edward Robinson's translation of *Being and Time* (1962).
65. Heidegger, *Being and Time*, 352/384.
66. Heidegger, *Being and Time*, 352/385.
67. Heidegger, *Being and Time*, 60/64.
68. Heidegger (1982), 165.
69. Heidegger, *Being and Time*, 208/226.
70. For debates regarding this issue, see David R. Cerbone, "Realism and Truth," in *A Companion to Heidegger*, ed. Hurbert L. Dreyfus and Mark A. Wrathall (Malden, MA: Blackwell Publishing, 2005), 248–64; William D. Blattner, *Heidegger's Temporal Idealism* (Cambridge: Cambridge University Press, 1999), see esp. pp. 251–53; Piotr Hoffman, "Heidegger and the Problem of Idealism," *Inquiry: An Interdisciplinary Journal of Philosophy* 43 (2010): 403–12.
71. For an insightful discussion of the difference between Western *creation ex nihilo* and the Chinese model of co-creativity, see Roger T. Ames and David Hall, *Focusing the Familiar: A Translation and Philosophical Interpretation of the* Zhongyong. (Honolulu: University of Hawai`i Press, 2001), 12–13.
72. Heidegger, *Being and Time*, 66/70.
73. Chan, *A Source Book in Chinese Philosophy*, 109, with minor modifications.
74. Tu, *Centrality and Commonality: An Essay on Confucian Religiousness*, 81–82.

75. Ames and Hall, *Focusing the Familiar: A Translation and Philosophical Interpretation of the* Zhongyong, 39.
76. Heidegger, *Being and Time*, 204/222.
77. Heidegger, *Being and Time*, 112/118.
78. Heidegger, *Being and Time*, 121/129.
79. Ibid.
80. Heidegger, *Being and Time*, 130. Hubert Dreyfus explains these terms this way: an "*existential* understanding is a worked-out understanding of the ontological structures of existence, that is, of what it is to be Da-sein. *Existentiell* understanding is an individual's understanding of his or her own way to be, that is, of what he or she is." H. Dreyfus, *Being-in-the-World: A Commentary of Heidegger's* Being and Time, Division I (Boston: MIT Press, 1991), 20.
81. This essay was completed while I was a Berggruen Fellow at the Center for Advanced Study in the Behavioral Sciences at Stanford University. I thank the Berggruen Center for Philosophy and Culture, as well as CASBS for their generous support. This project was also partially supported by a research grant from Nanyang Technological University (M4011397). The author would like to thank Jim Behuniak, editor of this volume, for his valuable comments and suggestions on an earlier version of this essay. I dedicate this essay to Roger Ames, a *junzi* and a good friend.

Part III
ROLES

8

Building Bridges to Distant Shores

Pragmatic Problems with Confucian Role Ethics[1]

STEPHEN C. ANGLE

Late in 1987, having graduated from college and headed to Taiwan to study more Chinese, I decided to attend an international conference on Confucianism. At lunchtime on the first day I was sitting by myself, intimidated by the luminaries all around, when a smiling scholar sat down across from me, introduced himself as Roger Ames, and immediately made me feel at home. (Although he did question the wisdom of my intention to attend a graduate school other than Hawaii.) The year 1987 also saw the publication of *Thinking Through Confucius*, Roger's seminal collaboration with David Hall; shortly after I met Roger I obtained a copy and was inspired. This, I felt sure, was just the kind of thing that I wanted to do: engage deeply with the Confucian tradition in a manner that also challenged Western philosophy. A basic premise of *Thinking Through Confucius* is that the ideas and practices expressed in a text like the *Analects* are centrally relevant to philosophy; insofar as they differ from long-standing assumptions within Western philosophy, this has to do with the narrowness or even parochialism of the Western tradition, rather than with preordained limits to the practice of philosophy itself. Studying Chinese philosophy is therefore not just an intensely interesting interpretive project, but also an enterprise with great significance for the ways we moderns—no matter which "we" one may find most apt—understand our world.

Over the years since I have continued to be stimulated by the work that Roger has done, alone or in collaboration, and I have consistently felt a significant kinship between his general goals and my own. Although he was never formally my teacher, I have learned a great deal from him. I have repeatedly found myself sympathetic to his positions on controversial issues like transcendence, creativity, relational selfhood, the processual world, and so on. It is with some puzzlement, therefore, that I have recently found myself unable to agree with his views about Confucian Role Ethics (hereafter, CRE). Even if I have sometimes not agreed with a given formulation of one of his other views, I have generally felt that I endorsed its spirit; so what is different about CRE? Or is CRE finally revealing to me an underlying difficulty that I have long missed?

This essay aims to uncover what is at stake in my concerns with CRE by examining a series of potential objections to Roger's general approach, most of them methodological. Even if there are nuances to be gleaned from thinking about these concerns, I will find Roger to be on solid ground. Next I examine the context in which CRE emerged as an interpretation of Confucian moral philosophy. I then argue in the essay's final section that we should resist the CRE interpretation primarily because of pragmatic issues, especially focusing on the positioning of Chinese philosophy vis-à-vis Western philosophy today. We are now at a point when, for reasons that have their roots in contemporary China as much as in the United States, bridging gaps and emphasizing common conversations are at least as important as keeping our distance and emphasizing our differences.

1. Rebutting Methodological Challenges

I begin with several key difficulties that any given aspect of Roger's interpretive-cum-philosophical project may face. One premise of my approach here is that together with important collaborators like David Hall and Henry Rosemont Jr., Roger has developed a broadly consistent method and that many of his specific findings follow from the broader picture. In this section I identify four central features of this approach, each of which may appear to be vulnerable to criticism. On balance, though, I find Roger's rebuttals to these criticisms to be quite convincing, which is precisely why our difference on CRE is intriguing.

Different Sameness

In many different ways throughout his writings, Roger has emphasized the differences between the assumptions and approaches of Chinese traditions, on the one hand, and those of Western traditions, on the other hand. Near the beginning of *Thinking Through Confucius*, we find:

> This present book is written in the belief . . . that in the enterprise of comparative philosophy, difference is more interesting than similarity. That is, the contrasting presuppositions of the Chinese and Anglo-European traditions are . . . a presently more fruitful subject for philosophical reflection than are the shared assumptions.[2]

We will have ample opportunity to reflect later in this essay on the significance of David and Roger's caveat that the difference-emphasizing approach is "presently more fruitful." For now, given that in all of Roger's work this stress on difference has continued, it seems fair to ask why difference is so important—and to examine whether, for all his talk of difference, Roger simply relies on a different form of sameness.

The basic worry about sameness is that too often, observations of cross-cultural similarity are the result of "inadvertently . . . foist[ing] upon an alternative culture a set of criteria drawn from our own tradition."[3] Starting from categories that are familiar to us, we unwittingly misconstrue the ideas of others by interpreting them as saying the same types of things as we do. Sometimes this process is more consciously chosen: in *Anticipating China*, David and Roger emphasize the role of what they call the "transcendental pretense," according to which the scientific rationality that emerged in the sixteenth century in Europe "names a universal norm for assessing the value of cultural activity everywhere in the planet."[4] Those in the grip of the transcendental pretense look for uniformities, patterns, and regularities—in other words, for "rational order."[5] Their goal is a single set of categories that can be applied everywhere. While David and Roger distinguish between "transcendental monism" and "transcendental pluralism," even the latter insists that there is a single best metatheory of philosophy, a single taxonomy into which all philosophical views across all cultures may be placed. In contrast, David and Roger favor an "interpretive pluralism" that emphasizes the unique, irreplaceable elements that are found in "aesthetic order."[6]

The history of cross-cultural encounters makes it clear that Roger's worry about misunderstanding stemming from hasty identification of similarities is well-founded. Later I will raise a concern about his suggestion that different philosophical discourses may be "incommensurable" with one another, but for now my attention is on a different issue. Let us accept that we often go awry by relying on familiar categories when interpreting others. My question is: do David and Roger do the very same thing? Notice that one of the ways in which they characterize their "interpretive pluralism" is as based in a "distinctly literary, historicist, 'Jamesian' form of pragmatism."[7] Their indebtedness to American pragmatism and to process philosophy are of course well-known and not at all hidden. In their earlier book, David and Roger acknowledge that they are relying on contemporary Western ideas in order to "sharpen [their] focus" on the ideas of Confucius.[8] Why is this not a straight-forward instance of the overfondness for sameness that they elsewhere reject?

The first thing to say in response is that no one can ever completely eschew the familiar and still hope to communicate. Some reliance on "sameness" is necessary. But this does not get us very far, since the more monistic approaches to comparative philosophy can also make this same move. David and Roger's main reply is to stress the value of unusual or esoteric elements of one's home tradition:

> Alterations in the character of Western culture have called attention to unusual elements in our own milieu that strongly resemble the ideological mainstream of the classical Chinese. To the extent that we are able to shift our perspective away from the dominant toward some of the more esoteric of the elements of our cultural milieu we are in a position to recognize and appreciate the distinctive significance of classical Chinese thought.[9]

I take it that the point here is not that esoteric elements of one's own culture are always central to understanding another culture's thought, but rather that: first, the presence of multiple strands or elements within our culture provides us with a wider range of starting points when trying to understand another; and second, in this particular case, the specific esoteric elements on which David and Roger focus are in fact helpful in understanding classical China.

Let me elaborate on each of these points. An excellent lens through which to view the first point is offered in Jeffrey Stout's *Ethics After Babel: The Languages of Morals and Their Discontents*. Stout argues that all creative ethical thinking involves what he calls "moral *bricolage*." *Bricolage* is originally employed by the Claude Lévi-Strauss to describe the so-called "primitive" mind: "drawing on a collection of assorted odds and ends available for use and kept on hand on the chance they might prove useful." Stout's insight is that we all engage in linguistic *bricolage* when working out what to make of a foreign other; Lévi-Strauss's distinction between the *bricoleur* and the ("modern") engineer is completely unhelpful.[10] Unlike some theorists who think of a language or culture as a monolithic set of concepts and values, Stout emphasizes the plurality of resources that we have at hand, some currently dominant, others esoteric or even all-but-forgotten. Stout argues that intellectual creativity is to "take the many parts of a complicated social and conceptual inheritance and stitch them into a pattern that meets the needs of the moment;" he says that it is no accident that our greatest moral thinkers—he cites Aquinas, Jefferson, and King—were as eclectic as they were.[11] Precisely the same is true, I would say, for those of us working on cross-cultural philosophy. We must be *bricoleurs*, open to all resources, very much including the unusual and esoteric.

The second point above was that Roger's *bricolage*, employing elements of pragmatism and process thought in order to understand classical Chinese philosophy, is in fact quite successful, but this is a contingent fact rather than a necessary one. For any given foreign tradition that we are trying to understand, it could turn out that we make more headway by relying (mainly) on mainstream or dominant ideas, rather than anything esoteric. It also may turn out that we need to leave our familiar categories even further behind than do nondominant contemporary views like pragmatism. For example, Brook Ziporyn makes a powerful argument that Roger is still too beholden to the traditional Western distinction between realist and nominalist (and between objective and subjective) to fully grasp the central role that "coherence" plays in Chinese thinking.[12] However we adjudicate that particular dispute, it clearly could be correct, and so there is nothing magical about embracing a given set of esoteric terms. Indeed, the final point to make for now is that Roger's pragmatism quite explicitly avoids prejudging what counts as "success" in a cross-cultural encounter. Understanding will almost always be a desideratum, but rarely will purely intellectual, de-contextualized understanding be the only thing that matters. I will return to this point below.

Counterexamples

Broad claims of the kind that we find throughout Roger's work on Chinese thought generally live in fear of one of the basic weapons in philosophical argumentation, the counterexample. In light of these types of criticisms, it is striking to hear David and Roger assert that "comparativists will be prevented from making sense of a culture if they do not diligently avoid the Fallacy of the Counterexample."[13] They continue, asserting that generalizations about cultures are often vindicated rather than falsified by the "resort to counterexamples" because even the successful search for counterexamples can be an indication of precisely how dominant a given overall view is within the culture. David and Roger therefore reject the idea that the "mere presence" of a given idea or doctrine has real significance, insofar as their goal is to map the "cultural determinants" of classical China. Critics might worry, though, that what is really happening is that they are insulating their grand theory against any evidence that might falsify it. Is the Fallacy of the Counterexample itself fallacious?

I believe that we should endorse Roger's position here, albeit with one significant caveat. We should endorse it because cultures, traditions, and discourses are complex, contested, and often made up of competing elements that we can call, following David and Roger, dominant and recessive. If an interpretive theory tells us that the dominant cultural problematique is X, then pointing out that someone says "not-X" is not a problem for that theory unless one can show that not-X is itself a central concern. To put this in less abstract terms, consider the view that early Chinese conceptions of knowing center on the ability to understand something and make relevant distinctions, rather than on propositional belief. As Chris Fraser summarizes:

> Perhaps the most frequent use of the word *zhi* (know) in early Chinese texts is in contexts in which it is best interpreted as "knowing-of" or "knowing-about," a sort of recognition, familiarity, or understanding. A second common use is to mean roughly "know-to" or "know-how-to," referring to a kind of competence or ability. Occasionally, *zhi* is used in contexts in which it is interpretable as "knowing that" and seems to refer to propositional knowledge.[14]

What are we to make of Fraser's concession that *zhi* sometimes seems to mean "knowing that"? Is this a counterexample to the interpretive theory he expresses here? No, probably not, because these uses can probably be explained as either: (1) a second, recessive strand of thought that competed with the dominant view, or (2) a special type of one or the other more general types. If either of these explanations is successful, then we are not faced with a genuine counterexample.

The caveat that I would like to register is related to the word "if" in the previous sentence. It must be the case that apparently countervailing evidence is taken seriously and has the potential to have an effect on the overall theory. As we have learned from Thomas Kuhn and others, large-scale theories are rarely subject to straight-forward tests of falsifiability. But by examining the ways in which a theory handles anomalies, and comparing this with the ways that alternative theories do so, we can do our best to judge whether a given explanation is "successful." As Roger (the pragmatist) will certainly agree, these judgments of success will be relative to our current purposes, but those purposes themselves will adapt over time. A theory that is judged successful at one point may be judged less successful at another.

The Goal(s) of Comparative Philosophy

In *Anticipating China*, David and Roger write, "Our ultimate purpose is to create a context within which meaningful comparisons of Chinese and Western culture may be made."[15] I am troubled by this formulation of their goal, as it suggests to me an ultimately passive outcome, and implies that the most we can hope to accomplish is to discover how one thing (Chinese culture) relates to one other thing (Western culture). Notwithstanding its name, "comparative philosophy" should not be, in my view, merely about comparison. This is not to trivialize the amount of work that is necessary to arrive at meaningful comparisons, but to insist that the fruits of such labors should provoke active transformations among all concerned. In fact, on closer examination of David's and Roger's position I think we can see that they are largely in agreement with me, even if their collaborative project focuses more on the comparative stage than on the transformative one.

The most obvious reason for taking a second look at what David and Roger might mean in the sentence quoted above is that in *Thinking Through Confucius* they say the following:

> One main consideration we are attempting to defend through this work is that the differences of emphasis that exist between the rich and diverse fabrics of Confucian and Anglo-European cultures are not merely meant to be charted or celebrated in some dispassionate manner. On the contrary, we hold that it is precisely the recognition of significant differences that provides an opportunity for mutual enrichment by suggesting alternate responses to problems that resist satisfactory resolution within a single culture.[16]

This both suggests that cultures are not single, unified entities but instead are "rich and diverse fabrics," and also points directly toward transformative outcomes. Indeed, the idea of "mutual enrichment" here sounds quite a bit like what I have come to call rooted global philosophy: that is, taking one's own philosophical tradition as a point of departure, but being open to stimulus from other philosophical frameworks as one strives to make progress (as progress is measured from one's own, current vantage point). So perhaps the reference to "meaningful comparison" from *Anticipating China* really means "mutual transformation," and there is no problem?

Perhaps. One reason for hesitation is David and Roger's skepticism about what they call "real philosophical progress" emerging out of "dialectical engagement among alternative theories which aim at getting at the truth."[17] To be sure, there are notions of "progress"—for example, as assuming a universal and/or linear convergence on a single set of truths—that we can well do without, but we do not have to conceive of progress as "progress-toward" a specific end. Instead, we can think of "progress-from": an improvement as compared to our own previous state. The determination that a given change is an improvement, resting as it does on the standards to which we are currently committed, is itself defeasible. In situations of considerable complexity, it will also often be at least somewhat unclear whether a given change is an all-things-considered improvement. Be this as it may, I see no reason why philosophers should be barred from aspiring to precisely this kind of progress. Given that David and Roger imagine that their work may facilitate the discovery of "alternate responses to problems that resist satisfactory resolution within a single culture"—alternate responses which are, I presume, more "satisfactory"—then it seems that they, too, endorse the aspiration for this kind of progress. Indeed, in the Prologue to *Thinking from the Han*, they explicitly endorse an approach to cross-tradition encounters according to which, "traditions as historical narratives [can] . . . at a practical, concrete level, intersect and even overlap. At this level, comparisons can be formulated and understood that are productive in identifying alternatives to familiar modes of expression and action."[18] Contrary to the sense one sometimes gets from their talk of "aestheticism" and sometimes even "incommensurability," in short, they very much endorse the idea that actual encounters between traditions can lead to positive, transformative effects.[19]

Our Practical Predicament

Writing in 1987, David and Roger say that "[it] is abundantly clear from the situation of Chinese philosophy in Western institutions of learning, [that] the sort of commonality that eventually will allow thinkers to engage in important conversations grounded in shared values and concerns is yet to be realized between Chinese and Western societies."[20] Based on this evaluation of the practical situation—that is, the pragmatic needs of the moment—they proceed with their project of stressing the differences between mainstream Chinese philosophy and mainstream Western philosophy. I have no disagreements with their assessment. However, as a way of clearing space for the argument I will make in section 3, let me note three limitations of David and Roger's characterization of the predicament we face. First, of course, things might have changed in Western institutions of learning, or in Western culture more generally, over the course of three decades. Second, given what we have seen so far it is not clear to me why transformative cross-tradition encounters must be "grounded in shared values and concerns." There must be some level of mutual understanding, but a grounding in shared values may be setting the bar too high. Third, it is striking that David and Roger refer only to the situation in the West. To be fair, they do make a few references to contemporary China (such as questioning how deep the influence of Marx really goes[21]) and they make a point of saying that they are writing for Sinophone as well as Anglophone audiences (the former can access the books in Chinese translations). Over his career, Roger is among the top North America-based scholars in terms of his efforts to reach audiences in China and to be open to what he can learn from them, in turn. So my point is not that he and David were ignoring China, but rather to emphasize that as "we" (however defined) consider "our" current practical situation, we may well want to take seriously the pragmatic effects that our scholarly choices will have in China as well as elsewhere.

2. The Emergence of Confucian Role Ethics

I now turn to a summary of the discourse context into which Roger and Henry Rosemont Jr., intervened with their articulation of CRE, and an overview of CRE itself. Because of the roles played in both Roger's and my arguments by assessments of the pragmatic impact of comparative philosophy, it makes sense to go into some detail on how we have reached the present moment.[22]

Anglo-European Moral Philosophy and the Rise of Virtue Ethics

In the mid-twentieth century, moral theory (like the era's psychology) was dominated by questions related to behavior and "right action." The key question was "what should one do?"; the key notions were individual duty, liberty, and so on. In 1958, Elizabeth Anscombe's scathing essay "Modern Moral Philosophy" questioned the foundations of this enterprise, arguing that it was based on an abandoned conception of divine moral law and on an inadequate approach to psychology.[23] These general lines of critique were reemphasized by Iris Murdoch a decade later when she argued that matters of inner agency—such as motivation and perceptiveness—were at least as important to morality as were our actions.[24] A good example of mainstream moral philosophy's reaction to these challenges is John Rawls's 1971 *A Theory of Justice*.[25] On the one hand, Rawls gives considerable attention in the later sections of his opus to motivation, moral education, and psychology. On the other hand, such issues only penetrate to a limited degree into his conception of morality. His influential taxonomy of morality is still based on the idea of right action, and is divided into "teleology" (i.e., those theories that determine the moral action through the maximization of some "end") and "deontology" (i.e., those theories for which moral rightness is defined independently from the goodness of our ends). This closely matches the slightly earlier dualism proposed by John Silber, according to whom teleological moral theories were "homogeneous" because they derived the moral good from the non-moral good, and deontological moral theories were "heterogeneous" since they viewed moral and non-moral goodness as fundamentally distinct.[26]

Through the 1970s and into the 1980s, the centrality of right action and the exhaustive dichotomy between teleological and deontological theories continued to characterize moral philosophy. The volume of critics' voices was rising, however. Alasdair MacIntyre's influential 1981 book *After Virtue* argued that the biggest difference among moral theories was actually between those, like Aristotle's, that were committed to a substantive end (such as nobility or virtue), and those that were not. On this account, utilitarianism had more in common with deontology than either did with Aristotle, despite the fact that on Rawls's account, both Aristotelianism and utilitarianism had been versions of teleology.[27] As more and more attention started to be paid to virtuous character as an end, Gary Watson offered another critique of Rawls, arguing in considerable detail for a threefold typology of "teleological/maximizing" or "ethics of outcome"; "teleological/non-consequentialist" or "ethics of virtue"; and "deontological" or "ethics of requirement."[28] Over the last two decades, MacIntyre's and Watson's efforts to define the territory of virtue ethics have been complemented by those working to articulate more clearly what "virtue" or "character" is, as well as some attempts to spell out full-fledged systems of virtue ethics. Rosalind Hursthouse's *On Virtue Ethics* marked a new level of confidence on the part of virtue ethicists; in the 2000s, we can say that virtue ethics was increasingly firmly ensconced in the now-enlarged field of Anglophone moral philosophy.[29] In addition, one of the critical developments in virtue ethics from the 2000s to the present has been its pluralization. Aristotle had been the touchstone for almost all prior writers in the field (Murdoch being a significant exception), but now it is widely accepted that many philosophers in the Western canon can be read as virtue ethicists, including not just Stoics and medievals, but also moderns such as Hume and Nietzsche.

The recent expansion of the scope of virtue ethics has by no means led to an end to the controversy over the category of "virtue ethics," though; a number of theorists have emphasized the degree to which Kantianism and some forms of consequentialism can accommodate a significant role for virtue and inner psychology, and some have argued on this basis that the category of "virtue ethics" is in the end unnecessary or even incoherent. In response, it has become common to distinguish between "virtue theory," which is the portion of a moral theory dealing with issues like virtue (no matter how peripheral it might be to the overall theory), and "virtue ethics," which is (at least purportedly) a distinctive category of moral theory itself.[30] For our purposes, one of the more interesting kinds of resistance to the category of virtue ethics comes from Martha Nussbaum, herself often identified as a virtue ethicist. To the contrary, she argues that virtue ethics is a "misleading category" because the ideas really shared by all so-called virtue ethicists are too few to support an independent category, and are in fact also shared by some non-virtue-ethical theories. She argues that it is more perspicuous to divide the purported virtue ethicists into two clusters, those who are pro-reason and anti-utilitarian, and those who are pro-sentiment and anti-Kantian; she places herself in the former group.[31] The problem with such a taxonomy is that while it might be true to the genealogy of current views, it defines its categories around existing approaches in Western philosophy, and is thus necessarily Eurocentric. It does not even make sense to ask whether Confucius is an anti-Kantian, nor are we likely to find very many Chinese philosophers who are "pro-reason" in Nussbaum's sense—at least, if anything like Roger's core argument about different conceptions of order is correct.

Despite Eurocentric thinking like Nussbaum's, the idea that Confucian ethics are centrally concerned with virtue—and perhaps should be characterized as forms of virtue ethics—gradually began to find some traction in U.S. academia.[32] The idea of virtue in the *Analects* and, especially, the *Mencius* loomed large in a series of important lectures given by David Nivison at Stanford in the early 1980s, though the lectures were not published until 1996.[33] Another important step was the publication in 1990 of *Mencius and Aquinas* by Nivison's colleague at Stanford, Lee Yearley. Yearley's book shows the fruits that can come from a detailed, sophisticated reflection on the idea of virtue in an early Confucian work.[34] With the nurturance of Nivison and Yearley, Stanford proved fertile ground for virtue-ethical readings of Confucianism. The writings of Philip J. Ivanhoe, Stephen Wilson, Edward Slingerland, Bryan Van Norden, and Eric Hutton—all with PhDs from Stanford—over the course of the 1990s and early 2000s increasingly come to make explicit arguments that early Confucianism should be interpreted through the lens of virtue ethics.[35] The year 2007 is a watershed year for Anglophone virtue-ethical readings of Confucianism, with three books published that defend such a thesis.[36] In the last few years, finally, scholars of Confucianism have begun explicitly engaging with contemporary developments in virtue ethics.[37]

Aristotle has loomed large in many of the virtue-ethical approaches to Confucianism that I have reviewed so far, both directly and *via* MacIntyre's version of contemporary Aristotelianism. Still, it is important not to conflate virtue ethics with Aristotle, and in this section's final paragraph, I mention some ways in which current thinkers have examined Confucianism in light of certain non-Aristotelian approaches to virtue ethics. First, though, it makes sense to look at the most explicitly Aristotelian approaches of all. Two books came out in 2007 arguing for significant similarities between Aristotle and Confucius; according to both authors—Jiyuan Yu and May Sim—we should interpret the *Analects* as a work of virtue ethics.[38] Both books are complex and have occasioned considerable debate; in the context of the present essay, it is only possible to touch on certain key themes. In both books, the conclusion that early Confucianism offers a virtue ethics is more the outcome of the larger comparison than a specific theme: they do not argue against alternative (Kantian or other) interpretations, but rather present considerable evidence that key Aristotelian ideas have correlates in Confucius, and *vice versa*. Both Sim and Yu hold that while Confucius and Aristotle share a great deal, each one also has some insights from which the other can learn, and the juxtaposition reveals certain lacunae in the thought of each. For example, according to Sim, there is a striking difference between the role of the individual, metaphysical soul in Aristotle's account, and the pure, role-based relationality she finds in Confucius. She suggests that both approaches leave something to be desired: Aristotle lacks the capacity to handle the thick relationality that his ethics in fact requires, while Confucius needs some independent substrate to anchor moral norms that would allow criticism of existing role relationships.[39] For his part, Yu sees less difference on this score. He argues that Aristotelian *eudaimonia* and Confucian *dao* are quite analogous to one another, and that Aristotle's understanding of humans as "political animals" is tantamount to Confucius's emphasis on the relational nature of the self.[40] I will return to this issue below, because the question of relationality turns out to be crucial to Roger and Henry's argument that Confucianism presents a role ethics rather than a virtue ethics.

The large majority of the analyses and arguments that I have canvassed so far take Aristotle, or at least contemporary developments of Aristotelianism, as their point of departure for understanding virtue ethics. It is vital to recognize that virtue ethics need not be tied so tightly to Aristotle's distinctive approach. Some of the most creative developments within Western virtue ethics over the last decade have been decidedly non-Aristotelian. In order to create the most room for a juxtaposition of Confucianism and virtue ethics to spark insightful interpretation and fruitful dialogue, we would be wise to think broadly about what virtue ethics can encompass. Indeed, there are already signs that Confucianism may fit better into an expanded understanding of virtue ethics. Among Chinese scholars, Chen Lai and Wong Wai-ying are notable for arguing that Confucian ethics can be constructively viewed as virtue ethics only so long as we recognize the important differences between Confucian ethics and the theories of Aristotle: Confucian ethics has its own distinctive concepts and emphases, from which Western virtue ethics may well want to learn.[41] For their part, American philosophers have also been looking for broader models. Philip J. Ivanhoe has suggested that in Western traditions we see both "virtue ethics of flourishing" and "virtue ethics of sentiments," and has then gone on to argue that representative Confucian thinkers actually cross-cut these two categories, implying that virtue ethics cannot be satisfactorily understood simply in terms of extant Western models.[42] In recent work, Amy Olberding has drawn on yet another emerging strand of Western virtue ethics, the "exemplarism" of Linda Zagzebski, to help us understand the *Analects* in particular.[43] It is evident that no one model is dominant, but this is probably as it should be; in the words of Christine Swanton, virtue ethics is a "genus" that contains many particular species.[44]

Confucian Role Ethics

For Roger and Henry, "Confucian Role Ethics" is simply a name meant to refer to the moral and religious vision that they find in early Confucianism. In the Preface to his 2011 book on Confucian role ethics, Roger notes that Henry began developing the idea of Confucian role ethics as early as a 1991 essay that drew a contrast between the "rights-bearing individuals" of Western moral theories and the "role-bearing persons" on Confucian ethics.[45] As far as I know, though, Roger and Henry only began using the term "Role Ethics" in print in 2009.[46] At the heart of Confucian role ethics is "a specific vision of human beings as relational persons constituted by the roles they live rather than as individual selves."[47] The roles that Roger and Henry have in mind are, in the first instance, family-based: son, daughter, mother, older sibling, grandfather, and so on. Traditional Confucian roles of ruler, subject, husband, wife, minister, and friend fill out the picture. Their point is not that these roles themselves are distinctively Confucian, but rather that the idea of humans as fundamentally constituted by our on-going living in roles ramifies throughout Confucian thinking in a way that renders it dramatically different from Greek or contemporary Western alternatives.

Their argument in favor of a role-ethical interpretation of early Confucianism depends on two important premises. The first is a wide-ranging interpretation of early Confucian thinking that emphasizes its anti-foundational, anti-essentialist, and processual character; part of the argument for this reading can be found in their individual and collective writings on CRE, but much of the background has been laid in the earlier scholarship that I have discussed above. The second premise is that even though Confucian role ethics comes closer to virtue ethics than to Kantianism or consequentialism, relying on virtue-ethical vocabulary to understand Confucianism "forces the Master and his followers more into the mold of Western philosophical discourse than they ought to be placed . . . and hence makes it difficult to see the Confucian vision as a genuine *alternative* to those with which we are most familiar."[48] This claim should be familiar, given what we saw in section 1. As Roger and

Henry see it, Confucian ethics is both similar and different from Western ethics, and they are choosing to emphasize the differences. This is a strategic choice, reflecting not just the degree of difference but also our contemporary situation in which differences with dominant Western frameworks tend to be downplayed. Roger and Henry note several instances in which, in the course of their comparisons of Aristotle and Confucius, Sim and Yu stress what seems to be lacking, missing, absent, or ignored in Confucian ethics, when seen in the light of Aristotle.[49] To be fair, both Sim and Yu announce that their projects are to see what each of their subjects can learn from the other, and both Sim and Yu note problems for Aristotle, including that his "insistent individualism . . . fails to account for the thick relations his own theory requires,"[50] and that his overly strong distinction between virtue and activity "inappropriately reduces the value of having virtue."[51] I will not try to settle here whether Sim or Yu in fact gives us problematic comparisons, but the fact surely remains that comparative philosophy overall has been characterized by what Kwong-loi Shun has called an "asymmetry" between Western and Chinese categories, and it is with this in mind that Roger and Henry "want to resist tailoring what we take to be a distinctively Confucian role ethics into a familiar category of Western ethical theory."[52]

3. An Amesian Defense of Virtue Ethics

In section 1, I reviewed four types of concerns that might be expressed about Roger's general argumentative strategy, and in section 2 examined some of the contexts out of which contemporary Western virtue ethics, virtue ethical interpretations of Confucianism, and CRE have emerged. It is now time to ask why I am so resistant to CRE, which I will do by returning to each of the topics from section 1 with virtue ethics and CRE in mind. My basic argument is that Roger's own methodological commitments should incline him toward virtue ethics, rather than insisting on a *sui generis* category like CRE.

Sameness Revisited

A summary of Roger's reaction to the current prevalence of virtue-ethical interpretations of Confucianism might run something like this: as English-language efforts to interpret Confucian ethics in philosophical terms emerged in the 1980s and 1990s, scholars helped themselves to the Western language of virtue in order to understand the Chinese texts, thus reenacting the same error that Western analysts have been making ever since the Jesuits first encountered what they labeled as "Confucianism" in the sixteenth century.

In contrast to this reliance on sameness, Roger and Henry have advocated the CRE interpretation in order to stress difference.

There is certainly some degree of accuracy in this account. However, we might note two further facts. First of all, as I mentioned above, Anglo-American moral philosophy has been dominated for the last century by variations on two schools of thought: Kantian deontology and the heirs of British utilitarianism. It is only quite recently that what we now are calling "virtue ethics" has started to be taken seriously again. Second, over the last century in the Sinophone world, the dominant philosophical interpretation of Confucian ethics has been based on Kantian deontology. I will not rehearse the history here, but from the early twentieth century down to the present day, the mainstream position in Chinese scholarship is that Confucianism is a form of autonomous, duty-based ethics.[53] Based on these two facts, it is possible to see the idea of Confucianism as virtue ethics in a different light: not as the imposition of hegemonic Western categories, but rather as exploring an interpretation based on a minority—even "esoteric"—position within Western thought. To draw on virtue ethics would then be to use a "different sameness" in order to emphasize broad East-West differences, much as David and Roger did by using ideas from pragmatism to stress differences between mainstream Chinese and Anglo-European assumptions. This is all the more attractive as a way of understanding the role of virtue ethics if we move away from an exclusively Anglophone context and enter a discourse that attempts to bridge Chinese and English scholarship: as I have said, virtue ethical readings of Confucianism are rare, even heretical, in most Chinese-language contexts today.[54]

So from a broader perspective, virtue ethics might be just the stance we need to adopt in order to see Confucian moral thought in its true distinctiveness. A related reason why Roger should find virtue ethics appealing is that powerful arguments have been made to the effect that the ethical thought of Dewey and other American philosophers is itself a form of virtue ethics.[55] I will not attempt to summarize or adjudicate these claims here, but this is a good place to reiterate the crucial idea that the contemporary understanding of virtue ethics is not confined to the frameworks of Aristotle. Even without taking Confucianism into account, virtue ethics has been rapidly diversifying. Admittedly, there are on-going debates about how to understand the scope of virtue ethics and whether seemingly related views like "care ethics" should also be understood as part of a single genus. It is too soon to judge how these debates will work themselves out, but in my view the value of an inclusive "virtue ethics" is evident, not least because of the ways it allows for substantive conversations across Eastern and Western traditions, as I will go on to emphasize here.

One final point before moving on: it is worth noting how close Roger already comes to something that we can easily call virtue ethics. In one place where he discusses *de* (which is often translated as "virtue"; he renders it "excelling morally"), Roger says:

> Each of these [terms that make up the vocabulary of Confucian role ethics] is a perspective on the same event, and functions to highlight a particular phase or dimension in achieving the consummate life. There is a sense in which *de* is used as the more general term for expressing the cumulative outcome of coordinating the shared experience effectively—both the achieved quality of the conduct of the particular person and the achieved *ethos* of the collective culture. Hence, the other terms we have explored above are all implicated in excelling morally (*de*).[56]

Roger makes it clear elsewhere that his concern with the term "virtue" is with its implication that virtues are reified, metaphysically independent things, rather than as aspects of our complex, socially articulated experience. Instead, he insists that "whatever we call virtue . . . is nothing more or less than a vibrant, situated, practical, and productive virtuosity."[57] Seen in this light, I wonder whether his ideas are really, at bottom, about roles. When we foreground virtuosity and interdependent flourishing instead, it starts to sound like such a "virtuosity ethics" has things to teach to, and things to learn from, virtue ethics—and indeed, that they may ultimately be two species of the same genus.

Counterexamples

As discussed above, David and Roger encourage us to avoid the Fallacy of the Counterexample. If readers are willing to grant that virtue ethics today is much broader than merely about Aristotle, then one of the core arguments used to buttress CRE—namely, that it is fundamentally different from Aristotle—starts to look like an over-reliance on a single counterexample. We can readily grant the difference with Aristotle but reply that Aristotle is only one strand of virtue ethics: that CRE is "not-Aristotle" does not mean that it is "not-virtue ethics." Henry and Roger, in other words, have themselves committed the Fallacy by over-emphasizing a single counterexample. This is not to say that any Western examples of virtue ethics is exactly like any specific instance of Confucian ethics: Cicero, Hume, Dewey, and Swanton all have certain areas where there are strong resonances with particular Confucian positions and other areas in which the differences are apparent, and the same can be said for Aristotle. That there are significant differences with Aristotle is not enough to end the conversation.[58]

The Present State of (Comparative) Philosophy, East and West

In addressing the pragmatic challenges faced by Chinese and Anglo-European philosophers today, I combine the final two issues from section 1. There, we saw that Roger and I are in general agreement that comparative philosophy aims at positive, transformative effects on participating traditions of thought. I also agreed that the situation in 1987 was not terribly conducive to constructive conversations across traditions, and thus that David and Roger's stress on differences—on striving for an account of early Chinese philosophy that better captured its distinctive concerns than did then-current interpretations—was very valuable. Here, I argue that the pragmatic situation is significantly different today, both in the United States and in China.

To begin with, there is more openness to non-Western philosophy as philosophy, with things to teach "us," in the American philosophical world than was the case three decades ago. This can be seen in several ways. Some significant pan-philosophical institutions now routinely include material on Chinese and other "non-Western" traditions: examples include all three major encyclopedias of philosophy, the most active online philosophical book review site, the major volunteer-run online site indexing philosophical publications, and the only proprietary bibliographical database on philosophy.[59] Panels, conferences, and anthologies have put specialists in Western and non-Western traditions into conversation around particular topics. And there have been instances of "mainstream" philosophical journals publishing articles in which non-Western traditions are major foci or major sources of inspiration. Admittedly, there are other ways in which things have not changed very much: most notably, it is still the case that very few graduate programs in philosophy have a specialist in any form of non-Western philosophy. But if our question is whether it is more likely now, than thirty years ago, that challenges arising from non-Western traditions will be taken seriously, the answer is certainly affirmative.

If this modest change in the United States were the only factor to be considered, my case for the pragmatic importance of viewing Confucian ethics as virtue ethics would be fairly weak. Consider, however, the changes that have taken place in China. Certainly, China's traditions are much more discussed and much more carefully studied in China today. (When I was traveling as a student on a train in China in 1986 and told a fellow traveler that I was interested in Chinese philosophy, his reply was "Oh, you mean Marxism and Leninism?") But some of the main ways that they are being framed is very worrying. A good example of the potential problems is the growth of *Guoxue*, or National Studies. The National Studies paradigm encourages Chinese to think of their traditions as a holistic body of knowledge and values, to be studied and revered but not criticized, relevant in the first instance only to Chinese.[60] The increasing numbers of Schools and Institutes of National Studies fit well with the current government-supported efforts to promote a relativist resistance to "universal values" (generally seen as exclusively Western). Instead of seeing Confucian (and other Chinese traditional) values as themselves universal—that is, as making claims on all people, Chinese and otherwise—the anti-universal values discourse suggests that Confucianism is a "cultural resource" or (in the view of some) a "religion" relevant only to Chinese.[61] Insofar as these trends are motivated by a desire to avoid forcing Chinese traditions into preexisting (and perhaps problematic) Western molds, it is easy to sympathize. But rather than withdrawing from global conversations, a better answer is challenging the sufficiency of potentially problematic Western frameworks, such as a conception of philosophy as purely professional, of little or no relevance to daily life.

A central reason why withdrawal from conversation is unsatisfactory is that it discourages critical engagement with Chinese traditions. Some contemporary Chinese philosophers have indeed recognized that for Confucianism to be relevant today, it must also be vulnerable to critique and open to change. Writing in 2001, here is Zheng Jiadong:

> As an ancient spiritual tradition, Confucianism is facing a more serious test than it has ever before encountered. This test will not be resolved by shouting stirring slogans about how this next century will be the "Asian Century" or the "Confucian Century." From another perspective, though, this kind of test can at the same time provide contemporary Confucianism with a favorable opportunity for self-transformation and development. A simultaneous test and opportunity, a crisis and a turning point: this is the fundamental reality that Confucianism today must face.[62]

While Prof. Zheng's open-minded attitude is shared by some, the National Studies movement pushes in the other direction. My chief concern about CRE is that at this point, emphasizing the uniqueness of Confucian ethics has the effect of resisting efforts to pursue piecemeal, critical dialogue. It plays into the hands of the relativism represented by National Studies.

The form of universalism that I favor—open-ended and open-minded critical conversations aimed at improving one's own values and institutions—does not suffer from the "transcendental pretense" about which Roger is concerned. I make no assumption that we will eventually converge on a single set of values or concepts. I readily grant that the dangers about which Roger is concerned are real and must be avoided. But we have reached a point at which the dangers of encouraging both West and East to think of their philosophies as fundamentally different are also increasingly pressing. We should search for ways to keep differences in mind even while we engage in constructive conversations. One way to do this is to find ways to undermine the idea that the West is the sole source of worthwhile methodologies and metatheories, a project to which Roger is one of the important contributors.[63] If we are cautious, we can build on the foundation that Roger has established in order to provoke more pluralistic and more productive philosophical conversations both at home and abroad.

Notes

1. My thanks to Max Fong for his assistance preparing this essay and for discussion about its contents, and to Jim Behuniak for his helpful comments.
2. David Hall and Roger T. Ames, *Thinking Through Confucius* (Albany: State University of New York Press, 1987), 5.
3. Ibid.
4. David Hall and Roger T. Ames, *Anticipating China* (Albany: State University of New York Press, 1995), xiv.
5. Ibid., 116.
6. Ibid., 143f.
7. Ibid., 144.
8. Hall and Ames, *Thinking Through Confucius*, 7.
9. Ibid.
10. Jeffery Stout, *Ethics After Babel* (Boston: Beacon Press, 1988), 74.
11. Ibid., 292.
12. Brook Ziporyn, *Beyond Oneness and Difference: Li and Coherence in Chinese Buddhist Thought and its Antecedents* (Albany: State University of New York Press, 2013), 42.
13. Hall and Ames, *Anticipating China*, xv.
14. Chris Fraser, "Knowledge and Error in Early Chinese Thought," *Dao: A Journal of Comparative Philosophy* 10 (2011), 131n9.
15. Hall and Ames, *Anticipating China*, 111.
16. Hall and Ames, *Thinking Through Confucius*, 5.
17. Hall and Ames, *Anticipating China*, 152.
18. David Hall and Roger T. Ames, *Thinking from the Han* (Albany: State University of New York Press, 1998), xv.
19. David and Roger say that the "pragmatist approach . . . accedes to the incommensurability of discourses whenever there is a lack of common conventions to

which all parties to a dispute appeal in the attempt to adjudicate conflict." They do not particularly emphasize incommensurability, though, and reject the cogency of claims that radical translation can fail. Hall and Ames, *Anticipating China*, 153–54 and 174–75.

20. Hall and Ames, *Thinking Through Confucius*, 5.

21. Hall and Ames, *Anticipating China*, xv.

22. The next few paragraphs are substantially drawn from Stephen C. Angle, "The Analects and Moral Theory," in *Dao Companion to the Analects*, ed. Amy Olberding (New York: Springer, 2013): 225–57.

23. Elizabeth Anscombe, "Modern Moral Philosophy," *Philosophy* 33:124 (1958), 1–19.

24. Iris Murdoch, "The Idea of Perfection," in *The Sovereignty of the Good* (New York: Routledge, 1970), 1–45.

25. John Rawls, *A Theory of Justice* (Cambridge, MA: Harvard University Press, 1971).

26. Silber develops this idea in a variety of articles; see, for example, John Silber, "The Copernican revolution in ethics: The good reexamined," in *Kant: A Collection of Critical Essays*, ed. Robert Paul Wolff (Notre Dame: University of Notre Dame Press, 1959–60). Lee Ming-huei notes that a similar distinction is made in German moral discourse between "*Gesinnungsethik*" and "*Erfolgsethik*" in Lee Ming-huei, "Confucianism, Kant, and Virtue Ethics," in *Virtue Ethics and Confucianism*, ed. Stephen Angle and Michael Slote (New York: Routledge, 2013), 47–55.

27. Both on this specific point, and more generally concerning the topic of this section, I have found Wang Yunping, "Are Early Confucians Consequentialists?" *Asian Philosophy* 15 (2005): 19–34 to be very helpful.

28. Gary Watson, "On the Primacy of Character," in *Identity, Character, and Morality*, ed. Owen Flanagan, and Amelie Rorty (Cambridge, MA: MIT Press, 1990) 449–70.

29. Representative works include Rosalind Hursthouse, *On Virtue Ethics* (Oxford: Oxford University Press, 1999), Michael Slote, *Morals from Motives* (Oxford: Oxford University Press, 2001), Christine Swanton, *Virtue Ethics: A Pluralistic View* (Oxford: Oxford University Press, 2003), and Lisa Tessman, *Burdened Virtues: Virtue Ethics for Liberatory Struggles* (Oxford: Oxford University Press, 2005).

30. See Julia Driver, "The Virtues and Human Nature," in *How Should One Live? Essays on the Virtues*, ed. Roger Crisp (Oxford: Oxford University Press, 1996), 111–29. Various other terms are used to mark roughly the same distinction. Van Norden prefers to speak of a spectrum from moderate to "radical" virtue ethics in Bryan Van Norden, *Virtue Ethics and Consequentialism in Early Chinese Philosophy* (New York: Cambridge University Press, 2007). Adams refers to "the ethics of character as an important department of ethical theory" in Robert Merrihew Adams, *A Theory of Virtue: Excellence in Being for the Good* (Oxford: Oxford University Press, 2006).

31. Martha Nussbaum, "Virtue Ethics: A Misleading Category?" *The Journal of Ethics* 3:3 (1999), 163–201.

32. Although it has had little direct effect on English-language interpretations of Confucianism, it is worth noting that starting in the early 1990s, influenced by their

Catholic/Aristotelian training and stimulated by Alasdair MacIntyre's *After Virtue*, some Taiwanese scholars began arguing against the deontological readings of early Confucianism that were dominant in Taiwan, and in favor of a virtue-ethical interpretation. Vincent Shen (Shen Qingsong) is a good representative of this movement. See Vincent Qingsong Shen, "沈清松, "德行伦理学与儒家伦理思想的现代意义 [Virtue Ethics and the Modern Significance of Confucian Ethical Thought]," in 沈清松自选集 [*Vincent Shen's Self-Selected Works*] (Jinan: Shandong jiaoyu chubanshe, 2004), 315-45. For further discussion, see Angle, "The *Analects* and Moral Theory."

33. See David Nivison, "'Virtue' in Bone and Bronze," in *The ways of Confucianism: Chinese philosophy*, ed. Bryan Van Norden (Le Salle, IL: Open Court, 1996), 17-30, and David Nivison, "The Paradox of "Virtue," in *The Ways of Confucianism: Investigations in Chinese Philosophy* (Le Salle, IL: Open Court, 1996), 31-44.

34. As can be seen from his glowing back-cover endorsement, Alasdair MacIntyre was also clearly aware of the book. This is perhaps an apt moment to mention MacIntyre's fairly extensive engagement with Confucian ethics—as seen in Alasdair MacIntyre, "Incommensurability, Truth, and the Conversation Between Confucians and Aristotelians About the Virtues," in *Culture and Modernity*, ed. Eliot Deutsch (Honolulu: University of Hawai`i Press, 1991); Alasdair MacIntyre "Once More on Confucian and Aristotelian Conceptions of the Virtues: A Response to Professor Wan," in *Chinese Philosophy in an Era of Globalization*, ed. Robin R. Wang (Albany: State University of New York Press, 2004), 151-62; and Alasdair MacIntyre, "Questions for Confucians," in *Confucian Ethics: A Comparative Study of Self-Autonomy, and Community*, ed. Kwong-loi Shun, and David B. Wong (New York: Cambridge University Press, 2004), 203-18.

35. This is more implicit than explicit in Ivanhoe's dissertation (published as Philip Ivanhoe, *Ethics in the Confucian Tradition: The Thought of Mencius and Wang Yangming* (Atlanta, GA: Scholar's Press, 1990)), though it is explicit in that work's revised second edition: Philip Ivanhoe, *Ethics in the Confucian Tradition: The Thought of Mencius and Wang Yangming*, 2nd ed. (Indianapolis, IN: Hackett, 2002): ix, 2n5, 9. The theme of virtue is also central in Philip Ivanhoe, *Confucian Moral Self Cultivation*, 2nd ed. (Indianapolis: Hackett, 2000), the first edition of which was published in 1993. See also Stephen Wilson, "Conformity, Individuality, and the Nature of Virtue: A Classical Confucian Contribution to Contemporary Ethical Reflection," in *Confucius and the Analects: New Essays*, ed. Bryan W. Van Norden (Oxford: Oxford University Press, 2002) 94-115, and Edward Singerland, "Virtue Ethics, the *Analects*, and the Problem of Commensurability," *Journal of Religious Ethics* 29:1 (2001): 97-125. The most mature statement of Van Norden's position is Bryan Van Norden, *Virtue Ethics and Consequentialism in Early Chinese Philosophy* (New York: Cambridge University Press, 2007), on which see below.

36. In addition to Van Norden, *Virtue Ethics and Consequentialism*, two important comparative studies of Aristotle and Confucius were published, May Sim, *Remastering Morals With Aristotle and Confucius* (New York: Cambridge University Press, 2007) and (Jiyuan Yu, *The Ethics of Confucius and Aristotle: Mirrors of Virtue* (New York: Routledge, 2007).

37. Eric Hutton's Stanford PhD thesis is an early instance of this trend, see Eric Hutton, "Virtue and Reason in *the Xunzi*" (PhD diss., Stanford University, 2001). In addition, see many of the recent essays by Huang Yong, of which Yong Huang, "The Self-Centeredness Objection to Virtue Ethics: Zhu Xi's Neo-Confucian Response," *American Catholic Philosophical Quarterly* 84(4) (2010): 651–92, is a good example; Bryan Van Norden, "Response to Angle and Slote," *Dao: A Journal of Comparative Philosophy* 8 (2009): 305–09; Stephen C. Angle, *Sagehood: The Contemporary Significance of Neo-Confucian Philosophy* (New York: Oxford University Press, 2009); Philip J. Ivanhoe, "McDowell, Wang Yangming, and Mengzi's Contributions to Understanding Moral Perception," *Dao: A Journal of Comparative Philosophy* 10 (3): 273–90; and Edward Slingerland, "The Situationist Critique and Early Confucian Virtue Ethics," *Ethics* 121:2 (2011): 390–419.

38. For example, Sim says, "ethics for both [Confucius and Aristotle] centers on character"; Sim, *Remastering*, 134. For his part, Yu begins his first chapter by saying, "For both ethics of Confucius and Aristotle, the central question is about what the good life is or what kind of person one should be. More strikingly, both ethics answer this central question by focusing on virtue. . . ." Yu, *Mirrors of Virtue*, 24.

39. Sim, *Remastering*, 135.

40. Yu, *Mirrors of Virtue*, 108.

41. Chen Lai 陈来, "古代德行伦理与早期儒家伦理学的特点 [Ancient Virtue Ethics and the Special Characteristics of Early Confucian Ethical Learning]," 河北学刊 [*Hebei Academic Journal*] 22:6 (2002): 31–39; Chen Lai, "Virtue Ethics and Confucian Ethics," *Dao: A Journal of Comparative Philosophy* 9 (2010): 275–87; Wong Wai-ying, "Confucian Ethics and Virtue Ethics," *Journal of Chinese Philosophy* 28, no. 3 (2001): 285–300; Wong Wai-ying, "Confucian Ethics and Virtue Ethics Revisted," in *Virtue Ethics and Confucianism* ed. Stephen C. Angle and Michael Slote (New York: Routledge, 2013) 74–79.

42. Philip Ivanhoe, "Virtue Ethics and the Chinese Confucian Tradition," in *Virtue Ethics and Confucianism* ed. Stephen Angle and Michael Slote (New York: Routledge, 2013), 28–46, and see also Michael Slote, "Comments on Bryan Van Norden's *Virtue Ethics and Consequentialism in Early Chinese Philosophy*," *Dao: A Journal of Comparative Philosophy* 8:3 (2009): 289–95, and Van Norden, "Response," 2009.

43. Amy Olberding, *Moral Exemplars in the Analects: The Good Person is That* (New York: Routledge, 2011).

44. Swanton, *A Pluralist View*, 1.

45. Roger T. Ames, *Confucian Role Ethics* (Honolulu: University of Hawai`i Press, 2011), xv.

46. Rosemont Jr., Henry, and Roger T. Ames (trans.). *The Chinese Classic of Family Reverence: A Philosophical Translation of the* Xiaojing (Honolulu: University of Hawaii Press, 2009).

47. Roger T. Ames and Henry Rosemont, "Were the Early Confucians Virtuous?" in *Ethics in Early China*, ed. Chris Fraser, Dan Robins, and Timothy O'Leary (Hong Kong: Hong Kong University Press, 2011), 17.

48. Ames and Rosemont, "Early Confucians," 17.

49. Ames and Rosemont, "Early Confucians," 18.
50. Sim, *Remastering*, 164.
51. Yu, *Mirrors*, 194.
52. Ames and Rosemont, "Early Confucians," 18. For Shun's asymmetry argument, see Shun Kwong-loi, "Studying Confucian and Comparative Ethics: Methodological Reflections," *Journal of Chinese Philosophy* 36, no. 3 (2009): 455–78.
53. I sketch this history and some of the attendant arguments at more length in Angle, "The *Analects* and Moral Theory."
54. I do not mean to imply that Roger eschews Chinese-language scholarship. To the contrary, in many ways he shows that he takes it seriously; witness, for example, the central role that the twentieth-century philosopher and scholar Tang Junyi plays in Roger's writings.
55. See, e.g., Philip Cafaro, *Thoreau's Living Ethics: Walden and the Pursuit of Virtue* (Athens: University of Georgia Press, 2004), and Jennifer Welchman, *Dewey's Ethical Thought* (Ithaca, NY: Cornell University Press, 1995).
56. Ames, *Role Ethics*, 207.
57. Ibid., 181.
58. It also bears noting that in a fascinating series of blog posts, William Haines has argued that, "in most respects, Aristotle accepted Confucian role ethics as Roger Ames and Henry Rosemont describe [it]." William Haines, March 22, 2012, "Comment on Stephen Angle, 'Role ethics as virtue ethics?'" Accessed July 13, 2015. https://warpweftandway.wordpress.com/2012/03/07/role-ethics-as-virtue-ethics/.
59. I refer respectively to the Stanford Encyclopedia of Philosophy (http://plato.stanford.edu/), the Routledge Encyclopedia of Philosophy (https://www.rep.routledge.com/), and the Internet Encyclopedia of Philosophy (http://www.iep.utm.edu/); Notre Dame Philosophical Reviews (https://ndpr.nd.edu/recent-reviews/); the PhilPapers site (http://philpapers.org/); and the Philosopher's Index (http://philindex.org/).
60. John Makeham, "Disciplining Tradition in Modern China: Two Case Studies," *History and Theory, Theme Issue* 51 (2012), 89–104, offers an excellent, critical account of National Learning.
61. There are a number significant countervailing voices, including not only liberals who deny that issues like human rights and rule of law are distinctively Western concerns, but also "New Cosmopolitans" who seek to discover new international possibilities inspired in part by Chinese traditions, as well as those contemporary Confucian who argue for the universal relevance of (a possibly updated version of) Confucianism. For some discussion, see Stephen C. Angle, "Western, Chinese, and Universal Values," *Telos* 171 (2015): 112–17.
62. Zheng, Jiadong 郑家栋. 断裂中的传统: 信念与理性之间 *[Fractured Tradition: Between Belief and Reason]* (Beijing: Zhongguo Shehui Kexue Chubanshe, 2001), 519.
63. See also Leigh K. Jenco, ed., *Chinese Thought as Global Theory: Diversifying Knowledge Production in the Social Sciences and Humanities* (Albany: State University of New York Press, 2015).

9

Does Confucianism Need a Metaphysical Theory of Human Nature?

Reflections on Ames-Rosemont Role Ethics[1]

PEIMIN NI

Confucius says, "Walking along with two others, I am certain there is my teacher among them."[2] Roger Ames is one of those that I have had the good fortune to "walk along with," and who has taught me more than most of my other teachers (in a good way, of course). His views may sometimes be controversial, but they never fail to be inspiring and thought provoking. A happy coincidence, for me, is that another highly inspiring teacher of mine who I had the privilege to study under in a more formal way, Henry Rosemont Jr., turns out to be a close collaborator with Ames. Together, they have presented us with their signature theory—"role ethics," which is also their interpretation of classic Confucianism. It seems to me appropriate that in this volume in honor of Roger Ames, I shall offer some reflections on this role ethics with the hope of getting more instructions from them and from others who come to "walk along" with us.

Due to the enormous scope of philosophical issues to which the theory of role ethics is relevant, I shall focus my reflections on a more specific aspect of it, namely the role of metaphysics in Confucianism. I will put it in the context of their dispute with the Aristotelian virtue ethicist reading of Confucianism.

I

The rise of virtue ethics and, along with it, the interest in Aristotle's ethics as an alternative to deontology and utilitarian ethics, have caught a lot of attention in recent decades, and they have significantly affected the study of Confucianism. Given the central place of *de* 德 and other concepts such as *ren* 仁 (human-heartedness) in Confucianism, terms that are easily identified as virtues within the Western conceptual framework, and given the Confucian emphasis on becoming *junzi* 君子 or exemplary persons, it seems quite natural to take Confucianism as a form of virtue ethics.[3] Indeed, this is the way many in the field of Confucian scholarship have taken it.[4]

One central issue related to this trend is the role of metaphysics, because apparently what counts as a virtue has to depend on the metaphysical nature, if not "*telos*," of the subject. The authors of two recent books on the comparative study of Aristotle and Confucius, Jiyuan Yu (*The Ethics of Confucius and Aristotle*) and May Sim (*Remastering Morals with Aristotle and Confucius*), both maintain that metaphysics plays a key role in evaluating the respective theories. Sim argues that Aristotle's metaphysics allows him to justify his theory of virtue without reliance on any social and political conditions, whereas in absence of an adequate metaphysical theory, the Confucian theory of virtue relies heavily on the past, such as traditional rituals, which are inseparable "from the society within which these proprieties are exercised."[5] It further relies on the authority of the *Book of Songs*, which is an "accident" in itself; the formation of the book presupposes an authority that selects what to include and what to leave out.[6] Comparing the idea of the mean in the *Nicomachean Ethics* and the Confucian classic, the *Zhongyong* 中庸, Sim says that even though the *Zhongyong* contains a metaphysic of heaven and human nature, the book fails to provide an adequate metaphysical justification for Confucian virtues. She writes:

> Apart from telling us that heaven is all encompassing and that it nourishes everything, that its way is *cheng* 誠, not much else is said about what it is or how we know it. Nor is there any suggestion about how we are to bring this way of heaven to human practice except by practicing the *li* 禮 of authoritative tradition in an earnest manner. . . . We are never provided with a rationale for why the Zhou *li* is over all others the *li* to be practiced, other than the assertion that it does in fact embody heaven's way.[7]

The comparison leads Sim to the conclusion that "a Confucian could profit from Aristotle's example of a more explicit metaphysics and elaborate on the *Zhongyong*'s metaphysics of heaven."[8] In her analysis of the notion of the moral self, Sim concludes with a similar view that Confucius could use a better metaphysical account of the person that will allow him to rely less on custom or ritual, and be able to criticize one's own roles and norms.[9]

Jiyuan Yu agrees with Sim on the importance of metaphysics for justifying Confucian virtue ethics, but disagrees with her on the lack of an adequate metaphysics in Confucianism. He says that "an examination of this issue reveals a counterexample to the general impression that Aristotle's ethics is well argued, whereas Confucian ethics is not. It turns out that while Mencius at least attempts to explain why there is an original good nature in us, Aristotle does not really argue for the thesis that rationality is what is essentially human."[10] P. J. Ivanhoe also shares this general view. He writes, "Despite [Confucius's] lack of a specific theory about the character of human nature, it is clear that his philosophy relies upon a general and distinctive concept of human nature and its flourishing."[11]

Contrary to these views, Ames and Rosemont argue that Confucianism is not a form of virtue ethics; instead, it is better to characterize Confucianism as "role ethics." They argue that while Aristotle's virtue ethics focuses on the character traits of individual persons, Confucianism bases its entire theory and practice on family based relational virtuosity. In other words, their bases of normativity—the *conceptions of what it means to be a human*—are fundamentally different. The Aristotelian notion of a person is a teleological one. There is a predetermined *telos*, or end, that is built into being a human, which then determines the virtues of the human. Just like the nature of an acorn determines what it means to be a good acorn, and that the good "life" of an acorn is to grow into an oak tree, our defining feature, the intellect, determines what is best for our own lives, and determines this to be inseparable from the use of reason. But according to Ames and Rosemont, most acorns do not turn out to be oak trees; they become squirrels instead. The goodness of an acorn and its life is not determined by what it is but by its relationship with others in an environment. In the Confucian view of moral life, say Ames and Rosemont,

> we are not individuals in the discrete sense but rather are transactional persons living—not 'playing'—a multiplicity of roles that constitute who we are and that allow us to pursue a unique distinctiveness and virtuosity in our conduct, which combines our intellect and our emotions. We are, in other words, the sum of the roles we live in consonance with our fellows, cognitively and affectively.[12]

With this contrast, Ames and Rosemont propose a reading of Confucianism that pays attention to the fact that while early Confucians "are by no means in agreement on the constitution of human nature," "they all presume that human beings—or in the Confucian case, perhaps 'human becomings'—are open to and shaped by culturally generated patterns of behavior and taste."[13] Such a view embraces an open-ended, "holistic, prospective, and contextual account of what it means to *become* human—a *human becoming*, as it were."[14] They argue that, "since for the Confucian person one's 'potential' arises *pari passu* within one's always shifting transactional relationships rather than being resident in one's person from the outset, 'potential' as such can only be determined after the fact."[15]

Ames and Rosemont also argue that while Aristotle uses reason to discover and determine what is moral, Confucius uses moral *imagination*. Since we do not have a fixed nature, we must continue to shape our relations locally through the art of contextualization (*ars contextualis*) while being aware that there are always possibilities both inside and beyond the existing patterns of relations to be reconfigured and newly nurtured. Hence, there is a central importance given to imagination in achieving human flourishing. According to this view, virtues are not "some predetermined ideal that is to be actualized as personal character traits through the proper cultivation of human experience;" they are rather, "virtuing," or the activity of relating itself.[16]

In Ames and Rosemont's view, the open-endedness of Confucianism entails the denial of any abstract preset universal standards of right and wrong or good and bad. "From the Confucian perspective, what we need instead is a phenomenology of experience as a basis for describing what it means to act in such a way as to enhance our relations. That is, we have to ask: What makes this situation comprised of these particular relations better, and what makes it worse? We take the substance of morality to be nothing more or less than positive growth in the constitutive relations of any particular situation."[17] Looking at our conventional discourse from a Confucian perspective, the main problem in the way we have come to think about virtues is that we tend to "*metaphysicalize*" them and thus render them as one more iteration of what John Dewey has dubbed "*the* philosophical fallacy." In so doing, we take the fixed and final to come before experience. We mistakenly take kinds and categories as an adequate expression of what are complex, relationally defined, social situations. We think that because we have abstract names, we also have "things" that match up with them. In Ames and Rosemont's view, human actions become "virtuous" by reference to how they come together within a specific context rather than by being "virtues-in-themselves." Virtue, then, is nothing more or less than a *practical and productive virtuosity*. The following statement nicely summarizes their view about the normativity of this Confucian role ethics:

> Ren is not *a* "good" but an efficacious "good at, good in, good to, good for, good with" that describes a relational dexterity within

the unfolding of social experience. *Ren* is "right" conduct only in so much as it is "right on"—whatever it takes to be timely in strengthening relations that is appropriate to our shared purposes. It is "correct" behavior only in so much as it is a corrective—making those adjustments in relationships needed to maximize the shared possibilities available in the circumstances. It is not primarily a retrospective "what" but a prospective "how." By requiring that the quality of (inter)action be determined and evaluated relationally—that is, in asking after what persons do with their interdependence and mutuality both in motivation and consequences—*ren* is the difference between efficacy and waste, between elegance and ugliness, between healthy relations and injurious ones.[18]

In Confucian role ethics, moral excellence, like a work of art, is a specific expression of virtuosity and imagination assessed as a quantum of satisfaction, and only in that sense and against that measure can it be judged in degree by applying the general terms of right or wrong, correct or incorrect.[19]

II

With regard to this role vs. virtue controversy, I am largely inclined toward the Ames-Rosemont side. Readers may refer to my article on May Sim's book for my reservations about virtue ethicist interpretation of Confucianism.[20] Here I would like to offer some observations about the Ames-Rosemont position. I shall first identify two distinctive theses of their position, the "open-endedness thesis" and the "relational person" thesis, and examine them against some possible challenges. This will be followed by, in section III, my defense of their position from the *gongfu* perspective, which is already implicit in their writings. Finally, I will conclude this paper with section IV, in which I shall explain how a more consistent and thoroughgoing application of the *gongfu* perspective will allow role ethics to be appreciated within the context of its "role" in cross- and inter-cultural philosophical dialogues.

The "open-endedness thesis" refers to Ames-Rosemont's view that the defining characteristic of the Confucian view on what constitutes human is openness, i.e., that human beings are "human becomings," "open to and shaped by culturally-generated patterns of behavior and taste." This view denies "presumed biological and metaphysical uniformities"[21] and upholds that virtues are nothing but "virtuings," or dexterity within the unfolding of social experience. The "relational person thesis" refers to Ames-Rosemont's view that humans are relational so much so that we do not *play* our roles; we *are* our roles or we *live* our roles. In contrast with the notion of "autonomous individual," the Confucian understanding of person is always within specific relations and interactions with others.

With regard to the open-endedness thesis, it is reasonable to say that no one would object that, for all Confucians, humans are open-ended in the sense that we are malleable, especially when we are young, and we should therefore cultivate ourselves. This is what Confucian learning is all about. But if this open-endedness is taken to mean free from the postulation of any biological or metaphysical uniformities that might be considered "human nature," then it can become controversial: If we are nothing but human becomings, then, as Sim, Yu, and Ivanhoe would ask, how do we justify our view about rights and wrongs? From where do we get the notion of what we "should" be? Furthermore, how do we reconcile this with the obvious fact that major Confucian classics, such as the *Zhongyong* and the *Mencius*, contain quite elaborate theories of human nature? What about the Song-Ming Confucians who developed the theories into more sophisticated doctrines of *tian li* 天理, or the principle of heaven? How do we explain the fact that these theories became the mainstream view within the Confucian tradition? These Confucians certainly emphasized some of our "natural tendencies" (as Ames would put it) to the degree that they constitute who we essentially are and what we should strive to retain and develop.

With regard to the "relational person thesis," most people would agree that Confucians characteristically understand human persons relationally in terms of their roles as *mother, wife, friend*, and so on. But if it is pushed so far as to deny the existence of individuals separated from their roles, it will raise many eyebrows. Not only does it seem contrary to our experience as self-determining beings, it also seems hard to square with the fact that within classic Confucianism there is a spirit of strong subjectivity or self-determination. Statements such as "The three armies may be deprived of their commander, but even a common man cannot be deprived of his resolution," and "Faced with a matter of human-heartedness, yield not even to your teacher,"[22] appear to suggest exactly the image of autonomous individuals.

Furthermore, Ames and Rosemont take the relational understanding of person to be so characteristic to Confucianism that they even named it as "role ethics," an ethics the normativity of which is inseparable from specific roles of specific persons in specific times. A problem with this is how then to define the goodness of each role, specific or general. In feudalist China, the doctrine of "three obediences"—i.e., a woman should obey her father at home, obey her husband when married, and obey her son when her husband dies—were considered the proper role for a woman. If social roles themselves define rights and wrongs, does that mean women ought to follow these three obediences? If not, how do we determine the proper role of a good daughter, a good wife, and a good mother? What if the "shared purposes" of a particular family, including its female members, were shaped by the culture to be such that part of it is exactly to strengthen the three obediences? We may recall that the author of *Nü Jie* 女戒, *Lessons for Young Women*, in which the doctrine of three obediences was articulated in detail, was Ban Zhao 班昭 (3–53 CE), a most highly educated and intelligent woman of the time.

Placing the "open-endedness thesis" and the "relational person thesis" next to each other, we shall further notice a tension between them. If we are truly open-ended human becomings, then why can't we become autonomous individuals? Why does the goodness (or virtuosity) we create have to be the kind that is "timely in strengthening *relations* that are appropriate to our *shared purposes*" (italics mine), but not "timely in strengthening one's independence and personal aspiration"? Why do our actions have to be *inter*actions, and why is their quality determined and evaluated *relationally* but not separately?

Moreover, the relational person thesis is itself a metaphysical position— namely the position that humans are metaphysically relational beings. Would this contradict Hall and Ames's claim that Confucianism does not commit itself to any pre-existing metaphysical principles? If humans are nothing but "human becomings," and virtues are nothing but "virtuings," then can they turn out to be non-relational or individualistic? If it is not up to us to turn out that way because we are doomed to be relational beings, why can't a virtue-ethicist generate a "role virtue" ethic here, which advocates predefined excellences for each role, such as "the virtue of motherhood" and "the virtue of brotherhood"?

The above challenges seem to boil down to a dilemma at the center of the matter: If we hold the view that there is no metaphysical theory of human nature in Confucianism, we shall have difficulty explaining a major line of metaphysical theories running from the *Zhongyong*, the *Mencius*, and all the way down to the Song-Ming doctrines of *tian li* or the principle of heaven. Indeed, these theories have been conceived as providing justifications for the Confucian views about what constitutes the goodness of human life. On the other hand, if we maintain a relational notion of human persons, we seem to be accepting a metaphysical view of human nature which itself needs justification, not to mention its apparent contradiction with the "open-endedness" thesis. Does or does not Confucianism need a metaphysics of human nature?

III

In my view, the answer to the above question is twofold. First, I would say that Confucianism does not need a metaphysical theory of human nature *as its justification.* Scholars such as May Sim seem to have taken for granted that the absence of a metaphysical thesis means the absence of a standard of justification.[23] I think Ames and Rosemont will agree with me that Confucianism is essentially a *gongfu* system, as the Song-Ming neo-Confucians have characterized it. It does not intend primarily to provide a descriptive theory of what the world is (i.e., a metaphysics), nor even an ethical theory of what we are morally *obligated* to be or to do, but a systematic instruction about how to cultivate ourselves so that we can live better lives and achieve human flourishing. This understanding is stated clearly as early as in the "Introduction" of their joint translation of the *Analects*, where they say,

> Chinese philosophers in general, and Confucius in particular, were teachers in a very different way than their peers steeped in the Greek and Abrahamic traditions. For Chinese teachers do not seem to have been so much concerned with describing and thereby conveying knowledge about the world as they were to have their students learn how to get on in the world.[24]

Confucianism can be justified in the same way that any practical instruction is justified, namely through its effectiveness and beauty. This is what Ames and Rosemont mean when they say that "*ren* is the difference between efficacy and waste, between elegance and ugliness, between healthy relations and injurious ones."[25] If one does not have to have a metaphysical theory to justify eating proper food as an effective way of maintaining health, why does Confucianism have to have a metaphysical theory for justifying its instructions about living a good human life? Speaking about practical effectiveness as justification, we can find many such justifications in Confucian classics. The *Zhongyong*, for instance, justifies *cheng* 誠 (sincerity) by saying that it will lead to *ming* 明 (understanding), to *qiang* 強 (being strong), to *bian* 變 (change), to *hua* 化 (transformation), to *qianzhi* 前知 (foreknowledge), and to *jiu* 久 (endurance).[26]

This does not mean to deny the existence of metaphysical theories of human nature within the Confucian tradition, such as in the *Mencius* or in the *Zhongyong*, nor does it entail that the metaphysical theories in these works serve no purpose. Insofar as all our modes of behavior are based on our fundamental view about what the world is, who we are, and how the two are related, metaphysics serves a fundamental role in shaping a person's conduct. In this sense, that is, the sense in which metaphysical theories of human nature are not descriptions of reality, but fundamental conceptions that shape our modes of behavior, Confucianism does need metaphysical outlooks on human nature. Our notion of self is a metaphysical construct that affects our way of living profoundly. Rosemont insightfully points out that "Whether we are ultimately autonomous individuals or co-members of the human community is of course not an empirical question, and I know of no conclusive rational argument for one or the other, *a priori* or otherwise."[27] Then why did he and Ames say that we should take the relational view of self? Certainly they believe that the relational view of person is more consistent with our concrete life experience than the view of the autonomous individual, but ultimately it is because of its practical implications. Rosemont argues that when the Enlightenment notion of the individual is applied to our social practice as the basis of prescriptive principles, it generates deep social problems. Since individual rights and social justice are very likely incompatible, there is no way we can resolve the "prisoner's dilemma" and the maldistribution of the world's wealth without rejecting the Enlightenment's notion of the autonomous individual human being. The collective good will never be obtained, and everyone will be worse off if our mode of behavior is based on such a notion. "Worse," he says, "these differing views are in many ways self-prophetic; the more we believe ourselves to be essentially autonomous individuals, the more easily we become such."[28]

If a metaphysical notion of self is needed, not as *a description of some truth*, but as *an outlook that guides human life and cultivation*, then our notions of self should be judged according to whether they are conducive to a better life or not. In other words, to hold the view that the goodness of life is to be judged according to whether it matches a certain metaphysical view is nothing more than to place the cart before the horse.

Examining Mencius's theory of human nature closely, for example, we can find that even though Mencius presented the theory as if he believed that the four incipient good tendencies constitute our human nature (*xing* 性), what he really meant is that it is better for us to hold such a view.[29] This is most clearly revealed in the following remarks in the *Mencius*:

> It is due to our nature that our mouths desire sweet taste, that our eyes desire beautiful colors, that our ears desire pleasant sounds. . . . But there is also fate (*ming* 命) [whether these desires are satisfied or not]. The superior man does not say they are man's nature [and insist on satisfying them]. The virtue of humanity in the relationship between father and son, the virtue of righteousness in the relationship between ruler and minister . . .—these are [endowed in people in various degrees] according to fate. But there is also man's nature. The superior man does not [refrain from practicing them and] say they are matters of fate.[30]

By recommending the choice of identifying ourselves with the four incipient tendencies, Mencius is teaching people a method or *gongfu* of how to become an exemplary person. Commenting on the above quoted passage (7B:24), Zhu Xi says,

> These two kinds of tendencies are both in our nature that are given to us by heaven. Yet ordinary people take the first five [that our mouths desire sweet taste, that our eyes desire beautiful colors, that our ears desire pleasant sounds, and so on] as human nature, and when they don't have the desired objects, they insist on having them. They take the latter five [The virtue of humanity in the relationship between father and son, the virtue of righteousness in the relationship between ruler and minister, and so on] as fate, and once they don't have them, they give up. This is why Mencius speaks on what needs to be emphasized with regard to each in order to advocate one and discourage the other.[31]

Mencius 7B:24 reveals that Mencius's intention behind his theory of human nature is not to offer us an objective description of a metaphysical fact of human beings as a natural kind. If his intention were to make this kind of assertion, he would more likely choose to side with Xunzi or Gaozi, because, compared to other natural tendencies, the four tendencies are no more ubiquitous, and where they are found, they tend to be more frail and obscure than the other tendencies. 7B:24 shows that the theory is actually more a recommendation of value and a methodological instruction about how to obtain the value. Even though it is usually stated in the form of a description of fact, what he does can be viewed, in Richard Rorty's terms, as a "re-description" or a creation of a "taste" by which he wishes we can be judged, and, more importantly, a method of reaching an ideal. Contemporary Confucian scholar Tang Junyi 唐君毅 tells us that

> Initially, I followed Song-Ming Confucians' teachings . . . thinking that only because human heart-mind *is* good, is it possible for everyone to become Yao and Shun [sages]. . . . However, recently I suddenly came to the realization that the intent behind Mencius' teaching about human nature to be good is to *teach people to follow the goodness* that they originally have, come up with a resolution themselves, and uphold the eternal ideal. . . . Hence I became aware of the spirit of the entire teachings of Mencius—it contains a way of *stimulating everyone's resolution* to rise up from the low and to establish themselves. . . . This way, to put it simply, can be named *the way of establishing people*.[32]

Looking from this perspective, the difference between Mencius's and Xunzi's theories of human nature becomes essentially the difference of two rival recommendations. While Mencius instructs people to look at themselves as good by nature to build up their confidence and resolution to become good, Xunzi recommends people be cautious about their natural tendencies to be bad and recognize the need to cultivate themselves. If we take these theories as descriptions of metaphysical truth, they would indeed be contradictory to each other and we could never give a final verdict on which one is correct. Yet looked at as instructions, they can be regarded as complementary to each other. Our way of treating little children, for instance, is typically Mencian. When we say to them "you are so good!" we are not so much *describing* a feature of their action as we are *encouraging* them to be good and better. On the other hand, the way we deal with alcohol and drug abusers is "Xunzian" when we urge them to recognize their problems first. These different *gongfu* methods complement rather than contradict each other, as they can be appropriate to different persons in different contexts.

Returning to Ames and Rosemont's role ethics interpretation of Confucianism, I think when they claim that there is no given universal metaphysical nature to be discovered among human beings, but always changing configurations of relations, what they really mean is that in Confucianism there is neither such a theory as a *description* of transcendental truth, nor does Confucianism need such a theory, because the aim of Confucianism is not to offer a theoretical account of reality. Its aim is to offer concrete instructions about life. Yet on the other hand, Confucianism does need metaphysical notions of what it means to be a human being for *guiding* our life. It is in this sense that they find in Confucianism a metaphysical outlook of relational and process-oriented understanding of human person. But this is necessary because, whether consciously or subconsciously, these notions determine our modes of behavior. Comparing Aristotle's teleology with the Confucian relational notion of human being, we find their profound differences in orientating human life. The difference is that the metaphysical content in Aristotle's system leads one toward the ideal life of a self-sufficient morally neutral contemplator more than anything else, whereas the metaphysical content in the *Zhongyong* and the *Mencius* leads one toward an exemplary person who is fully immersed in social relatedness and practical and moral life. As Ames and Rosemont rightly observe, while Aristotle does assume some general notion of community, the community is not in all cases *necessary* for him since many of the virtues may be cultivated in solitude. That is, the basic excellences he champions *may* be cultivated in social situations, but they need not be. "We can resist the temptation for third helpings of dessert when we are dining alone; test our courage by sky-diving, bull-fighting, or in many other ways defy death that does not require others; and of course we read, and usually reflect on things, by ourselves."[33] Compared to this orientation, a Confucian relational metaphysical outlook is much more conducive to the cultivation of socially responsible and conscientious persons.

If the relational person thesis is understood more as a prescriptive recommendation than a descriptive metaphysical truth, then there is no contradiction with the open-endedness thesis. As a *gongfu* system, Confucianism does not need a metaphysical theory for *justification* because it is justified by its effectiveness; yet also because as a *gongfu* system it will take the *guiding* function of our metaphysical notions seriously. A relational notion of person is valuable because, in Ames and Rosemont's view, it is much more conducive to human flourishing than its alternatives, particularly the notion of autonomous individuality.

IV

With clarification from the *gongfu* perspective, not only does the central dilemma stated in section II disappear, other related issues can be addressed more adequately as well.

Ames and Rosemont have foreseen the danger of metaphysicalizing roles that preset standards of right and wrong. They emphasize that they take "role" in a "highly particularistic" sense.[34] That means instead of presuming a single preset right way of being a mother, they allow for culturally and situationally specific ways or styles of being a good mother. In other words, their "role ethics" is not a theory that determines rights and wrongs *according* to preset standards of abstract, generalized roles (like the "three obedience" doctrine), but rather determines them *through* particular interactions within the context of the roles that relevant persons live. The goodness of actions is derived from their *effectiveness* and to the extent to which all participants flourish.

It is important, however, to be clear about the nature of the distinction between "abstract" and "particular" that is involved here. Let us take martial arts learning as a paradigm example of *gongfu* (although we do not want to take *gongfu* as *equivalent to* the martial arts, as this would be too narrow). In learning the martial arts, one begins with following standard routines and generalized rule-like instructions, but the excellence of one's *gongfu* is ultimately judged according to the effectiveness and the elegance of one's performance rather than according to how much it conforms to the standard routines and rule-like instructions. Indeed, standard routines and generalized rule-like instructions in martial arts themselves emerge through particular practices because of their effectiveness, although there can always be exceptions in which they do not apply. This reminds us of Confucius's characterization of the highest perfection of learning—*quan* 權, or the art of using discretion. In the *Analects* 9.30, the Master says,

> There are some with whom we may pursue learning, but not go along in pursuing the Way. There are some with whom we may go along in pursuing the Way, but not take a stand together. There are some with whom we can take a stand together, but not jointly exercise discretion (*quan*).

The word *quan* originally meant "scale," and thus the action of "weighing" or "making discretion" as well. According to the *Gongyang* version of the *Spring and Autumn Annals* 公羊傳 (dated probably in the Warring States period, ca. 475–221 BCE), "*quan* means goodness resulting from transgressing well-established canons."[35] As a master artist of life, Confucius is fully aware of the importance of using names to define roles. This may be conceived exactly as his recognition of the need to set general, not-so-particular standards for guiding people's behavior before they are able to respond appropriately to all specific conditions. Only real masters can fully embody the ability to use discretion. To be clear about this helps us to see that, as a *gongfu* system, Confucianism does not deny the practical function of generalized and somewhat abstract standards. Confucius's fairly general remark, "Let a ruler be a ruler, a minister be a minister, a father be a father, and a son be a son"[36] is but one example of the distinctively Confucian method of the "rectification of names" (*zhengming* 正名) for standardizing roles. But exactly because of this, it would fall short of characterizing the "highly particularistic" art of using discretion at the advanced level that Ames and Rosemont intend to stress. As Mencius suggests, in a situation where one's sister-in-law is drowning, the role-specific ritual of keeping oneself free from having physical contact with her would no longer apply.[37] If we say that the term "role ethics" is vulnerable to misinterpretation because it may be conceived as taking generalized roles to be preset standards of rights and wrongs, such interpretation would not be groundless if one looks at it from the perspective of *gongfu*. As we know, names of roles are inevitably generalizations, and as generalizations, they are descriptions of "types" rather than "tokens." So, although the name of a role itself has the tendency to lead people toward the type that lacks particularity, according to Confucianism, general instructions or standards set up through the rectification of names are indispensable in learning *gongfu*.

Another issue that may gain more clarity through the application of the *gongfu* perspective is, to put it bluntly, "who decides what is good and bad, or appropriate and inappropriate in role ethics?" Roles certainly carry with them normativity.[38] But one should neither rely solely on the roles one happens to be in, nor solely on the shared aim of all the related parties, to determine what is right or good, for otherwise a slave society in which all the slaves are brainwashed to accept their role would find no way out. People tend to have a misconception about the Confucian sense of relatedness as if it is contrary to subjectivity, independence, and self-determination, and as if it requires us to simply accept whatever relations we happen to have. Actually, recognizing our social relatedness is no more incompatible with self-determination and creativity than causal determinism is to free will. While it may be hard to reconcile the apparent conflict between the two in theoretical discourse, no one feels that it is difficult to reconcile them in practical life. We may well recognize our social relations and roles without surrendering the ability to make our own judgments and to stand on what we believe to be right, even if it means going against our superiors, or the majority, or the tradition. In fact recognition of our relatedness will sometimes require us to uphold our subjectivity against others—not as a way of denying our relatedness, but of affirming it. When Confucian officials remonstrated against their tyrannical rulers, they did so to *fulfill* rather than to relinquish their duties as subjects. Yet under other circumstances, refusing or cutting off a relation to retain one's integrity may be considered appropriate also. Confucius never meant that one should accept whatever role one happens to be in and act accordingly. Although he highly admired the culture of the *Zhou*, he still endorsed Boyi and Shuqi, who went into self-imposed exile and starved themselves to death because they refused to eat the grain of the *Zhou*. In doing so, Boyi and Shuqi retained their role as subjects of the *Shang* and refused to accept the role of becoming subjects of the *Zhou*. When his disciple Ran Qiu was collecting and hoarding excessive tax for the *Ji* house to increase their wealth, the Master said, "He is not my disciple. Young men, you may beat the drum and assail him!"[39] Here he is cutting off his teacher-disciple relation with Ran Qiu and calling upon his other disciples to cut off their classmate relation with him as well. If the Way does not prevail, it is all right to resign from one's post and even leave one's own state, as Confucius himself did. None of these examples show a non-relational way of thinking, but they all suggest that thinking and living through roles does not mean that one should only navigate through them, act one's best to strengthen them, negotiate within their constraints, and never resist any of them.

Characterizing Confucianism as a *gongfu* system reminds us of the difference between the common fellow and the master who is a connoisseur—an expert of a certain kind of art—who has a developed sense or taste for what is good. To borrow an example from Rosemont, Toscanini, Leonard Bernstein, and Dmitri Rostropovich can have their distinctive styles of conducting music. Similarly one can be a good mother, good son, and good friend in many different and creative styles. But an abusive mother cannot argue that her way of ignoring her child is just another style of mothering any more than a noise-maker can say that his noise is just another beautiful style of music. While the master conductors' different kinds of music are all good in different ways, the noise-maker's is simply not good. Even the ability to appreciate the masters' brilliance has to come from cultivation. To a non-musical ear, the master's performance may not be much different from the noise of the noise-maker. Here, the goodness has to go *through* the relation, but it is not *solely determined by* the relation. Whether the aim is *shared* by all the parties in a relation or not, we need to put more weight on the real master's opinion with regard to whether the relation itself is worth retaining and strengthening, and if it is, what sense of excellence should be cultivated among the parties involved.

Of course it is difficult to judge who is a real master. If one were to laugh at a teenager who thinks that he knows better than his well-educated parents about what is a good parent-child relationship, consider the period early last century when some influential Chinese intellectuals (e.g., Kang Youwei) wanted to abolish marriage and family. Confucians are supposedly experts on family relations, but they also have debated on the subject of same-sex marriage. Like any form of art, the art of life must open itself to competing visions of excellence and an infinite number of creative styles—but that does not mean we have to reject objectivity and turn the matter simply to everyone's shared opinion. While this point may not easily come through the term "role ethics," it can be brought to light once we start to use the *gongfu* perspective.

It is important to recall that, in countering the Aristotelian virtue as character traits, the key insight of Ames and Rosemont is their characterization of Confucian relational virtuosity. A Confucian master's ability to discern what is *yi* 義 or appropriate is exactly manifested in his or her holistic, relational vision. It is this vision of interrelatedness manifested through particular roles that provides a stark contrast with the practical implications of Aristotle's metaphysics and the abstract notion of the autonomous individual. Yet once we more thoroughly apply the *gongfu* perspective, we will gain a better understanding of the "role" of this way of thinking as well. As we know, the Confucian soil has been perceived to be fertile for developing socially responsible persons, but less so in generating persons with a strong sense of personal rights and freedoms. This has been taken as a liability generated from conceiving the self as nothing but a part of the whole to which it belongs. But if one understands the relational self dynamically and holistically, one will realize that respect for each other's personal rights and freedoms is an inevitable product of healthy, caring relations. If I, as a conscientious role-bearing person, care for your wellbeing, I will respect your rights and freedoms, which will naturally increase your likelihood of doing the same to me. But as Rosemont points out, the converse does not hold. Respecting people's rights and freedoms does not necessarily lead to healthy and caring relations. As a self-induced, free, rational, and autonomous individual, I can respect your freedoms and rights by simply ignoring you.[40] Taking both notions of self as different *gongfu* recommendations, we see more clearly which one is more conducive to human flourishing. But understanding Confucianism as a *gongfu* system will help us to appreciate its unique art style without having to reject whatever effectiveness and beauty alternative styles of life may have to offer. If we really appreciate the highly particularistic relational way of thinking, we should then, by the same token, recognize that in some particular situations and to some particular kinds of human practices, non-relational thinking may be more effective and appropriate. Faced with the situation in which a child is about to fall into a well, the most appropriate response would be to take the quickest effective action to save the child. Except for the intuitive realization that in the most general sense a child is in danger, all other relational particularities, such as whose child it is, how the child is related to you, what has led the child to being in danger, how the child's family and the community would react to your action, should rightly be put aside as irrelevant. Non-relational thinking is not characteristically Confucian, and yet since Confucianism is a *gongfu* system, and the highest perfection of this *gongfu* is, as Confucius puts it, the art of using discretion (*quan*). It might actually be *more* Confucian than otherwise to think in terms of the autonomous individual within some particular situation. For the same reason, I wonder if the relational outlook and the individualistic outlook, conceived as different *gongfu* approaches to life, might become complementary in certain particular situations. Having said that, I remain convinced that given the overall particularities of the world today, it is much more urgent and profitable to advocate the relational outlook, as Ames and Rosemont have been tirelessly doing. Even if in some situations the individualistic outlook may lead to desirable outcomes, the side effects of this outlook must be carefully considered.

In summary, I suggest a more consistent and thoroughgoing application of the *gongfu* perspective. Already entailed in Ames and Rosemont's writings, this perspective will enable role ethics to clear away some misplaced charges and perform its "role" more effectively and adequately within the context of cross- and inter-cultural philosophical dialogues.

Notes

1. This is a substantially revised and expanded version of a paper I presented at the 2009 Society of Asian and Comparative Philosophy Conference in Asilomar, California, and at the "International Academic Symposium on Exchange and Creativ-

ity: Dialogue between Chinese and Western Philosophy" held at Zhejiang University, China, in the summer of 2012. It appeared in "Role, Virtue, or *Gongfu*?—Some Reflections on Interpreting Confucian Ethics," in *Zhedong Xueshu* 浙東學術 [*Academics of East Zhejiang*], 3 (Hangzhou: Zhejiang University Press, 2013): 134-48, under the title "Role, Virtue, or *Gongfu*?—Some Reflections on Interpreting Confucian Ethics."

2. The *Analects* of Confucius (my own translation, based on the Chinese version in *Shisan Jing Zhushu* 十三經注疏 [*Commentaries of the Thirteen Classics*]. Shanghai: Shanghai Guji Chubanshe 上海古籍出版社, 1997), 7.22.

3. In this article I will make no fine differentiation between a virtue ethicist interpretation of Confucianism and a character ethics interpretation of it, as represented by Joel Kupperman. Though Kupperman disagrees with the former, virtues are still largely conceived as character traits, and hence the concept of character is used frequently by virtue ethicists. Kupperman's main reservation against virtue ethics is that it compartmentalizes character traits. See Joel J. Kupperman, *Character* (New York and Oxford: Oxford University Press, 1991), 112-14.

4. See, for example, Philip J. Ivanhoe, "Kongzi and Aristotle as Virtue Ethicists," in *Moral Cultivation and Confucian Character, Engaging Joel J. Kupperman*, ed. Chenyang Li and Peimin Ni (Albany: State University of New York Press, 2014), 47-64; Lee H. Yearly, *Mencius and Aquinas: Theories of Virtue and Conceptions of Courage* (Albany: State University of New York Press, 1990); and Edward Slingerland, "Virtue Ethics, The *Analects*, and the Problem of Commensurability," in *Journal of Religious Ethics*, 29 no. 1 (2001): 97-125.

5. Sim quotes Ivanhoe and Michael Martin on this in May Sim, *Remastering Morals with Aristotle and Confucius* (Cambridge: Cambridge University Press, 2007), 36-37. This view is also shared by Chad Hansen.

6. Sim, *Remastering Morals*, 38-39.

7. Sim, *Remastering Morals*, 127.

8. Sim, *Remastering Morals*, 131.

9. Sim, *Remastering Morals*, 14.

10. Jiyuan Yu, *The Ethics of Confucius and Aristotle, Mirrors of Virtue* (New York and London: Routledge, 2007), 67, see also 53, 63-64.

11. Ivanhoe, "Kongzi and Aristotle," 48.

12. Roger T. Ames and Henry Rosemont Jr., "Were the Early Confucians Virtuous?" in *Ethics in Early China: An Anthology*, ed. Chris Fraser, Dan Robins and Timothy O'Leary (Hong Kong: The University of Hong Kong Press, 2011), 20.

13. Ames and Rosemont, "Were the Early Confucians Virtuous?" 31.

14. Ames and Rosemont, "Were the Early Confucians Virtuous?" 34.

15. Henry Rosemont Jr., and Roger T. Ames, *The Chinese Classic of Family Reverence: A Philosophical Translation of the Xiaojing* (Honolulu: University of Hawai`i Press 2009), 41.

16. Ames and Rosemont, "Were the Early Confucians Virtuous?" 34.

17. Ames and Rosemont, "Were the Early Confucians Virtuous?" 7.

18. Ames and Rosemont, "Were the Early Confucians Virtuous?" 22.

19. Ames and Rosemont, "Were the Early Confucians Virtuous?" 23.

20. Peimin Ni, "How Far is Confucius an Aristotelian?—Comments on May Sim's *Remastering Morals with Aristotle and Confucius*," in *Dao, A Journal of Comparative Philosophy*, VIII 3 (2009): 311–19.

21. Ames and Rosemont, "Were the Early Confucians Virtuous?" 31.

22. *Analects*, 9.26 and 15.36.

23. See Sim, *Remastering Morals*, 36.

24. Roger T. Ames and Henry Rosemont Jr., *The Analects of Confucius: A Philosophical Translation* (New York: Ballantine Books, 1998), 33.

25. Ames and Rosemont, "Were the Early Confucians Virtuous?" 22.

26. *Zhongyong*, see *Focusing the Familiar, A Translation and Philosophical Interpretation of the Zhongyong*, by Roger T. Ames and David L. Hall (Honolulu: University of Hawai`i Press, 2001), chapters 20, 23, 24, and 26.

27. Henry Rosemont Jr., *Rationality and Religious Experience—The Continuing Relevance of the World's Spiritual Traditions* (Chicago and La Salle, IL: Open Court, 2001), 91.

28. Ibid. Readers may also refer to chapter 4 of Henry Rosemont Jr., *Against Individualism, A Confucian Rethinking of the Foundations of Morality, Politics, Family, and Religion* (Lanham/Boulder/New York/London: Lexington Books, 2015) for a more elaborate discussion of the negative practical implications of the belief in the autonomous individual taken normatively.

29. See Peimin Ni, "A Comparative Examination of Rorty's and Mencius' Theories of Human Nature," in *Rorty, Pragmatism, and Confucianism*, ed. Yong Huang (Albany: State University of New York Press, 2009), for a more detailed discussion of Mencius's view of human nature.

30. *Mencius*, trans. by D. C. Lau (Harmondsworth: Penguin Books, 1970), 7B:24.

31. Zhu Xi 朱熹, *Mengzi jizhu daquan* 孟子集注大全 [*Complete Collection of Commentaries of the Book of Mencius*], in *Siku Quanshu* 四庫全書 (Wenyuange version 文淵閣本, Classics Part 經部, The Four Books Section 四書類), vol. 14, 23.

32. Tang Junyi 唐君毅, *Zhongguo zhexue yuanlun, yuandao pian* 中國哲學原論 · 原道篇 [*On the Origins of Chinese Philosophy, The Chapter on the Origin of Dao*, volume 1 (Hong Kong: Research Institute of the New Asia College 新亞書院研究所, 1974), 212, my emphasis.

33. Ames and Rosemont, "Were the Early Confucians Virtuous?" 31.

34. Rosemont, *Against Individualism*, 105.

35. *Gongyang Zhuan* 公羊傳 [*Gongyang version of the Spring and Autumn Annals*], "Duke Huan, Year 11," in *Shisan Jing Zhushu*, 2220.

36. *Analects*, 12.11.

37. See: *Mencius*, 4A:17.

38. See: Rosemont, *Against Individualism*, 102–06 for articulation of this.

39. *Analects*, 11.17.

40. Rosemont points out that it is easier to generate first generation human rights (civil and political rights, such as freedom of speech, equality before law, freedom of religion, the right to vote) from second-generation human rights (economic, social, and cultural rights such as the rights to food and health care) than the other way

around. This is essentially because it is easier to generate a sense of personal rights and freedoms from role-bearing socially responsible persons than it is to generate a sense of social responsibility from autonomous people with a sense of their personal rights and freedoms, because the latter would have no sense of the need to care for others (see Rosemont, *Against Individualism*, 65–68 and 110–12).

10

Roles, Community, and Morality
Comment on *Confucian Role Ethics*

Daniel A. Bell

I have known Roger for many years and he is a good friend. I am also a great admirer of his groundbreaking philosophical work on Confucianism, and I make use of his excellent translations of the early Chinese classics. *Confucian Role Ethics: A Vocabulary* is an important contribution to an impressive, decades-long academic output of lasting value. A Confucian way of life, in my view, is a constant quest for self-improvement and Roger is a wonderful model for young and formerly young academics. Let me now turn to some questions about Roger's book with the hope that Roger's answers will clarify some key issues.[1] I will focus on chapter 4, which specifically deals with Confucian role ethics, beginning with some questions about terminology and then raising some questions about role ethics and morality.

Terminology

One of the delights of reading Roger's book is that he explains the etymology of key Confucian ethical terms and shows how the characters bear on the meaning of the terms. Roger's approach is also admirable because he seeks to understand Confucian ethics from the inside, without forcing categorization into "Western" philosophical vocabulary. Still, there are two terms that seem to come from outside the Confucian ethical tradition(s), and I hope Roger can provide some clarification.

The first term is the word "community," which comes up several times in Roger's book. In the preface, Roger quotes approvingly from Henry Rosemont Jr.:

> We are all born and reared in a specific cultural community, each with its language, values, religious orientation, customs, traditions, and concomitant ideas of what it is to be a human being. There are not, in short, any culturally independent human beings. Each of us has specific hopes, fears, joys, sorrows, values, and views which are inextricably linked to our definitions of who and what we are, and these definitions have been overwhelmingly influenced by the cultural community of which we are a part. (xv)

But what exactly is "the" community that "overwhelmingly" shapes our identity? In fact, one might ask, what is the Chinese/Confucian term for "community"? The term has been used by contemporary Western communitarian thinkers, but is it part of the Confucian tradition(s)? The contemporary Chinese translation of community—*shequn* 社群—is not a key concept in any of the Confucian classics that I am familiar with. It is odd that Roger, who otherwise seeks to understand Confucian ethics in its own terms, invokes a term that has not been an important part of Confucian ethics and does not seek to provide any sort of etymological explanation.

The mystery deepens in chapter 4. Roger says that "shame is such a powerful expression of moral awareness that, when properly nurtured, can become a pervasive value that enables the community to be both inclusive and self-regulating" (172), and he refers to a passage in the *Analects* (2.3), but that passage does not mention anything about "the community." Elsewhere, Roger mentions the famous passage from the *Great Learning* about the need to extrapolate family roles so that they "inform one's dealings with the community more broadly" (183) but that passage refers to the state (*guo* 国) and the whole world (*tianxia* 天下), not the community. In another passage, Roger explicitly contrasts the community with the state: "family is the ultimate source and ground of political order, and in the absence of the flourishing family and the thriving community it enables, political order is a sham or worse. It is for this reason that any formal pretense to be a strong state independent of the thriving community is an empty abstraction."(168) In short, the community that shapes our identity—our roles—is located somewhere between the family and the state, but Roger does not tell us what it is. Nor does he refer to any part of the Confucian tradition that may shed light on this question. I raise the issue of how to define "the community" not to be pedantic, but because it plays such an important role in Roger's account of Confucian role ethics: it shapes the roles that are supposed to tell us what to do.

Roger's reply recognizes that "there is no specific mention of 'community' per se" in the Great Learning (643) but suggests that the "central message of this terse yet comprehensive document is that while personal, familial, social, political, and indeed cosmic cultivation is ultimately coterminous and mutually entailing, it must always begin from a commitment to personal cultivation" (643). Still, we are not provided with an account of the kind of community that shapes our roles. Roger adds that several of the early texts underscore the social dimension of the ideal of the junzi (君子) "when they define the term jun 君 paranomastically—that is, by semantic and phonetic association—as qun 群 (to gather around)" (644) but again we are not provided with any account of the all-important community that is supposed to shape our roles.

Another key concept in Roger's account of role ethics is the idea that we are *constituted* by our relations: "From the Confucian perspective in which persons are constituted by their relations and in which the goal of becoming a person is to become consummately so, these self-other and means-end distinctions have no purchase" (180). In the epilogue, Rogers adds: "To transform the world into a family, according to this Confucian sensibility, is to promote a model of interdependent relationships that will best accomplish the goal of getting the most out of your constitutive relations" (261). In short, we should recognize that our identity is constituted by our constitutive relations, and our goal (the way to self-realization, as well as our moral goal) is to "get the most" out of those relations. But which relations are constitutive of our identity, and which ones are contingent? Some family relations may be constitutive (our relations with our parents and children?) but some may not be (our relations with our cousins?). What about relationships with friends, religion, nation, profession, and sexual orientation? Are they constitutive of our identity, meaning that it makes no sense, either descriptively or from a moral point of view, to seek to shed those "elements" of our identity? At least, we can agree that some relations are more contingent, such as membership in a neighborhood homeowner's association, or a local sports team. There will be no major damage to my identity, I trust, if I change those relations, and it seems hard to object on moral grounds if those relations do more harm than good. But how do we distinguish between "constitutive" and "contingent" relations? Here too, I hope Roger can provide some clarification. My aim, again, is not to be pedantic. It is an important question because Roger's account of Confucian role ethics places so much emphasis upon the descriptive and moral importance of constitutive relations, so it would be helpful to know what those relations are and how they differ from more contingent relations.

Let me suggest that the insights of contemporary Western communitarians may help to shed some light on these terminological issues (while one should welcome Roger's efforts to defend Confucian ethics in its own terms, there is good reason to borrow insights from other traditions if those insights can help to develop the Confucian tradition, as Roger recognizes when he engages with the arguments of American pragmatists). Communitarians distinguish between "constitutive" communities and "contingent" attachments: constitutive communities start with how people define themselves, they provide a largely background way of meaningful thinking, acting, and judging, and one typically loses a commitment to a constitutive community at the price of being thrown into a state of severe disorientation where one is unable to take a stand on many things of significance.[2] So for example, the relation with my parents is constitutive of my identity—I define myself in terms of those relations. I cannot really fully understand how my life is shaped by ties with my parents and I know deep down I cannot shake off that influence, and making a conscious effort to "free" myself from my parents' influence may be ineffective if not counterproductive—whereas none of these considerations apply when I think of my attachment to, say, my local hockey team in Beijing. Such distinctions might be helpful for thinking about the obligations that arise from "role ethics": only constitutive communities generate strong moral obligations in terms of how we should treat other people; in contrast, the decision to join or leave contingent attachments can and should be determined first and foremost by whether or not such communities contribute to personal happiness. In other words, my role qua son is fundamentally different than my role qua Beijing hockey player, and communitarian theorizing can help to make sense of that difference. Confucians may provide distinctive answers to the question of what counts as a constitutive communal relation—perhaps prioritizing the "five relationships"—but they cannot avoid the need to distinguish between constitutive and contingent communal relations.

Confucian Role Ethics and Morality

That said, there is a need to further clarify the relation between Confucian role ethics and morality in the sense of the obligations we owe to other people (I leave aside such questions as the obligations we owe to animals and the environment). I would like to distinguish between two claims: the strong claim that the (constitutive) roles we occupy determine the content of our moral obligations, and the weaker claim that our (constitutive) roles set constraints upon what we ought to do. I think the weaker claim is more persuasive, but Roger's formulations suggest he wants to defend the first, stronger claim.

Consider what he says on page 168:

> Let me be clear about what Confucian role ethics asserts. Confucian role ethics would content that those family roles and the extended relations we associate with community that designate a specific configuration of activity—the roles of father, mother, son, daughter, teacher, friend, and neighbor, for example—are themselves a normative vocabulary more compelling than abstract injunctions. Such roles recommend in the most concrete of terms an existentially informed disposition and the search for a course of conduct that is the ground of family and community life. In Confucian role ethics, "to mother" and "to neighbor" are not merely descriptive; they serve as ethical injunctions, and unlike abstract principles, they serve as concrete guidelines that help us to determine what to do next.

Later on, Roger asserts that "since morality is *nothing more* than those modalities of acting that conduce to enhancing relations, any kind of conduct that has a disintegrative effect on the fabric of family or community is perceived to be fundamentally immoral" (pp. 171–72; my emphasis). Here, morality is equivalent to doing what's good for our constitutive relations, and immoral behavior consists in harming those relations. If I am puzzled about what to do from a moral point of view, I should realize that my obligation is to promote the good of my constitutive relations. Hence, I should reflect upon my constitutive roles rather than consult abstract moral principles, and this will determine what I should do.

But surely it cannot be that simple. For one thing, the obligations associated with particular roles change over time, and awareness of one's role *per se* cannot always (or even usually) serve as a useful guide for action, particularly in times of change. Most obviously, the role of "wife" has evolved over time, and no doubt Kongzi (and almost all other pre-twentieth-century thinkers) would have been shocked by the "modern" assumption that women can be men's moral and intellectual equals both within the family context and in "the community" at large. Today, we argue about same-sex marriage—can somebody from the same-sex assume the role of "wife" in a marriage?—and it is unclear how Confucian role ethics can help us answer the question. At minimum, we need some sort of moral standard external to the role to help us determine what we should do.

A second problem is that different roles can point to conflicting obligations, and here too we need some sort of external moral standard to help us make morally informed judgments. Roger does discuss the (in)famous passage in the *Analects* about the need to cover up for a son or a father who steals a sheep, where doing what is right from the family's point of view seems to conflict with doing what is right from a societal point of view. From the perspective of Confucian role ethics, Roger suggests that the two obligations can and should be balanced: for example, a child should protest (remonstrate) against the conduct of an erring parent rather than call the police; hence the moral wrongness of the deed could be exposed and the wrong rectified without undermining the harmony of the family. Roger then invokes a contemporary example to illustrate the "moral" of Kongzi's story.[3] Roger suggests that parents who discover that a child has been shoplifting should use the power of shame to reform the child's conduct rather than summon the police. But what if a close family member has committed a more serious crime? Was the Unabomber's brother wrong to denounce him to the authorities? Or should we praise Seif Qaddafi for taking his father's side and threaten "rivers of blood" at the start of the uprising in Libya? How do we decide between obligations qua citizen and obligations qua family member? If the Confucian perspective is that our obligations qua family member should always have priority, it might lead to morally perverse consequences.

One possible response is to say that we should do our best to seek the good of our "constitutive relations" so long as it does not involve the gross violation of human rights, such as the murder of innocent people. But Roger seems to object to an appeal to any sort of moral principle (such as human rights) external to our roles that set constraints upon what we should do for the good of our constitutive relations. In the epilogue, he defends "an ethic in which models, rather than principles, are the final arbiters of proper conduct and cultural values—that is, appeal to the excellent person rather than an abstract standard . . . Confucian ethics avoids intractable moral conflict by abjuring any appeal to universals" (265).[4] But what underpins human rights is not a view about what it means to be an "excellent person"; rather, it's a view about basic human interests—for example, nobody likes to be subject to violent death at the hands of other—that underpin any conception of human excellence in any society. In other words, people of different times and places can all agree that we have certain universal biological needs—like an aversion to extreme pain—that underpin such basic human rights as the right not to be tortured. Why can't a view about basic human interests grounded in human biology serve as an "abstract standard" that sets limits upon the sorts of obligations that stem from our constitutive roles? This kind of defense of human rights is no more "metaphysical" than Mengzi's example of the universally felt compassion for a baby who is about to fall into a well.

Roger replies "that lived roles are themselves the ultimate source of [. . .] standards and principles . . . if courage or justice does have a referent, it is primarily as a generalization that is derived from acting courageously or justly within our family and community roles and relations" (645–46). It may be true that principles, to an important extent, are generalizations from lived roles in history: for example, we may have settled on the generalization that individuals have a fundamental interest in not being tortured at least partly because of hundreds of years of experience with people who lived the roles of torturer and tortured, and we learned that no good has ever come out of this relationship from the perspective of the tortured and society at large,[5] and we label this conclusion the right not be to tortured.[6] That is fine, but we do not have to personally experience these roles in order to appeal to them as a standard for thinking about how we should lead our lives: in that sense, they are external moral standards and they are experienced as such by the decision maker. In other words, these generalizations need not be the product of our *own* lived roles. Roger writes: "In the extreme cases of Seif Qaddifi, the son of Muammar, and the Unabomber's brother . . . I don't think many of us would have much difficulty in deciding which of their roles must take precedence and wherein appropriateness lies" (647). But it is only obvious because there is a widely recognized view that nothing can justify the murder of innocent people: again, it could be argued that this view emerged from a realization in history that there was something fundamentally wrong about assuming the role of killing innocent people, but today it is no longer a question of selecting between the obligations associated with our own roles; rather, it is a conflict between the obligations generated from our own roles and an external moral standard, even if that standard may have originated at least partly from lived roles by other people in past human society.[7]

In short, Confucian role ethics, if it is to provide morally informed practical guidance, needs to be constrained by moral standards external to the roles. Still, I do not mean to suggest that Confucian role ethics does not say anything interesting about the content of human morality. If it is true that some of our roles are constitutive of our identity—like my role *qua* son—and I should not try to shed those roles (unless seeking the good of those roles has the effect of violating the basic human rights of others), then it does determine to an important extent how I should lead my life. More precisely, my constitutive relations may not provide much detailed guidance about what to do in situations that call for new interpretations or balancing different roles, but they can at least tell me what I *cannot* do. According to the standard liberal view about ethics, once I reach the age of reason (say, 18 years old), then I should have the choice to stick with, or withdraw from, particular roles. I can choose to be a filial son, but it is no great moral sin if I choose not to. The Confucian perspective—one that still informs ethical thinking in East Asian societies and contrasts with more liberal ethical systems in Western societies that prioritize individual autonomy—is that such constitutive relations are not matters of individual choice. I cannot, and should not, withdraw from the role of filial son: I have a lifelong obligation to care for my parents, and in a fundamental sense, it is not up to me, no matter how I am treated by my parents. In short, constitutive relations set constraints upon what we ought to do.[8] But they cannot tell us what to do in all, or even most, situations in a fast-changing world with conflicting moral obligations.

Notes

1. This comment draws on "A Comment on Confucian Role Ethics," *Frontiers of Philosophy in China* 2012, 7(4): 626–31, as well as Roger's response to my comment in the same issue ("Author's Reflections and Responses," 642–47). Bracketed page numbers in this comment refer to Roger's book *Confucian Role Ethics: A Vocabulary* (Honolulu: University of Hawai'i Press, 2011), except for my references to Roger's reply which refer to his "Author's Reflections and Responses."

2. I develop these points in my book *Communitarianism and Its Critics* (Oxford: Oxford University Press, 1993).

3. Regrettably, such examples are only too rare in Roger's book. It is odd that Roger often objects to "abstract" theorizing, yet his own account of Confucian role ethics often seems quite abstract. In my view, the book would have benefitted from more examples meant to illustrate his theory, along with a more detailed effort to draw out practical and political implications.

4. At the very end of the book, to be fair, Roger does put forward a "Confucian" argument for impartiality that qualifies a role based ethics of partiality: "Rather than invoking some transcendental moral standard or some faculty of impersonal reason as a strategy for claiming such impartiality—a strategy that is inevitably hobbled by the contingencies of circumstances—the Confucian tradition in developing a notion of impartiality has remained true to the family metaphor . . . [I]mpartiality is served practically by extending one's range of concern . . . The Confucian formula of "putting oneself in the other's place" . . . is another variation on this deferential attempt to keep one's range of concern open in determining what is moral" (267–68). But "putting oneself in the other's place" is also an important idea in the universal moral reasoning of the liberal, Judeo-Christian, and Kantian ethical traditions (among others), and it is unclear how Roger's account of the Confucian view of impartiality remains "true to the family metaphor" or differs in interesting ways from those traditions.

5. Perhaps we would have a different view about torture if it was shown to be an effective way of, say, identifying witches or preventing mass terrorist attacks.

6. Such generalizations may be the product of both lived roles in history and basic biological facts, such as an aversion to extreme pain.

7. At some level, there is a self that allows for individuals to distinguish between contingent attachments and constitutive relations and also to subordinate the

obligations of constitutive relations when they conflict with external moral standards, such as basic human rights. For an argument that early Confucian thinkers did regard human beings as capable of self-reflection and direction, having the capacity to reflect both on one's place in the social order and to redirect one's life on the basis of such reflection, see Kwong-loi Shun, "The Person in Confucian Thought," in *Confucian Ethics: A Comparative Study of Self, Autonomy, and Community*, eds. Kwong-loi Shun and David B. Wong (Cambridge: Cambridge University Press, 2004), ch. 8.

8. The idea of "constraint" suggests closure rather than openness of possibilities, but the opposite may be true: just as constraints on language allow for the creative use of language (otherwise human sounds would be random, with no meaning), so constraints on roles allow us to express our creativity (see Henry Rosemont Jr., *Against Individualism: A Confucian Rethinking of the Foundations of Morality, Politics, Family, and Religion* (Lanham, MD: Lexington Books, 2015), 103–04).

11

Performance in Confucian Role Ethics[1]

Kathleen M. Higgins

Roger Ames and Henry Rosemont characterize the Confucian ethical framework as a version of role ethics. In this essay I will consider this view as Ames interprets it in his book *Confucian Role Ethics: A Vocabulary*, but although my discussion will focus on Ames's analysis in that context, it should be recognized that it applies to Rosemont's views as well. I will briefly consider the debate about whether the Confucian view should be characterized as a form of virtue ethics, but focus most of my attention on the performative character of roles on Ames's interpretation.[2] Comparing some of his claims about role performance to those of Judith Butler in connection with gender, I will raise the question whether Confucian role ethics might reinforce roles that are oppressive, despite its idealistic character. I conclude that as valuable as it is for tapping into noble relational aspirations, Confucian role ethics should be supplemented by efforts to undermine demands for conformity to social roles that can result in oppression of sexual minorities and others who perform their roles atypically.

The Confucian Ethical Vision

The primary focus on Confucianism is ethical, and cultivating and enhancing interpersonal relationships is the ongoing ethical project. Confucianism, according to Ames, is about "attaining relational virtuosity."[3] This contrasts with the major emphases of the Western ethical tradition, which variously focus on the attainment of happiness understood primarily as individual flourishing, the development of criteria for right action, or some combination of the two.

The Confucian project, according to Ames, reflects a worldview that originated in Chinese antiquity, according to which everything in the world, including the human being, is configured *qi* (energy) operating in a larger field of energy. This model is dynamic and interactive, where continuous change is assumed and energies interact and affect one another. This counters the Western view that originated in Greek thought, which (with important exceptions) tends to take stasis as the norm and movement to require explanation. Chinese thought presupposes the opposite. The cycles of nature, not transcendent eternal ideas, are the starting point for understanding everything, including human reality. Like everything else, we are embedded in a world in which everything transforms and interacts. Contrary to the model typically assumed in the West, in which individuals are discrete beings who act in a world that is external to them, the Chinese model does not, even theoretically, separate the person from the ongoing, changing situation.

Confucian ethics begins with this dynamic, interactive model. Provocatively, Ames contends that we are not even human until we develop through our interactions. One becomes human "by cultivating those thick, intrinsic relations that constitute one's initial conditions and that locate the trajectory of one's life force within family, community, and cosmos."[4] Effectively, for Ames and Rosemont, the project of becoming human is one and the same as the Confucian ethical agenda. The central aim is becoming *ren*, consummate as a human being.

This project literally "begins at home," in the family, within the relationships in which one initially finds oneself.[5] We first develop skill in relating to others by learning how to interact with family members, and we rely on the skills honed within this context as we attempt to extend our relational virtuosity through ever-widening circles. We thrive as human beings only interactively, relating to our families, communities, and world, and it is through such relating that we find meaning in our lives. Accordingly, Ames sees the Confucian ethical project as ultimately religious. The project of attaining virtuosity in relation to others is the center of Confucian religiousness, which he defines as "the spirituality achieved when members of family and community *aspire* to contribute themselves utterly in their relations with others, and thus live *inspired* lives."[6]

The cultivation of relationships in the Confucian project is not a matter of freewheeling interactions. Instead, it builds on societally established roles. Traditional Chinese thought took five relationships as basic: ruler-subject, parent-child, brother-brother, husband-wife, and friend-friend. These relationships are part of the Chinese correlative cosmology. They are correlated with the five phases (or elements or aspects)—wood, fire, earth, metal, and water—that are considered to be the basic ways that the processes *yin* and *yang* manifest themselves concretely in nature. The relationships are also correlated with numerous other basic sets of fives in Chinese cosmology (for example, directions, colors, body parts, seasons, metals, musical tones of the pentatonic scale, etc.). Thus these relationships are considered natural, much as are the other basic sets of five.

The conception that there are "natural" relationships might be questioned, given that roles are always given specific content in particular historical contexts. Indeed, to foreshadow a later point, the illusion that contingently constructed roles are "natural" renders those who perform them atypically socially suspect, a problematic result if the thriving of everyone is an ethical aim. The five traditional relationships are also inherently hierarchical, in that it is assumed that one party has the dominant status within each. Certain patterns of deference are built into what is expected of those participating in these relationships. While Ames does not restrict the relational roles enjoined by Confucian ethics to the five traditional relationships,[7] he accepts the Confucian notion of *shu*, often translated as deference, which he translates as "putting oneself in the other's place," as essential to relating in a virtuosic way.

The specific behavior that roles require, however, is determined particularistically. That is, what behavior is appropriate depends on the situation and on who is involved. *Yi* (or appropriateness) is therefore an important consideration for determining how one should act in particular circumstances. However, social roles do have their characteristic content. Fulfilling one's roles involves the observance of *li* (or ritual propriety), the performance of the social rituals that are partly constitutive of the role. Ames characteristically interprets *li* quite broadly, defining it as "being committed to the pursuit of propriety in one's familial and communal roles and relationships."[8] Traditionally, however, emphasis is placed on the procedures deemed proper to a role, extending from general practices of politeness to very specifically codified forms. Book X of the *Analects* itemizes some of Confucius's own detailed observances, giving some impression of how specific ritual prescriptions could be.

Roles and Virtues

In light of its emphasis on ideals as *shu*, *li*, and *yi*, and also on *xiao* (filial piety), one might take the Confucian ethical vision to be a form of virtue ethics. But Ames rejects this characterization. He focuses attention on virtuosity as opposed to virtues as such.[9] One could say the same of Aristotelian ethics, which takes the goal to be the activity of living well, and the means to be various virtues, defined as traits that facilitate living in a way that is objectively good. However, Ames, along with Rosemont, takes Confucius's ethics to be importantly dissimilar from Aristotle's.[10] Aristotelian ethics is individualistic both in its aim of individual flourishing and its conception of virtues, which are traits of an individual. Confucian ethics, by contrast, takes the flourishing of relationships as the primary goal.

Others, however, have challenged the idea that Confucian ethics is not a form of virtue ethics. One of these is P. J. Ivanhoe.[11] Although he concurs with Ames that Confucian ethics distinctively emphasize social roles, Ivanhoe contends that, "what matters is not so much the role that one plays but *how* one plays it." Thus, he sees the stress as lying really on the virtues one exhibits in playing particular roles as opposed to the roles themselves.[12] Ivanhoe thinks this characterization helps one to see the contemporary relevance of Confucian ethics, since the virtues encouraged are readily transposable to present-day concerns, while some of the roles emphasized by early Confucians have become outmoded (that of king, for example, at least in many societies). The early Confucians placed considerable importance on being parents, while we would presumably want a theory that allows non-parents to live ethically good lives as well. Ivanhoe also observes that many of the character traits that enable one to play a particular role well often enable one to play other roles well in addition. Thus the value of virtues transcends their usefulness within particular roles.

Ames, however, considers Ivanhoe's proposal that Confucian ethics is a form of virtue ethics as remaining within the individualistic paradigm of Western ethics that he wants to criticize.[13] Ames promotes Confucian ethical thought as a corrective to the excessive individualism that he takes to underlie most ethical thought in the West. As he sees it, Ivanhoe's interpretation of Confucian ethics preempts its potential to offer a different way of modeling ethical life from the dominant Western tendency.

Ames does not think the Confucian emphasis on roles has relevance only for roles that existed in Confucius's own society. Confucianism is a living tradition, and it is able to accommodate changes in the ways that roles have developed over time. Thus, while many contemporary societies lack kings, in virtually all societies certain individuals still have political power over others, and societal wellbeing arises from political leaders and other citizens playing their roles well and cooperatively.

Similarly, although Ivanhoe correctly notes that the ancient Confucians took being a parent as essential to good living (a view they shared with Aristotle, one might add), the family-centered orientation of Confucianism does not require that contemporary families be structured like families in Confucius's China. Whether or not we have children, relational roles within our families remain foundational to how we learn to interact with others, and flourishing relationships with others in our families (however organized) are still important to us. The new challenges faced by adults with aging parents in this era of extended longevity draws attention to the importance of family roles and intergenerational relationships, even among mature people who are not parents themselves.

Ames's position can thus be defended against Ivanhoe's critique. Ivanhoe's point that the Confucian emphasis on roles encourages the cultivation of certain virtues also seems apt, however. In that a person committed to the Confucian Way is enjoined to practice self-cultivation, one might say that cultivation involves developing certain virtues within the context of one's roles. To the extent that self-cultivation is encouraged, some focus on one's personal ethical development is part of the Confucian picture. Accordingly, it might be said that role ethics does entail concern with what might be called virtue, so long as it is understood within a relational context.

Christine Swanton claims that the converse is also true. She contends that "standard virtue ethics entails belief in role ethics," for what counts as virtuous behavior depends on the particular role a person plays.[14] Moreover, she contends that "being good as a human being is itself shaped by role demands."[15] Thus, while she would distinguish role ethics from virtue ethics (claiming that there can be deontological role ethics and consequentialist role ethics as well as virtue ethical role ethics), she certainly sees no incompatibility between the two approaches.[16]

Swanton would question whether or not virtue ethical theories should be categorized as individualistic in orientation. She certainly does not think that virtue ethics should be equated with the Aristotelian approach, with its emphasis on individual excellence. This does seem to be the presupposition of Ames and Rosemont in their defense of Confucian role ethics. Within the domain of virtue ethics, they give Aristotelian ethics pride of place, and while they seem to allow that certain virtues on the Aristotelian might typically benefit relationships (good temper would be an example), they take the goal of the Aristotlelian virtuous person to be one's personal best, not the relational best. By contrast, Swanton thinks Aristotelian ethics is only one of many possible versions of virtue ethics. She herself has developed a Nietzschean virtue ethical approach, and though Nietzsche is certainly individualistic in his orientation, she has more recently been using the more relationally focused work of Martin Heidegger as a point of departure.[17]

Does it matter whether or not Confucian role ethics can be described as a form of virtue ethics? An answer to this question, I suspect, depends upon one's agenda within contemporary philosophy. Ames and Rosemont want to underscore the impact of the different starting points of Confucianism and Aristotelian virtue ethics, particularly with regard to the underlying conception of the human individual presupposed in these two ethical frameworks. They see the emphasis on relationality as a major contribution that Confucianism offers to contemporary ethical discussion.

If, however, one is excited about what contemporary virtue ethics has brought into ethical consideration, such as emphasis of character and living well as opposed to the best procedures for determining right action, one might be more inclined to see Confucianism as contributing to this conversation. Someone with this concern, such as Swanton, might well take virtue ethics to be a broad category that encompasses many possible specifications, only some of which are Aristotelian. On this view one might reasonably see Confucian ethics as a form of virtue ethics that distinctively insists that character development should occur within a relational context in which people stand in various roles toward one another.

Ames's Particularism

Ames's interpretation of Confucian ethics is very particularistic, and as a consequence, it sees Confucianism as extremely open with respect to behavioral specifics. In Ames's account, *yi* ("optimizing appropriateness") is emphasized over the procedural dictates of *li*. The details of how one behaves should be tailored to the particularities of those involved in given relationships. This flexibility is one of the positive features of Confucian role ethics, according to Ames.[18] It allows for a range of ways of articulating a role, enabling participants in a relationship to draw on their particular strengths and to make use of the affordances offered by the situation. It also enables one to fine-tune one's behavior and gestures to the unique relationship given its specific trajectory.

Ames rejects an ossified interpretation of roles. Thus, although he acknowledges that *zhengming* does involve the "rectification of names" (the common translation of the term), the satisfaction of "the stipulated meanings of names and ranks," he sees it as encompassing considerably more. It involves a recognition that language is living, "sensitive to the specifics of the always changing context" and respectful of "the uniqueness of the persons involved in the conversation."[19]

Confucian ethics is also very accommodating to the peculiarities of individuals on Ames's account. Even though he rejects an individualistic conception of the human being, Ames sees Confucianism as respecting the particularity of the person. He points to Confucius as a model in the way he approached his students, demonstrating sensitivity to their individual uniqueness as well as to the contextual situation.[20] Confucian ethics also appreciates the individual contributions of the parties to a relationship, their differential strengths providing means through which they help each other to flourish.

Ames emphasizes the themes of interdependence and the impossibility of flourishing on one's own. Both are evident in ancient Confucian texts;

Ames's interpretation also draws on neo-Confucians who were influenced by Chinese Buddhism. His emphasis on interdependence fits well with the Buddhist interpretation of reality as empty of separate selves and Buddhism's idealistic orientation, according to which one should do what one can to help bring an end to suffering regardless of whether others are enlightened enough to assist in this effort. The model of the compassionate Buddha who preached using skillful means to intervene in even the most intransigent situation seems akin to what one might expect from the Confucian who is committed to the Way on Ames's account.[21]

It is worth noting that commitment to Confucian ethics on Ames's view has a decidedly performative character, another aspect of the openness that he sees in the Confucian model. Individual creativity can be brought to bear on how one lives out one's role, and one is encouraged to use one's imagination in determining how best to enhance the flourishing of relationships in which one is involved.[22] Ames notes the affinity between the aesthetic and the ethical in the Confucian framework.[23] The arts that particularly resonate with ethics on the Confucian model are the arts of performance, and Ames characterizes the implicit goal as "a human and a cosmic 'musicality.'"[24]

Indeed, the Confucian association between ideal human relating and music suggests some of the artistry involved in good performance in either sphere. The "Record of Music" calls for "the blending together without any mutual injuriousness," effectively an admonition to maximize harmony through deference.[25] Good ensemble performers attune themselves to the others' timing in great detail, so fluent in responding to each other's cues that the music seems to emerge from one musician.[26] The Confucian ideal for conducting relationships involves a similar attunement. Another parallel is the importance of facilitating others' efforts in both frameworks. Doing what one can to set up the other performers for their own consummate performance is a part of musical excellence. Jazz saxophonist Steve Lacy reports gaining insight that reoriented his understanding of performance when Thelonious Monk told him to make the drummer sound good.[27] Confucius says something remarkably similar in the following remark from the *Analects*:

> [The Master:] Authoritative persons establish others in seeking to establish themselves and promote others in seeking to get there themselves. Correlating one's conduct with those near at hand can be said to be the method of becoming an authoritative person.[28]

As many parallels as there are between musical excellence and relational virtuosity on the Confucian model, however, perhaps the art that is most pertinent to role ethics is the art of the theater. Like the actor, we perform our humanity, and we do so by enacting roles that in some sense have already been assigned to us. Our context within families and communities provides us with general scripts, but these scripts only come to life when interpreted in a performance. We give meaning to the roles we play by making them our own, much as an actor does.

Reflection on this performance emphasis, however, can lead us to recognize certain potential problems with the emphasis on roles in Confucian ethics. Just as great acting is compromised by inadequacies in the script, so is commitment to the Way if one is locked into oppressive or straitjacketing roles. Thus it is important to consider whether some of the roles that Confucian ethics fosters are not oppressive or in other ways harmful.

Relational Role and Performance Problems

If we are going to adopt a version of role ethics, we need to be clear about which roles we are talking about. Five traditional relationships were emphasized by the early Confucians, and each involved specific ritual demands.[29] These five relationships had a decidedly male bias, in that certain of the relationships were unavailable to women, either intrinsically or in practice. By definition a woman could not be a father, a son, or an elder or younger brother, and practices that restricted women's activities in the public sphere could effectively prevent them from having friends outside the household.[30] We can, of course, reinterpret the father-son relationship in less gender-specific terms as parent-child. But there is room for considerable debate about whether or not a father's relationship with a child is different from a mother's relationship, and on whether any differences that might exist are necessary or contingent. The traditional assumption that husbands held the hierarchically dominant position within the husband-wife relationship presupposes gender inequity. Certain formulations of neo-Confucian thinkers, such as those of Zhu Xi and Cheng Yi, seem explicitly to justify sexist practices, but one can find sexist statements in earlier Confucian texts, too, such as the *Analects* and *Mencius*.[31]

This historical background does not pose a problem for Ames's view. The "concrete familial and social roles" that are central to Confucian ethics are now structured in accordance with more egalitarian ideals than was the case in Confucius's time. By taking its cues from the concrete ways that we relate to others, as opposed to abstract codes of conduct, Confucian ethics reflects changes in societal conceptions of what particular social roles entail.

Thus historical sexism in the interpretations of roles is not essential to Confucianism. In fact, Confucianism can help us to recognize some of the harms of sexism, since sexism interferes with the flourishing of relationships by undercutting the wellbeing of some who are part of them.³² Another set of considerations, however, might raise questions about the impact of Confucian ethics on women. Some commentators have noted striking similarities between Confucian ethics and feminist care ethics, in that both take the flourishing of relationships to be the central goal as well as the basis on which one should determine how to act.³³ Although care ethics has been developed within feminist thought, some feminists have criticized it on grounds that might apply to Confucian role ethics as well.³⁴ Specifically, they contend that care ethics can rationalize the exploitation of women by encouraging women to give their utmost in relationships, regardless of whether or not their commitment is shared by men. This is particularly worrisome in that traditional gender roles have made care the province of women, with the result that women have often devoted themselves utterly to the wellbeing of their families at the expense of their own wellbeing. Many feminists who take the care perspective seriously have, in light of this, taken considerations of rights and justice to be essential, along with an orientation based on care.³⁵

One might raise similar criticisms of the Confucian role ethical framework. If women have been socialized to devote themselves utterly to the flourishing of their families while men have not, Confucianism would seem to reinforce patterns of male exploitation of women. The fact that arrangements that were oppressive toward women have historically been defended by reference to Confucian principles suggests that this concern is not idle. Conventional associations with gender have certainly affected how the respective roles of husbands and wives have been understood, both in China and elsewhere. This suggests that Confucian role ethics, centered as it is on the family, may endorse reigning conceptions of gender roles that are implicit in the way "family" is often understood.

The problem is that the ideal of performing one's relational roles to one's utmost presupposes that one has some idea of what those roles consist of, and that idea may be tainted by stereotypes that are sexist or in other ways oppressive. Even if the specifications of *li* for given social roles is more relaxed in our time than it was in Confucius's day, social expectations about what those roles involve can have pernicious consequences for those whose way of performing them is nonstandard.

Judith Butler has done much to theorize the problems lurking in the performance of reigning social roles. She focuses on the oppressive results for those who are members of sexual minorities. She is rightly renowned for her theory that gender is a performance and that gender identity is a fabrication created by the repeated performance of gender. Society demands that its members adopt certain styles and types of behavior associated with one of the accepted genders, and that each individual perform the gender that is taken to correspond to that person's biology. Those who perform as required succeed in creating the impression that they "have" one of the authorized genders, indeed that they have always already had it.

> Words, acts, gestures, and desire produce the effect of an internal core or substance, but produce this *on the surface of the body* . . . such acts, gestures enactments, generally construed, are performative in the sense that the essence or identity that they purport to express are *fabrications* manufactured and sustained through corporeal signs and other discursive means. That the gendered body is performative suggests that it has no ontological status apart from the various acts which constitute its reality. . . . In other words, acts and gestures, articulated and enacted desires create the illusion of an interior and organizing gender core, an illusion discursively maintained for the purposes of the regulation of sexuality within the obligatory frame of reproductive heterosexuality.[36]

The similarities and dissimilarities of Butler and Ames's accounts are striking. Like Ames, Butler rejects the Enlightenment model of society as composed of autonomous individuals. She defends a relational view of the human being, in which each of us is "a porous boundary, given over to others," operating in a "field of ethical enmeshment with others and a sense of disorientation for the first person."[37] Butler also agrees with Ames that personhood is not an innate internal core. They seem to disagree, however, about how one acquires personhood. Ames contends that one becomes a person through developing one's relationships, beginning with the familial relationships that are there from one's infancy. One grows into a person by developing a thick nexus of relationships, but this occurs almost inevitably, given that our very survival depends on relating to others.

By contrast, Butler sees personhood as socially conferred—or withheld. Speaking of those in sexual minorities, she contends that "norms of recognition . . . produce and sustain our viability as human,"[38] and that in the struggle for sexual rights, those in sexual minorities are "struggling *to be conceived as persons.*"[39] She draws attention to the fact that sanctions on those who do not conform to the system of compulsory heterosexuality are often severe, sometimes extending to violence and the denial of personhood altogether.

Ames and Butler also disagree about the nature of our performance-generated identities. Butler takes the identity that is conjured through the performance of gender to be productive of illusion—the illusion that this identity has always been there. By contrast, Ames takes an entirely positive view of the identity production accomplished through the performances of one's roles on the Confucian system. He stresses that such identities are historically situated, and that he does not want to enshrine ancient Confucian understandings of relational roles. But in light of Butler's analysis of the command performances required by the gender system, we might ask whether the relational roles as contemporary society conceives them are necessarily benign in their consequences.

Ames, however, does not seem to take gender roles, *per se*, to be among the roles that Confucian ethics seeks to cultivate. The role ethics that he finds in Confucianism focuses on reciprocal roles in relationships. Many aspects of gender roles have to do with individual style, preference, and manner of performance that do not appear to be relational in focus (even if gender roles are societally mandated as a means of governing sexual relationships and the reproduction that might ensue). Ames also thinks that the Confucian ethical vision can apply to social roles as they evolve. Nevertheless, its history suggests that this can apply within contexts in which the *status quo* assumes roles with exploitative practices. Of course, exploitation is not the aim, and the goal of mutual flourishing resists it.

The Confucian elevation of familial and social roles has a built-in conservative bias; these roles are understood on the basis of how they have been conducted in practice. This being the case, it is hard to see how gender roles, which have been pervasively taken for granted, could be entirely extricated from the roles Confucian ethics exhorts us to play.

Let us imagine the person committed to the Way who attempts to perform his or her relational roles so as to promote mutual flourishing. What does this person use for guidance in how he or she might do this? Presumably, he or she uses some general idea of what is entailed in the roles based on observation of role models and knowledge of societal expectations. Socially mandated features of role performance (such as the restrictions on acceptable performances of gender) will be modeled (at least approximately) by the vast majority of people one encounters, and one does not have to search hard to become aware of sanctions against those who deviate. Almost inevitably, the person's idea of his or her roles will take conventional form and include societal biases against approaches viewed as deviant.

Of course, one's background may be in some ways atypical, and this may affect one's understanding of what specifics are required by one's role. One may include idiosyncrasies of one's primary model in one's conception of successful role performance. One often finds young academics imitating their elder colleagues, perhaps unwittingly. A somewhat comical illustration is provided by those who have adopted the Oxbridge stutter. But the results are not always so harmless. Most people learn what is involved in parenting from their parents first of all, and children who are abused by their parents often become abusive parents themselves.

Ames might reply that looking to previous models for a sense of our relational roles is inevitable. We learn roles on the basis of forms that society has already developed, and we do not construct our ways of relating *de novo*. But there is room for worry that the Confucian emphasis on good form in one's relationships, combined with a role orientation that necessarily appeals to models, reinforces rather than resists societal compulsions that are oppressive to some part of the population.

Both Ames and Butler believe that social roles can evolve, though they both take such change to be gradual. Butler points out that gender is not accomplished through a single act, but maintained by means of repetition. Because one can alter the way one performs one's gender, one is able to contest the current gender system and the binarism that underlies it.

> The object is not *determined* by the rules through which it is generated because signification is *not a founding act, but rather a regulated process of repetition* that both conceals itself and enforces its rules precisely through the production of substantializing effects. . . . "Agency," then, is to be located within the possibility of a variation on that repetition. If the rules governing signification not only restrict, but enable the assertion of alternative domains of cultural intelligibility, i.e., new possibilities for gender that contest the rigid codes of hierarchical binarisms, then it is only *within* the practices of repetitive signifying that a subversion of identity becomes possible.[40]

In other words, alternative performances to those required by the disciplinary system that produces gender are the means by which its demands can be resisted and undermined, at least to a certain extent. Butler does not think that one "puts on" and "takes off" gender roles.[41] Much of one's performance is unconsciously directed. Nevertheless, repetition of deviant performances can have an impact on how gender identity is understood when it provokes a shift in societal expectations.

Ames interprets Confucian ideals in sufficiently general terms to see them as resources for improving human relationships and for promoting less oppressive or inequitable arrangements. The radical particularism of Ames's interpretation of Confucianism does not accommodate efforts to subvert reigning conceptions of roles in general.[42] Nevertheless, he thinks that by making particular adjustments and contributions to one's relationships in concrete contexts, one nudges the social world toward concern with the flourishing of all human relationships, a commitment that would resist oppressive forms. Like Butler, he takes positive change in social roles as achievable through the steady repetition of revisionary gestures. He does not, however, target some of our reigning social roles as inherently oppressive or encourage projects of role subversion, projects that Confucian role ethics would not facilitate.

Conclusion

Ames himself acknowledges certain limitations of the Confucian vision, which he grants is "not entirely benign" in its effects.[43] Thus, he recognizes some legitimacy to the complaint that Confucian ethics gives "an excess of attention to intimate relations" while being insufficiently concerned with "guarantees that derive from more impartial considerations," and thereby enables certain kinds of cultural corruption.[44] He also grants that the partiality that Confucian ethics defends can be an obstacle to public spiritedness, and that it can nurture parochialism.

The previous section suggests additional reasons for doubting that Confucian role ethics, on its own, necessarily tends toward a world in which all would flourish. Despite the Confucian view's relational focus, those who occupy roles in an atypical manner are not protected from various kinds of social exclusion, perhaps to the point that their very humanity may not be recognized. If implicit scripts that constitute social roles have oppressive consequences, they should not be the touchstone for the good life, important as interpersonal roles of some sort may be for enabling us to participate meaningfully in the social world. As much insight as it might contribute to our way of conceiving ethical life, Confucian role ethics appears insufficient on its own for addressing contemporary failures to extend respect and benevolence to all within our communities.

The great promise of Confucian ethics on Ames's interpretation is its power to focus our aspirations. Ultimately, the aim of Confucian role ethics as Ames interprets it is "to transform the world into a family" in which interdependence is acknowledged and all parties to relationships recognize the concerns of the others as their own. "Role ethics applies the logic that when another member of your family does better, you do better too."[45] Ames has an extremely idealistic vision of family, in which this logic is assumed to apply. Family, in his view, is an unmitigated good, at least taken as an ideal. It seems to exclude no one in principle, and it makes allowances for other family members' peculiarities, whatever they happen to be.

The problem with idealistic visions is that very few come close to living up to them. As opposed to the benign ideal of family in Ames's interpretation, we need to consider real families that are quite other than this, in which power dynamics are exploitative and even brutal, and in which the modeling of roles is perverse, if not perverting. And we also need to recognize that families do not always actually accommodate those who are different, even among those in their midst.

In keeping with his idealistic Confucianism, Ames would likely say the import of the Confucian vision is that no situation is intractable, but acknowledge that realistically many are difficult. Confucianism promotes the view that relationships are ongoing and improvable. Confucianism encourages us to approach our actual, flawed relationships by giving them "all that you've got," by using imagination in confronting relational impasses and rising to the occasion when offered the chance to relate with greater virtuosity.

Ames does not propose that Confucian role ethics is a panacea for our contemporary problems. But he rightly sees it as offering a vision that can help direct our course, so long as we are not blinded by the biases that disfigure our conceptions of roles. One may need to interpret Confucianism as flexibly as he does to see the extent of its contemporary promise. But Ames shows that Confucian devotion to furthering one's family can prompt the endeavor to render all relationships fully humane. He urges us to expand the notion of family to the full matrix of our human connections, and to recognize that we best flourish when we help others flourish, too.

Notes

1. I am delighted to have the opportunity to contribute to this commemorative volume in honor of Roger Ames. As friend, mentor, and colleague over a long span of years, he has exemplified the person who truly lives his philosophy. I am sure I speak for many others, too, when I say that I count myself as tremendously fortunate to have been welcomed into Roger's extended family and treated with so much aloha.
2. Roger T. Ames, *Confucian Role Ethics: A Vocabulary* (Hong Kong: Chinese University Press, 2011).
3. Ames, *Confucian Role Ethics*, 87.
4. Ibid.
5. Ames, *Confucian Role Ethics*, 91.
6. Ames, *Confucian Role Ethics*, 92.
7. See Ames, *Confucian Role Ethics*, 100–01.
8. Ames, *Confucian Role Ethics*, 7.
9. Ames, *Confucian Role Ethics*, 157.
10. See Henry Rosemont Jr., and Roger T. Ames, "Introduction," *The Chinese Classic of Family Reverence: A Philosophical Translation of the "Xiaojing,"* trans. and ed. Henry Rosemont Jr., and Roger T. Ames (Honolulu: University of Hawai'i Press, 2009), 40–45.

11. See Philip J. Ivanhoe, "The Shade of Confucius: Social Roles, Ethical Theory, and the Self," In *Polishing the Chinese Mirror: Essays in Honor of Henry Rosemont Jr.*, ed. Marthe Chandler and Ronnie Littlejohn (New York: Global Scholarly Publications, 2007), 33-48. Another is May Sim. See her "Why Confucius' Ethics Is a Virtue Ethics," in *The Routledge Companion to Virtue Ethics*, ed. Lorraine Besser-Jones and Michael Slote (New York: Routledge, 2015), 63-76.

12. Ivanhoe, "The Shade of Confucius," 38.

13. It is worth noting that some defenders of feminist care ethics, with its focus on relationships, have similarly resisted the description of care ethics as a form of virtue ethics. See, for example, Virginia Held, "Care and Justice in the Global Context," *Ratio Juris* 17:2 (2004), 143.

14. Christine Swanton, "Virtue Ethics, Role Ethics, and Business Ethics," in *Working Virtue: Virtue Ethics and Contemporary Moral Problems*, ed. Rebecca L. Walker and P. J. Ivanhoe (New York: Oxford University Press, 2007), 207. See also 217.

15. Swanton, "Virtue Ethics, Role Ethics, and Business Ethics," 211.

16. Note that the roles that Swanton has primarily in mind are those that arise because of one's participation in a particular profession, such as law, medicine, or business.

17. For her Nietzschean account of virtue ethics see Christine Swanton, *Virtue Ethics: A Pluralistic View* (Oxford: Oxford University Press, 2003). For a more Heideggerian discussion see Christine Swanton "Heideggerian Environmental Virtue Ethics," in *Journal of Agricultural and Environmental Ethics* 23 (2010): 145-66. In contrast to most interpreters who see Nietzsche as an individualist, Julian Young argues that he has communitarian concerns. See Julian Young, *Nietzsche's Philosophy of Religion* (Cambridge: Cambridge University Press, 1997).

18. Ames, *Confucian Role Ethics*, 161.

19. Ames, *Confucian Role Ethics*, 101.

20. Ibid.

21. Cf. Peter Hershock, *Liberating Intimacy: Enlightenment and Social Virtuosity in Ch'an Buddhism* (Albany: State University of New York Press, 1996).

22. See Roger T. Ames and David L. Hall, "Introduction: A Philosophical Interpretation of the Zhongyong," in *Focusing the Familiar: A Translation and Philosophical Interpretation of the "Zhongyong,"* trans. and ed. Roger T. Ames and David L. Hall (Honolulu: University of Hawai`i Press, 2001), 30-35.

23. Ames, *Confucian Role Ethics*, 169.

24. Ames, *Confucian Role Ethics*, 168-71.

25. "Yo Ki, or Record of Music," in *The Sacred Books of China* in 6 vols. in *The Sacred Books of the East* in 50 vols., ed. F. Max Müller, Vol. XXVIII, trans. James Legge. *The Texts of Confucianism*, Part IV: *The Li Ki* (Delhi: Motilal Banarsidass, 1885; reprinted by Clarendon, 1966), 101.

26. See Alfred Schutz, "Making Music Together: A Study in Social Relationship," *Social Research* 18:2 (1951): 76-97.

27. Steve Lacy, interview by Terry Gross, *Fresh Air*, produced by WHYY-FEM/ Philadelphia, distributed by National public Radio, November 20, 1997, cited in William Day, "Knowing as Instancing: Jazz Improvisation and Moral Perfectionism," *Journal of*

Aesthetics and Art Criticism 58 (Spring 2000), 108. Day points out that Lacy tells essentially the same story in Thomas Fitterling, *Thelonious Monk: his Life and Music*, trans. Robert Dobbins, a foreword by Steve Lacy (Albany, CA: Berkeley Hills Books, 1997), 13–14.

28. *The Analects of Confucius: A Philosophical Translation*, trans. and ed. Roger T. Ames and Henry Rosemont Jr. (New York: Ballantine Books, 1998), 6.30, 110.

29. Obligations in mourning, for example, depend on one's relationship to the deceased person, the appropriate funeral ceremonies, as well as the person's own status. See Mencius 1B.16.

30. Zhu Xi, for example, contended that women's position was inside the home, by contrast with that of men, which was outside. See Chenyang Li, "Introduction," *The Sage and the Second Sex: Confucianism, Ethics, and Gender*, ed. Chenyang Li (Chicago: Open Court, 2000), 5.

31. See Li, "Introduction," *The Sage and the Second Sex*, 5.

32. See David L. Hall and Roger T. Ames, *Thinking from the Han: Self, Truth, and Transcendence in Chinese and Western Culture* (Albany: State University of New York Press, 1998), 100.

33. See Nel Noddings, *Caring: A Feminine Approach to Ethics and Moral Education* (Berkeley and Los Angeles: University of California Press, 1984); and Sara Ruddick, *Maternal Thinking: Toward a Politics of Peace* (Boston: Beacon, 1989). See also Henry Rosemont Jr., "Classical Confucianism and Contemporary Feminist Perspectives: Some Parallels and their Implications," *Culture and the Self: Philosophical and Religious Perspectives, East and West*, ed. Douglas Allen (Boulder, CO: Westview, 1997).

34. For a summary, see Hilde Lindemann, *An Invitation to Feminist Ethics* (New York: McGraw-Hill, 2005), 94–96. See also Eva Feder Kittay, *Love's Labor: Essays on Women, Equality and Dependency* (New York: Routledge: 1999).

35. See, for example, Carol Gilligan, *Joining the Resistance* (Cambridge: Polity Press, 2011).

36. Judith Butler, *Gender Trouble: Feminism and the Perversion of Identity* (New York: Routledge, 1990), 136.

37. Judith Butler, *Undoing Gender* (New York: Routledge, 2004), 25.

38. Butler, *Undoing Gender*, 33.

39. Ibid.

40. Butler, *Gender Trouble*, 145.

41. See Judith Buttler, "Gendering the Body: Beauvoir's Philosophical Contribution," in *Women, Knowledge, and Reality: Explorations in Feminist Philosophy*, ed. Ann Garry and Marilyn Pearsall (Boston: Unwin Hyman, 1989), 256.

42. Ames characterizes Confucianism as having a notion of justice, but it "references the complex, creative process of achieving what is most appropriate in the specific, usually inequitable relations and situations that locate us within family and community. The resolutely hierarchical and dynamic pattern of the human experience that begins in family relations is going to have to be included in the equation that expresses a Confucian notion of justice" (Ames, *Confucian Role Ethics*, 123).

43. Ames, *Confucian Role Ethics*, 261.

44. Ibid.

45. Ibid.

12

Role Ethics

Problems and Promise

HENRY ROSEMONT JR.

It is indisputable that there is much wrong with the world today. Many people of good will think the problems are basically political and economic, but Roger and I believe that the politics and economics are embedded in a conceptual framework of moralities grounded in one type of foundational individualism or another, none of which is even capable of addressing those problems competently any longer, in our opinion, much less contributing to their solutions. Thus we believe new moralities are needed (containing some very old elements), with intellectual and psychological resources that more closely resemble the hopes, fears, dreams and aspirations of actual people than the disembodied individuals who tend to populate our current patterns of moral thinking. For us, role ethics presents one such conceptual framework for working through a morality we believe is appropriate for the present day, and more than that, can appeal to liberals and conservatives alike, with room for both the faithful and the skeptics, and proffering a vision of the good life for human beings that can provide highly useful guidelines for addressing our problems—political, economic, environmental, and perhaps even spiritual—in a more cooperative manner.

We both came to these views through the study of classical Confucianism, and later by working closely together on Confucian translation and interpretation projects for a number of years, and I thought it might be appropriate for his *Festschrift* (i.e., commemorative volume) to briefly sketch the history and development of these collaborative efforts as I experienced them.[1] But hoping that our collaborative endeavors are not yet over, I want to stimulate his thinking by then taking up a couple of themes we will have to tackle if we wish to advance the case for a Confucian-inspired role ethics to a higher level. The first of these is metaphilosophical, reflecting on the extent to which the content of our arguments for role ethics must needs affect the manner of their presentation, and reflecting as well on how to bridge the gap between *understanding* a way of experiencing the world and actually experiencing it that way. I will then take up the issue of democracy in the context of role ethics, for reasons that I will explain in due course. In all three of my accounts, my overall goal will be to stimulate Roger's thinking afresh, as we have so often done for each other in the past.

Coming to Role Ethics

The concept of role ethics by which we tend to be known had its genesis in a paper I wrote for another commemorative volume—for Herbert Fingarette in 1991—wherein I suggested that seeing the Chinese as flesh and blood role-bearers rather than potential candidates to be abstract rights-holders might give Western trained philosophers a better background for reading early Confucian texts.[2] Roger began to work with the idea in some depth before I did, contextualizing it with the centrality of the family for developing an ethics of roles. I then picked up on Roger's discussions of family by working to find an appropriate English vocabulary for describing such a morality because it had no close counterpart in the history of Western ethics, and he picked up the cudgels to do the same for refining the Chinese lexicon in order for the early Confucians to be able to speak more clearly and faithfully in their own voices yet expressing views applicable to the present.[3] Roger also developed the notion of paronomasia to explicate the Chinese lexicon,[4] and I began to think less of concepts and words, and more of concept-clusters, especially, but not confined to terms central for philosophers, particularly in ethics, politics, and religion.[5] Against the background of these three shared interrelated themes—role ethics, family, and language/translation—what followed were our two collaborative translations (*Lunyu* and *Xiaojing*),[6] a half-dozen joint articles, and two separately authored books, his *Confucian Role Ethics: A Vocabulary* (2011)[7] and my *Against Individualism: A Confucian Rethinking of the Foundations of Morality, Politics, Family and Religion* (2015).[8]

At first we attempted to articulate Confucian role ethics somewhat unreflectively in terms that could conceivably be descriptive of free, autonomous individual selves as well as role-bearers—even though we were increasingly suspicious of the former—especially as we undertook our translation of the *Analects*. We confirmed our suspicions fairly quickly, however, because we encountered two major difficulties: (1) While passages in the text pertaining to the conduct of human beings as role-bearers abounded, we could find none that described their activities in terms of freedom or autonomy, and very few (e.g., 18.7) in which any of the participants were not discussed in terms of close relationships to others; and, (2) As we continued to think about and began to develop role ethics, we increasingly found less work for the concept of the free, autonomous (and rationally choosing) individual self to do, or even to *be*, once Roger began to speak of human beings as always *becoming*. Instead, more and more it seemed to us that describing the proper performances of the role participants with the appropriate attitude toward the performance and the other(s) with whom they were engaged, sufficed to articulate an ethics that seemed both to give the greatest consistency and coherence to the text, and also to conform to our human daily experiences much better than the abstract accounts thereof reflected in the writings of the heroes of Western moral philosophy, past and (near) present.

By the time we came to translate the *Xiaojing*, we were willing to jettison the concept of the free, autonomous individual self altogether, for several reasons. First, we increasingly became puzzled when trying to make clear sense of what it meant to be a free, autonomous individual self—apart from its psychological pull—supported in our growing doubts by recent work in the neurosciences as well as in philosophy. Second, we were able to begin work with both Chinese and English to capture the vision of Confucius as we saw it without doing violence to the text, and to explicate more generally what an ethics of roles might be like.

Third, we came to believe—and argue for—the idea that an insistence on the paromouncy of individual freedom in ethical and political theories was at the expense of equality and social justice, and consequently moral arguments on behalf of the latter that were also grounded in the concept of individual human freedom could be easily met by counter arguments equally moral. And purchased at the expense of social and economic justice, as the libertarians have been (unintentionally) making clear for some time now. Moreover, although interpreting the *Analects* as a role ethics met with initial skepticism, we did not receive any critiques of what was wrong with our translations or our interpretations of it, and that has held for our *Xiaojing* efforts as well. If we were correct in our claim that championing the freedom and autonomy of individuals came at the expense of social justice, then clearly we would not be doing the early Confucians any favors by attributing a concept of autonomous individualism to them.

And finally, a fourth reason for abandoning the fiction of an autonomous individual self was that it seemed increasingly to be the case that all of the important *good* work done by deontological, consequentialist, or virtue ethics based on individualism could also be captured by an ethics of roles, hence the concept of human beings as free, autonomous individual selves could be dispensed with in accordance with Ockham's Razor, and Confucius did not at all have to be seen as a second-class moral philosopher.

Believing that every society worth living in must be characterized by a robust sense of social justice and a fair measure of economic equality, we have thus been led in recent work to abandon altogether *every* ethical theory grounded in what we have come to call "foundational individualism," which includes pragmatism, care ethics, Marxism, and the communal anarchism of Peter Kropotkin no less than the strictly individualist version of Max Stirner, and almost all other philosophers in between, as otherwise different as Rousseau, Rawls, Sandel, MacIntyre, Nel Noddings, and Charles Taylor. If we are correct that all ethics and politics grounded in the freedom and autonomy of individual selves hinders significantly the achievement of social (distributive) justice in a society, and if many of the horrors confronting the world today have poverty and inequality at their root, then, to repeat, it becomes clear that we do no favors to the early Confucians to ascribe an individualist foundation to their thinking, for they then can have little to say about solving those problems, and we would be reduced to reading the *Analects* for its antiquarian interest.

We may be wrong in some or all of these beliefs: it may be that there is an ethics and politics grounded in individualism that can indeed claim the moral high ground for social justice and wealth redistribution, which we urge our colleagues to continue to attempt to develop. But because we believe that foundational individualism is a major *cause* of our contemporary malaise we are not optimistic that any theory accepting it can contribute to its cure; thus far we have not seen any plausible candidates, and until we do will continue to push the envelope for an ethics and politics grounded in the roles lived by interrelated persons, whose sole constant is change.

Is Dialogue or Debate on Role Ethics Possible?

Much work in role ethics of course remains to be done; we seem to have only begun to explore the possibilities and problems attendant on such a major reorientation of how to think about morality and politics, and by extension, the family, society, economy, and religion. How can, or should, we view these and similar institutions differently as role-bearing persons rather than as free, autonomous individuals? Perhaps the most basic concern is how to establish ground rules for dialogues with people who disagree with our claims but are as committed as we are to the view that fundamental change in contemporary society in the United States is necessary, but that it cannot come about unless the overall moral perspectives of the American peoples undergo a sea change with respect to their foundations. Put differently, given the Ames-Rosemont ontology of relations, transformations and becoming rather than essences, constancy and being, how best do we debate or engage in dialogue with colleagues much more accustomed to dealing with essences, constancy, and worrying about *being* who want to criticize the concept of role ethics either as the best interpretation of the *Analects*, or as a viable ethical position today?

Taking the former challenge first, it poses few problems of a narrative sort, largely thanks to Roger's close philological work; the matters are significantly textual and logical, not ontological, and hence can be discussed without undue misunderstanding, it has seemed to me. Following Roger, we attempted to make a full case for an ethics of roles together as the best interpretation of the *Analects* in our follow-up translation of the *Xiaojing*, proffering philological evidence and philosophical arguments which Roger further elaborated at length in his *Confucian Role Ethics*. We have not had any serious critiques of those arguments and evidence yet, save for the question of who or what it is that lives all their roles if not an individual self. And I have addressed *that* question in some detail in *Against Individualism*, so the ball is still in the other court on this score as far as we can determine.

Relatedly, we have been criticized for not arguing in any detail against the position of Confucianism being a type of virtue ethics, but we have not seen any critiques of our position by proponents of virtue ethics, and no defense of the concept of the Confucian individual self to which the Confucian virtues are supposedly attached.[9] Again, Roger and I have both proffered arguments against this position at some length apart from Confucian concerns: the idea of an autonomous individual self is a fiction, and has become a pernicious fiction; it is incoherent when spelled out, and inconsistent when spelled out further. Neuro-scientific research is rendering the idea ever more implausible, and when taken in a spiritual sense becomes positively bizarre.[10] Whether and/or to what extent our arguments have been suasive or at least seem reasonable it is too early to tell, because reasonableness will not be the sole criterion by which our position will be evaluated—which takes us to the second, more serious dimension of the problem of engaging in dialogue with opponents of our views.

One complication for dialogue or debate is that it is difficult to raise an objection to our position without begging the question against us. That is to say, reservations about role ethics are almost invariably grounded in a foundational individualistic framework. It is indeed a criticism of our view that human beings are fundamentally and always encumbered, hence not free in the modern Western moral sense. But it is a criticism only if it has been assumed in advance (presupposed, actually) that we are free, autonomous individual selves. If we are role bearers, the society/state must insure that no one is constrained from securing the wherewithal necessary to meet their role responsibilities—education, work, health care, etc. as well as options for electing how best to fulfill their roles—but that is a long way from what virtually every moral philosopher has meant by "freedom;" role-bearing persons are never unencumbered.

Similarly, for us, it seems clear that human beings have responsibilities in roles they have not chosen (my brother and I did not negotiate to be brothers), whereas in modern Western moral and political philosophy—especially social contract and rational choice theories—this would not generally be so, and abstractly regrettable when it was. But this objection has force only under the condition that the contracts and choices have been made by free, autonomous individuals, not interrelated role-bearing persons who cannot be described, even imaginatively, as having their relationship contracted, except perhaps in economic situations between strangers. We cannot answer any questions about what the essence of role-bearing persons might be because we do not believe they have any "essence," nor any "being" either, as they are always becoming. Change is the norm, constancy an aberration.

Our narrative problem (Roger's and mine) is on all fours with anyone else who wants to claim the truth of a negative existential statement. We may affirm the unlikelihood of there being unicorns in our world, but only God could *prove* that there weren't any. Thus, if someone says to us that, even though they cannot directly meet our arguments against their having a free, autonomous individual self, they are nevertheless certain that they do, then there is nothing more for us to say. Roger and I can still claim that such a belief tends to prevent achieving social justice in democratic societies, but we cannot say that the belief is false. By the same token the foundational individualist cannot *prove* that a role-bearing person is not really who she thinks she is; obviously cannot claim, in other words, that such a person does have a self, but just doesn't realize it. This, too, however, is not an easy argument to make convincing. Moreover, arguments showing the perniciousness of the concept of human beings as free, autonomous individual selves will have force only in proportion to the closeness of social and economic justice to freedom on the value scale of those who hear the arguments; if human freedom is an unalloyed good for you and justice ranks much lower or not at all in your value prioritization the impact of our arguments will approximate zero for you. In short, Roger and I claim that the concept of free, autonomous individual selves as definitive of *homo sapiens* is misguided because there are no such things, and we should rather see each member of the species as defined by the sum of the roles they live interrelatedly with others, or at least entertain the possibility that such might be the case. Our opponents will affirm just the opposite in both circumstances.

There seems to be, in short, no conceptual place where true *engagement* with our fellow philosophers might take place; both sides seem to have little choice but to be *confrontational*. We offer arguments on behalf of our claim that we believe are fairly strong, but admit straightaway that they are not, cannot be conclusive. It is difficult to ascertain how the dispute might be resolved because it is neither fully empirical nor *a priori*. And there does not seem to be any vantage point from which to analyze and evaluate the two positions neutrally; in this case, as in so many others, there is no "view from nowhere." We cannot simultaneously see an autonomous individual self and an interrelated role-bearing person. Like the optical illusion of a young woman in a Victorian hat in a picture, which if viewed a different way, is a picture of an old crone. Or two black silhouette profiles against a white background, or a white urn against a black background—or a duck looked at one way, but then becomes a rabbit when the paper is turned. In all of these and similar instances, you can see one or the other, but cannot hold them both in view simultaneously.

What makes this point relevant to our concerns here is that pre-philosophically, the psychological pull of the belief that we each have about being an autonomous individual self is *extremely* strong. We feel in our bones that there is no one just like us, and that we are free to have chosen otherwise than we did virtually all of the time. And we feel as well that no matter how much affection is bestowed on our loved ones, or bestowed on us by them, we are fundamentally *distinct* from them then, now and forever. An argument and/or evidence that a stranger has done something really bad might be accepted by us fairly easily. A little more argument and/or evidence will be required for an acquaintance, but perhaps no argument and/or evidence will ever convince us that an old and cherished friend has done a dastardly deed. In just the same way, we tend to be pretty intimate friends with ourselves, and find it very difficult to entertain the possibility that we may not be the abstract autonomous individual self we have always thought we were.

Of course this difficulty applies to Roger and me no less than to our individualist challengers. We have a slight edge on them, however, for we both viewed the world as individuals for many, many years before its spell began to weaken after working with classical Confucian texts closely for a long while, and reflecting at philosophical length on what, exactly, it meant to be or to have a unique autonomous individual self. Eventually we both made the change. Speaking for myself at least, it was not an "aha!" event, a quick gestalt switch, but came slowly, over time, as I attended more closely to my behavior in my roles, and reflected on them afterwards. But Roger has long been much farther down this road than I have been, which is one reason I have raised the issue here: to me, Roger exemplifies *ren* more than almost anyone I know, a compliment I do not make lightly. He not only understands experiencing the world from a role-bearing perspective, he is experiencing it himself. One small example: when he was giving the Ch'ien Mu lectures at the Chinese University of Hong Kong in 2008, he said that he was spending time most afternoons with his mentor D. C. Lau, who was becoming quite frail by then. When I complimented him for doing his duty as a student in such an exemplary fashion he said that it wasn't a duty at all, or at the least that he didn't experience it as such; rather he "experienced joy" at having "the honor and the privilege" (the terms are all his) of contributing to the well-being of his teacher. I believed him then, and even more so now; but you will not understand him, or why I am so fond of him, if you think of his actions as "altruistic."

In sum on this score, my sense is that the two orientations toward what it is to be a human being do not seem to be commensurable; if we see ducks, we don't see rabbits. Roger and I might be construed as issuing "a call to be heard,"[11] except that we are not taking up matters of faith, but matters of reason, with a psychological twist.

Perhaps the impasse can be resolved by expanding the issue, adding to it the further question of what major implications follow from the conflicting views of what it is to be a human being. If it is not possible to resolve the issue yea or nay on its own, I'd like to suggest to Roger that it is now time for us and other supporters of role ethics to begin addressing crucial questions as to its applicability today. How might government, the economy, family, community, legal system, etc., be seen and structured differently in a role-bearing culture than in an individualistic one? How can, or should, we view these and similar institutions differently as role-bearing persons rather than as free, autonomous individuals?

Put another way, even if we accept that an ethics of roles much more nearly conforms to our lived experiences than the more abstract theories definitive of the major Western theories, so what? Are there any implications of role ethics for how we construe democracy? How different will economic exchanges look in societies governed morally by a role ethics? How about the legal system? Is it even minimally realistic to think of returning to extended family living patterns in this day when there are as many divorces as marriages? How can extended families be housed as the trend toward hyperurbanism continues?

I thus want to suggest that viable answers to these questions will be needed if role ethics is to be taken seriously by a wide range of people, and providing those answers will be strong support for the position overall. If the moral and political implication of role ethics can be seen as salutary for our fractured world today, the spell of foundational individualism may continue to weaken, and it may be possible to answer the question "When might everyone accept role ethics?" with the one given by Max Planck when he was asked when all physicists would accept Einstein's theories: "When all those who don't have died."

To one such concern that Roger has taken up in the past—prior to our full commitment to an ethics of roles for a Confucian past and global present—I now want to turn.

A Political Corollary for Role Ethics: Democracy

The concept of democracy broadly construed must occupy a prominent place in any fleshed-out account of role ethics in general, and for a Confucian-inspired role ethics in particular. I will first offer some reflections on Roger's earlier treatment of the topic, then briefly consider some recent work dealing with Confucian democracy, and then insert my own two cents worth into the discussion. My hope is to nudge Roger into taking up this issue again, or to at least offer some further reflections on it, just as I hope he will do for the other issues I have touched on in this essay.

All efforts to argue for the applicability of the Confucian vision for today's world—not alone our role ethics—must take up the patterns of democracy that might emerge from it, or are, at the least, consistent with it (assuming that authoritarian systems are not on the table). This is so because at the heart of the vision is an ethical ideal, and there is fairly uniform agreement that ethics is linked to (what we would classify as) politics in Confucianism. But "politics" for the Master was a long way from democracy. He was unequivocal about the necessity for governors to take seriously the hopes, fears, dreams and wellbeing of the peasantry, and that addressing these concerns was the first duty of rulers, but he never hinted at the possibility of having popular elections for the governors. Merit was needed, as defined by both knowledge and wisdom; winning a popular vote was never even mentioned. We must, therefore, inquire as to whether a very different political order than the one Confucius inherited would have an effect on the contemporary significance of his ethical ideal, and if so, of what kind?

It is of course possible to think of an ethics of roles apart from a Confucian orientation, but it is largely that orientation, for me at least, and I believe for Roger as well, that makes the concept of a Confucian-inspired role-bearing person a uniquely positive model of human beings, no matter what one's cultural background, because it not only seems to approximate our actual lived lives more than any other ethics, but is also not culture-specific despite its distinctive Chineseness, and does indeed embrace an ideal most people would find admirable. Moreover, as I will argue later, a number of fundamental changes in the way the United States is governed are needed, and an ethics of roles is much better suited to provide a moral conceptual framework for such changes than moralities grounded in one form of individualism or another. What, then, might a Chinese-style, role-based Confucian-inspired democracy look like compared to those now current in the West?

Roger began to address this question in an earlier work with David Hall, *The Democracy of the Dead*:

> We do not ignore the serious defects of traditional Confucianism illustrated by the isolation of minorities, gender inequities, and an overall disinterest in the rule of law. In spite of these past failings, we argue that, on balance, there are resources within the Confucian tradition for constructing a coherent model of viable and humane democracy that remains true to the communitarian sensibilities of traditional China while avoiding many of the defects of rights-based liberalism.[12]

They later sketch out a Chinese communitarian model of democracy along lines espoused by John Dewey in the name of Pragmatism. But their sketch is no more than that, a sketch; there is very little specificity to their position, except to establish that accepting Dewey does not require abandoning many traditional Chinese cultural norms. Moreover, when *Democracy of the Dead* was being written, Roger, like me, had not yet entirely given up the idea of the individual as a locus of value in beginning to develop role ethics beyond the early Confucian texts, and in the context of the centrality of the family in that development. Roger did not return to the theme of a Confucian-style democracy in *Confucian Role Ethics* except to note that, "Without the balance accorded by an appropriate regimen of institutionalized regulative ideals . . . dependence on intimate [family] relations can be a disintegrative source of . . . parochialism and corruption."[13] Thus one or both of us must sooner or later say more about how role ethics can mesh with a robust democratic politics. Does a contemporary society composed of interrelated role-bearing persons truly require "institutionalized regulative ideals?" If so, which, and whence do they come? *Prima facie* role ethics should engender some different ways of thinking about politics. For example, if we are all individuals and self-interested, why should I be impressed with the "One man. One vote" idea; who wants all that competition? Role-bearers might distinguish public from private morality very differently than individuals seem to be inclined to do. Procedural justice might consistently give way to substantive justice, retributive justice to restorative; or more generally, a society of role-bearers may want its elected governors to seek the good, not the right.

To help our thinking on this score we may examine some of the most recent scholarship dealing with Confucianism significantly as a political philosophy. I do so quickly because almost all of it will not answer *our* questions. The authors, knowledgeable scholars all, have their own agendas. Some of what they have to say can clarify our thinking, but each of the four authors I will take up very briefly has his own audience in mind, which all differ somewhat from ours.

First, there is much discussion among Chinese intellectuals today about the role of Confucianism in contemporary China. Not all of it has to do with politics, but much of it does. Many of the discussions, however, are altogether specific to the Chinese context, as Roger knows well, and consequently can only be of minimal help in addressing the question of what a Confucian democracy might look like in a broader context. Some scholars, for example, will insist that the politics of Confucianism require also making it a, or *the* state religion, supported by the government, which in the United States would be a complete non-starter except in the hearts-and-minds of a few Christian fundamentalists.

Probably China's most well-known thinker of twenty-first-century Confucian politics is Jiang Qing, whose major work has been translated into English along with some responses to it, and his replies, in *A Confucian Constitutional Order*.[14] Therein he outlines a tricameral legislature in conformity with the ancient tripartite Chinese symbolism of Heaven, Earth, and Man (only in the latter house can people elect representatives to the government). The Head of State is of even greater symbolic significance in terms of the entirety of Chinese culture, and hence the only qualified candidates for the position must be direct descendants of Confucius. (This point should not be taken lightly; in both form and function very few people can succeed Elizabeth II). Much of the actual governing power would be in the hands of scholars, which is indeed in keeping with Chinese tradition, but ill accords with American sensibilities. We may entrust the higher education of our offspring to the professors, but certainly not the governance of the country. I do not wish to belittle Jiang Qing's work in the slightest. It surely deserves the attention it has received in China, and has much to recommend it. And parts of it, I suspect, will find a place in the future government of China. But while Jiang Qing's constitutional order is indeed neither neoliberal Western nor revived/revised Marxism, it is not a fully viable model even for China domestically; I believe, much less for export.

Closer to home, among comparative philosophers Stephen Angle has been writing at length on the relationship of Confucian ethics to politics, especially in his *Contemporary Confucian Political Philosophy: Towards Progressive Confucianism*,[15] wherein he links the two with an argument as forceful as it is straightforwardly simple: (1) Moral progress is of the essence of Confucian ethics; we must constantly work to become better persons. (2) Becoming a better person requires political progress as well, in the light of the greatly changed environmental and cultural circumstances in which we think, feel, and act today. Therefore, (3) contemporary Confucians must adopt a progressive politics if they are to remain true to its ethical ideals. Q.E.D.

In this way, Angle is able to introduce contemporary political concerns into the vision of the Confucian ethical ideal that is appealing, without diminishing that ideal in any way. If we now ask what the criteria are for "progressiveness" in politics, the answer is again straightforward: whatever conduces to the continued approximation of the Confucian ethical ideal. The argument becomes circular, but not viciously so. Angle—unfortunately, in my opinion—obscures these good arguments by his concern with a particular subset of the qualities of the Confucian sage, the major theme of Joseph Chan's review of Angle's book.[16] In keeping with the clearly stated beliefs of the early Confucians, Angle accepts that sagehood is possible, even though he personally is skeptical that there have ever been any. Indeed, *anyone* can approximate the ideal if they devote themselves wholeheartedly to the task. And sages must devote themselves to serving the people well and altogether unselfishly, without coercion and with full impartiality. Their job is to exercise their authority to rule such that peace, order, and at least a measure of prosperity are brought to all. But this poses problems for introducing a democratic politics into the social fabric of the ethical ideal. If someone really did clearly reveal all the qualities of a sage, why on earth would we need elections, at least until the sage passed to her reward, and no replacement was in sight? To answer this question, Angle develops a theme from Mou Zongsan about "self-restriction" that applies even to sages: if they want everyone to approximate sagehood—as they should if they are true sages—and if full sagehood requires using one's sagely authority (doubtful; Confucius was an "uncrowned sage"), then clearly sages must restrict themselves both as subjects of a constitutional democracy and as rulers of it; everyone must have the opportunity to participate in the exercise of both power and deference; thus the ethical ideal of Confucianism *requires*, on Angle's view, a progressive participatory politics grounded in the idea of self-restriction, and appealing to the value Confucians place on deference and humility, and more solidly grounding his claim that the Confucian ethical ideal requires the kind of political progressivism he champions.

If Angle is basically concerned with the relationship between ethics and "progressive politics," Joseph Chan is primarily concerned with Confucianism as a contemporary political philosophy, full stop. In his review of Angle's book he argues that Angle's views of self-restriction and the importance of political participation are either irrelevant (if there are no sages) or unnecessary (instrumental arguments do not require self-restriction). Chan's primary focus on political philosophy is evident in his own recent book, *Confucian Perfectionism*.[17] Beginning with the title: "perfectionism" is a term of art in political theory, denoting one theoretical model of the state in which institutions are justified as they are designed to help achieve the perfectibility of its citizens; it is not a hyper-idealistic Confucianism Chan is considering. The book has much to recommend it, certainly by expanding the dialogue between and among political theorists East and West. To my mind, however, Chan's book does not provide much guidance for Roger and myself, for he accepts a foundational individualism that we have rejected, and I confess that his distinction between personal and moral autonomy seems forced, if not a case of special pleading. Roger, however, attended a small conference on Chan's book in May, 2015 that I didn't, so I will trust him to add or subtract from my words here.

The last recent work dealing with democracy, China, and Confucianism that I should mention is Daniel Bell's *The China Model: Political Meritocracy and the Limits of Democracy*.[18] As the title suggests, the book is in the first instance a cogent critique of contemporary Western-style democracy in a number of countries, not least the United States, followed by a series of arguments suggesting that if China can get its act together—ending corruption, strengthening the legal system, not crushing dissent, etc.—it might be a more suitable political model for many developing countries than the troubled democracies we are currently living with, and under. In Bell's own words,

> ... [My] central area of concern is the question of how to maximize the advantages and minimize the disadvantages of a political system that aims to select and promote political leaders of superior virtue and ability, particularly in the contemporary Chinese context.[19]

Bell's critique of democratic institutions is somewhat shrill, but should be read by every American because of our tendency to glorify those institutions, and thus overlook their significant shortcomings, especially in their own country, where they are almost surely the most serious. But overall, his focus is on China serving as a counter-model to the United States for developing political institutions in countries in the early stages of modernization. Turning to a meritocratic government in the U.S., however, is not a credible possibility (Bell doesn't say that it is); thus, his work too, like the others, has a *problematik* that differs from my concerns (and Roger's I hope). It is to a consideration of these concerns that we now turn.

We focus on the United States and its democracy, just as Roger did. I do not apologize for this, because in my opinion it has been largely a terror in the politics among nations for many, many years now, and internal reforms are a precondition for freeing up other states to contemplate establishing political (and economic) institutions other than those foisted on them by our foreign policies, military adventurism, and international trade arrangements. But internal reforms are difficult to achieve because our democracy has become so dysfunctional as to make governing nigh unto impossible, and almost totally incapable of representing well the people who elected those who govern.

But it is a democracy, insofar that our leaders must be legitimated by popular vote at prescribed intervals, and that fact must serve as the basis for linking politics to a role ethics with Confucian characteristics. We have no history of meritocratic governance, nor rule by scholars; no tradition of a symbolic head of state; many Americans remain proud of the fact of universal suffrage even though the choices have been pretty much reduced to Tweedle Dee and Tweedle Dum; and much more. Our traditions and our symbols, such as they are, are intimately tied to the concept of democracy, and hence it must be restored, revitalized, reformed. It is what our founding fathers bequeathed us (if we were free, property-owning, white males).

Moreover, in my view a democracy that functioned well would be altogether compatible with Confucian ideals, ethical and otherwise, and assumed as much while writing *Against Individualism*. The dysfunctional elements of our contemporary democratic institutions are less with the institutions themselves as much as they are with the justifications given for some of them, which prevent their modification, and with the ideological uses to which they have been put. For example, the U.S. Senate is obviously not a particularly democratic body. Two "aye" votes by the California delegation can be cancelled by the two "nay" votes from their Senate colleagues from Wyoming. But the Californians represent over 36 million people, while the Wyoming pair have a little less than a million constituents. Forty-one senators representing only 18 percent of the voters can stop any piece of legislation from being passed. Today, the clear Republican majority in the Senate represents only 46 percent of the electorate; what is democratic about all this?

The clear answer, of course, is that there is very little that is democratic about that particular legislative arrangement; it was put into place at the constitutional convention of 1787, supposedly to secure passage of it by the smaller states, thus to protect the rights and interests of minorities. The compliance of the smaller states was secured two centuries ago, which today then leaves only the argument for the protection of minorities. But given that Blacks, women, and many others enjoyed few if any rights at the time, and that no single denomination made up a religious majority, which minorities were the Founding Fathers worried about? James Madison gave us the answer as he defended the idea of the senate:[20]

> In England, at this day, if elections were open to all classes of people, the property of the landed proprietors would be insecure. An agrarian law would soon take place . . . Our government ought to secure the permanent interests of the country against innovation. Landholders ought to have a share in the government to support the invaluable interests and to balance and check the other. They ought to be so constructed as to protect the minority of the opulent against the majority. The senate, therefore ought to be this body, and to answer these purposes, they ought to have permanency and stability.

(Senators were originally appointed by the legislators of each state; full popular election came only in 1914). Now if we replace Madison's "opulent minority" with "the 1%" we will have a keen insight, I believe, into why our government is as it is today. Changes in the *status quo* were needed then, and they are needed even more now. But the "opulent minority" then and now are doing very well under the *status quo*, and hence will be opposed to change. But there are only two ways fundamental changes can come about now: *via* the ballot box, or by revolution, which could not be but violent. To rehearse briefly an argument I made in *Against Individualism*, this fragile planet can no longer endure the exploitation it has undergone in the last two centuries; if the economic pie can no longer be substantially enlarged without irreparable harm to our water, air, and land, then the extant pie will have to be apportioned differently if any significant measure of equality is to be achieved and poverty overcome. But such can only come at the expense of the currently well-to-do. We should therefore not be surprised that the well-to-do will do all within their power to elect representatives who promise not to support any significant increases in taxes, nor to endorse enlargements of social services, etc.

There are fairly simple and straightforward means of making our democracy much more democratic: model the British parliamentary system, or by instant runoff balloting, by proportional representation, by electronic voting, by sharply limiting campaign time and campaign financing. But procedural issues make the changes Herculean, largely because of the ideology of the priority of the right (procedures) over the good (substantive), and the moralities that flow from the image of voters as free, autonomous, self-interested, and competitive individuals continues to suggest that the citizens of big states might well want to lord it over the others for their own interest. I personally doubt that the good citizens of Delaware stand in fear of the tyrannical yearnings of their neighboring Pennsylvanians. But at the same time I do believe we all have good reason to fear the political machinations of the 1%.

This is not the place to take up the ancient problem of the right vs. the good; there are extensive arguments on both sides, but I'd like to suggest that much of the seeming intractability of the problem relies on the idea that it is individuals who will be most affected either way. The basic argument for opting for procedures (the right) over the good is that the good is not agreed upon—there may be almost as many definitions thereof as there are participants in the debates. But how do we know these things? Is it impossible that the great majority of the American peoples today might want to have a government that governed for the common good of *all* citizens? A majority seriously worried about environmental destruction and wanting a government to stop it as quickly as possible, and compensate the citizens adversely affected by the needed changes? One, as well, of a much more deeply moral nature on issues such as gun control, the abolition of the death penalty, health care, etc., as well as desirous for the common good—also moral wants—such as parks, public transportation, and more?

I may well be wrong in framing the questions in this optimistic manner. The issues certainly need fleshing out, but my strong sense is that role-bearing persons will be much more inclined to give affirmative answers to them than rights-holding autonomous individuals. If I define myself basically in family terms first, then in terms of the manifold web of relations in which I stand to others and they to me, and see morality basically as meeting my role responsibilities to others as others meet theirs toward me, then the good, I believe, will loom large in my thinking at all levels, and the right will not.

In any event, this is one direction I believe it will be productive to take up in some detail in linking family, role ethics, Confucianism, and democracy much closer together, which I take to be the import of a statement of Roger's at the close of *Confucian Role Ethics*: "[P]erhaps the most profound insight Confucianism has to offer the world today lies in prompting us to rethink the role of family as the ground and primary site of the consummate life and by extension, of a truly robust democracy."[21] I hope, dear friend, there is enough material somewhere in these remarks to encourage you to contemplate additional collaborative efforts. In the meantime, thanks for being just who you have been, are now, and will continue to become.

Notes

1. I focus only on our collaborative history here because I have already discussed, with Carine Defoort, Roger's overall philosophical orientation and style in an earlier work, an "Introduction" to a special issue of *Contemporary Chinese Thought*

devoted to a series of articles by Chinese scholars on Roger's contributions to Chinese philosophy (Autumn, 2010).

2. Henry Rosemont, "Rights-holding Individuals and Role-bearing Persons," in *Rules, Rituals and Responsibility: Essays in Honor of Herbert Fingarette*, ed. Mary Bockover. (Chicago and LaSalle, IL: Open Court Pub. Co., 1991).

3. These works are all referenced in a forthcoming anthology of our joint essays being published by NTU Press in 2016, *Essays in Role Ethics*, edited by the two of us.

4. Roger T. Ames, "Paranomasia: A Confucian Way of Making Meaning," in *Confucius Now*, ed. David Jones. (Chicago and LaSalle, IL: Open Court Pub. Co., 2008).

5. Discussed in several essays from 2001 on. See recently Rosemont, *Against Individualism: A Confucian Rethinking of the Foundations of Morality, Politics, Family and Religion*. (Lanham, MD: Rowman & Littlefield/Lexington Books, 2015), ch. 2.

6. Ames and Rosemont, *The Analects of Confucius: A Philosophical Translation* (New York: Random House/Ballantine Books, 1998), and Ames, *The Chinese Classic of Family Reverence: A Philosophical Translation of the* Xiaojing (Honolulu: Univ. of Hawai`i Press, 2009).

7. Ames, *Confucian Role Ethics: A Vocabulary* (Hong Kong: The Chinese University Press, 2011).

8. Rosemont, *Against Individualism: A Confucian Rethinking of the Foundations of Morality, Politics, Family and Religion*. (Lanham, MD: Rowman & Littlefield/Lexington Books, 2015), ch. 2.

9. In his review of an anthology, with one of our essays included in it, Timothy Connolly, for instance, criticized us for not confronting virtue ethics in a more sustained manner, and claimed, without argument, that we had made a "straw man" of Aristotle in our article—all of which amounts to little more than name-calling. *Journal of Chinese Philosophy*, 41, nos. 1–2, March–June 2014, 210.

10. These are the central themes of the 3rd and 4th chapters of my *Against Individualism, op. cit.*

11. Pierre Hadot, *The Present Alone is Our Happiness: Conversations with Jeannie Carlier and Arnold Davidson* (Stanford, CA: Stanford Univ. Press, 2008), 21.

12. David Hall and Roger T. Ames, *The Democracy of the Dead* (Chicago and LaSalle, IL: Open Court Pub. Co., 1999), 12.

13. Ames, *Confucian Role Ethics* (Hong Kong: The Chinese University Press, 2011), 263.

14. Jiang Qing, *A Confucian Constitutional Order*, ed. Daniel Bell and Ruiping Fan, trans. by Edmund Ryde, Princeton, NJ: Princeton University Press, 2013.

15. Cambridge, UK: Polity Press, 2012.

16. Angle, "'Self-Restriction' and the Confucian Case for Democracy," in *Philosophy East & West*, 64, no. 3 (July, 2014).

17. Joseph Chan, *Confucian Perfectionism* (Princeton, NJ: Princeton University Press, 2014).

18. Daniel Bell's *The China Model: Political Meritocracy and the Limits of Democracy* (Princeton, NJ: Princeton University Press, 2015).

19. Daniel Bell's *The China Model: Political Meritocracy and the Limits of Democracy* (Princeton, NJ: Princeton University Press, 2015), 12.

20. Finding this source is not easy. It comes from the "Secret Debates on the Constitution" in the summer of 1787. These remarks of Madison's were made on June 25. To the best of my knowledge, Noam Chomsky was the first to call attention to the passage, found in the archives at the Yale library. The link is http://avalon.law.yale.edu/18th_Century/yates.asp.

21. Ames, *Confucian Role Ethics: A Vocabulary* (Hong Kong: The Chinese University Press, 2011), 268.

Part IV
REPLIES

Roger T. Ames Responds

ROGER T. AMES

Thomas P. Kasulis

Tom Kasulis has always been a person of enormous intellectual integrity—a person who says what he thinks. The revealing story he rehearses of the two of us as young colleagues beginning our careers across the hall from one another at the University of Hawai`i, is certainly true in all of its parts. As he has noted, when I was hired at UH, there were serious deficiencies in my own philosophical training (although I didn't think anyone noticed). And at that juncture, Tom had only recently come to the lifelong challenge of achieving real proficiency in his Asian languages, both modern and classical.

I benefitted enormously from Tom's philosophical mentorship during these early years, and truth be known, still do today. When Tom talks, like most others, I listen very carefully. In this sense, I might fairly claim that Tom was the first in my promiscuous career of professional collaborators. And I can also say that my first several years at UH were spent doing a lot of reading—that is, discussing Western philosophical texts in the regular series of collegial reading groups Tom organized. I also did close readings of original Buddhist texts with Tom's many graduate students, trying to get them up to the standard of linguistic competence they would need for real credibility in their research on the philosophical texts of East-Asian Buddhism.

Tom reflects on the challenges we have both faced in careers that have been dedicated to cultural interpretation by invoking one of the most fundamental philosophical questions: Where does meaning come from? And he is certainly right in observing that, in my own research, the different stipulated "meanings" of meaning—reference, sense, and intention—must necessarily be at play in any responsible introduction of Confucian philosophy into the Western academy.

Meaning as reference requires that we strive with imagination to locate the Confucian text within its own interpretive context and allow it to speak on its own terms without overwriting it with cultural importances that are not its own. This has certainly been one of the hobbyhorses I have ridden throughout my career by bringing under scrutiny many of the existing translations that purport to give us access to the philosophical canons of the Confucian tradition, and by often impugning the integrity of the Chinese-English dictionaries on which they are based. Both our received translations and our lexicons are freighted with religious and ontological assumptions that have little relevance for the persistent Chinese process cosmology as it was captured and delineated early on in the first among the Chinese philosophical classics, the *Yijing* or *Book of Changes*.

As Tom reports, Frege uses the distinction between "the morning star" and "the evening star" to illustrate the nuance needed to distinguish between "reference" to the same "star" (Venus) and the different complex "senses" these terms express—the very different contexts of "morning" and "evening." But when we move to a Chinese process cosmology that favors gerundive "events" over discrete "things" as points of reference, this distinction between sense and reference becomes very blurred indeed. Rather than Frege's Venus, we might take as our example the naming practices used for putatively one and the same person across the human narrative.

The person we know as "Sun Yat-sen," for example, has the genealogical name of Sun Deming 孫德明, locating him in the web of family by sharing the second character *de* with both his brother and relatives of the same generation. Born in the Guangdong village of Cuiheng 翠亨, he comes to Hawai`i at age 13, and is known to his family and community by his intimate "nursing name," Sun Dixiang 孫帝象, a name that remembers and celebrates the local village god of Cuiheng, Beidi 北帝, the "God of the North." This name in its Cantonese pronunciation, Tai Tseong, is found on Hawai`i's Punahou School ledger, and because English lacks the Cantonese phoneme "tseong," it becomes Tai Chu. When he is baptized in Hong Kong at age 17 he takes the name Sun Rixin 孫日新 ("daily renewed," an expression that alludes to the *Book of Changes*) and in the same year a mentor gives him the name Sun Yixian 孫逸仙 ("liberated immortal," pronounced "Yat-sen" in Cantonese) that he will from then on use within his English-speaking world. In any official Chinese documents, however, and in his calligraphy too, he uses his "big name" (大名), Sun Wen 孫文. And along the way, he assumes the courtesy name (字), Sun Daizhi 孫戴之, from the familiar expression "literature is how way-making is conveyed" 文以載道 as a play on his "big name" *wen* 文. The major cities in China today remember Sun Yat-sen with their "Zhongshan" parks and main streets, and the city of Guangzhou has its Zhongshan University 中山大學. But where did this name come from? Sun Zhongshan 孫中山, and more often, "Dr." Sun Zhongshan 孫中山先生 is taken from his Japanese alias "Nakayama Shō 中山樵" that he used in hiding from the Qing court spies and agents who dogged him relentlessly in Japan and around the world as he schemed to foment a revolution that would topple the Qing dynasty. And finally in death, Sun Yat-sen has come to be known affectionately by a grateful China as *guofu* 國父: "Father of our Nation."

Meaning as "sense" requires that we acknowledge the narrative function of language wherein the social and political context is always integral to its meaning. Sun Yat-sen's many names tell his complex story. The application of such correlative pragmatics in amplifying meaning is the substance of philosophizing itself, and is importantly prospective as well as retrospective, constantly being deployed to extend our complex, continuous and evolving philosophical narratives. As A.N. Whitehead observes:

> The Fallacy of the Perfect Dictionary divides philosophers into two schools, namely, the 'Critical School' which repudiates speculative philosophy, and the 'Speculative School' which includes it. The critical school confines itself to verbal analysis within the limits of the dictionary. The speculative school appeals to direct insight, and endeavours to indicate its meanings by further appeal to situations which promote such specific insights. It then enlarges the dictionary. The divergence between the schools is the quarrel between safety and adventure.[1]

When as philosophers we acknowledge Whitehead's fallacy of the Perfect Dictionary, we opt for prospective speculation over mere textual criticism, and for new philosophical adventures over safety.

In our *intra*-cultural translation—that is, "carrying over" within an interpenetrating cultural ambiance rather than between or among putatively discrete cultures—we must think in terms of organically related and polysemous clusters of terms and their mutually amplicatory connotations, and further of the primacy that the later Wittgenstein gives to language as "use" in his notion of "language games." Tom appeals to the organic intertextuality of the early corpus of philosophical texts and its evolving commentarial traditions, where commentary is not secondary or epiphenomenal, but has always been integral to the very notion of "text" itself. Indeed, as Tom observes so eloquently, we contemporary Western students of Confucian philosophy, while determined to unearth the roots of Confucianism, are ourselves at the same time nothing less than a later hybrid blossoming of this old Confucian tree. In thinking *through* Confucian philosophy as a source of human flourishing for our own time and place, we must make the important choices about what to endorse and what to reject, and more importantly, what to leave fallow and what to continue to nurture and grow.

This then leads us to meaning as "intention," where we need to ask after the existential and transformative force of these texts as a source of continuing education as an "educing" from them. The questions is: What do we intend and affirm as our own *dao* 道—our own process of "way-making" as a philosophical journey that has in degree, taken its bearings and trajectory from the signposts we have inherited from the tradition, and that in degree, requires of us that we forge our own unique pathways forward?

Tom brings these three "meanings" of meaning—reference, sense, and intention—to ask after my recent work on Confucian role ethics. In responding I will need to reverse their order by beginning from *intention*. Only then can I explain the evolving *sense* and *reference* that is entailed by Confucian role ethics, not as one more ethical "theory," but rather as the antique and evolving Confucian vision of the moral life.

In our own time, but with deep roots in the classical Greek philosophical narrative, individualism has become a default, commonsense assumption, if not an ideology. That is, individualism has become a dogma when, in our own post-Marxist, post-collectivist era, it has garnered a monopoly on human consciousness without any serious alternative to challenge it. I argue that the contemporary ethical discourse to the extent that it appeals to the vocabulary of agents, acts, generic virtues, character traits, autonomy, motivation, reasons, choices, freedoms, principles, consequences, and so on, introduces a cluster of distinctions that assume this foundational individualism as its starting point.

Confucian role ethics by contrast begins from the wholeness of experience, and is formulated by invoking a radically different focus-field cluster of terms and distinctions with fundamentally different assumptions about how meaningful personal identities emerge in our human narratives, and how moral competence is expressed as an achieved virtuosity in the roles and relationships that come to constitute us. To fail to distinguish what I will call individual human "beings" from relationally constituted human "becomings," then, would mean that we have willy-nilly insinuated a contemporary and decidedly foreign notion of person into our investigation of Confucian philosophy before it has even begun.

But as Tom would surmise, "Confucian" role ethics is only the deep root of this old tree, and that a full-blown role ethics grafted on to it for our own time and place will require that, in the fullness of time, we bring this tradition into conversation with Western ethical theory as both a complementary and a disruptive critique.

Hans-Georg Moeller

Hans-Georg Moeller has provided us with a synoptic overview of the history of the comparative philosophy movement as it has evolved over the past few centuries, and provided us with both the narrative structure and the distinctions needed to identify our own phase in this continuing story. He is able to identify and abstract four importantly different modalities of comparative philosophy out of a cultural narrative that dates back to seventeenth-century Europe and one of our earliest and most formidable comparative philosophers, G. W. Leibniz.

Leibniz, in his writings on China (Preface to *Novissima Sinica*, is a good example) had, without reference to the specific philosophical terms such as "family reverence" (*xiao* 孝) and "the achievement of propriety within one's roles and relations" (*li* 禮), a penetrating insight into these prime moral imperatives of Chinese culture. Leibniz made an earnest effort to learn from what he took to be the superior "civil philosophy" of the Chinese—their ethics, and social and political philosophy—and incorporate it into his universalizing project: that is, his vision of formulating a federalist world government, a universal morality, an ecumenical religion, a fundamental binary system for mathematics and logic, a universal language, and so on.

A long century later, a condescending G. W. F. Hegel, by contrast with Leibniz, saw the Chinese tradition as the most primitive and nascent form of philosophy. And predictably, this same inchoate Asian *Geist* was, in its evolution through history, to find the maturation of its self-consciousness in the Absolute Spirit of German Idealism. It was this same Hegelian perception of the impotency of a beleaguered China—China's abject weakness in the face of the crushing imperialist incursions from Europe—that came to dominate the Western "impact-response" reading of Chinese history that persisted through the first half of the twentieth century.

During this same period, sinological missionaries bent on saving the soul of China, interpreted Chinese philosophy through the interpolation of Christian categories into the Chinese sources, a Christian iteration of the earlier "classifying meanings" (*geyi* 格義) method of correlating Buddhist ideas with Chinese categories in third-century China. As one would anticipate, just as Buddhism became radically sinocized through such reductive correlations, these figurist Christian missionaries were hugely successful in discovering in China the early stirrings of an always second-rate version of their own Christian values and ways of thinking.

And finally, in the late nineteenth and early twentieth centuries, with the disenchanting forces of a new scientism, syncretic Western religious scholars found in Chinese philosophy a resource that would at least complement if not provide a novel alternative for the waning "spirituality" of their increasingly secularized cultures.

Up through at least the first half of the twentieth century, professional philosophy within the Western academy remained largely ignorant of Asian and comparative philosophy in the sense of "ignoring" it. And as an academic discipline, its own self-understanding was that philosophy is an Anglo-European adventure: Outliers need not apply. While during this same period in which Western academic culture had found sometimes intense interest in the poetry and wisdom literature of China, on the other side of the world, an evolving Chinese academic ethos that introduced the European-style universities wholesale was appropriating and absorbing mainstream Western philosophy as integral to its own curriculum. Many Western-trained Chinese philosophers themselves came to conceptualize and theorize their own Chinese philosophical narrative through a Western framework and its increasingly familiar vocabulary. At the same time, while standing in the shadow of the powerful Western philosophical tradition, yet other Chinese philosophers—Liang Shuming, Feng Youlan, Tang Junyi, Fang Dongmei, Mou Zongsan, and many others—argued not only for the inclusion of Chinese philosophy within a world philosophical narrative, but also for its value as a compensatory spiritual and aesthetic corrective on the rationalistic and secular limitations of the Western tradition.

In the recent generation, a sometimes controversial kind of contrastive comparative philosophy has evolved within the European cultural sphere that continues to argue for a distinction between Chinese and Western ways of thinking. Such proponents—François Jullien being a prime example—have come under severe criticism for first purportedly essentializing both the West and their own exotic East, for then attempting to formulate a Chinese way of thinking that cannot make any sense when it fails to respect foundational Western assumptions such as impersonal reason and a universal logic, and finally at the end of the day, for arguing shamelessly for a pernicious relativism.

There is much insight and everything to agree with in Hans-Georg's summary of our shared "whence" in comparative philosophy. Hans-Georg having rehearsed this history, then turns his reflections upon the work that I and my trusty collaborators—importantly, David Hall and Henry Rosemont—have undertaken in our own phase of this narrative, categorizing our work under the rubric of "post-comparative" Confucian philosophy. What does Hans-Georg mean by this neologism?

In the journey that has lead up to our present pass, comparative philosophers have tried to achieve a unity in their efforts at "de-barbarizing" the Chinese tradition in one of two ways: by either advocating for a deeper understanding of it and including its differences within a broader purview of philosophy itself, or by denying these same differences in asserting our universal and thus shared rational and cognitive structures as human beings.

As Hans-Georg observes, in our own efforts to allow this Chinese philosophical tradition to have its own voice and to speak on its own terms, we collaborators have certainly been advocates of a deeper cultural understanding and an extension of the boundaries of the discipline of philosophy by the inclusion of features that are unique to, or more pronounced in, Chinese ways of thinking and living. In my own recent work, then, I appeal to familiar historical and philological criteria, and to this extent I am still properly to be numbered in the ranks of "comparative philosophers." As Hans-Georg avers (and I wholly agree), "the post-comparative dimension of *Confucian Role Ethics* is . . . firmly grounded and embedded in the comparative dimension of Ames's work."

But according to Hans-Georg, I have also had bigger, and indeed most importantly, "philosophical" fish to fry. In not only introducing Confucian role ethics but advocating for it, I seek to challenge the ideology of individualism with a robust, conceptual alternative: what I have termed the Confucian relationally-constituted human "becoming." In so doing, I offer a disruptive critique of some of the persistent and uncritical assumptions of the prevailing ethical discourse—that is, I seek "to quite thoroughly question contemporary individualism-centered moral philosophies."

While I would readily accept Hans-Georg's generous reading of what I have been trying to accomplish as a "post-comparative philosopher," my only reservation would be to pretend that I and my collaborators have some special or exclusive claim on this most productive direction in comparative philosophy. For example, the "Afterword" and conclusion in the new book of essays in *Comparative Philosophy without Borders* edited by Arindam Chakrabarti and Ralph Weber was going to be called "Beyond Compare," heeding as they do the exhortation of Dayaji (Daya Krishna) to go beyond "superficial comparativism." And even closer to home, in Hans-Georg's own recent work, *The Moral Fool: A Case for Amorality*, he appeals to the "moral foolishness" of "amoral" philosophers in the pantheons of the Daoist and Zen traditions, as well as our own Wittgenstein and Luhmann, as a critique on the dangerous dogmatism of our standard Western moralists who assume that their rigid ethical catechisms provide us with a way forward (rather than backward) in our best efforts to optimize the human experience. In trying to move beyond self-conscious comparisons and to just do philosophy, I and my collaborators are thus walking in the best of company.

Robert Cummings Neville

Turning now to Robert Cummings Neville; this grand gentleman muses upon how we collaborators as a small group of American Confucians with our considerable intellectual, philosophical, and personal differences, have in many ways over our shared narratives actually "become" one another—as good Confucian friends are wont to do. Indeed, Confucius, in his several reflections on friendship as they are remembered in the *Analects*, begins by suggesting that there are significantly different expectations in his contrast between our family relations and those we develop with our professional peers:

> Zilu asked Confucius, "What must one be like to be called a scholar-official (*shi* 士)?"
> The Master replied, "Persons who are critical and demanding, yet amicable can be called scholar-officials. They need to be critical and demanding with their friends, and amicable with their brothers."[2]

This is the same Confucius who says more than once in the same canonical text that: "Exemplary persons . . . do not have as a friend anyone who is not as good as they are."[3]—an exhortation that, on the surface, seems to promise that the number of friends owned by scoundrels will be legion while exemplary persons will have few indeed. But on further reflection, this statement on friendship reflects Confucius's insight that both personal growth and its diminution are a function of associated living. Confucius does anticipate that friendships can in many ways be more challenging than intimate family relations. After all, one can fairly take for granted the love and protection of one's immediate family, while successful life in the public sphere requires a much higher degree of discrimination and a more critical sense of engagement. On the other hand, the sustained dividends to be reaped from enduring friendships over a lifetime are not only substantial, but indeed transformative: indeed, this is Bob's point. In this Confucian tradition, to "make" friends is quite literally to participate in the "making" of each other to the extent that it is the friendship that is most concrete, while the putative "individuals" who participate in this matrix of relationships become increasingly only an abstraction from it.[4]

For Confucius, it is the ways in which friends are qualitatively superior to and profoundly different from each other in what they bring to their relationships, that provides the opportunity for a collaborative advancement. Indeed, it is the nurturing process of such "appreciating" relationships in the sense of value-added that is the ultimate source of meaning itself. The Confucian conception of friendship is a classic illustration of the many versions of Confucius's familiar mantra: "Exemplary persons seek harmony rather than uniformity; petty persons are the opposite."[5]

I have begun my response to Bob here with his reflections on "making friends" because this intensely personal "first problematic" experience we have shared together over our careers can serve as an object lesson in how David Hall and I tried to challenge the prevailing asymmetry in the culture of comparisons—that is, our attempt to overcome the unrelenting theorization of Chinese philosophy through Western categories. As Bob astutely observes, for David Hall and me, it has been this intellectual adventure of the culturally romantic Western-trained philosopher and the philosophically inclined sinologist, beginning as we do from our oft-assailed thick generalizations about Chinese and Western culture, that has allowed us as self-consciously "philosophers of culture" to advocate for "a reappraisal of Western comparative culture itself." We have endorsed the primacy of *ars contextualis*—the open-ended aesthetic of first problematic, correlative and analogical thinking—over the many variations of second problematic rationalization available to us on the carousel of systematic philosophy. Our concern from the beginning has been with the excavation of the "uncommon assumptions" that serve as alternative grounds for the continuing cultural discourses within the two traditions themselves. And such contrastive assumptions can only be identified and made available for mutual edification and critique through a process of responsible and responsive comparisons.

Certainly the clearest and most robust statement of our *ars contextualis* methodology to date is found in Robert W. Smid's *Methodologies of Comparative Philosophy*, and it should be a surprise to no one that this monograph is a revision of a Boston University dissertation certainly researched and crafted by Smid himself, but also with Smid having the benefit of the clear-eyed guidance of his supervisor, Robert Neville.[6]

In reading Bob's synoptic characterization of the Hall and Ames collaboration, especially with respect to our contrast between transcendence and "correlative causation," and the corollary distinction between substantial human "beings" and relational human "becomings," I can only delight in the extent to which I think he not only "gets it" (and so many so far do not), but how he is able to reach into his own continuing philosophical ruminations to describe our project much better than we have been able to do so ourselves. This intervention is most timely for me.

My recent monograph, *Confucian Role Ethics: A Vocabulary*, and other work I have done in collaboration with Henry Rosemont on the same subject published recently in our volume, *Confucian Role Ethics: A Moral Vision for the Twenty-first Century?* was a part of our concerted effort to challenge the gross asymmetry in theorizing Confucian ethics by appeal to an always Western vocabulary. In these publications, we have self-consciously tried to allow the tradition to speak on its own terms—that is, to use its own vocabulary. Our argument simply put is that the encounter of Confucian ethics with Western ethical theory is not its defining moment.

But on reading the peer evaluations of our work on Confucian role ethics that often default to the discrete individual in framing their critiques, I have been deeply worried that we have not yet succeeded in expressing our conception of the Confucian notion of the relationally constituted human "becoming" in clear enough terms. Indeed, in an effort to address this failure specifically, I have set aside my sequel to *Confucian Role Ethics* tentatively entitled *Confucian Role Ethics: Doing Justice to Justice*—that is, a conversation with Western ethical theories on the shared theme of "justice"—to go back and work on another monograph, *Theorizing "Persons" for Confucian Role Ethics: A Good Place to Start*.

G. W. F. Hegel in the introduction to his *Encyclopaedia Logic* famously observes that one of the most difficult problems in any philosophical investigation is the question of where to begin. In this new monograph I argue that the appropriateness of categorizing Confucian ethics as either role ethics or virtue ethics turns largely on the conception of person that is presupposed within the interpretive context of classical Chinese philosophy. And Bob has much of importance to say on this topic:

> Suppose the self, then, is a continuum beginning from the inner center of responsiveness, that is, the intentionality of orientation, functioning specifically to take on orientations in body and mind to the close things of the intimate body, to things and persons of direct contact such as family, friends, and coworkers, and then to social situations, historical places, nature, and the vast cosmos—the ten thousand things each with its own rhythm, *dao*, and discernible grain. . . . In the theory of orientations, the boundaries of the self are functions of differing orientations, and the continuity of the self has to do not with an underlying fixed essence or character but with the history of the person's poise efforts, with the ongoing shifting harmonization of the changing things to which the person must take up or correct orientations.[7]

In this new project, I am much indebted to and inspired by Bob's own contribution to articulating this new Confucian model of person using his "theory of orientations" and his emphasis upon "ritual forms." We "two"—that is, Bob and I—have certainly become a collaborating "one" in our own orientations, and there is much of real ritual in the sincerity of our hugs.

Graham Parkes

Graham Parkes, like Tom Kasulis, was a colleague and the very best of friends during our many happy years together at the University of Hawai'i, and as with Tom, I benefited much from his philosophical mentorship. In his contribution to this volume, Graham ranges far and wide through the classical Chinese canons to share with us some of his most recent thoughts on the cosmological assumptions that serve as the interpretive context for Chinese philosophy, and advocates for the ways in which these assumptions might be instructive in our own time and place with our shared advocacy of environmental flourishing. In my response to Graham, I want to use this occasion to play the Hui Shi and Zhuangzi gambit that makes the *Zhuangzi* such an exhilarating read—that is, to play off of and respond to Graham's insights abductively to continue the discussion by making some hopefully productive and yet always open-ended and happily inconclusive correlations.[8] Like his graduate students, many of Graham's colleagues too have been inspired to do some of our own best thinking with Graham as our intrepid interlocutor. Graham says that he wants to "complement and compliment" my early *Art of Rulership* monograph, and I want to return the favor by engaging Graham's insights and joining him in common cause by further elaborating upon one Confucian concept that is immediately relevant to his environmentally inspired exposition.

One main theme in Graham's exposition of traditional Confucian attitudes toward the environment is "the mandate of Heaven" (*tianming* 天命) as a window on the perceived interdependence of the human being and the naturally numinous within the Chinese worldview. In his discussion, Graham resources the canonical texts to rehearse the history of this concept and to argue for the pervasiveness in Chinese cosmology of the assumed mutuality and collaterality among the "three powers" (*sancai* 三才): that is, the powers of the heavens and the earth, and the contribution the human experience makes to cosmic order as it unfolds between them. Throughout this antique tradition from the very earliest records there are exhortations for the human being to coordinate the human experience with the natural environment and to live in a manner that conduces to both human and natural flourishing. In giving his account of *tianming*, Graham further emphasizes the correlation between the impartiality of the numinous aspect of our natural environs which registers all interests as pertinent, and good rulership within the human world that is likewise catholic and inclusive of our natural context. With *tian* 天 serving as metonym for *tiandi* 天地—"the heavens and the earth," this assumption is properly captured in the mantra, "the inseparability of the natural and cultural context, and the human experience" (*tianrenheyi* 天人合一).

What further thoughts does Graham's discussion of *tianming* occasion and inspire for me? The first thing that comes to mind is Tang Junyi's 唐君毅 insistence that "the mandate of Heaven" (*tianming*) references a bilateral relationship rather than unilateral agency:

> The term "*ming*" represents the interrelationship or mutual-relatedness of Heaven and man. . . . [W]e can say that it exists neither externally in Heaven only, nor internally in man only; it exists, rather, in the mutuality of Heaven and man, i.e. in their mutual influence and response, their giving and receiving.[9]

Tang Junyi's point is that in this cosmology, *tian* and *ren*, far from designating two discrete things that then have to be fitted together, in fact reference both the primacy and the mutuality of their relatedness, where the challenge is to optimize the possibilities of this relationship. In my enduring friendship with Graham, as an example, it is our narrative of friendship that is primary and concrete, and the erstwhile discrete "individuals" in the relationship are only mental abstractions from it. Consistent with the mutually implicated dyadic pairs such as *yinyang* 陰陽 and *daode* 道德, this *tianren* mantra describes the deliberate growth of constitutive relations that are already defining of the human and cosmic orders as continuous and inseparable aspects of the human experience.

In our understanding of *tianming*, we are immediately aware of the imperative of human beings comporting themselves according to the ostensive will of *tian*, but given our uncritical and default assumptions about the aseity of God, we might not be sufficiently cognizant of and even overlook the perceived human capacity and responsibility to extend and deepen the meaning of *tian* itself.

Graham cites John Knoblock's translation of the *Xunzi* that has been misread "as advocating the exploitation of the natural world" and offers as his own corrective interpretation that this text in fact expresses "an ongoing interaction, more complex and mutually responsive than exploitation." Indeed, I would revise Knoblock's translation with this important insight in mind in the following way:

How can taking advantage of things to increase their numbers be better than harnessing their capacities and transforming them? How can merely contemplating things and instrumentalizing them be better than understanding them according to the opportunities they present? How can being preoccupied with how things grow be better than considering what they can be used to accomplish? Thus, to set aside the human collaborator and merely contemplate the natural is to lose sight of what the myriad of things really are.[10]

The *Zhongyong*—a text that Zhu Xi elevates as the most profound statement of the Confucian project—is even more explicit as a rhetorically powerful celebration of the co-creative role that humanity has in cosmic flourishing. Perhaps in response to the challenge of an expansive Daoist cosmology, the *Zhongyong* goes beyond the earlier Confucian texts in extending the compass of its concern beyond our immediate human limitations to apply the transformative force of human feeling to the cosmos more broadly. And the first two characters that open this *Zhongyong* text are nothing other than *tianming*:

> What *tian* commands is called natural tendencies; drawing out these natural tendencies is called the proper way; improving upon this way is called education.[11]

Indeed, the theme that is expanded upon as the axis of this entire text is a Confucian interpretation of this opening line that, as a deliberate and pointed rejection of the more theistic Mohist assumptions about the asymmetrical relationship between *tian* and the human order, celebrates the singularly human capacity to produce culture in collaboration with the heavens and the earth. The message of this text, far from modestly encouraging us to "use restraint"—to "conserve" or "sustain" or "protect" the natural environment—exhorts humanity with its capacity for making meaning, to step up boldly and take responsibility for "appreciating," aestheticizing, and indeed transforming our world, with our natural context being one important and irreducibly precious aspect of it. Graham cites the *Zhongyong* in which Confucius as the paradigmatic human exemplar is described in the language of nature itself:

> Confucius . . . modeled himself above on the rhythm of the turning seasons, and below he was attuned to the patterns of water and earth. He is comparable to the heavens and the earth, sheltering and supporting everything that is. He is comparable to

the progress of the four seasons, and the alternating brightness of the sun and the moon.[12]

But the *Zhongyong* does not end with human beings merely modeling themselves on the natural order. Indeed, it requires nothing less of us than the transforming of a natural deposit of ore into the iconic meaning of a Shang dynasty bronze, and resolving discord in the world with love and reverence for all living creatures.

> An achieved equilibrium and focus is the great root of the world, and harmony is the advancing of the proper way in the world. When equilibrium is sustained and harmony is fully realized, the heavens and the earth maintain their proper places and all things flourish in the world.[13]

For a tradition that, in abjuring any nature/nurture dualism, instead acknowledges their symbiotic, contrapuntal relationship, the production of human culture—material and political—far from being epiphenomenal or secondary, is integral to the measurement of our environmental responsibility, and it is this capacity that makes us the counterpart of the heavens and the earth:

> Only those of utmost sagacity in the world: . . . Everywhere that boats and carriages ply, everywhere that human strength penetrates, everywhere that is sheltered by the heavens and is borne up by the earth, everywhere that is illumined by sun and moon, everywhere that the frosts and dew settle—all creatures that have breath and blood revere and love them. Thus it is said that they are the complement of *tian*.[14]

To make my point here, I would merely point out how Graham, with the formidable artistry of his tide-pools and rock-shows, has made himself an astral complement to *tian* in precisely this Confucian sense.

Richard Shusterman

Richard Shusterman, having developed his *sui generis* notion of the somaesthetic over the past few decades, takes us from the aesthetic of Graham's "rock shows" and "rock gardens" to Shusterman's now uncontested status as an academic "rock star." His work has occasioned nothing less than a somatic turn in mainstream philosophy, including as it does the all too often ignored Chinese current within this same intellectual conduit. Indeed, I take some considerable pride in Richard's habit of kindly announcing to his colleagues that I am his "teacher of Chinese philosophy," thus associating me with his own stellar rise over the Chinese world wherein his most important books are circulating widely in accurate and accessible translations made by some of China's best philosophers.

In Richard's essay for this volume, he reflects upon and interprets the arts of the bedchamber as this theme has come to be understood within the antique Chinese tradition. Locating Chinese sexuality as one aspect within the holistic narratives of healthy and happy persons committed to the project of personal cultivation, Richard places himself in stark contrast to the problematic if not orientalist interpretation of Michel Foucault who ascribes to the Chinese tradition an *ars erotica* committed to the pursuit of the highest, unbridled intensity of sexual pleasure as Foucault's own pointed critique of Greek and Roman sexual "scientism" and Christian puritanical prudery.

Sexuality and eroticism too are most interesting topics within the context of the Chinese tradition, and as we see in Richard's essay, there is a lot to say about them. On the one hand, Richard begins his essay by thanking colleagues, including me, for cautioning him about being too explicit about the erotic dimensions of the somaesthetic within the more conservative Chinese academic community, but further allowing that with this present essay, such reserve is not really an issue because he is writing for a largely American audience. Richard here is alluding to the self-sensorship and seemingly muted interest within popular Chinese culture in explicitly sexual subjects, especially eroticism, and a reticence to engage this particular topic in the mainstream scholarly literature.

Two anecdotal examples might be helpful in making Richard's point. I was teaching at Peking University some years ago with an attractive American PhD student as my teaching assistant, and I remember her volunteering that she enjoyed spending time in a culture in which she was not constantly being "checked out." I think this is a fair observation on her part that does register a palpable difference between these two worlds. Another instance of this gap was when in an early Zhang Yimou movie the knothole voyeurism of someone watching the lovely Gong Li enjoying her own body was widely and critically interpreted in China as Zhang Yimou shamelessly playing to a Western audience.

On the other hand, and seeming to contradict this reticence, Richard makes reference to the many erotic manuals compiled in China across the centuries that promise explicit and often illustrated tutoring on how good technique in sexual congress—the contrapuntal, responsive rhythm of nine shallow strokes to one long, deep thrust, for example—conduces to a long and healthy life for both man and woman. The role of the male as described in this literature requires him to constantly regulate the intensity of the coupling in order to refrain from surrendering his own *yang* ejaculation while accumulating *yin qi* from the female's secretions. Such a cadence in lovemaking would seem to be a deliberate strategy that guarantees extended sensual arousal for both intimates and optimum orgasmic pleasure for his female partner.

If both of Richard's observations are on the mark—that is, sexology in the Chinese world is at once colorfully explicit, and at the same time, private, and hidden away out of view of the conservative public gaze—then where do we situate and how are we to understand sexuality within the broad terrain of Chinese culture?

We have to allow that, given the holistic, focus-field notion of person that is pervasive in this Chinese cosmology, Richard properly locates sexuality as one aspect within a person's narrative of roles and relations that, with one's sexuality itself being a subject of personal cultivation, is intimately connected with growth in relations and an achieved propriety (*li* 禮) within the intergenerational family lineage of ancestors and progeny. This sexual aspect of achieved "propriety"—making one's role fully one's own—is an aesthetic achievement in Whitehead's sense of every detail being relevant to the totality of the effect. And this virtuosity must be assessed by appeal to the ethical vocabulary of consummate conduct in one's roles and relations (*ren* 仁) and an optimal appropriateness (*yi* 義) in these roles. As Richard insists, healthy sexual relations are integral to one's insistent particularity and one's potency that is captured in the aesthetic *ethos* of human "virtuosity" (*de* 德). Citing several of the Daoist canons, Richard also ponders a perceived tension between self-forgetting spontaneity and deliberate reflection in effective sexual performance. But as he concludes himself, this is only a seeming conflict in the life of the novice that is resolved through an achieved virtuosity in which what was once purposeful and reflective has become spontaneous as second nature, like Butcher Ding's carving of the ox.

And just as John Dewey would argue that there is no separate and isolatable "aesthetic" or "religious" experience—that an aesthetic and religious quality ought to be aspired to as an aspect of every pulse of the human experience—so human sexuality is an aspect of continuing healthy and happy, lived relations. The heat, intensity, and prolonged pleasure of virtuosic copulation between husband and wife cannot be separated from the warm embrace of a grandmother around her grandson, or the laughter around a welcoming family dinner table in the glow of hearth and home. Richard aptly cites the *Classic of Rites* (*Liji*) to argue *contra* Foucault that "the Chinese erotic arts were primarily designed for health, procreation, and the harmonious management of a polygamous household."

There is another classic that might be relevant in understanding the sense of privacy that attends Chinese sexual sensibilities: the *Book of Songs* (詩經). Human sexuality like poetry is the outside of an inside, a shared musical discourse that gives access and reveals a person most intimately to another person. In the "Great Preface" to this work, it states:

> Poetry is where one's purposes have carried one to. Whilst in one's own heartmind, it is what one purposes; when given voice in language it becomes poetry. Feelings being stirred within are given shape in words. When words are inadequate, we express such feelings in sighs and moans. When sighs and moans are inadequate, we give them expression in song. And when song is inadequate, we impulsively dance these feelings out according to the beat of our hands and feet.[15]

Poetry like our sexuality is a discourse, a relationship in the sense of "a relating to," "a giving an account of." As we ascend from the more public medium of a love poem spoken in words to the increasingly intimate and personal expression in sighs, then song, and ultimately to our rhythmic bodily gestures, we move into a complex space wherein increasing vulnerability and increasing privacy intersect. As the serenading lover through his song lowers his defenses and provides his Juliet with a deepening access to his inner most, private person, such increasing intimacy is responded to by his lover and serves as ground for the kindling and growth of affection in a deepening yet increasingly private conversation. That is, the quality and the intensity of the intimacy is enhanced by the extent to which it is a private affair—theirs alone—and it is again likewise compromised to the extent that in the same form it becomes a public matter. The private and intimate "dancing" of our lovers becomes the parody of pornography if and when it becomes theater.

Brook Ziporyn

A central concern for me in interpreting the classical Chinese canons has always been to register and respect the interpretive context. To thus receive Brook Ziporyn's penetrating and constructive reading of our best efforts to apply this strategy in our translation of the *Daodejing* is high compliment in itself. As is abundantly clear from his essay, there are very few scholars indeed who can come near his depth of insight and broad erudition in parsing these texts, and in getting the most out of them. The "childlike eyes" he ascribes to me that ostensibly allow me to read the text in seemingly novel but defensible ways takes me back to my years of working under the guidance of my mentor, D. C. Lau. Professor Lau (I could never call him anything else) spent his life learning many of the world's languages—certainly Chinese and English, but also Latin, Greek, German, Japanese, and together in London, we studied Pali too. The gift I would usually bring Professor Lau when continuing to work with him for many years after he returned to Hong Kong would be one more volume of the Loeb classics series. His motivation behind this commitment to study languages was not to become the cosmopolitan linguist who would "master" these languages and traverse the world speaking and writing them, but rather to be the philosophical archaeologist going down the portal to the other side of the looking glass and recovering from these languages the many different ways of interpreting the human experience that they reveal. His starting point was the recognition that languages speak people as much as people speak languages. One among too many examples of his discoveries was the occasion on which he asked me if I had noticed that much of the Chinese epistemic language (*zhidao* 知道, *lijie* 理解, *liaojie* 瞭解, *tongda* 通達, and so on) seems to infer a kind of "mapping" and "reconnoitering" rather than a "grasping" or "getting"—a way of knowing that allows us to negotiate our way forward rather than discovering some eternal truth. Where does one leave off trying to harvest the implications of such an insight?

One of the uncommon assumptions that I have glommed onto along the way in trying to think through the interpretive context for the *Daodejing* that might have relevance for responding to Brook's generous commentary on our translation is the primacy given to vital relationality in this text. Many, if not most of Brook's observations, beginning with his title, "Vast Continuity versus the One," take us back to the corollaries that follow from relationality as first order actuality in the process, event, cosmology that serves as the context for reading this text. Certainly we are on the same page with Brook's arguments for giving privilege to reading the term *yi* 一 as a complex, concrete, boundless and evolving "continuity" rather than as an abstracted and individuated "one," and in choosing our terms of art, for favoring the gerundive form over nouns with their isolating definite ("the") or indefinite ("a") articles. Of course what follows from this observation is the inadequacy of Aristotle's "what" question when asking after the eventful contents of our experience, and the privileging of the "whence" and "whither" questions in the Chinese cosmology that provide a narrative explanation for the "way-ing" of erstwhile "things." Perhaps the *Taiyi shengshui*, rather than providing an answer to "What exactly *is* this Great One?"—an answer that would only serve to arrest, circumscribe, and deracinate this event—instead tries to say something in answer to the question: "How did this process come about and what are its consequences?"

With this insight of relational primacy in hand, I join Brook in understanding Tang Junyi's cosmological postulate of 一多不分觀 (*yiduo bufenguan*) as "the continuity between one and many" rather than appealing to language of unification—the unifying of putatively separate things. The mantra of 天人合一 (*tianren heyi*) for example is better read as "the inseparability of the heavens and the earth" rather than "the unity or unification of the heavens and the earth." That is, we are not putting two erstwhile separate things together, but rather deepening what is first and foremost a relationship, and only secondarily acknowledging two aspects or horizons that can be abstracted from our continuing experience. Of course this continuity would mean that we might do better to think of *tiandi* 天地, for example, not as "two ends of any particular way" or "endpoints" in a process, but as two horizons from within our own particular experience of the unbounded cosmological continuity.

Brook's reflections on our work are mostly corroborative, and sometimes delightfully speculative and instructive—a flash of something I had not thought of, but that I am now glad to have. As such, his comments are a source of confidence that our always evolving interpretation of this text has in many parts the endorsement of such a fine scholar. This being the case, I want to try to take up one of the questions he poses that plays into a criticism he makes of our interpretation. Brook asks: "Dao is supposed to mean something like 'The Way.' Why would it produce anything? What is there about a 'way' that produces? And why would it produce 'The One?' " "Producing" here references the term *sheng* 生 that is usually translated as "birthing, living, growing." With such a conventional rendering, it reinforces our sense of priority and sequencing—after all, the mother must precede the progeny. But we must ask the question, what does *sheng* mean in a cosmogony in which *dao* 道 and *wanwu* 萬物 do not have the creator/creature relationship that is commonsense in metaphysical cosmogonies, but are instead two "aspectual" and nonanalytic ways of looking at the same phenomenon? Certainly "the indeterminate is the fetal beginning of the cosmos and the determinate is the mother of the myriad things," but as we are further told in this same chapter, "these two aspects have the same source but different names."[16] And that source—whence they arise—is *ziran* 自然—the "self-so-ing" of the cosmos. Certainly "*dao* emulates *ziran*," but "the common people all say of themselves we are *ziran*" as well.[17] Both *dao* and *wanwu* are explained through the vital interface between the indeterminate and the determinate, and the holography in this focus-field cosmology means that the totality is implicated in each of the foci. Which comes first, focus or field? They come together. What comes first, mother or child? They arise together.

Again, it seems almost impolite to take up and dispute the one point that Brook describes as "interpretive overreach" on our part "that raises the hackles of the anti-Ames party, and weakens the Amesian case." But Brook will forgive me for trying to make my case. His concern is that we cannot ascribe reversibility to the relationship between *dao* and *wanwu*—that *dao* must have priority over the myriad things. I think Brook's position here—that *dao* has priority over *de*—would vitiate Tang Junyi's postulate, "the continuity between one and many" (*yiduo bufenguan* 一多不分觀) and the focus-field holography that follows from it as it applies to the *Daodejing*. And the textual evidence I would cite on behalf of reversibility would be:

> Way-making (*dao*) brings things to life,
> Their virtuosity (*de*) provides them with nourishment,
> Environing things shape them,
> And their contextualizing circumstances (*shi*) usher them to completion.
> It is thus that all things revere *dao* and esteem *de*.
> As for this reverence and esteem,
> It just arises spontaneously without anything decreeing it to be so.[18]

Shi 勢 is a generic term that expresses the complex, holistic dynamics of the process of "trans-*form*-ing" (*tiyong* 體用) as it occurs within the evolution and consummation of any particular situation. First, there is the element of cultivation and enhancement that is captured in the etymology of the term as "sowing and cultivating" (*yi* 埶) and in its cognate term, the "performing arts" (*yi* 藝). Situations do not just happen; they emerge in their complexity as a growing pattern of changing relations that are vital, and display the possibilities of incremental design as well as an achieved, aesthetic virtuosity. Situations by definition also have a morphology or "habituated" aspect—a localized place with its insistent particularity and its own persistent yet always changing configuration. But as observed above, we must see the relationality as first order, actual reality and all individual actors as conventionally abstracted and derived from them.

Putative "things" are horizons, and thus only convenient abstractions from persistent and continuous matrices of interdependent relations. And these relations do not terminate anywhere, but reach out to the furthest limits of the cosmos. Any particular "thing" or situation emerges at the pleasure of every other situation, and is thus at once a cause and an effect. Another way of capturing this relationship between particular focus and unbounded field would be "self-so-ing" (*ziran* 自然). *Ziran* means that all of a thing's relations that come to constitute it as its "self" (*zi* 自) conspire to give life to its unique presencing or arising (*ran* 然) that makes it insistently so.

And there is a second passage in the *Daodejing* that might be an even clearer statement of this focus-field holography:

> Sages are ever without a heartmind (*xin*)
> In their taking the heartminds of the common people as their own.[19] . . .
> As for the presence of sages in the world,
> In their efforts to draw things together they make of the world one muddled mind.
> The common people all fix their eyes and ears on the sages,
> And the sages treat them as so many children.

In this *Daodejing* passage, implicated in the narratives of the sages are the lives of the common people. In order to make sense of this passage—a passage that is reminiscent of the Mencian claim that "the myriad happenings of the world are all implicated here in me"[20]—we need to invoke the holographic alternative to our common sense understanding of the "inner" and the "outer" as two separate domains. The ordinary people certainly look to these sages for direction in finding their bearings, but they also retain the spontaneity (*ziran* 自然) needed to live their own diverse lives in a way that retains the indeterminacy of so many children, with everyone being given the space to create their own unique narrative in the world. Without any specific regimen being imposed upon them, the world around them is simply the unsummed totality of many different orders, allowing everyone to enjoy the diversity of participating whole-heartedly and like-mindedly in a happily muddled *xin* in which their differences make a difference for each other, and for the sage as unsummed totality as well.

Li Chenyang

Over the past decade, Li Chenyang has made an enormous and highly visible contribution to the archaeology of Chinese philosophical terms, most notably the distinctively Confucian conception of what is conventionally translated as "harmony" (*he* 和). In his essay, Chenyang turns his attention to the key philosophical term *cheng* 誠. He rehearses the history of how its meaning has been parsed in the translation of the Chinese philosophical canons as these texts have been introduced into the Western academy—beginning from *cheng* as a human psychological category meaning "sincerity," "authenticity," "integrity," raising it to an ethical and ontological category of "true," "truth," and then further elevating it to become a cosmological or metaphysical category meaning "reality" and "creativity." For Chenyang, it is only when all of these dimensions of meaning are registered in the translation of *cheng*—psychological, ethical, ontological, and metaphysical—that we have a comprehensive understanding of this term, and have done justice to its depth and scope.

In generously acknowledging my own contribution to our current understanding of *cheng* as part of this process, Chenyang allows that Ames has connected "the dots between 'sincerity,' 'integrity,' and 'creativity.'" But although Chenyang would acknowledge that I have covered some of this terrain, he perceives that there are still two "weak links" in my conceptualization of *cheng*. As the first of these, although I have taken "creativity" to be the core meaning of *cheng*, it is an understanding of "creativity" that in being committed to how affect ("sincerity") enables the growth of interpersonal familial and communal relations, is only a psychological and social reading of creativity that lacks the ontological depth as a special mode of being in which human "*beings*" are true to themselves and to others. His second concern is that to the extent that I have given *cheng* any ontological consideration at all, I have invoked a process cosmology that is too fluid and unstructured to do justice "to being, to human reality." For Ames, says Chenyang, "everything is in the flux of 'becoming'" and thus "reality has been replaced with process." By contrast, D. C. Lau and Tu Weiming have been able to recover the ontological and metaphysical implications of being true to oneself and others as "a mode of being," "a state of being," "a way of being."

Chenyang then provides his own conceptualization of *cheng* as having three main dimensions. First, *cheng* means to be true to oneself, to others, and to the world, giving "sincerity" the necessary ontological depth that it requires by extending the mental state to encompass a way of authentic being. Second, as Ames and Hall have argued, *cheng* means "creativity" as a human capacity to transform the world. And third, *cheng* means reality; beyond whatever there is, *cheng* signifies how the world truly exists—the ultimate reality.

Because Chenyang has invoked the ontology of "being" and "reality" as a necessary aspect of *cheng* that echoes the Heideggerian project, he marshals Heidegger's protean voice and his always tortured language to shed "new light on our understanding of the Confucian notion of *cheng*." Heidegger, "by setting human creativity within an already established yet continuously renewing referential framework . . . presents more stability for being than Ames provides."

In responding to Chenyang, I want to invite the later Heidegger and his project of *Destruktion* to my side and claim him as a fellow traveler who I think in challenging and rejecting the old metaphysics (*The End of Metaphysics*) by striving to overcome onto-theological thinking, makes my case rather than Chenyang's. Heidegger, in his attempt to find a historicist, hermeneutical path beyond our own nihilistic Nietzschean age, is concerned that the persistent eliding of ontology and theology has led to the "forgetfulness of being" by reducing theology to ontology, and vice versa. Mystery has become mere technological efficacy enabled by our understanding of the order of being, and philosophical rigor is given over to unjustified belief.

In mounting his argument for his interpretation of *cheng*, Chenyang gives us an all too familiar theistic reading of the *Zhongyong*—a strong divine command theory—that reduces the *Zhongyong* ontology to theology. He claims that for the *Zhongyong*, "human nature is Heaven-endowed and hence is in accord with the Way. To be authentic is to be true to one's nature." What then is the nature of the human contribution in its putative co-creativity (or bi-creativity) with the cosmos? For Chenyang, "humanity is not an arbitrary creator in any sense. It is destined toward the Way of Heaven. Individual persons need to cultivate themselves in order to come into attunement with the Way." "A person of full truth is one who is completely one with Heaven."

Chenyang certainly tries to nuance this kind of a reading that stabilizes ontology with his implicit theology with claims such as "humanity is definitely a creative force and aims to bring out a humanized world." But when creativity is reduced to actualizing a nature that is predetermined by a divine source and comporting oneself according to the way of that same source to become one with it, it is a *creatio ex nihilo* creativity that reduces humanity to nothing.

If I were Chenyang, I would have been critical of the Ames/Hall translation of *cheng* as "creativity" for another reason. The *Zhongyong* for Zhu Xi is the highest and most profound statement of the Confucian project. It is nothing less than an impassioned celebration of not only the human capacity, but also our responsibility to be co-creators with the heavens and the earth. The Confucians, in arguing against the Mohist soft theism—the assertion that cosmic order is divinely imposed in some degree—are not simply advancing the claim that human beings have an active role in the production of cosmic order, but moreover, in this aspiration to live inspired lives, human beings contribute in an intense way to its refulgent spirituality. Moreover, this spirituality is not unilateral and singular in purpose (*tianzhi* 天志), but is multivalent, pluralistic, and inclusive. The myriad things obey no single unifying principle, but achieve their harmony and diversity through the interpenetrating differences among things that come to make a difference for all of them. In many ways, the structure of the *Zhongyong* is an object lesson in Confucian metaphysics as it inspires its readers to exercise their capacity to "extend the way" (*hongdao* 弘道) and through *ars contextualis*, to strive to realize a profound harmony and coalescence in their relations with all those things present-to-hand: that is, to aspire to the co-consummation of person and world (*chengji chengwu* 成己成物) that is the axis of the *Zhongyong*.

Given that *cheng* clearly means "creativity" in the most robust sense of this term, the weakness does not lie in translating *cheng* as such, but rather that we have not sufficiently considered the fact that this radically situated and relational meaning of "creativity" is unfamiliar to the English-speaking readers who are the target audience for our translation. When they read the word "creativity," given the *creatio ex nihilo* Abrahamic and Promethean assumptions sedimented into this word within our own tradition, they stand the real danger of overwriting the Confucian cultural importances with their own. Such readers would undoubtedly have been better served if we translated it as "co-creativity," thereby alerting them to this specific, revisionist, and historicist sense of creativity.

Steve Angle

Steve Angle is not only a generous person, he is a generous philosopher. His questions herein are first asked and then happily answered himself without the need of help from me. That is, Steve poses good questions about some of the different assumptions my collaborators and I have had in doing what we have done over the years, and then gives them his own best answers. And in most cases there is little for me to add or to disagree with. Roger's *bricolage*, for example, that draws piecemeal upon whatever resources I can find in our own tradition that can serve as either associative or contrastive analogies for engaging Chinese philosophy, pragmatism and process being favorites among them, is a generous way to get past the familiar charge that I am just substituting pragmatic or process language for the vocabulary drawn from Greek or Christian or German sources. And I certainly do anticipate that once we have given the Chinese tradition its full value through the comparative (and contrastive) stage, the encounters between our traditions will lead to the optimum measure of positive, transformative effects.

Over the years, I have found Steve's rigorous scholarship on Confucianism to be an important source of reassurance and the best kind of corroboration because, although we have very different methodologies, we are usually not far apart in our conclusions. The fact that, so far, I have not been able to win him and scholars like him, over to Confucian role ethics has occasioned an abrupt turn in my own research plan. When I published *Confucian Role*

Ethics: A Vocabulary in 2011, I was keenly aware of and concerned about addressing the asymmetry that prevails in comparative studies in both the English and the Chinese scholarly literature, where the persistent pattern has been to theorize Chinese culture through a Western conceptual vocabulary. In my monograph on Confucian ethics, I made the argument that China's encounter with the Western academy is not its defining moment, and that we must try with imagination to allow this tradition to speak with its own voice and on its own terms. To this end, I abjured appealing to Western ethical theory and its discourse, and instead attempted to use the Confucian vocabulary itself to give an account of what I take to be a *sui generis* vision of the moral life. Having made my argument for pursuing a clear understanding of Confucian ethics itself as step one—what Steve has called the "comparative stage"—I then moved on to the "transformative" stage in a sequel volume tentatively entitled: *Confucian Role Ethics: Doing Justice to Justice* by trying to put Confucian role ethics into conversation with Western ethical theory on the specific topic of social justice.

But in registering the reception that my first book has garnered among many open-minded and well-intended scholars within the academy, Steve being one of the most prominent among them, I have become persuaded that I have yet to make my argument for Confucian role ethics sufficiently clear, especially on the topic on which I believe it has the most to offer, that is, an alternative conception of person. While many, if not most scholars of Confucian ethics, Chinese as well as Western, would choose to categorize this tradition as a variation on virtue ethics, I and my collaborators have contended that only in allowing that Confucius offers us a *sui generis* role ethic are we able to appreciate its important contribution to contemporary ethical discourse.

Whence came this turn to virtue ethics as the category of choice for interpreting Confucian ethics? And here I would rehearse the history a little differently than Steve. As an immediate example of the problem of theorizing China according to Western concepts, it is at the very least an interesting coincidence that most of our most influential scholars on Chinese ethics—Feng Youlan and Guo Qiyong would be good representative examples—early on proffered a purely principle-based interpretation of this tradition. But when Elisabeth Anscombe in her 1958 "Modern Moral Philosophy" essay accused deontology and utilitarianism of being legalistic and for lacking any moral psychology, and in so doing precipitated a revisionist direction in the Western ethical discourse with publications such as Alasdair MacIntyre's *After Virtue*, our interpretations of Chinese ethics changed too.[21] That is, our own turn from principle-based ethics to virtue ethics in Western normative theory occasioned by Anscombe's challenge, is also the story of an interpretive turn in our reading of Confucian ethics where we have come to embrace the newly revived virtue ethics as the most apposite reading of this antique tradition. While some Chinese scholars themselves might demure and allow that virtue ethics only has some relevance for understanding Confucian ethics (Chen Lai) but is by no means the whole story, almost all of the Chinese scholars who do Western ethics would use virtue ethics to describe the Confucian tradition (Shi Yuankang, Yu Jiyuan, Huang Yong).

G. W. F. Hegel in the introduction to his *Encyclopaedia Logic* famously observes that one of the most difficult problems in assessing any philosophical investigation is to ask the question of where it begins. I would argue that the appropriateness of categorizing Confucian ethics as either role ethics or virtue ethics turns largely on the conception of person that is presupposed within the interpretive context of classical Chinese philosophy.[22] If our goal is to take the Confucian tradition on its own terms without overwriting it with our own cultural importances, we must begin by first self-consciously and critically theorizing the Confucian conception of person as the starting point of Confucian ethics, and only then introduce it into our contemporary discourse. For this reason, I have set aside my *Doing Justice to Justice* book temporarily, and am now working on a sequel to *Confucian Role Ethics*, that is, *Theorizing "Persons" for Confucian Ethics: A Good Place to Start*.

In our own time, but with deep roots in the classical Greek philosophical narrative, individualism has become a default, commonsense assumption, if not a flat-out ideology. That is, individualism has become an ideology to the extent that, in our own post-Marxist, post-collectivist era, it has garnered a monopoly on human consciousness without any serious alternative to challenge it. Although Steve believes that what I am calling role ethics, with virtuosity doing the work of virtue, can quite comfortably be housed within the tent of a rapidly diversifying virtue ethics that some argue even includes Dewey (I think most Deweyans would reject this claim), it is the robust and significant alternative to individualism in Confucian role ethics that warrants this separate category. In this new manuscript on persons, I argue that the language of virtue ethics broadly, in appealing as it does to the vocabulary of agents, acts, generic virtues, character traits, autonomy, motivation, reasons, choices, freedoms, principles, consequences, and so on, introduces distinctions that assume this foundational individualism as its starting point.

And further, I claim that Confucian ethics by contrast begins from the wholeness of experience, and is formulated by invoking a radically different focus-field cluster of terms and distinctions with fundamentally different assumptions about how personal identities emerge in our human narratives, and how moral competence is expressed as an achieved virtuosity in the roles and relationships that come to constitute us. To fail to distinguish what I will call individual human "beings" from relationally constituted "human becomings," then, would mean that we have willy-nilly insinuated a contemporary and decidedly foreign notion of person into our investigation before it has even begun.

Peter Hershock, in his work on the value of diversity that I appeal to herein, has made the argument that "something that is good for each of us, considered individually, may not be good for all of us."[23] If individual autonomy and equality are high values within the virtue ethics discourse—values that necessarily bring with them corollaries such as rationality, freedom, rights, and personal choice—the counterparts to these values in Confucian role ethics are relational equity and an achieved diversity. Autonomy and equality give us a relatively barren sense of variety—we certainly have differences among us that we do our best to register and tolerate, but we are still equal as individuals. Such variety stands in rather stark contrast with the real diversity that can only be achieved by fully activating and appreciating our differences from each other—that is, not just differing from each other, but differing for each other. Both autonomy and equality are grounded in a doctrine of external relations that subordinate our relations to our individual selves, subordinate our interdependence with each other to our personal integrity, and subordinate our differences to our sameness. That is, maintaining comparative equality and individualism guarantees that difference can only be variation (variety) rather than diversification (diversity), and relations can only be external rather than intrinsic and constitutive. In Confucian role ethics, the alternative to comparative equality and individualism is *equity* (as the heightened realization of dynamically shared wellbeing) and *diversity* (as the full appreciation of the creative possibilities of any situation by conserving and coordinating differences).

Steve believes that much has changed over our past generation in the way in which Chinese philosophy has been received within our Western philosophical world, and even more importantly, in the way in which Chinese philosophy is being done within China itself. Steve reads what he translates as "National Studies" (*guoxue* 國學) as having the markings of a xenophobic withdrawal from global conversations, and our emphasis on the *sui generis* nature of Confucian ethics giving encouragement to such cultural purists. And it is for pragmatic reasons—keeping the conversation going—that we should relent. While allowing that Steve's counterexample to our emphasis on difference certainly has some merit—there is some scholarship that makes his point—I think that generally speaking, the return within China to confidence in its own traditions, and the resurgence of Confucianism across Asia as a global resource for a changing world cultural order is in everyone's best interest, not just China's. While Confucianism might not be the answer to the predicament of the gathering perfect storm that humanity is confronting in our own historical moment, it certainly deserves a place at a table from which it has been all but excluded these past two centuries.

Peimin Ni

The remaining four papers in this volume all concern themselves with Confucian role ethics. In the first of them, Ni Peimin opens his essay with a cogent summary of the position Rosemont and I have laid out in arguing for role ethics as our best explanation of Confucian moral philosophy. Holding us up in contrast with Aristotle, Peimin identifies three important, uncommon assumptions. First, while Aristotle offers a predetermined conception of persons as a *telos* of intellect (human "beings"), our Confucian notion of person emerges from "culturally generated patterns of behavior and taste" as contextually emergent human "becomings." Second, while Aristotle appeals to reason to discover and determine what is moral, Confucius would look to the exercise of moral imagination as our resource for moral artistry. And third, while Aristotle understands virtues as antecedent ideals that can be actualized as personal character traits, a practical Confucian virtuosity emerges through the activity of productive relations.

Peimin expresses some personal sympathy with several of our assumptions: to wit, our underlying conception of the relational person, and our open-ended thesis expressed in the language of "human becomings." Having tried to give us our best argument, Peimin then offers a set of challenging questions—very penetrating questions—that provides me with an opportunity to try to further clarify what we mean by role ethics.

Peimin's first question concerns the limits of relationality. If role ethics presses relationality to the extent that it would "deny the existence of individuals separated from their roles," it would offend against the "spirit of strong subjectivity" and "self-determination" that invoke "the image of autonomous individuals" in the Confucian canons. "Why," asks Peimin, "do our actions have to be *inter*actions, and why is their quality determined and evaluated *relationally* but not separately?" Indeed, for Peimin it would be a misconception of the Confucian sense of "relateds" to treat this relatedness as "contrary to subjectivity, independence, and self-determination."

I am glad to have this question because how persons are theorized is really necessary for responding to a second important question he poses on the source of normativity in Confucian role ethics. And in the tension between Peimin's both accepting the relationality constituted person associated with

Confucianism, and at the same time, wanting to hang on to the conditions of the default autonomous individual, has been our greatest obstacle in trying to get our peers to understand our position.

What we are calling Confucian role ethics begins from the primacy of vital, constitutive relationality of our lived roles and relations. We will need to distinguish between our commonsense understanding of external relations among discrete individuals and a less familiar and perhaps counterintuitive doctrine of internal relations in order to make this point. Peter Hershock offers a rather clear and uncontroversial account of internal, constitutive relations in diagnosing the problem we have in our culturally specific and recalcitrant habit of seeing the world as being comprised of preexisting, discrete "things" that then enter into external relations among themselves:

> Autonomous subjects and objects are, finally, only artifacts of abstraction.... What we refer to as "things"—whether mountains, human beings, or complex phenomena like histories—are simply the experienced results of having established relatively constant horizons of value or relevance ("things"). They are not, as commonsense insists, natural occurring realities or [things]. Indeed, what we take to be *objects* existing independently of ourselves are, in actuality, simply a function of habitual patterns of relationships.[24]

Hershock goes on to offer us an intellectual cure for our culturally bound, default assumption that discrete "things" (or persons) are primary, allowing us to see "through the conceit that relations are second-order realities contingent upon pre-existing actors." A doctrine of internal relations requires of us a different commonsense:

> This amounts to an ontological gestalt shift from taking independent and dependent actors to be first order realities and relations among them as second order, to seeing relationality as first order (or ultimate) reality and all individual actors as (conventionally) abstracted or derived from them.[25]

The Confucian tradition resists our seemingly default assumption that individuals as discrete entities are concrete existents rather than second order abstractions from their narratives. It offers instead a "gerundive" and holistic, focus-field reading of persons, and goes on to further claim that such persons cannot be accurately described, analyzed, and evaluated independently of their contextualizing environments, including first and foremost their dealings with other human beings.

Stated simply, the relationally constituted person starts from the bare fact of associated living—an empirical fact that does not need to be argued for. It is the way things are. And the notion of the discrete, independent, and autonomous individual is a fiction. We do not live our lives inside our skins. Our claim here is that nothing and no one does anything by itself. All of our physical and conscious activity as persons is collaborative and transactional. Importantly, such embeddedness within our vital context does not deny subjectivity or individual purpose or uniqueness, but requires that we understand these conditions differently.

Rather than embracing our commonsense realist notion of a mind-independent world that serves as warrant for the independence of subjectivity from world, in the human experience as it is understood in Confucian philosophy, world and person are mutually entailing, coterminous, and inseparable. Experience can be more or less subjective, but it is never subjective to the degree that it is independent of context. Indeed, the content and quality of such subjectivity would be a function of the degree to which one coalesces with one's various natural, social, and cultural environments. And subjectivity and objectivity far from being dualistic categories that allow for separation, have the *yinyang* 陰陽 correlative and interdependent relationship assumed with the language that translates subject and object into Chinese: *ke* 客 and *zhu* 主.

One's individuality understood differently is not a discrete starting point exclusive of relationships. Our lives from the beginning are lived *in media res* as narratives within narratives, and such lives as intertwined narratives are constituted by relations all the way down. In this narrative understanding of persons, we become distinctive and even distinguished not exclusive of our relations, but by virtue of the quality we have been able to achieve in the cultivation of these same relations. Importantly, such relationally constituted individuality entails an individual uniqueness that is more pronounced than the familiar understanding of persons that assumes an essential sameness—for example, the metaphysical claims about a reduplicative human nature true of all instances of human beings that would reduce all differences to being merely incidental.

But where associated living is merely descriptive, as soon as we stipulate our various kinds of associations as roles, they become normative. A person's specific roles then—daughters and grandpas, teachers and neighbors, shopkeepers and lovers—are simply stipulated kinds of association that in their specificity take on a clear normative cast: Am I a good daughter? Am I a good teacher? Role ethics begins from the assumption that, in any interesting moral or political sense, persons cannot be understood apart from the other persons with whom they interact, and that in fact persons are best described and evaluated in terms of the specific roles that guide their actions in their transactions with these specific others. Simply put, what is moral is conduct that conduces to growth and flourishing in the roles and relations we live together with others, and what is immoral is the opposite.

This leads to Peimin's second important question. With respect to "human becomings," Peimin asks, do not the rather elaborate, mainstream theories of human nature in texts such as *Mencius* and *Zhongyong* provide a metaphysics of person that serves as a standard for adjudicating right and wrong and as a normative vision of what we "should" be: "what we essentially are and what we should strive to retain and develop?" Here Peimin would ask after the source of normativity in Confucian role ethics.

Daniel A. Bell

I want to carry Peimin's second question about the source of normativity in Confucian role ethics over to my answer to Daniel Bell, and then on to Kathy Higgins, because they too express similar concerns about normativity, albeit in their own language. Daniel has had the advantage of spending most of his professional career in China, and from this vantage point, has become one of the most prominent and most intelligent voices on the increasingly important role of Confucianism in the emergence of a new China. His several questions are important ones, and I will address them here carefully.

One of the claims of my *Confucian Role Ethics* is that I am seeking to allow Confucianism to use its own vocabulary in speaking for itself, and to resist what I take to be a familiar asymmetrical pattern of shoehorning Confucian axiology into Western ethical categories. And Daniel points out rightly that a prominent theme in my text is how family and communal relations function as the site for developing moral competence. This being the case, if we are trying to let Confucianism speak for itself, what, Daniel asks, is the Chinese term that does the work of "community" in these canonical texts? Indeed, the mantra in the *Expansive Learning* (*daxue* 大學) that is often cited as the radial and reflexive process of personal cultivation is: "Once their hearts-and-minds knew what is proper, their persons were cultivated; once their persons were cultivated, their families were set right; once their families were set right, their state was properly ordered; and once their states were properly ordered, there was peace in the world." There is certainly no mention of "community" in this passage, and if there is not an equivalent for "community" in these texts, am I not perhaps importing insights from the contemporary Western communitarian tradition to define Confucian role ethics?

My first point would be that this Confucian project as stated in the *Expansive Learning* is clearly holistic, and even though there is no specific mention of "community" *per se*, the radial, rippling pattern of cultivation is inclusive of the direct, shared sense of identity and the significant quality of relationships that we associate with the communal dimension. The central message of this terse yet comprehensive document is that while personal, familial, social, political, and indeed cosmic cultivation is ultimately coterminous and mutually entailing, it must always begin from a commitment to personal cultivation, with the cosmic context providing the resources available for such cultivation.

A second argument that I would make on behalf of an implicit sense of community is that, historically, "family" (*jia* 家) in this same *Expansive Learning* mantra is inclusive of community. Yan Fu makes the argument that during the two millennia of imperial China, at best 30 percent of social order was derived from empire; the other 70 percent was a function of lives lived within family lineage (*jiazu* 家族 or *shizu* 氏族) and the social fabric such communities provided.

Yet another way of arguing that the notion of community is integral to Confucian role ethics is to derive community from the ubiquitous use of the term "exemplary person" (*junzi*) in the early Confucian canons. It is a commonplace that Confucius as depicted in the *Analects* reinvents this term *junzi*, transforming it from denoting nobility of birth and blood (king, ruler, vassals, high ministers) to nobility of conduct (persons who serve as exemplary models for family and community). This being the case, *junzi* still retains a social and political reference in the sense that human beings can only become exemplary in their conduct through full participation in the social and political life of their family lineages and communities. Several of the early glosses and texts—the *Er Ya*, the *Hanshiwaizhuan*, the *Baihutong*, and others—underscore this social dimension when they define the term *jun* 君 paronomastically—that is, by semantic and phonetic association—as *qun* 群 "gathering around:" as Daniel notes, the same term used to translate "community" in modern Chinese. That is: "*Junzi* are those to whom the community repairs."

A second concern that Daniel voices is with my claim that we are constituted by our relations. He suggests that while some of our relations might be "constitutive" (our immediate family relations, for example), others might well be "contingent" (second cousins and shopkeepers). I am assuming that Daniel is suggesting that some relations are more essential to our identity than others. As I have argued above, while all of our roles are constitutive of who we become (those important family relations over which we have little control as well as those that are incidental and that we might choose quite arbitrarily), some are more important and thus more defining of personal identity than others. I have tried to respond to this same question in my answer to Ni Peimin above, and would refer Daniel to what I have said there.

But Daniel's main concern has to do with his worry over the relationship between role ethics and moral obligation. He distinguishes between two claims: "the strong claim that the (constitutive) roles we occupy determine (or are the main source of) the content of our moral obligations and the weaker claim that our (constitutive) roles set constraints upon what we ought to do." He rightly associates my position with the former stronger claim, while he himself wants to advocate for the latter. Daniel's position in sum is that if "role ethics is to provide morally informed practical guidance, it needs to be constrained by moral standards external to the roles."

For Daniel, we need to consult abstract principles rather than just lived roles for two reasons. First, roles change over time. There is clearly a difference between the role of "wife" in classical China, in the contemporary world, and the "wife" that would emerge in a same-sex marriage. And second, our lived roles often entail conflicting obligations—he references the obligations of citizen versus family member in the cases of Seif Qaddafi and the Unabomber's brother.

I do not dispute the functional value of regulative ideals, nor have I overlooked the many abstract standards appealed to in the Confucian texts. But I would argue that it is roles as they have been lived that are themselves the ultimate source of our standards and principles and obligations. Where do our values come from? In guiding our actions, we are inclined to presume uncritically perhaps that because we have a word, we have a "thing." Not only does "courage" or "justice" or "*ren* 仁" or "*cheng* 誠" have some immediate referent, but this referent is somehow independent of our actions, and thus has either causal status as a given principle antecedent to what we do, or a teleological status as a predetermined goal for our actions. To the extent that we think of courage or justice as *principles*, there is a strong sense of antecedence, generality of application, and derivation. Indeed, the idea of principle carries just such connotations: a basic source, an essence or determining characteristic, an original faculty or endowment, an originating or actuating force, a higher-order norm from which lower and more specific rules of behavior are derived, a fixed or predetermined mode of action, an axiom of conduct, and so on.

But in fact, on reflection we can argue from a Confucian perspective that if courage or justice do have referents, it is as generalizations derived from specific human beings acting courageously or justly within their family and community roles and relations. Courage is an abstracted characterization of the unrelenting tenacity of this mother protecting her child from this danger, and justice is the deliberate, circumspect evaluation of the applications of these students by this teacher. Rather than being fixed and retrospective, such principles point most concretely to the historical unfolding of complex configurations of always-unique, always-specific relations as they are informed by analogy with past experience. Similarly, putative "virtues" are in fact a virtuosity that has been abstracted from past human experience—a quality of conduct itself when it is informed by our best efforts at cultivation and personal growth, thereby making our actions efficacious and qualitatively productive.

Since the lived roles of human beings are themselves the ultimate source of erstwhile principles, standards, virtues, and values, the content of these abstracted (rather than abstract) principles, like the roles themselves, also change over time. The question we must ask, then is: Since most of our moral lives are lived close to home, does not the role or the role model more often give us better guidance for practical actions than the derivative, abstracted principle? For example, the principle of justice as it is to be understood in a classical Chinese family will be different from a contemporary Western family, and from the same-sex family as well, and to assume that it can be applied objectively is simply a contemporary conceit that will disrespect the differences and do violence by enforcing sameness. Because of the abstract, ambiguous, and only purportedly objective sense of justice, it is not sufficiently capacious to provide us with the same quality of guidance that appeals to the roles of "wife" and "husband" have that are being redefined and reauthorized in our own time and place.

When I reflect on what it means to be a good husband to my wife, I find an enormous disconnect from what "husband" meant even in my father's generation, and I wonder if these traditional but changing terms are meaningful for members of a same-sex family, or whether they would want to stipulate a different role that is more appropriate to their familial relationship—"partner," for example. What is optimally appropriate in the husband-wife relationship in my home is certainly retrospective in being informed by the past experience of my parents, but it is also prospective in being determined ultimately by the needs of the two persons in this specific relationship. The virtue of giving privilege to the lived roles of "wife" and "husband" is that it allows me to focus on the satisfactions of my own specific relationship without doing violence to it by having to tailor it to conform to some ostensibly objective norm.

Let me say this another way. Does not the appreciation of real differences—those of gender, generation, and most importantly, personal differences—give the lie to the idea that social justice is to be achieved by treating all people according to the same principle or standard? Ironically a heavy-handed conception of justice that, in imposing some codifiable standard of equity on family, would fail to respect the processual, phasal, and resolutely hierarchical nature of family life, is itself reductive and violent, becoming a procedural strategy for enforcing conformity at the unacceptable expense of excising real differences and their creative possibilities. In failing to accommodate family roles lived through richly textured and constantly changing patterns of both natural and socially constructed differences, such a theory is an anathema to the optimizing of the family experience for all of its members. And after all, it must be this aspiration to optimize the family experience that is surely the ultimate goal of any conception of real, actualized justice.

With respect to Daniel's concern that our roles often present us with conflicted obligations, of course this is true. And the Confucian process recommended for dealing with such cases requires an appeal to deference (*shu* 恕) and the application of the quantum of moral imagination it entails that will enable us to discover and act upon what is most appropriate for all concerned within the specific circumstances—what in the Confucian vocabulary is captured in the term *yi* 義. The problem is that the determination of what is appropriate cannot be disengaged from the specifics of the roles and circumstances. In the extreme cases of the son Seif Qaddafi and the Unabomber's brother that Daniel cites, I don't think many of us would have much difficulty in deciding which of their roles must take precedence, and wherein an optimal appropriateness lies.

Kathleen M. Higgins

Kathleen Higgins, like several of the other voices in this volume, addresses my work as a seamless collaboration with my fellow travelers—David Hall, Henry Rosemont Jr., D. C. Lau, and others. On her chosen topic of Confucian role ethics, I am at once inseparably Henry and Roger. In a very explicit and satisfying way, deference in the collaboration of all of life's various activities and the first-order primacy of our relationality over the second order of abstracted individuals is immediately relevant to our advocacy of Confucian role ethics.

Kathy provides a most articulate and persuasive account of Confucian role ethics that brings with it its own cosmological assumptions and its own conception of how particular persons emerge within their roles in families and communities through an achieved propriety in patterns of conduct called *li*. She acknowledges both the prescribed nature of these patterns and the particularistic demands that always qualify such prescriptions—that is, the profoundly unique and inimitable project of making full use of the affordances offered in being *this* daughter to *this* dad. Indeed, it is the emphasis on this particularity that provides a clear affinity between the aesthetic and the ethical, and that makes the artistry of musical performance an analogy to the efficacy of role performance in the key Confucian binomial, *liyue* 禮樂.

Kathy takes up the debate between virtue and role ethics, opining that when virtue ethics is disengaged from just Aristotle and given its full contemporary compass, these two positions focusing as they both do upon the consequences of personal cultivation might at least be complementary if not even fully elided. Still, she recognizes that what is at stake in the discourse is an alternative, robust, relationally constituted conception of persons that might serve as a counterweight to the prevailing ideology of individualism.

At the same time, Kathy also worries over how the Confucian emphasis on the performance of roles might have the real negative consequence of reinforcing demands of conformity to prevailing social expectations to the extent that such imposed uniformity suppresses if not excludes utterly minority voices and their alternative values. And this is not an unwarranted concern. Certainly *li* 禮 must be understood as the institutions and life forms that serve as a living embodiment of traditional cultural authority, and family and social roles are the medium through which such authority is passed on from generation to generation. *Li* provides role models for our roles, and such prescribed patterns of conduct carry with them very real social expectations expressed as both approbation and censure. There is certainly high value invested in shame in Confucian culture in both its positive function of encouraging participation in shared life forms to meet such social expectations, and in its negative function of punishing the deviant and recalcitrant who would do otherwise.

In my own critique of Confucianism, as Kathy has observed, I have expressed concern about how the seemingly liberating emphasis upon family and intimate relationships—the culture of *guanxi* 關係—is at the same time the source of cronyism and a pervasive culture of corruption throughout China. Such corruption has metastasized throughout every institutionalized stratum of the social order, from government to education to the military, and left unconstrained, it is arguably China's single greatest obstacle to a distinctively Confucian process of democratization in our own historical moment.

A companion worry to this corruption is how an exclusive sense of the *li*-generated identity of a people (*minzu* 民族) can and often is expressed systemically as the tyranny of the majority. In our *Democracy of the Dead* (1999) that we wrote in anticipation of the trajectory that China might take in its democratic evolution, the greatest concern that David Hall and I had with what we perceived as an ineluctable process, was what we described as "the myth of the Han"—the putative "family resemblance" of 94 percent of the population. We interpreted this "Han" politics as family writ large, and saw in it the deliberate construction of a putative centripetal center of Chinese identity that has the twin functions of forestalling the centrifugal forces of a powerful regionalism, and at the same time, of generating an "oriental orientalism" bent on marginalizing if not assimilating those minorities that lay beyond its boundaries. The fact that this section of the book was excised by censors when it was translated and made available to a Chinese audience several years after its English publication would seem to make our case.

But the Confucian response that would be made in favor of the importance invested in intimate relations, in the centrality of the institution of family, and in the socially redeeming dividends of promoting the continuing identity of a people (*minzu*) is that these values, even as they are so often perverted, are still our best hope. Life in association—*guanxi*—is a fact. And just because relations when misused and abused lead to corruption, does not provide us with some benign alternative to *guanxi*. Rather, it requires of us that we generate the social intelligence and regulative ideals necessary to guarantee that these same relations function to conduce to optimal family and communal flourishing. And these regulative ideals are the substance of *li* and its institutions. To make the often-made case that Confucianism is the source of corruption because it is centered on and celebrates these familial values is to deprecate the intergenerational renewal of the best strategies the cultural tradition has been able to produce for deploying relationships in an optimally productive way. And to fail to acknowledge the extent to which a shared *minzu* identity grounded in both the authority and the aesthetics of *li* has been a positive factor in promoting and sustaining harmony not only among a national population, but a continental population, is to overlook the scale of China's challenge—a China that in population exceeds every continent save Asia itself. China, with respect to the tensile strength of its social fabric, is to be compared to the complexities and diversity of an Africa or a Europe, not to a Canada or Japan.

This same point arises in the positive if not idealistic representation of Confucian role ethics advocated by Rosemont and Ames in its contrast with the sometimes negative characterizations of family and the performance of its often oppressive roles that we find in Judith Butler. One contribution of Butler that resonates with our understanding of role ethics is her interpretation of gender identity as a fabrication engendered through habitual performance that creates the illusion of some "interior and organizing core." At least two points might be made here, the first being that the radically different way that gender is both achieved and constituted within the Chinese tradition when set in contrast with other traditions certainly supports Butler's argument that gender is largely the product of social practices. The second reflection would be that in the Confucian tradition not just gender identity, but the performance of personal identity broadly through our embodied roles and our lived bodies follows much this same creative, irreducibly social process.

As Kathy duly notes, we and Butler are theorizing the performative nature of relationally constituted human identity and our how our agency as persons is constituted in similar terms, but while one of us underscores the positive possibilities for achieved growth and diversity that such an understanding of the human experience invokes, the other would emphasize the real oppression and the exploitative practices that the social construction of person brings with it for certain populations. For the Confucian, our humanity is a personal achievement won through the cultivation of our roles in family and community, while for Butler this same humanity is conferred upon us (or withheld) by our societies. Butler's concern here would certainly apply as cautionary for the Confucian case as well, but to locate the agency and energy of the attainment of personal identity on the social context alone without allowing for the commitment to the cultivation of relationships of the unique person emerging in that context might be too asymmetrical. And in the same vein, in this tension between idealities and realities, it is not the case that the former is some Pollyannic fiction while the latter is the way the world really is. Idealities are historical too, and such aspirations are often formulated to light our way during our darkest days. Indeed, we could not survive our ordinary lives for an hour without the energy and lift that such cherished aspirations encourage. At the end of the day, we must not give up on our ideals, but we must also resist naïveté by giving full credence to the reality check that the sobering critique of Butler brings to our idealistic assumptions about the social construction of persons.

Kathy's concerns require us to make one point clearly: It will only be a self-critical, revisionist, and practicable form of Confucianism that will have any real relevance as a resource for the inevitable changing world cultural order.

Henry Rosemont Jr.

Henry Rosemont Jr., begins his contribution to this volume by rehearsing the history of the happy collaboration we have shared over these past several decades that has united us in common cause against the ideology of individualism. And I am delighted to have his honest testimony that he has found our work together as much a source of pleasure and satisfaction as I have. On his account, we have translated Chinese canonical texts together, written commentary upon and interpreted these classical documents together, and quite boldly invented a new brand of ethics—what we are calling "Confucian role ethics"—together. Alluding to the language of Bob Neville above, in having shared this piece of life in its so many dimensions, with most of our activities accompanied by significant quantities of red wine, we have as friends become one together, thus allowing Kathy Higgins and others in this volume to address issues giving primacy to our relationship rather than treating us as two persons.

In Henry's essay, he expresses a frustration we have both experienced in the reception that our Confucian role ethics has had among our academic peers who almost always ground their reservations within a framework that assumes a foundational individualism. But I do not think that we need give up on the conversation; I think we need more of it. As Henry himself avers, we still have much work to do. As I have expressed in my response to Bob Nevillle, I do not think Henry and I have as of yet been able to make our position sufficiently clear, and in particular, we need to provide a stronger account of the counterintuitive, Confucian alternative to individualism—the relationally constituted, focus-field conception of person—an account that will be necessary if we want to precipitate the gestalt shift from duck to rabbit among well-intended colleagues who quite understandably are defaulting to the kind of entrenched individualism that has become their commonsense. After all, Henry himself notes the extremely strong *psychological* pull of the individual self, and also recalls our own only gradual and incremental turn from assuming this notion of the autonomous individual as everyone else seems to do, to being inspired by the Confucian texts to develop our very different view that this pervasive and seemingly invincible assumption of the free and autonomous person is in fact, anathema to social justice.

In his always kind remarks about his old collaborator, Henry alludes to the wonderful relationship I had with Professor Lau even during the last few years of his long life before his passing in April 2010, when it was the contrast between the extraordinary strength of his mental capacities in his full stride that made us all aware of their gradual waning. And Henry, with this aside, gives me an occasion to remember this singular relationship, and to reinforce the important point that Henry is making here, and that must not be missed.

As I am writing, I have just responded to an email from Robin Ling Ling Wong who as always is organizing a visit by a group of us, no less than twenty persons in number, to the peaceful Buddhist temple in the New Territories where Professor Lau's ashes and his tablet are kept. Professor Lau and his three siblings were all unmarried and produced no continuing family members to take care of them, and as he grew older, a network of former students (me and Ho Che-wah), students of students (Florence and Wing), other colleagues and their students, and other important friends gathered around Professor Lau, and each in their own different way, cared for him, both early on, and as his days came to a peaceful end. In my *Confucian Role Ethics* published shortly after his death, my dedication read:

> For D. C. Lau and his CUHK family: The ordinary lives of these extraordinary people teach us more about Confucian role ethics than any book could pretend to do.

What is different with this year's visit is that the October occasion has now become a complement to the usual assemblage on Professor Lau's birthday in early March.

As Henry keenly observes, to reduce the shared feelings that galvanize and continue to strengthen this matrix of relationships to "altruism"—that is, the expression of disinterested and selfless concern for the wellbeing of another—would diminish these feelings utterly. First, without Professor Lau, none of us would be who we are—indeed, we would all be much less. We are all located and flourish within the web of relationships that constituted him and his narrative. Certainly, in this continuing practice there is a powerful deference and affection for my old teacher, but it is not about him or about me—it is about our teacher-student relationship as it deepened, and by extension, about all of us in our evolving relations. And far from being the expression of some disinterested or selfless concern, it is how we extend our shared interest in each other, and in so doing, strengthen our own persons through the quality of the relationships we are able to achieve. Teachers do not come before students, parents do not come before children, and credible friends do not come before trust; these roles must come together or not at all.

In what remains of Henry's essay, he takes the conversation from Confucian role ethics to "role politics" by asking the question: "What, then might a Chinese-style, role-based Confucian-inspired democracy look like compared to those now current in the West?" Allowing that David and I began to respond to precisely this question in our *Democracy of the Dead: Dewey, Confucius and the Hope for Democracy in China* (1999), Henry brings in and explores four recent important contributions to the notion of Confucian democracy.

Joseph Chan's *Confucian Perfectionism* as one configuration among many argues that contemporary Confucians should draw upon Western liberal institutions to the extent that they can provide effective measures of governance, while at the same time modifying these modern democratic resources in such a way and to the extent needed to keep alive the compelling spirit of the Confucian ideal. Recently, Sungmoon Kim, in advancing his own version of Confucian democracy, identifies the alternatives to it: the competing particularism thesis that advocates for a unique kind of democracy "most suitable to East Asia's particular cultural context" (such as Jiang Qing), the communitarianism thesis that assumes an incompatability between rights-based liberal individualism and Confucian values (such as Sor-hoon Tan, Hall and Ames, and Rosemont), and the meritocracy thesis that challenges egalitarian assumptions that ground the principle of universal suffrage with governance by the "best and brightest" (such as Daniel Bell). In advancing his own model of Confucian democracy, Kim explicitly (and Chan too) asserts that, "democracy can mean or include many different things, but at its core, it is a political system and a sociopolitical practice, not a philosophical idea or an ethical precept."[26] While I too want to advocate for a Confucian democracy, I like Henry think this effort has to be guided philosophically by a clear understanding of the several "ideas" or "ideals" that are at issue.

Confucian role ethics is grounded in the way in which an achieved propriety in our roles and relations (*li* 禮) brings full resolution to and thus aestheticizes the human experience:

> Master You said: "An optimizing harmony is the most valuable function of achieving propriety in our roles and relations. In the ways of the Former Kings, this optimizing harmony through achieving propriety made them elegant, and was a guiding standard in all things large and small. But when things are not going well, to realize harmony just for its own sake without regulating the situation through an achieved propriety in our roles and relations will not work."[27]

Given the relational focus-field nature of person, this is a Confucian formula for everyone-in-community aspiring to achieve an optimal propriety in their roles and relations that resonates immediately with John Dewey and A. N. Whitehead's assumptions about the grounding premises of real democracy: a social and political mode of association that optimizes the human experience. In *The Public and Its Problems*, Dewey looks for the real substance of democracy in the informal, the concrete, and the everyday—the lives and relationships of particular people in their own particular communities—and thus defines "the democratic idea in its generic social sense" in the following terms:

> From the standpoint of the individual, it consists in having a responsible share according to capacity in forming and directing the activities of the groups to which one belongs and in participating according to need in the values which the groups sustain. From the standpoint of the groups, it demands liberation of the potentialities of members of a group in harmony with the interests and goods which are common.[28]

We must be careful here because Dewey's language if misunderstood—and it frequently has been—can betray his deeper meaning. For Dewey, the "individual" and the "group" are neither separate nor separable entities. On the contrary, given Dewey's commitment to the wholeness of experience as the starting point of all reflection, lives lived together have priority over discrete individuals, and concrete situations have priority over the abstraction of agency.

If we need further corroboration for the intimate relationship between what Dewey has identified as the "idea" of democracy with its religious and cosmological grounding, Whitehead in his own language, but in the same spirit as Dewey, sees the cosmological "ideal" of democracy as an aesthetic and moral achievement that optimizes the creative possibilities of the human condition:

> The basis of democracy is the common fact of value experience, as constituting the essential nature of each pulsation of actuality. Everything has some value for itself, for others, and for the whole. This characterizes the meaning of actuality. By reason of this character, constituting reality, the conception of morals arises . . . Existence, in its own nature, is the upholding of value intensity. Also no unit can separate itself from the others, and from the whole. And yet each unit exists in its own right. It upholds value intensity for itself, and this involves sharing value intensity with the universe. Everything that in any sense exists has two sides, namely, its individual self and its signification in the universe. Also either of these aspects is a factor in the other.[29]

Translating an abstract Whitehead into concrete communal terms, unique persons certainly have their own integrity, but it is an integrity that has its moral meaning and aesthetic value not exclusive of their relations, but only by virtue of what these persons constituted by these same relations mean for each other and for the community as a whole.

At least at this theoretical level, we can confirm that at least the ideal of democracy if not the political system expresses ideals and values that are not only fundamental to Confucian role ethics, but to the cosmological assumptions that provide the interpretive context for this tradition.

Where the Confucian ideal differs from Dewey and Whitehead is the central heuristic role it gives to the family as the entry point for pursuing this optimization. For Tang Junyi, Chinese culture is grounded in the everyday lives of the people and the natural deference that pervades family living.[30] The meaning and value of family relations is not simply the primary ground of social order—it has cosmological and religious implications as well. Family bonds properly observed are the point of departure for understanding that we each have moral responsibility for an expanding web of relations that reach far beyond our own localized selves.[31] The family is the center of cosmic order, and as we have seen above in the *Expansive Learning*, all order ripples out in concentric circles from and returns to nourish this primary source.

Just as Dewey's "idea" of democracy is his vision of the flourishing communal life made possible by optimizing the contributions of the uniquely distinguished persons that constitute it, Tang Junyi's Confucianism is also directed at achieving the highest integrated cultural, moral, and spiritual growth for the individual-in-community. What makes the distinctively Confucian "values" ideal is that each one of them—"family reverence" (xiao 孝), "fraternal deference" (ti 悌), "achieving propriety in one's roles and relations" (li 禮) "personal cultivation and consummation in our roles and relations" (ren 仁), "way-making" (dao 道) through "virtuosity in conduct" (de 德), and so on—functions within this aestheticism to optimize the creative possibilities that are available in the evolving culture.

Of course the Confucian appeal to family as the organizing metaphor for the human experience is not altogether benign. While being the most profound insight of this Chinese tradition in rethinking the ground of real democracy, as I have opined above in my response to Kathy Higgins above, the intimate relations we associate with family as a source of endemic corruption have also been the main obstacle on its road to democratization. While the primary problem Dewey is addressing in invoking the "idea" of democracy is his attempt to overcome the aggregating inertia of form that if left unreformed will stifle the life of the really democratic community, the problem that the "idea" of Confucianism faces if it is to be realized as a Confucian democracy is precisely the opposite. With so much investment in intimate and informal familial relationships, the Confucian tradition has been slow to produce the formal, more "objective" institutions necessary to sustain its own Confucian version of democracy, and when it has produced them, these same institutions are often compromised and ultimately eroded by the excessive attention paid to personal as opposed to civic relationships. Indeed, as democracy emerges in China, we are witnessing that the cure for the ills of a Confucian democracy is a transparent and effective appeal to rule of law and the establishment of those formal civic institutions of democracy that will be able to contain the excesses of family feeling.

Notes

1. A. N. Whitehead, *Modes of Thought* (New York: Free Press, 1938), 173.

2. *Analects* 13.28: 子路問曰：「何如斯可謂之士矣？」子曰：「切切、偲偲、怡怡如也，可謂士矣。朋友切切、偲偲，兄弟怡怡。」

3. *Analects* 1.8: 君子 . . . 無友不如己者 (repeated in 9.25). See also 19.3.

4. A. N. Whitehead's related fallacies of "simple location" and "misplaced concreteness" immediately come to mind. See his earliest formulations in *Science and the Modern World* (New York: The Macmillan Company, 1925; New York: The Free Press, 1967).

5. *Analects* 13.23: 君子和而不同，小人同而不和。

6. I have tried to summarize this methodology myself in "Philosophizing with Canonical Chinese Texts: Seeking an Interpretive Context," in Sor-hoon Tan (ed.), *Research Handbook on Methodology in Chinese Philosophy* (London: Bloomsbury Press, 2016).

7. See Robert Cummings Neville, *Ritual and Deference: Extending Chinese Philosophy in a Comparative Context* (Albany: State University of New York Press, 2008), 159–60.

8. In "Philosophizing with Canonical Chinese Texts: Seeking an Interpretive Context," in Sor-hoon Tan (ed.). *Research Handbook on Methodology in Chinese Philosophy* (London: Bloomsbury Press, 2016). I have suggested some resonances between interesting interpretations of Peircian abduction and the *ars contextualis* that inspires Chinese correlative, analogical thinking.

9. Tang Chun-yi [Tang Junyi], "The *t'ien ming* (heavenly ordinance) in pre-Ch'in China," *Philosophy East and West* 11 (1962), 195.

10. *Xunzi* 荀子天论17: 因物而多之, 孰與騁能而化之！思物而物之, 孰與理物而勿失之也！願於物之所以生, 孰與有物之所以成！故錯人而思天, 則失萬物之情。

11. *Zhongyong* 中庸 1: 天命之謂性, 率性之謂道, 修道之謂教。

12. *Zhongyong* 中庸 30: 仲尼 . . . 上律天時, 下襲水土。辟如天地之無不持載, 無不覆幬, 辟如四時之錯行, 如日月之代明。

13. *Zhongyong* 中庸 1: 中也者, 天下之大本也；和也者, 天下之達道也。致中和, 天地位焉, 萬物育焉。

14. *Zhongyong* 中庸 31: 唯天下至聖 . . . 舟車所至, 人力所通, 天之所覆, 地之所載, 日月所照, 霜露所墜；凡有血氣者, 莫不尊親, 故曰配天。

15. *Book of Songs* (诗经大序) 诗者, 志之所之也, 在心为志, 发言为诗。情动于中而形于言, 言之不足故嗟叹之, 嗟叹之不足故永歌之, 永歌之不足, 不知手之舞之足之蹈之也。

16. *Daodejing* 1: 無名天地之始；有名萬物之母。 . . . 此兩者, 同出而異名, 同謂之玄。玄之又玄, 衆妙之門。

17. *Daodejing* 25: 道法自然. And 17: 百姓皆謂我自然。

18. *Daodejing* 51: 道生之, 德畜之, 物形之, 勢成之。是以萬物莫不尊道而貴德。道之尊, 德之貴, 夫莫之命常自然。

19. *Daodejing* 49: 聖人恆無心 , 以百姓心為心。。。。 聖人在天下, 歙歙為天下渾其心, 百姓皆注其耳目, 聖人皆孩之。The received text of *Daodejing* 49 has 聖人無常心: "Sages are without a constant heartmind." On the basis of a Mawangdui text, a variant that has 聖人恆無心, Liu Xiaogan 劉笑敢 uses received commentaries to argue for the cogency of this alternative: "Sages are ever without a heartmind." See his *Laozi Past and Present* (老子古今) (Beijing: Zhongguo shehuikexue chubanshe, 2006) vol. 1, 487.

20. *Mencius* 7A4: 孟子曰: 萬物皆備於我矣。反身而誠, 樂莫大焉。強恕而行, 求仁莫近焉。 Mengzi said, "Is there any enjoyment greater than, with the myriad happenings of the world all implicated here in me, to turn personally inward and to thus find resolution with these happenings? Is there any way of seeking to become consummate in my person more immediate than making every effort to act empathetically by extending myself into the places of others?"

21. G. E. M. Anscombe, "Modern Moral Philosophy," *Philosophy*, 33 (1958).

22. It should be noted that we need the term "role" in the English expression "Confucian role ethics," but it is redundant to use the Chinese because "role" is already

there in the language of "Confucian ethics" (儒學倫理學) with the term *lun* 倫 itself meaning "human roles and relations." Although *lunlixue* as a translation of "ethics" is a modern term, the binomial *lunli* dates back to Han dynasty sources. That this same term *lun* also means "category" and "class" suggests that the construction of such discriminations as "categories" is a function of correlations and analogy rather than assumed essences.

23. Peter D. Hershock, *Valuing Diversity: Buddhist Reflection on Realizing a More Equitable Global Future* (Albany: State University of New York Press, 2012), 133.

24. Peter Hershock. *Buddhism in the Public Sphere: Reorienting Global Interdependence* (New York: Routledge, 2006), 140.

25. Hershock, *Buddhism in the Public Sphere*, 147.

26. Sungmoon Kim, *Confucian Democracy in East Asia: Theory and Practice* (Cambridge: Cambridge University Press, 2014) 9.

27. *Analects* 1.12: 有子曰：禮之用和為貴。先王之道, 斯為美；小大由之。 有所不行, 知和而和, 不以禮節之, 亦不可行也。

28. *The Essential Dewey*, edited by Larry A. Hickman and Thomas A. Alexander (Bloomington: Indiana University Press, 1998), vol 1, 294–95.

29. A. N. Whitehead. *Modes of Thought* (New York: Macmillan, 1938) 111.

30. Tang Junyi, *Complete Works* Tang Junyi, *Complete Works* 唐君毅全集 (Taipei: Xuesheng shuju, 1988), vol. 4, 219–302.

31. Tang Junyi, *Complete Works*, vol. 4, 210–15.

Contributors

Stephen C. Angle is Mansfield Freeman Professor of East Asian Studies and Professor of Philosophy at Wesleyan University. He specializes in Chinese Philosophy, Confucianism, Neo-Confucianism, and comparative philosophy, and is a recipient of two Fulbright grants, a Berggruen Fellowship, a Millicent C. McIntosh Fellowship, and a Chiang Ching-Kuo Postdoctoral Research Fellowship. Angle is the author of *Human Rights and Chinese Thought: A Cross-Cultural Inquiry* (2002; Chinese edition, 2012), *Sagehood: The Contemporary Significance of Neo-Confucian Philosophy* (2009; Chinese edition, 2017), *Contemporary Confucian Political Philosophy: Toward Progressive Confucianism* (2012; Chinese edition, 2015), co-author (with Justin Tiwald) of *Neo-Confucianism: A Philosophical Introduction* (2017), and co-editor of two other volumes. His blog on Chinese and comparative philosophy is warpweftandway.com.

Daniel A. Bell is Dean of the Faculty of Politics and Public Administration at Shandong University and Professor at Schwarzman College and the Department of Philosophy at Tsinghua University (Beijing). He is the author of *The China Model: Political Meritocracy and the Limits of Democracy* (2016) and of four other books on East Asian politics and philosophy published by Princeton University Press. He is also the editor of the Princeton-China series. He publishes in leading media outlets in China and the West and his works have been translated into twenty-three languages.

Kathleen M. Higgins is Professor of Philosophy at the University of Texas at Austin. Her main areas of research are aesthetics (especially musical aesthetics), philosophy of music, continental philosophy, and philosophy of emotion. She is author of several books, including *The Music Between Us: Is Music a Universal Language?* (2012), *Comic Relief: Nietzsche's "Gay Science,"* (2000), *The Music of our Lives* (1991), and *Nietzsche's "Zarathustra"* (1987) and three others with Robert C. Solomon, *What Nietzsche Really Said* (2001), *A Short History of Philosophy* (1996), and *A Passion for Wisdom* (1998). She has edited or co-edited several other books, on such topics as aesthetics, ethics, erotic love, Nietzsche, German Idealism, non-Western philosophy, and the philosophy of Robert C. Solomon. Among these are *From Africa to Zen: An Invitation to World Philosophy* (1993) and *World Philosophy: A Text with Readings* (1995), both with Robert C. Solomon. She has been a Visiting Fellow at the Faculty of Psychology and Educational Sciences of Katholieke Universiteit Leuven, the Australian National University Philosophy Department, and the Canberra School of Music, as well as Resident Scholar at the Rockefeller Foundation's Bellagio Study and Conference Center. She has been a frequent visitor to the Philosophy Department of the University of Auckland, and she is currently President of the American Society for Aesthetics.

Thomas P. Kasulis is past Chair of the Department of Comparative Studies and also of the Department of East Asian Languages and Literatures at the Ohio State University. He was also the founding director of OSU's Institute for Collaborative Research and Public Humanities. He has written numerous books and scholarly articles on Japanese religious thought and Western philosophy, including *Zen Action/Zen Person* (1989) and *Shinto: The Way Home* (2004). He has co-edited for SUNY Press a three-volume series comparing Asian and Western ideas of self in different cultural arenas: *Self as Body in Asian Theory and Practice* (1993), *Self as Person in Asian Theory and Practice* (1994), and *Self as Image in Asian Theory and Practice* (1998), as well as *The Recovery of Philosophy in America: Essays in Honor of John Edwin Smith* (1997). He is the author of *Intimacy or Integrity: Philosophy and Cultural Difference* (2002), a comparative cultural philosophy of relationship based on his Gilbert Ryle Lectures of 1998. He is also co-editor of *Japanese Philosophy: A Sourcebook* (2011).

Chenyang Li is a Professor of Philosophy and the Founding Director of the Philosophy Program at Nanyang Technological University, Singapore. He is the author of *The Tao Encounters the West: Explorations in Comparative Philosophy* (1999), *The Confucian Philosophy of Harmony* (2014), *Confucianism in a Pluralist World* (in Chinese), and of over 100 journal articles and book chapters. He is also editor of *The Sage and the Second Sex* (2000), *The East Asian Challenge for Democracy* (with Daniel Bell, 2013), *Moral Cultivation and Confucian Character* (with Peimin Ni, 2014), *Chinese Metaphysics and its Problems* (with Franklin Perkins, 2015), among others. He was the founding president of Association of Chinese Philosophers in North America, a Senior Visiting Fellow at the City University of Hong Kong, an ACE fellow with American Council on Education, and an inaugural Berggruen Fellow at the Center for Advanced Study in the Behavioral Sciences in Stanford University.

Currently he serves as President of International Society for Chinese Philosophy and on the editorial/academic boards of over two dozens of scholarly publications and organizations.

Hans-Georg Moeller obtained his MA and PhD degrees in Chinese Studies, Philosophy, and European Ethnology at the University of Bonn in Germany. Currently, he is Professor of Philosophy at the University of Macau. His research focuses on Chinese and (Post-)comparative philosophy and on Social and Political Thought. He is co-author of *Genuine Pretending: On the Philosophy of the Zhuangzi* (with Paul D'Ambrosio, 2017) and author of *The Radical Luhmann* (2011), *The Moral Fool: A Case for Amorality* (2009), *The Philosophy of the Daodejing* (2006), and several other academic books and articles.

Peimin Ni is Distinguished Professor of Philosophy at Beijing Normal University and Professor of Philosophy at Grand Valley State University. He has authored eight books, including *Understanding the Analects of Confucius: A New Translation of Lunyu with Annotations* (2017), *Confucius: The Man and the Way of Gongfu* (2016), *On Confucius* (2002), *On Reid* (2002), *Wandering: Brush and Pen in Philosophical Reflection* (co-authored with Stephen Rowe, 2002), and around seventy journal articles and book chapters. Ni served as Executive Vice Director of the Institute of Advanced Humanistic Studies at Peking University, Visiting Professor at the University of Hong Kong and the University of Hawai`i at Manoa, President of the Association of Chinese Philosophers in America (ACPA) and the Society of Asian and Comparative Philosophy (SACP), and is the Editor-in-Chief of the ACPA book series on "Chinese and Comparative Philosophy" with Global Scholarly Publications in New York.

Robert Cummings Neville is Professor of Philosophy, Religion, and Theology at Boston University. He has been president of the American Academy of Religion, the International Society for Chinese Philosophy, the Metaphysical Society of America, the Institute for American Religious and Philosophical Thought, and the Charles S. Peirce Society. His most recent books are *The Good Is One, Its Manifestations Many: Confucian Essays in Metaphysics, Morals, Rituals, Institutions, and Genders* (2016) and *Defining Religion: Essays in Philosophy of Religion* (2018). Roger Ames once remarked that Neville publishes everything he thinks, which is obviously false because he publishes much more than that.

Graham Parkes was born and raised in Glasgow and educated at Oxford and the University of California, Berkeley. He taught Asian and Comparative

Philosophy at the University of Hawai'i for twenty-five years, punctuated by three years as a Visiting Scholar and Fellow at Harvard. After seven years as Professor of Philosophy at University College Cork in Ireland, he moved to Vienna, where he is a Professorial Research Fellow at the Institute of Philosophy, University of Vienna. He is also Visiting Professor in Philosophy (one month a year) at East China Normal University in Shanghai. Among his publications are: *Heidegger and Asian Thought* (ed. 1987), *Nietzsche and Asian Thought* (ed. 1991), *Composing the Soul: Reaches of Nietzsche's Psychology* (1994), and translations with commentaries of Keiji Nishitani's *The Self-Overcoming of Nihilism* (1990), Reinhard May's *Heidegger's Hidden Sources: East-Asian Influences on His Work* (1996), François Berthier's *Reading Zen in the Rocks: The Japanese Dry Landscape Garden* (2000), and Friedrich Nietzsche's *Thus Spoke Zarathustra* (2005). He has also published over a hundred journal articles and book chapters on topics in Chinese, Japanese, and European philosophies.

Henry Rosemont Jr., received his PhD in Philosophy from the University of Washington, and pursued postdoctoral studies in Linguistics (and politics) with Noam Chomsky at MIT. His areas of research and writing include Chinese Philosophy & Religion—especially early Confucianism—moral and political theory, philosophy of religion, and philosophy of language. He was George B. & Willma Reeves Distinguished Professor of the Liberal Arts at St. Mary's College of Maryland, as well as Visiting Scholar of Religious Studies at Brown University, and spent three years in China as Fulbright Senior Lecturer at Fudan University in Shanghai. Professor Rosemont is the author of *A Chinese Mirror* (1991), *Rationality & Religious Experience* (2001), and *Is There a Universal 'Grammar' of Religion?* (with Huston Smith, 2007), *Against Individualism* (2016), and *Confucian Role Ethics: A Moral Vision for the 21st Century?* (with Roger T. Ames, 2016). He edited and/or translated ten other books, including *Explorations in Early Chinese Cosmology* (1984), *Leibniz: Writings on China* (with D. J. Cook, 1994), *Chinese Texts & Philosophical Contexts* (2000), and with Roger T. Ames, *The Analects of Confucius: A Philosophical Translation* (1998), and *The Classic of Family Reverence* (2008).

Richard Shusterman is the Dorothy F. Schmidt Eminent Scholar in the Humanities and Director of the Center for Body, Mind, and Culture at Florida Atlantic University. His major authored books (in English) include *Thinking through the Body* (2012), *Body Consciousness* (2008), *Surface and Depth* (2002), *Performing Live* (2000), *Practicing Philosophy* (1997), *T. S. Eliot and the Philosophy of Criticism* (1988), *The Object of Literary Criticism* (1979), and *Pragmatist Aesthetics* (now published in fifteen languages, 1992). All of these books except the one on Eliot exist in Chinese translation. After completing a BA and MA from Hebrew University in Jerusalem, Shusterman received his doctorate in philosophy from Oxford University. He has held visiting academic appointments in France, Germany, Norway, Denmark, Israel, Italy, China, and Japan. The French government honored him as a Chevalier de l'Ordre des Palmes Académiques, and Aalborg University awarded him a Doctor Honoris Causa. Shusterman has developed two projects for UNESCO and was awarded research grants from the National Endowment for the Humanities, the Fulbright Commission, American Council of Learned Societies, and the Humboldt Foundation. Since 2010, he has included performance art as a mode of research, an account of which is published in *The Adventures of the Man in Gold: Paths between Art and Life* (2016).

Brook Ziporyn is a scholar of ancient and medieval Chinese religion and philosophy. Professor Ziporyn received his BA in East Asian Languages and Civilizations from the University of Chicago, and his PhD from the University of Michigan. Prior to joining the Divinity School faculty, he taught Chinese philosophy and religion at the University of Michigan (Department of East Asian Literature and Cultures), Northwestern University (Department of Religion and Department of Philosophy), Harvard University (Department of East Asian Literature and Civilization) and the National University of Singapore (Department of Philosophy). He is the author of *Evil And/Or/As the Good: Omnicentric Holism, Intersubjectivity and Value Paradox in Tiantai Buddhist Thought* (2000), *The Penumbra Unbound: The Neo-Taoist Philosophy of Guo Xiang* (2003), *Being and Ambiguity: Philosophical Experiments With Tiantai Buddhism* (2004), *Zhuangzi: The Essential Writings with Selections from Traditional Commentaries* (2009), *Ironies of Oneness and Difference: Coherence in Early Chinese Thought, Prolegomena to the Study of Li* (2012); *Beyond Oneness and Difference: Li and Coherence in Chinese Buddhist Thought and its Antecedents* (2013); and *Emptiness and Omnipresence: The Lotus Sutra and Tiantai Buddhism* (2016).

Index

Aesthetic Order, 59, 161
Allan, Sarah, 3
Angle, Stephen
  on Confucian ethics and politics, 239–241
Anscombe, Elizabeth, 167, 273
Aristotle
  as comparative philosopher, 31
  and virtue ethics, 168–170

Bell, Daniel
  on Chinese democracy, 288
  on democracy in China, 241
Boodberg, Peter, 4
Brandom, Robert, 51
Buber, Martin, 36
Buck, Betty, 6
Bultmann, Rudolf, 26
Butler, Joseph, 2
Butler, Judith, 285–286
  on roles, 221–225

Callicott, J. Baird, 6
Carmen, Taylor, 146
Chakrabarti, Arindam, 255
Chan, Joseph, 240–241, 288
Chan, Wing-Tsit, 4
  on cheng 誠, 135–136
Cheng 誠, 269–270
  Ames and Hall's interpretation of, 139–142
  Chan's interpretation of, 135–136
  and "creativity," 139–142, 149–150, 271–272
  Graham's interpretation of, 136–137
  Lau's interpretation of, 138
  Legge's interpretation of, 134–135
  Munro's interpretation of, 136–137
  Tu's interpretation of, 137–138
  in the Zhongyong, 190
Chinese sexology
  as aesthetic, 99–105
  Foucault's understanding, 93–99
  as reflective, 105–108
  and yin/yang 陰陽, 96–99, 102, 104, 264
Coherence
  Ziporyn on, 119
Communitarianism
  and role ethics, 206
Comparative Philosophy
  and asymmetry, 172, 273
  and counterexamples, 50, 163–164, 174–175
  four historical forms, 32–36
  goals of, 164–166, 175–177
  and philosophy of culture, 48–51
  with respect to sameness and difference, 160–163, 172–174
Correlative Thinking
  and transcendence, 54–57

Dao 道
  and transcendence, 115–116
  as "way making," 113–114, 117, 252

de Bary, Wm. Theodore, 4
De 德
   as virtue, 174, 184
Defoort, Carine, 7
Deforestation
   in China, 70
   and ox mountain passage, 72–73
Democracy
   and role ethics, 237–244
Deutsch, Eliot, 6
Dewey, John, 16, 23, 37, 48, 238, 264
   on democracy, 289–291
   on the philosophical fallacy, 186
   as virtue ethicist, 173, 274
Dissanayake, Wimal, 6
Driesch, Hans, 37

Edwards, Jonathan, 48
Elvin, Mark
   on environment in China, 69, 71, 73–74, 82
Emerson, Ralph W., 48
Engels, Friedrich, 32
Exemplarist Ethics, 171

Fang, Dongmei, 254
Feminist Care Ethics
   and Confucian ethics, 221
Feng, Youlan, 254, 273
   on Chinese philosophy, 38–39
Feuerbach, Ludwig, 129–130
Fingarette, Herbert, 4, 230
First and Second Problematics, 53–54, 257
Focus/Field Model, 58, 121, 277
   and oneness, 267–269
   and role ethics, 252, 287
Foucault, Michel
   on Chinese sexology, 93–99, 263–264
Fraser, Chris
   on zhi 知, 164
Frege, Gottlob
   on meaning, 15, 250

Gender Roles
   in Confucianism, 220–225
Graham, A.C., 2, 50, 77, 107
   on cheng 誠, 136–137
Guignon, Charles, 147
Guo, Qiyong, 273

Hall, David L., 112
   collaboration with Ames, 3–5, 14, 20, 42–43, 47–61, 160, 173, 257
   on philosophy of culture, 49–50
Hansen, Chad, 4
Hegel, Georg W.F., 258
   on Chinese philosophy, 32–36, 253
Heidegger, Martin, 37, 217, 270–271
   on Da-sein, 143–148, 150–151
Hershock, Peter, 6, 7
   collaboration with Ames, 23–24
   on discrete "things," 277
   on diversity, 275
Hughes, Donald, 74
Hume, David
   as virtue ethicist, 168
Hursthouse, Rosalind, 168
Hutton, Eric, 169

Interpretative Pluralism, 161
Intra-Cultural Translation
   as "carrying over," 251
Ivanhoe, Philip J., 169, 170–171
   and Confucian ethics, 216–217
   on Confucian virtue ethics, 185

James, William, 107
Jullien, François
   and contrastive philosophy, 39–40, 254

Kang, Youwei, 197
Kant, Immanuel, 34
Kasulis, Thomas P., 6
Kim, Sungmoon, 288
Knoblock, John, 260
Krishna, Daya, 255
Kropotkin, Peter, 232

Lai, Chen, 170
Lau, D.C., 2, 4, 236, 287–288
　on cheng 誠, 138
　on Chinese epistemic language, 266
Legge, James, 1, 9, 35
　on cheng 誠, 134–135
Leibniz, Gottfried W.
　on Chinese philosophy, 32–36
　as comparative philosopher, 33, 253
Li, Chenyang
　on harmony, 269
Liang, Shuming, 254
Luhmann, Niklas, 32
　on modernity, 40–41

MacIntyre, Alasdair, 58, 168, 232, 273
Madison, James
　on the opulent minority, 243
Marks, Joel, 7
Marx, Karl, 32, 166
Meaning
　as intention, 23–24, 249
　as reference, 16–18, 249–250
　as sense, 18–23, 249, 252
Merleau-Ponty, Maurice, 107
Moeller, Hans-Georg
　on moral fool, 255–256
Moore, Charles A., 6
Mou, Zongsan, 240, 254
Munro, Donald
　on cheng 誠, 136–137
Murdoch, Iris, 167

National Studies (Gouxue 國學), 176, 275–276
Neville, Robert C., 4
Ni, Peimin
　on the "open-endedness thesis," 187–189
　on the "relational person thesis," 188–189
Nietzsche, Friedrich
　as virtue ethicist, 168
Nivison, David, 169
Noddings, Nel, 232
Northrop, F.S.C., 49

Nussbaum, Martha
　as virtue ethicist, 168–169

Olberding, Amy, 171

Philosophy of Culture
　advantages of, 51–52
　and comparative philosophy, 48–51

Qing, Jiang, 239
Quan 權
　as discretion, 195

Rawls, John, 167, 232
Ren 仁
　Ames translation of, 1–3
Ricci, Matteo, 31
Roetz, Heiner, 40, 42
Role Ethics
　as challenge to individualism, 42–43, 58, 230–232
　collaboration of Ames and Rosemont, 7–8
　and communitarianism, 206
　and community, 204–205, 279–280
　and democracy, 237–244, 288–291
　development of, 230–232
　and family, 214, 225–226, 280–281, 284, 290
　and focus/field model, 252
　and human nature, 189–194
　and metaphysics, 57–60
　and morality, 206–210, 281–283
　and "open-endedness thesis," 187–189
　and "relational person thesis," 188–189
　and relationships, 205–206, 218–225, 276–279, 292–293n.22
　various meanings of, 25–29
　and virtue ethics, 167–172, 183–187, 215–218, 233, 273–274, 283–284
Rorty, Richard, 16, 19, 43
Rosemont, Henry, 4
　collaboration with Ames, 5–6, 7–8, 14, 20, 42–43, 160, 171, 230–232

Rosemont, Henry *(continued)*
  on the individual, 191, 197–198, 230–237
Rousseau, Jean-Jacques, 232
Russell, Bertrand, 37

Sandel, Micheal, 232
Shi 勢
  as transforming situation, 268
Shun, Kwong-loi
  on comparative asymmetry, 172
Silber, John, 167
Sim, May, 169–170, 172, 184, 187, 190
Slingerland, Edward, 42, 169
Smid, Robert W., 257
  on comparative philosophy, 50, 61–62n.8
Spinoza, Baruch
  on oneness, 128–130
Stirner, Max, 232
Stout, Jeffrey, 162
Sun, Yat-sen, 250–251
Swanton, Christine
  on virtue ethics and roles, 217

Taiyi 太一
  meaning as "Great One," 124–126, 267
Tang, Junyi, 119, 192, 254, 290–291
  on mandate of heaven, 260
Taylor, Charles, 232
Thompson, Paul, 3
Tian 天
  and mandate of heaven, 67–69, 259–260
  meaning of, 66–67
  translation as "Heaven," 2, 17
Transcendence
  and correlative causation, 54–57, 257
  and dao 道, 115–116
  and immanence, 123–124
  and reciprocity, 122–123
Translation
  and equivalence, 111–112
  as intra-cultural, 251
  and understanding, 17–18

Trauzettel, Rolf, 39
Tsao, Hsingyuan, 7
Tu, Wei-ming
  on cheng 誠, 137–138, 145, 149

Van Gulik, R.H., 96–97, 99, 101, 103
Van Norden, Bryan, 169
Virtue Ethics
  and Confucian ethics, 273–274
  resurgence of, 167–171
  and role ethics, 183–187, 215–218, 233, 273–274, 283–284

Watson, Gary, 168
Weber, Ralph, 255
Whitehead, Alfred N., 289
  on democracy, 290
  on "fallacy of the perfect dictionary," 251
Wilhelm, Richard, 35
Wilson, Stephen, 169
Wittgenstein, Ludwig, 20, 251
Wong, Wai-ying, 170

Xi, Jinping
  environmental policies of, 70–71

Yang, Yu-wei, 3
Yearly, Lee, 169
Yi 一
  as "continuity," 114
  as "one," 111–112, 118, 267
  as process term, 118–119
Yin/Yang 陰陽, 84, 278
Yu, Jiyuan, 169–170, 172, 184–185

Zagzebski, Linda, 171
Zhang, Dainian
  on cheng 誠, 133, 138, 145
Zheng, Jiadong, 176
Zhengming 正名
  as rectifiction of names, 195, 218
Ziporyn, Brook, 5
  on Ames and nominalism, 163
  on coherence, 119

www.ingramcontent.com/pod-product-compliance
Lightning Source LLC
Chambersburg PA
CBHW030747250426
43672CB00028B/1309